中国社会科学院中白发展分析中心
Chinese-Belarusian Analytical Center of Development, CASS

现代化与治理创新
中国与白俄罗斯的经验

张翼 马峰 等 ◎ 著
ZhangYi MaFeng et al

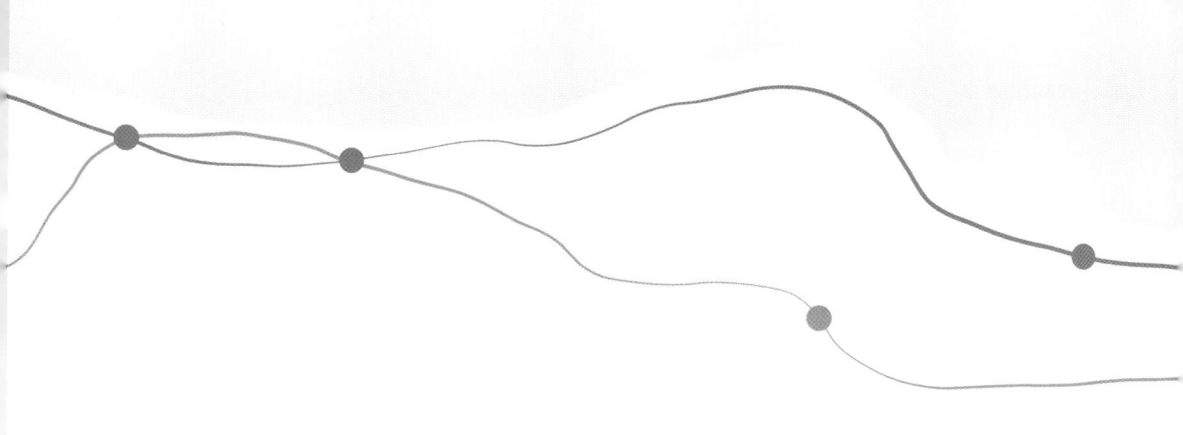

中国社会科学出版社

图书在版编目（CIP）数据

现代化与治理创新：中国与白俄罗斯的经验／张翼等著 . —北京：中国社会科学出版社，2021.10
ISBN 978 - 7 - 5203 - 8764 - 4

Ⅰ.①现… Ⅱ.①张… Ⅲ.①行政管理—现代化管理—研究—中国②行政管理—现代化管理—研究—白俄罗斯　Ⅳ.①D630.1 ②D751.143.1

中国版本图书馆 CIP 数据核字（2021）第 144568 号

出 版 人	赵剑英
责任编辑	张冰洁　侯聪睿
责任校对	夏慧萍
责任印制	王　超

出　　版	中国社会科学出版社
社　　址	北京鼓楼西大街甲 158 号
邮　　编	100720
网　　址	http://www.csspw.cn
发 行 部	010 - 84083685
门 市 部	010 - 84029450
经　　销	新华书店及其他书店

印刷装订	北京明恒达印务有限公司
版　　次	2021 年 10 月第 1 版
印　　次	2021 年 10 月第 1 次印刷

开　　本	710×1000　1/16
印　　张	27.25
插　　页	2
字　　数	433 千字
定　　价	148.00 元

凡购买中国社会科学出版社图书，如有质量问题请与本社营销中心联系调换
电话：010 - 84083683
版权所有　侵权必究

目 录

治理现代化与人的全面发展

中国人口变迁及未来治理政策架构 …………………… 张 翼(3)
人际信息交互与现代化治理机制 …………… Anatoly Lazarevich(23)

治理现代化与社会全面进步

当代中国社会治理发展历程与方位 …………………… 朱 涛(37)
构建更可持续的生态治理体系 ……………… Natalia Lazarevich(50)
中国社会治理现代化与创新发展机制 ………………… 马 峰(56)
白俄罗斯社会治理与性别平等 ………………… Volha Davydzik(69)

治理现代化与治理创新发展

中国增值税改革的宏观经济效应与经济治理
　效能 ………………………………………………… 娄 峰(79)
"一带一路"倡议与白俄罗斯国家治理
　现代化 ……………………………………… Dzmitry Smaliakou(94)
中国生态文明的制度和行动建构与生态环境
　领域治理现代化 …………………………………… 林 红(102)
白俄罗斯治理现代化进程中的人格
　认同 ………………………………………… E. V. Kuznetsova(120)

中国企业民主管理制度发展历程与新方位 ………… 孙兆阳(127)

治理现代化与民心相通

中国文化产业发展的特征与文化领域治理
  现代化 ……………………………………… 祖春明(143)
"一带一路"框架下中白旅游合作前景与
  治理创新 …………………………………… 张艳璐(153)
"一带一路"倡议背景下中白社会体育
  人文合作与展望 …………………………… 方正威(165)
中国人才发展与治理新格局 ……………………… 戈艳霞(172)

Contents

Modernization of Governance and All-round Development of People

China's Population Changes and Future Governance
    Policy Framework ·· Zhang Yi (181)
Interpersonal Information Interaction and Modern
    Governance Mechanism ······················· Anatoly Lazarevich (208)

Modernization of Governance and All-round Progress of Society

Changes of Social Governance in Modern Society
    in China ··· Zhu Tao (227)
Build a More Sustainable Ecological Governance
    System ·· Natalia Lazarevich (250)
China's Social Governance Modernization and
    Innovative Development Mechanism ······················ Ma Feng (259)
Social Governance and Gender Equality in
    Belarus ·· Volha Davydzik (278)

Modernization of Governance and Innovative Development of Governance

The Study of Macroeconomic Effect and Governance
    Effectiveness on the Reform of VAT in China ············ Lou Feng (291)
The BRI and the Modernization of National Governance
    in Belarus ································ Dzmitry Smaliakou (309)
Systems and Regulations and Action Construction on
    Ecological Civilization and Modernization of Ecological
    Environment Governance of China ···················· Lin Hong (319)
Personality Identity in the Process of Modernization of
    Belarusian Governance ······················ E. V. Kuznetsova (351)
China's Enterprises Democratic Management
    Researches ································· Sun Zhaoyang (361)

Modernization of Governance and People-to-people Bond

The Characteristics of the Development of China's Cultural
    Industry and the Modernization of Governance in the
    Cultural Field ································· Zu Chunming (383)
The Prospects and Innovation in Governance of
    China-Belarus Tourism Cooperation under the Belt
    and Road Framework ························ Zhang Yanlu (397)
Cooperation and Prospects of Society, Sports and
    Humanity between China and Belarus in the Context
    of the BRI ································· Fang Zhengwei (413)
New Pattern of China's Talent Development and
    Governance ································· Ge Yanxia (423)

治理现代化与人的全面发展

中国人口变迁及未来治理政策架构

张 翼

中国社会科学院社会发展战略研究院院长、研究员

在世界历史上，中国人口长期占世界人口的20%—25%。自鸦片战争以来，虽然战乱频发，但因基数庞大，中国人口仍保持了增长态势。1949年中华人民共和国的成立，消除了频繁发生的战祸，农民分得了耕地，工人获得了就业机会，人民的衣食基本有了保障，人口具备了迅速增长的必要条件。而医疗卫生状况的改善，传染病的控制，则大规模消除了消化系统疾病和呼吸系统疾病，这在人口出生率迅速上升中降低了死亡率，从而形成了"人口大爆炸"的潜在条件。

一 1949—1957年的人口变迁

新中国成立初期，国民经济基础极其薄弱。但基层政权的建立、物价的稳定、农村与城市经济制度的变革，给中国社会注入了新的活力。土改的推进，使无地或者少地的贫农分到了土地，实现了耕者有其田。随后实施的"党在过渡时期的总路线"[1]，在互助组基础上，促进了初级

---

[1] 1953年6月15日，在中央政治局的扩大会议上，毛泽东提出了"党在过渡时期的总路线"，后来正式表述为："从中华人民共和国成立，到社会主义改造基本完成，这是一个过渡时期。党在过渡时期的总路线和总任务，是要在一个相当长的时期内，逐步实现国家的社会主义工业化，并逐步实现国家对农业、对手工业和对资本主义工商业的社会主义改造"。1954年2月，七届四中全会批准了这个总路线，简称为"一化三改"或"一体两翼"。

社（土地入股）和高级社（土地公有）的建立，并最终完成了对农业的社会主义改造，使差不多五亿多的农民从个体小农经济转化为社会主义集体所有制经济。[①] 与此同时，城市没收官僚资本建立国营经济，保护民族工商业，稳定就业，破除封建把头制，逐步在企业建立工青妇组织，保护工人的基本权益，居民的收入水平得到改善。随后的合作化运动，也完成了对个体手工业和资本主义工商业的社会主义改造。农村与城市经济所有制的转型，使中国社会经济结构与性质发生了根本改变。社会主义改造的基本完成，为1956年党的八大的召开奠定了经济基础。党的八大指出"我国国内的主要矛盾已经是人民对于建立先进的工业国的要求同落后的农业国的现实之间的矛盾，是人民对于经济文化迅速发展的需要同当前经济文化不能满足人民需要的状况之间的矛盾"。新制度格局产生的新分配政策，改善了人民的生活，从整体上提升了生育水平（见表1）。

表1　新中国成立初期人口的出生率、死亡率和自然增长率　　单位：‰

年份	全国			市镇			县		
	出生率	死亡率	自增率	出生率	死亡率	自增率	出生率	死亡率	自增率
1949	36.00	20.00	16.00	—	—	—	—	—	—
1950	37.00	18.00	19.00	—	—	—	—	—	—
1951	37.80	17.80	20.00	—	—	—	—	—	—
1952	37.00	17.00	20.00	—	—	—	—	—	—
1953	37.00	14.00	23.00	—	—	—	—	—	—
1954	37.97	13.18	24.79	42.45	8.07	34.38	37.51	13.71	23.80
1955	32.60	12.28	20.32	40.67	9.30	31.37	31.74	12.60	19.14
1956	31.90	11.40	20.50	37.87	7.43	30.44	31.25	11.84	19.40
1957	34.03	10.80	23.23	44.48	8.47	36.01	32.81	11.07	21.74

数据来源：《中国统计年鉴》，中国统计出版社1987年版，第90页。

从表1可以看出，虽然1949年的出生率高达36‰，但因为1949年

[①] 1956年年底，加入合作社的农户达到全国农户总数的96.3%，其中参加高级社的总农户达到87.8%。这就是说，原来预计用18年完成的农业合作化，仅仅用7年时间就加速完成了。当然也存在一些农户的不满行为。

的死亡率高达20‰，所以自然增长率较低，仅仅为16‰。1950年到1954年，出生率一直稳定在37‰左右，但因为死亡率从1950年的18‰降低到1954年的13.18‰，所以，人口的自然增长率就从1950年的19‰上升到1954年的24.79‰。虽然目前缺乏1953年之前农村与市镇的人口出生率、死亡率和自然增长率的数据，但从1954年的情况可以看出，这一时期，市镇的出生率远远高于农村的出生率，市镇的死亡率又远远低于农村的死亡率，这就导致市镇人口的增速快于农村的人口增速。比如说，1954年市镇的自然增长率高达34.38‰，而农村的自然增长率仅为23.80‰。1955年，市镇的人口自然增长率为31.37‰，农村为19.14‰。由此可以看出，战争过后社会稳定时期的补偿性生育现象有所消退。为什么人口增长会如此迅猛呢？其主要原因在于：

第一，政策性鼓励生育，满足对战乱之后人民稳定祥和生活的需要。新中国成立之后，农民分到了土地，工人稳定了就业，结婚与生育的愿望非常强烈。

第二，实际初婚年龄较小。虽然1950年5月1日颁布的《中华人民共和国婚姻法》规定，女性法定结婚年龄为18周岁，男性为20周岁，但婚姻法从颁布到真正成为约束婚姻当事人的起作用的规范，存在一个过程。事实上，在广大农村地区，当时还存在早婚的现象，不管是男性还是女性，早婚的比例很高。[①]

第三，医疗卫生防疫体系的建立，迅速降低了婴幼儿的死亡率，提升了新生儿人口的存活率。

1953年进行的第一次人口普查发现，中国大陆的总人口已经达到5.94亿，这与1949年经常说的4.8亿人有非常大的出入。[②] 事实上，以普查数据为基数，以每年的出生率为标准，最后正式回推得到的1950年

[①] 原国家计生委1982年组织实施的"全国千分之一人口生育率抽样调查"资料显示，女性平均初婚年龄由1949年的18.57岁升至1960年的19.57岁、1980年的23.05岁，1981年微降，为22.82岁。王跃生通过对第五次人口普查数据的分析，发现在1950—1954年结婚的人当中，低于法定结婚的男性占30%，女性占25%。参见王跃生《法定婚龄、政策婚龄下的民众初婚行为》，《中国人口科学》2005年第6期。

[②] 1950年国家内务部公布的全国（包括台湾）人口数是4.8亿左右，财政部公布的数字是4.83亿左右。毛泽东主席在中国人民政治协商会议第一次会议的开幕词中说，中国人口总量为4.75亿。

的总人口数达到5.5亿。经过几年增长后，1955年全国总人口达到了6.1亿。

中国人口的出生率在1955年降低到32.60‰，在1956年降低到31.90‰，在1957年为34.03‰。从市镇人口出生率与农村人口出生率的比较上可以看出，市镇要远远高于农村。在人口自然增长率栏可以看出，市镇人口的增长率长期较高。

1949—1957年这一时期具有恢复性生育的特征，由于市镇的生活条件和医疗卫生条件好于农村，所以市镇的人口增长率快于农村。

二 1958—1976年的人口变迁

我国人口的变迁过程表明，自20世纪60年代始到70年代中后期，人口一直处于迅速降低的态势。当然，在1959年到1961年，中国人口的下降主要是农村人口增长率的下降（县的人口出生率的下降）。"大跃进"运动和"大炼钢铁"抽离了农村劳动力，从表2可以看出，在这一时期，一方面是县的人口出生率趋低，另一方面是县的死亡率趋升，导致了这几年的人口损失。尤其是在1960年，县的死亡率突破到28.58‰，而同年县的出生率仅为19.35‰，于是出现人口自然增长率 -9.23‰ 的负增长。即使到1961年，经过逐渐的恢复，中国县的人口自然增长率也才达到2.41‰。

1962年是中国人口增长史上极其重要的转折年。在此之前是市镇的出生率和自增率高于县，在此之后是县的出生率和自增率高于市镇。1962年市镇的出生率和自增率分别为35.46‰和27.18‰，县的出生率和自增率分别为37.27‰和26.95‰——出生率是县高于市镇。从1962年起，中国出现了新一轮补偿性生育。但总体趋势是全国人口出生率处于不断下降的态势，自1963年的43.37‰一直下降到1976年的19.91‰。所以，从人口出生率的下降、到随后补偿性生育的提高、再到人口出生率的逐步降低，中国完成了其历史性的人口转型过程。1962年中共中央、国务院发出了《关于认真提倡计划生育的指示》，1971年国务院转发了卫生部军管会、商业部、燃料化学工业部《关于做好计划生育工作的报告》，政府号召实行计划生育、晚婚晚育。

表2　　1959—1976年中国人口的出生率、死亡率和自然增长率　　　单位:‰

年份	全国 出生率	全国 死亡率	全国 自增率	市镇 出生率	市镇 死亡率	市镇 自增率	县 出生率	县 死亡率	县 自增率
1959	24.78	14.59	10.19	29.43	10.92	18.51	23.78	14.61	9.17
1960	20.86	25.43	-4.57	28.03	13.77	14.26	19.35	28.58	-9.23
1961	18.02	14.24	3.78	21.63	11.39	10.24	16.99	14.58	2.41
1962	37.01	10.02	26.99	35.46	8.28	27.18	37.27	10.32	26.95
1963	43.37	10.04	33.33	33.33	7.13	37.37	43.19	10.49	32.70
1964	39.14	11.50	27.64	32.17	7.27	24.90	40.27	12.17	28.10
1965	37.88	9.50	28.38	26.59	5.69	20.90	39.53	10.06	29.47
1966	35.05	8.83	26.22	20.85	5.59	15.26	36.71	9.47	27.24
1967	33.96	8.43	25.53	—	—	—	—	—	—
1968	35.59	8.21	27.38	—	—	—	—	—	—
1969	34.11	8.03	26.08	—	—	—	—	—	—
1970	33.43	7.60	25.83	—	—	—	—	—	—
1971	30.65	7.32	23.33	21.3	5.35	15.95	31.86	7.57	24.29
1972	29.77	7.61	22.16	19.3	5.29	14.01	31.19	7.93	23.26
1973	27.93	7.04	20.89	17.35	4.96	12.39	29.36	7.33	22.03
1974	24.82	7.34	17.48	14.50	5.24	9.26	26.23	7.63	18.60
1975	23.01	7.32	15.69	14.71	5.39	9.32	24.17	7.59	16.58
1976	19.91	7.25	12.66	13.12	6.60	6.52	20.85	7.35	13.50

数据来源:《中国统计年鉴》,中国统计出版社1987年版,第90页。

现在来看,这一时期前期人口的快速增长,一方面取决于人口死亡率的快速下降,另一方面取决于"赤脚医生"制度的实施控制了传染病的蔓延,由此逐渐延长了中国人的平均预期寿命。中国开始从农业社会的人口增长模式向工业社会的人口增长模式转变。

这一时期后期人口增速得以在控制中下降的主要原因是:第一,基层组织的组织化。人民公社、生产大队、生产队的"三级"所有模式,加强了对基层社会的组织化,通过上门做工作等措施有效控制了人口增速。

第二，知识青年上山下乡运动，① 使大量城市适婚青年流动到农村（总计涉及 1800 万—3000 万人）。刚开始是为了解决城市青年的就业问题，后来发展为运动。在这场运动中，有些知识青年在农村结婚了，但绝大多数希望回城再结婚。这种流动过程在一定程度上既降低了结婚率，也抑制了生育率。

第三，晚婚晚育政策的推行。"晚婚晚育"政策，打破了 1950 年《婚姻法》男性 20 周岁、女性 18 周岁的法定结婚年龄格局，倡导青年男女响应党和政府号召，自觉晚婚晚育，将精力主要用于社会主义现代化建设。因此，当时的实际登记结婚年龄，主要在男性 25 周岁，女性 23 周岁左右。在有些地方，如果婚龄差比较大，则实行男女双方相加接近 50 岁的晚婚政策。在北京、上海、天津这样的直辖市，实际登记结婚年龄甚至比这个年龄还要迟一些。

第四，第四个五年计划提出了人口控制的目标。"四五"（1970—1975 年）明确提出力争将城市人口自增率降低到 10‰左右，将农村自增率降低到 15‰左右——第一次在政府正式文件中提出了人口控制目标。1973 年成立了国务院计划生育领导小组，并在国务院计划生育领导小组办公室召开全国第一次计划生育工作汇报会，提出了"晚、稀、少"（晚婚、间隔生育、少生）的生育政策。事实上，到 1976 年，全国市镇人口增长率已经降低到 6.52‰，县人口增长率降低到 13.5‰，超计划完成了人口控制目标。

三　1978—2000 年的人口变迁

"文化大革命"结束之后，国家延续了控制人口增长的政策。为加快经济发展速度，降低人口增长对人均各项指标的负面影响，第五个五年

---

① 1953 年《人民日报》就发表社论《组织高校青年毕业生参加农村生产劳动》，1955 年毛泽东发出"农村是一个广阔的天地，在那里是可以大有作为"的号召。1966 年"文化大革命"开始，高校停招。1968 年很多初中和高中毕业生既无法升学，也不能在城市就业，出现劳动力闲置现象。1968 年《人民日报》发表了《我们也有两只手，不在城里吃闲饭》的文章。1969 年掀起了更大规模的知识青年到农村去安家落户的现象。直到"文化大革命"结束，高考恢复，知识青年才逐步回城。1980 年之后停止上山下乡运动。

计划提出要将市镇人口自增率降低到6‰，将县的自增率降低到10‰。从1978年开始，政府开始提倡一对夫妇生育子女数最好为一个，最多为两个。①"文化大革命"时期推行的"晚、稀、少"的计划生育工作重点转移到"少"上。

"文化大革命"结束之后，相继发生了三件对生育行为具有深远影响意义的重大事件。其一是在1980年9月由第五届全国人民代表大会第三次会议通过了新的《中华人民共和国婚姻法》，并明确在1981年1月1日起施行新的婚姻法。该法将法定结婚年龄从原定的男性20周岁、女性18周岁方可结婚修改为男性22周岁、女性20周岁方可结婚。虽然从法律意义上看，第二部婚姻法推迟了法定结婚年龄，但与事实上在"文化大革命"时实行的晚婚晚育"倡导"的男性25周岁、女性23周岁方可结婚相比，结婚年龄有所提前。其二是1982年在全国范围推行家庭联产承包责任制，即将原来人民公社、生产大队、生产队三级所有的集体生产组织方式，以责任田的方式划分给家户耕种，②客观上扩大了生产自由权、提升了社会流动的自主性。其三是1983年10月，中共中央、国务院发出了《关于实行政社分开，建立乡政府的通知》，实行政社分设，取消人民公社制度，在人民公社基础上重建乡镇，乡被确立为农村基层行政单位。客观上，基层组织的约束程度有所减弱。

新婚姻法的实施扩大了随后几年中国的结婚对数，包产到户解构了农村基层生产队和生产大队的组织方式，激发了家族主义传统的回归，激励了农村家大业大势力大以及多子多福的思想观念的流行。为加强计划生育工作，1982年修宪时，将"国家推行计划生育，使人口的增长同经济和社会发展计划相适应"和"夫妻双方有实行计划生育的义务"写入宪法。党的十二大又将计划生育确定为基本国策，并以中共中央和国务院的名义发出了《关于进一步做好计划生育工作的指示》，重申在20世纪末把人口控制在12亿以内。

---

① 见1978年10月中央批转的《关于国务院计划生育领导小组第一次会议的报告》。
② 即农村改革的所谓包产到户，其政策的核心是"交够国家的、留足集体的、剩下全是自己的"。中国农民长期受"大锅饭""平均主义"压抑的生产积极性，在这一制度改革中得到解放，并在短期内解决了困扰中国上千年的吃饭问题。

从表3可以看出，1978年的自增率为12‰，1979年为11.61‰，1980年为11.87‰，但恰恰在1981年却增加到14.55‰，自增率在计划生育制度成为基本国策之后不降反升，在市镇和县都表现出反弹状况：县在1981年的出生率达到21.55‰，在1982年达到21.97‰。市镇的出生率在1981年达到16.45‰，在1982年达到18.24‰。随后经过艰苦努力，虽然有所降低，但在1986年，县的出生率反弹到21.94‰，市镇的也反弹到17.39‰。

表3　　　　中国人口的出生率、死亡率和自然增长率　　　单位：‰

年份	全国			市镇			县		
	出生率	死亡率	自增率	出生率	死亡率	自增率	出生率	死亡率	自增率
1977	18.93	6.87	12.06	13.38	5.51	7.87	19.70	7.06	12.64
1978	18.25	6.25	12.00	13.56	5.12	8.44	18.91	6.42	12.49
1979	17.82	6.21	11.61	13.67	5.07	8.60	18.43	6.39	12.04
1980	18.21	6.34	11.87	14.17	5.48	8.69	18.82	6.47	12.35
1981	20.91	6.36	14.55	16.45	5.14	11.31	21.55	6.53	15.02
1982	22.28	6.60	15.68	18.24	5.28	12.96	21.97	7.00	14.97
1983	20.19	6.90	13.29	15.99	5.92	10.07	19.89	7.69	12.20
1984	19.90	6.82	13.08	15.00	5.86	9.14	17.90	6.73	11.17
1985	21.04	6.78	14.26	14.02	5.96	8.06	19.17	6.66	12.51
1986	22.43	6.86	15.57	17.39	5.75	11.64	21.94	6.74	15.20
1987	23.33	6.72	16.61	—	—	—	—	—	—
1988	22.37	6.64	15.73	—	—	—	—	—	—
1989	21.58	6.54	15.04	16.73	5.78	10.95	23.27	6.81	16.46
1990	21.06	6.67	14.39	16.14	5.71	10.43	22.80	7.01	15.79
1991	19.68	6.70	12.98	15.49	5.50	9.99	21.17	7.13	14.04
1992	18.24	6.64	11.60	15.47	5.77	9.70	19.09	6.91	12.18
1993	18.09	6.64	11.45	15.37	5.99	9.38	19.06	6.89	12.17
1994	17.70	6.49	11.21	15.13	5.53	9.60	18.84	6.80	12.04
1995	17.12	6.57	10.55	14.76	5.53	9.23	18.08	6.99	11.09
1996	16.98	6.56	10.42	14.47	5.65	8.82	18.02	6.94	11.08

续表

年份	全国			市镇			县		
	出生率	死亡率	自增率	出生率	死亡率	自增率	出生率	死亡率	自增率
1997	16.57	6.51	10.06	14.52	5.58	8.94	17.43	6.90	10.53
1998	15.64	6.50	9.14	13.67	5.31	8.36	17.05	7.01	10.04
1999	14.64	6.46	8.18	13.18	5.51	7.76	16.13	6.88	9.25
2000	14.03	6.45	7.58	—	—	—	—	—	—

注：1987年、1988年、2000年市镇与县的数据不详。

中央政府在1986年将本世纪末（2000年）的总人口控制目标放宽到12亿左右，在1987年放宽到12.5亿左右。在计划生育政策的执行中，逐步推进计划生育工作中的"三不变"（即坚持各级党政一把手亲自抓、负总责不变，现行计划生育政策不变和既定的人口控制目标不变）、"三为主"（计划生育工作要以宣传教育为主、避孕为主和经常性工作为主）和"三结合"（即把计划生育工作与发展经济、帮助农民勤劳致富奔小康、建设文明幸福家庭相结合）。

虽然"三为主"的制度探索开始于20世纪80年代早期，但"三为主"一直到2000年前后才基本在全国层面达标。计划生育的政策目标，在1987年放宽到12.5亿左右，后来这个指标又放宽到"把人口控制在13亿之内"。通过这些制度性改革，实现了"两个转变"，即由单纯的就计划生育抓计划生育向综合治理人口问题转变，由以社会制约为主向利益导向与社会制约相结合，宣传教育、综合服务、科学管理相统一的工作机制转变。这才出现了人口出生率掉头下降的态势。

通过非常艰苦的工作，中国人口逐渐从高出生率、低死亡率、高自增率向低出生率、低死亡率和低自增率转变。在1990年之后，全国出生率连年降低，1991年降低到19.68‰，1992年降低到18.24‰，1994年降低到17.7‰，1996年降低到16.98‰，1998年降低到15.64‰，1999年降低到14.64‰。与此同时，中国人口的自增率，也在1992年降低到11.6‰，在1995年降低到10.55‰，在1998年降低到9.14‰，在1999年降低到8.18‰，在2000年降低到7.58‰。

通过这些工作，2000年中国总人口达到了12.67亿，虽然超过了12

亿，但却没有达到13亿——并迎来了低生育水平。2000年人口普查表明，中国的总和生育率已经降低到1.4左右，其中城市的总和生育率为0.9，市镇为1.2，县为1.6。从分地区的总和生育率来看，最低的是北京和上海，都是0.7。①

四 2001—2018年的人口变迁

2001年12月颁布了《中华人民共和国计划生育法》，在具体执行过程中，城市、镇、农村地区，根据户籍人口的稠密程度并照顾到少数民族地区的情况，形成了以下格局：在全国的城镇地区以及四个直辖市加江苏和四川等地的农村，对汉族居民实行独生子女政策；在除以上各省市之外的农村，如果第一胎生育的是女孩，可以安排五年后再生育一个孩子；也有五个省和自治区规定可以生育两个孩子；如果夫妻双方均为独生子女，则可以生育两个孩子；对人数比较少的少数民族实行更宽的生育政策；在西藏等地区则不实行计划生育政策。

应该说，2000年人口普查的数据质量是较高的。其得到的1.22的总和生育率的结论与此前国家统计局于1995年1%人口抽样调查得到的结论具有趋势一致性。

2005年，1%人口抽样调查的结果继续表明，总和生育率为1.34。2010年第六次人口普查的结果显示，该年的总和生育率只有1.18，其中城市为0.88，镇为1.15，农村为1.43。在人口研究领域比较有影响的《人口研究》和《中国人口科学》这两个杂志中发表的文章，开始越来越多地讨论和评论原有计划生育政策的合理性。② 2015年1%人口抽样调查数据再一次证明，中国的总和生育率已经处于世界最低水平，仅仅为1.047（见表4）。

---

① 国家人口和计划生育委员会发展规划司、中国人口与发展研究中心编：《人口和计划生育常用数据手册》，中国人口出版社2006年版，第105页。
② 郭志刚：《中国人口生育水平低在何处》，《中国人口科学》2013年第2期。

表4　　　　　　1960—2017年中国的总和生育率（个）

年份	世界银行	国家统计局	年份	世界银行	国家统计局	年份	世界银行	国家统计局
1960	5.748	—	1980	2.63	—	2000	1.497	1.22
1961	5.919	—	1981	2.57	—	2001	1.508	—
1962	6.089	—	1982	2.56	—	2002	1.524	—
1963	6.237	—	1983	2.582	—	2003	1.54	—
1964	6.346	—	1984	2.623	—	2004	1.554	—
1965	6.396	—	1985	2.661	—	2005	1.565	1.34
1966	6.375	—	1986	2.675	—	2006	1.572	—
1967	6.286	—	1987	2.654	—	2007	1.577	—
1968	6.133	—	1988	2.593	—	2008	1.581	—
1969	5.92	—	1989	2.489	—	2009	1.586	—
1970	5.648	—	1990	2.35	2.3	2010	1.59	1.18
1971	5.322	—	1991	2.187	—	2011	1.594	—
1972	4.956	—	1992	2.021	—	2012	1.599	—
1973	4.57	—	1993	1.868	—	2013	1.604	—
1974	4.181	—	1994	1.739	—	2014	1.61	—
1975	3.809	—	1995	1.639	1.56	2015	1.617	1.047
1976	3.472	—	1996	1.571	—	2016	1.624	—
1977	3.18	—	1997	1.527	—	2017	1.631	—
1978	2.938	—	1998	1.503	—			
1979	2.753	—	1999	1.494	—			

数据来源：https://data.worldbank.org/indicator/SP.DYN.TFRT.IN?locations=CN，中国国家统计局数据根据历次普查或1%人口抽样调查数据整理。

2013年11月，党的十八届三中全会通过了《中共中央关于深化改革若干重大问题的决定》，提出实施"夫妇一方是独生子女的即可生育两个孩子的政策"。2014年年初，各省人大会陆续通过了新的计划生育条例，开始实施新的人口调控政策。通过表5可以看出，2014年全年出生人口数量达到1692万人（国家统计局公布数据是1687万），这个数据高于2013年的1644万人。但2015年全年的出生人口数量却下降到1659万人，低于2014年。"单独二孩"人口政策的红利仅释放了一年。2015年，党的十八届五中全会决定，坚持计划生育基本国策，完善人口发展战略，全面实施一对夫妇可生育两个孩子的政策，积极开展应对人口老龄化行动。2015年12月全国人大常委会审议了人口与计划生育法修正案草案。2016年1月，中共中央明确指出，生育二孩无须审批，家庭完全可以自主安排生育。

表5　改革开放以来中国历年出生人口、死亡人口和净增人口数

（单位:‰、万人）

年份	出生率	死亡率	自增率	总人口	出生人口	死亡人口	净增人口
1978	18.25	6.25	12.00	96259	1757	602	1155
1979	17.82	6.21	11.61	97542	1738	606	1132
1980	18.21	6.34	11.87	98705	1797	626	1172
1981	20.91	6.36	14.55	100072	2093	636	1456
1982	22.28	6.60	15.68	101654	2265	671	1594
1983	20.19	6.90	13.29	103008	2080	711	1369
1984	19.90	6.82	13.08	104357	2077	712	1365
1985	21.04	6.78	14.26	105851	2227	718	1509
1986	22.43	6.86	15.57	107507	2411	737	1674
1987	23.33	6.72	16.61	109300	2550	734	1815
1988	22.37	6.64	15.73	111026	2484	737	1746
1989	21.58	6.54	15.04	112704	2432	737	1695
1990	21.06	6.67	14.39	114333	2408	763	1645
1991	19.68	6.70	12.98	115823	2279	776	1503
1992	18.24	6.64	11.60	117171	2137	778	1359
1993	18.09	6.64	11.45	118517	2144	787	1357
1994	17.70	6.49	11.21	119850	2121	778	1344
1995	17.12	6.57	10.55	121121	2074	796	1278
1996	16.98	6.56	10.42	122389	2078	803	1275
1997	16.57	6.51	10.06	123626	2048	805	1244
1998	15.64	6.50	9.14	124761	1951	811	1140
1999	14.64	6.46	8.18	125786	1842	813	1029
2000	14.03	6.45	7.58	126743	1778	817	961
2001	13.38	6.43	6.95	127627	1708	821	887
2002	12.86	6.41	6.45	128453	1652	823	829

续表

年份	出生率	死亡率	自增率	总人口	出生人口	死亡人口	净增人口
2003	12.41	6.40	6.01	129227	1604	827	777
2004	12.29	6.42	5.87	129988	1598	835	763
2005	12.40	6.51	5.89	130756	1621	851	770
2006	12.09	6.81	5.28	131448	1589	895	694
2007	12.10	6.93	5.17	132129	1599	916	683
2008	12.14	7.06	5.08	132802	1612	938	675
2009	11.95	7.08	4.87	133450	1595	945	650
2010	11.90	7.11	4.79	134091	1596	953	642
2011	11.93	7.14	4.79	134735	1607	962	645
2012	12.10	7.15	4.95	135404	1638	968	670
2013	12.08	7.16	4.92	136072	1644	974	669
2014	12.37	7.16	5.21	136782	1692	979	713
2015	12.07	7.11	4.96	137462	1659	977	682
2016	12.95	7.09	5.86	138271	1791	980	810
2017	12.43	7.11	5.32	139000	1728	988	739
2018	10.94	7.13	3.81	139540	1527	995	532

数据来源：1978—2015 年数据来自 2016 年《中国人口与劳动统计年鉴》，2016—2018 年数据来自历年《中华人民共和国国民经济与社会发展统计公报》。历年出生人口、死亡人口和净增人口数据根据总人口与相应的出生率、死亡率和自增率计算得出。因为国家统计局公布的数据由四舍五入得出，故这里计算得到的数据与统计局公布的确切数据稍有出入，但差距很小。

2016 年中国出生人口上升到 1791 万（国家统计局公布数为 1786 万），比 2015 年增加了 132 万。2017 年出生人口数又降低到 1728 万（国家统计局公布数据是 1723 万）。2018 年出生人口数又开始下降，只有 1527 万（国家统计局公布数是 1523 万）。

为什么近年来人口出生率继续下跌？原因主要包括：第一，每年的结婚对数持续降低。在 1980 年实施独生子女政策时期出生的女性进入了结婚生育年龄。在整个 20 世纪 80 年代，每年出生人口差不多都在 2300 万左右，但在进入 20 世纪 90 年代之后，每年新出生的人口数量就降低到 1900 万到 2100 万，而且呈现越来越低的趋势。等到"85 后"和"90 后"开始结婚时，每年初婚的结婚对数就开始急剧下跌，比如说，2013

年初婚对数为1341.13万对，2014年初婚对数降低到1302.04万对，2015年初婚对数降低到1220.59万对，2016年初婚对数降低到1138.61万对，2017年初婚对数继续降低到1059.04万对，[①] 2018年包括了再婚对数的结婚对数只有差不多1010万对——初婚对数已经不足1000万对。初婚对数的降低，不仅会降低初婚后的出生率，长期趋势上还会降低整个社会的出生率。

第二，每年进入生育期的育龄妇女人数日益降低。现在生育旺盛期的育龄妇女，恰好是原计划生育政策严格执行时期出生的同期群，因为独生子女政策实施过程中出现了人口出生性别比的上升，即每出生100个女婴相对应出生的男婴数迅速上升，打破了原有的相对平衡特征。[②] 20世纪80年代之后人口出生性别比的上升，使这些出生队列进入婚姻期之后的女性适婚年龄人口不足，这会导致一部分男性因为找不到配偶而难以结婚生育。根据2017年1‰人口变动抽样调查，15—19岁年龄段的性别比是117.70，20—24岁年龄段的性别比是110.98，25—29岁年龄段的性别比是104.47。[③] 如果15—19岁年龄段人口进入婚育旺盛期，结婚难、结婚贵的问题还会趋于严重。但最严重的影响是：降低了婚育年龄段的女性人口数，一方面加大婚龄年龄段男性的结婚压力而形成婚姻挤压，另一方面也会降低出生率，使每年新出生的第一胎生育人口数量趋于减少。在整个新出生人口中，由育龄妇女的存量所生产的二孩比重已超过50%。

第三，离婚率的上升与初婚年龄的推迟。城镇化、高等教育的大众化、后工业化与女性收入的增长以及常态化的人口流动等，一方面提升了离婚率，另一方面也推迟了女性人口的初婚年龄。改革开放以后，中国先是普及了义务教育，接着又免除了义务教育阶段的学费，进入新世纪绝大多数地区都提升了高中阶段教育的入学率，[④] 最近又迅速提升了大

---

① 数据来源：2018年《中国统计年鉴》表22—表24。
② 人口出生性别比的正常值，介于103—107，超过107即属于高出生性别比，低于103即属于低出生性别比。如果介于103—107，则因为男婴或男童的死亡率高于女婴和女童，所以，到婚育年龄段之后的性别比会趋于平衡。
③ 数据来源：2018年《中国人口与劳动统计年鉴》表2—表3。
④ 2018年高中阶段毛入学率达到88.8%。

学毛入学率。1978年高等教育的毛入学率仅仅为1.55%，1988年是3.7%，1999年大学扩招。2002年上升到15%，2007年达到23%，2010年达到26.5%，2018年达到48.1%，2019年超过50%，从而使中国从大众教育阶段进入普及化阶段。这些因素使女性初婚年龄迅速推迟，从1990年到2017年，女性平均初婚年龄从21.4岁推迟到25.7岁。平均初育年龄也从23.4岁提升到26.8岁。在某些大城市、特大城市或超大城市，女性的初婚年龄会更迟，比如在上海或北京，女性初婚年龄甚至推迟到29岁或30岁左右。初婚年龄的推迟必然继替性地提升初育年龄，缩短婚龄女性的生育期，从而降低整个社会的出生率。

第四，生活成本的上升降低了生育愿望。自改革开放以来，中国步入了快速城镇化的轨道。在1978年，中国的城镇化水平仅仅为17.9%，但到2018年年底上升到59.6%左右。城镇化并不会均等地将各个年龄段人口都移入城市，而是有选择地将那些年纪较轻、劳动就业能力较强的人率先吸纳进城市，而这部分人口又恰恰是婚育旺盛人口。可最初城镇化的年轻人，一方面需要照顾家乡的老人（计划生育减少了这些出生队列的兄弟姐妹数量，加大了他们的养老负担），另一方面还需要养育自己的子女，满足当前的生活消费需要。但城市房价的上升，消费品价格的坚挺，使得他们的生育意愿难以提升。在避孕工具日益多样化和便捷化的过程中，生育意愿的降低直接消减了实际出生率。

第五，有待改善的生育环境抑制了整个社会的生育需求。"单独二孩"政策与"全面二孩"政策的实施，之所以难以释放出持续性的生育红利，一个重要的原因，就是其深受入托难、入学难、就业难、育儿难、看病难等现实问题的影响。家庭的小型化和流动化，以及"80后"结婚之后家庭观念和生活观念的变化，使原来依靠父母照顾小孩的支持体系有所减弱。家庭保姆价格的上升，也使一般青年夫妇很难雇得起保姆照顾小孩。社会竞争压力大，工作时间变相延长，缩短了青年一代的闲暇时间，也很难使现在的青年一代有足够的时间照顾孩子。孩子从出生到上学直到大学毕业，其间的花费居高不下。孩子要结婚，还得买房或添置嫁妆。农民工进入城市务工经商，但没有完全转变为城市市民，户籍制度还没有回归人口信息登记功能，城市公共服务还难以均等化。因此，不管是在职场还是在家庭生活领域，还需要继续建构有利于生育的家庭友好型社会。

正因为上述问题的影响,到目前为止,实际生育率还大大低于政策生育率。而一旦一个国家或社会陷入总和生育率长期低于1.5或1.4的低生育陷阱,则这个社会或国家就很难跳出低生育陷阱,并持续性地处于低生育陷阱之中不能自拔,从而影响人口的年龄结构和赡养结构,导致人口老龄化加速,缩小支撑整个社会的劳动力人口规模,形成奇高的养老金负债压力,使人口从红利阶段过渡到负债阶段,形成未富先老格局,滑落到易于造成中等收入陷阱的人口结构。事实上,在发展中国家中,人口陷阱与中等收入陷阱同构发生的案例比比皆是,这两个陷阱互相影响,形成有增长但无发展的局面,陷入低水平重复但却难以发展的困局。

五 面向未来的治理政策架构

中国的计划生育政策,从最初的节制生育,到后来的"一个不少、两个正好、三个多了",再到20世纪80年代推行"独生子女",最后发展到现在的"全面二孩",经历了社会反思性的回归过程。这个过程始终伴随着经济发展不同阶段生活资料供给与人口数量和人口结构的压力性矛盾,也伴随着国家计划生育基本国策与家庭计划生育偏好之间的矛盾。这些矛盾运动的过程,构成了人口发展与结构变化过程,也成为结婚、生育这种家庭行为与生育率这个政府控制指标的连接纽带。

制度设计的初衷在于缓解人口增长对国民经济发展压力。人口的生产与再生产和物质资料的生产与再生产之间的矛盾,是第二次世界大战之后世界各国共同面临的主要社会矛盾。第二次世界大战之后的"人口爆炸",也是世界人口史上发生的短期内规模最大的人口"爆炸"。中国为解决人口压力问题,面对当时的生产力发展水平和经济社会发展水平,采取了控制人口增长的措施。

实际上,这些措施控制了人口增速,有效缓解了人口存量和人口增量对生活资料的供给压力,提升了百姓的生活水平,使中国从农业国转变为工业国,基本建立起中国特色的工业体系,完成了GDP从以农业为主向以工业为主、再向以后工业为主的转变过程。计划生育缩小了家庭规模,减轻了家庭育儿压力,使家庭有能力积存资金,并将这些资金集中使用在孩子身上，顺利推进了9年义务制教育，相继提高了高中阶段和高等教育的入学率，促使中国从人口大国向人力资源强国转变。计划生育与独生子女政策的实施，客观上消解了盛行整个封建社会的男尊女卑思想，增加了女童和女青年在各个年龄别的入学率，从而提升了女性的人力资本，缩小了教育、就业和职业方面的性别差距。计划生育也在降低人口出生率的同时，大大降低了整个社会的少儿负担系数，减轻了抚养成本，促进了社会发展。计划生育与孕期检查，迅速降低了孕产妇死亡率，保障了胎儿的健康孕育，降低了出生缺陷率。计划生育还延长了女性的就业时间，改善女性的家庭地位和社会地位，大力促进了社会进步和社会发展。计划生育在城市和乡村的政策性区别，大大加快了城市的老龄化水平，为改革开放之后的农民工进城预设了劳动力人口的需求空间，加快了中国的城镇化速度。总之，计划生育的客观结果，在计划生育执行的后期渐显其积极意义，其在经济快速发展时期，源源不断地提供了人口红利。其在中国经济与社会的转型时期——尤其是在从高速增长转向高质量发展时期，减轻了国家的治理成本，在人口老龄化水平相对较低的时期形成过渡期，也在一定程度上降低了转型成本，为中国的现代化做出了不可磨灭的贡献。

但人口转型或人口转变，在发生正功能的同时，也衍生了负功能，并越来越强烈地显现负功能。人口实践证明，由人口转变制造出正功能的速度越快，其迎来负功能的可能性也就越快。人口的转型，是社会发展与计划生育两个因素促进的转型。政府和学术界在制定人口政策时，重视了政府之手的作用，但在一定程度上忽视了市场和社会之手的作用。自20世纪80年代起抑制的人口增长，逐步降低了后来的劳动力人口供给，并在2000年之后逐渐出现劳动力人口连年净减少的现象，从2018年开始出现就业人口净减少的问题。当前的人口老龄化，就是20世纪80年代和90年代之后连年少生的结果，这使中国成为世界人口史上老龄化速度最快的国家，人口金字塔底部的收缩速度快于所有发展中国家。政府促动的计划生育与家庭对男孩的需求之间的矛盾，也造成居高不下的出生性别比，现在正通过人口流动以放大其负面影响的方式形成了婚姻挤压。中国历史上形成的家庭网和亲缘网支持体系，在家庭的小型化过程中逐步弱化，使社会不得不建构新的支持体系以缓解冲击。从世界各国人口干预效果上得出的唯一可靠的结论是：政府能够有效降低生育率，但却很难通过刺激提升生育率。因为鼓励生育的政策实施成本远远大于抑制生育所投入的政策成本。从2000年开始中国65岁老龄人口占总人口的比重就达到7%左右，2018年已经达到11.9%（60岁以上人口已经达到17.9%）。部分计划生育执行较严的大城市、特大城市和超大城市户籍人口已经过渡到老龄型阶段（65岁及以上老龄人口占总人口的比重超过14%）。2018年北京市户籍人口老龄化水平已经超过25%——对于这类城市来说，其如果离开流动人口中的劳动力人口，将很难正常进行生产和再生产。现在及未来一个时期，伴随高生育时期人口进入退休年龄，老龄化速度会进一步加快。尤其是在人口金字塔顶部的老龄化和底部的收缩中发生的老龄化，其影响会更为严重，中国将在第十四个五年计划时期步入更快的老龄化过程。正是在这个背景下，省会城市和除北京与上海之外的一线城市才开始了"抢人大战"，大约从2012年开始，以户籍制度改革为借由，各地陆续推出积分落户政策，形成"人才大战"格局。但从2018年开始，地方不得不调低了"人才"的政策性解释门槛，将"人才大战"向"人口大战"推进。到2019年，面对经济下行压力，像石家庄、西安等城市已实质性将"人才大战"转变为"人口大战"了。总之，单纯依靠劳动力人口的无限供给所形成的农村蓄水池已经枯竭了。中国不可能再在劳动力人口的净增长中维持较低的人工成本。超大城市、特大城市、大城市等正在抽离中等城市和小城市的人口。由人口流动带来的资源流动将在农村的空壳化之后制造城镇和小城市的空壳化——人口转型正在倒逼经济转型形成新增长动能。但最可靠的动力来源依赖于科技进步。在人口红利消退之后，中国将在人口老化速度与科技进步速度之间展开长久的赛跑，如果科技进步跑赢人口老化速度，则发展将比较顺利；如果老化速度跑赢科技进步速度，则发展战略就需要长期进行波动性调整。①

我们从改革开放的实践中看到了生产关系等制度设施的改进对生产力的解放作用。千百年来，中国一直处于人口增长与饥饿风险分配的马尔萨斯陷阱之中，但改革开放以来的发展，彻底解决了中国人的粮食需

---

① 蔡昉：《人口转变、人口红利与刘易斯转折点》，《经济研究》2010年第4期。

求并改善了中国人的食物结构,使中国人从总体上摆脱了生存危机并真正开始消费升级。中国开始从人口总量的压力阶段进入年龄结构压力阶段。这一阶段形成与积累的风险比原来的总量压力所形成的风险所带来的压力更大。现在,养老问题比以往任何时候都显得重要。

在这种情况下,未来的人口政策将不得不在以下方面进行实质性调整:第一,适时废除《计划生育法》。在叫停《计划生育法》的同时,废除社会抚养费征缴制度,清理整个法律法规及政府文件中限制生育的条文,变限制生育的人口政策、或放松限制生育的人口政策为自由生育政策。虽然现代化水平越高,人类的生育率会越低,但终有一些夫妇存在生育孩子的偏好——这些生育在一定程度上会缓解断崖式下跌的生育水平,平缓人口下降趋势。

第二,适时出台"失独家庭保障条例"。对于在计划生育过程中认领了独生子女证的,独生子女又出现意外伤亡的脆弱家庭,提供从物资到心理的人道主义支持。尤其是对于逐渐进入老年失能阶段的失独家庭,必须提供与时代发展水平相一致的保障支持。

第三,建立生育友好型社会。优化社会公共服务,推进基本公共服务均等化水平,加强社区治理体系和治理能力的现代化建设,真正贯彻落实党的十九大提出的幼有所育、学有所教、劳有所得、病有所医、老有所养、住有所居和弱有所扶"七有"号召,建立家庭友好型社会或生育友好型社会。如果幼儿园入园价格奇高、学习费用难以降低、劳动收入差距不能缩小、看病难看病贵问题不好解决、养老压力加大、住房价格高企、脆弱群体得不到扶持,生育率就很难回升。当前的年青一代,既担忧父母的养老问题,也担心孩子的抚养压力,他们徘徊于养老与养小之间,很难做出生育决定,这才出现实际生育率大大低于政策生育率的现象。

第四,在全国建立免费的公立幼儿园。普及公立幼儿园,鼓励民营企业兴办托儿所或幼儿园,政府购买入园位。根据家庭收入水平制定差额入园费,即对低收入水平家庭免除入园费或少交入园费。等到国力发展到既定水平,则实行公立幼儿园完全免费的政策,减轻家庭育儿压力。

第五,以家庭为单位建立个税征缴体系。对以夫妇方式报税的,或者对以挈带子女生活家庭报税的,在一定程度上降低个税税负,或提高个税起征点。对生育了第二个子女的家庭，进一步降低税负。对生育了三个及以上子女的家庭，实行负所得税制，即对家庭人均可支配收入达不到某一标准的多子女家庭，将其收入补足到核定标准。

第六，鼓励地方政府出台刺激生育政策。采取先实验再普及的方式，率先在特大城市或超大城市这类户籍人口老龄化水平奇高的地区，出台刺激生育政策，为新出生的幼儿提供生活补贴费用。考虑到社会主义初级阶段的特征，可以为二胎实行既定额度的生活补贴政策。

第七，积极发展人工智能等机器人。提高生产效率，缩短工作时间、减轻劳动过程的人力消耗，延长假期、提升生活质量。从发达国家鼓励生育的政策实践可以看出，即使出台成本极高的鼓励生育政策，总和生育率也很难上升到 2.1 的更替水平。在这种情况下，为激发长远发展动力，需要集中力量开发机器人，并发展机器人替代人力的各种技能，在人口老龄化逐渐加深的背景中，保障国民经济的顺利发展，通过人机互动或人机社会的建设，减轻养老压力，增加新动能，争取早日实现中华民族伟大复兴中国梦。

以上建议可以概括为"三步走"：第一步，在 2020 年小康社会建成之后废止原有限制生育的政策。第二步，在 2021—2025 年实行家庭友好型社会建设，逐步而富有实效地减轻父母的育儿成本。第三步，2026 年之后实行鼓励生育的人口政策，先从第二孩开始为未成年子女提供一定生活补贴及其他可能的社会服务，从育龄妇女的存量和增量两个方面刺激生育。

人际信息交互与现代化治理机制

Anatoly Lazarevich
白俄罗斯国家科学院哲学研究所所长、教授

管理问题就其本质来讲是多层面的,可以根据应用领域对其进行区分。在评估社会生产方法结构的根本转变时,卡尔·马克思曾经写道:"……各种社会活动的组合充当生产者"①。在这种管理活动中可以明确地观察到两个层次:(1)作为转化和受控的自然过程参与技术过程的管理;(2)参与对合作过程的管理以及工作者活动按功能上的特定形式划分过程的管理。

科学、工程和技术领域的一般文明成就在解决管理问题方面发挥了显著作用。20世纪60年代美国杰出的经济学家和社会学家加尔布雷斯(J. Galbraith)提出了技术结构的概念。技术结构是一个主要由专家组成的层级组织:这些专家中包括普通工程技术人员、职业经理人和企业高管。加尔布雷斯认为,技术结构是一种精英统治,他们集中在国民经济的大型公司中。由于这些大型组织机构起着领导作用,因此技术结构的代表者们占据了社会的领导地位。

技术专家体制概念的变体之一是施泰因布赫(K. Steinbuch)的"精英控制论"理论。他认为现代社会中的权力应该属于数学家、经济学家和程序员,因为他们比其他的普通人更能判定管理决策的有效性。

本文将尝试从区分文化作为一种有机体和文明作为一种机制的观点

---

① Из неопубликованных рукописей К. Маркса. – Большевик. – 1939. – №11, с. 64.

来论述治理现代化的机制。机体与文明的统一性明显体现在现代"组织"（源自希腊语ὄργανον——工具）现象中，它是社会财富生产、交换、分配和消费的目的，也是专门的信息沟通结构和功能结构以及对这一过程有效管理的实现。作为控制的一种结构—过程催化剂，关于组织的知识是人类行为学（praxeology，源于古希腊语πρᾶξις——活动，和λογία——科学、学问，即关于人类活动组织有效性的科学）的一个重要组成部分。

马克思曾经在《费尔巴哈论》中写道：社会生活本质上是务实的。但是术语"praxeology（人类行为学）"是在1890年由埃斯比纳斯（A. Espinas）首次使用的。著名的经济学家冯·米塞斯（L. von Mises）继续推动了人类行为学的发展。在他的专著《人类活动》中，他创造了一个新的科学方向——"praxeology（人类行为学）"，即关于人类行为的科学。①

从人类行为学的角度来看，研究各类组织机构的管理功能和各类组织机构在现代信息交流过程中的作用至关重要。根据定义，组织是人员、结构和过程的系统。就像"组合总计工人"一样，也有"总计经理"。技术和经济学、社会和精神生活的复杂性不断增加。这就需要包括管理人员在内的劳动分工与合作，最重要的是，它需要列姆（S. Lem）提到的"技术总和"的支持。

原则上讲，组织效应是人类生命活动的永恒伴侣和催化剂，从其原始形式（原始社会狩猎期间的劳动分工）开始，再到伟大的古代文明（埃及金字塔的建造，东方宏大的灌溉工程）。恩格斯用一个简单的例子令人信服地证明了组织协同作用的效果。在非洲殖民期间，法国和阿拉伯骑兵（Mamelukes——奴隶骑兵）之间经常发生冲突。它的特征是200名奴隶骑兵总是能打败200名法国骑兵；双方都有500名骑兵时多次交战会各有胜负；但是由于有较高的组织性，1000名法国骑兵总是能击败1000名奴隶骑兵。

效率更高的组织以更高水平的组织能力为特征绝非自相矛盾。系统，

---

① Мизес, Л. Человеческая деятельность: Трактат по экономической теории. – 2 – е испр. изд. / Л. Мизес. – Челябинск: Социум, 2005. – 878 с.

特别是复杂的系统，具有分层结构的特征，即按一定顺序将较低级别的系统包含到较高级别系统中。在复杂组织，特别是人类的系统中，组织和管理过程被作为一种特定特征加以区分，并且已从一种社会生产模式转变为另一种社会生产模式。

工业社会就是一个像机器一样的利维坦（Leviathan——庞然大物），它需要严格集中的、线性的和分级的治理。马克斯·韦伯（M. Weber）在他的"官僚组织"理论中表达了这一能够确保社会中有效人类活动的特征。"技术智能"赋予它以下特征：忽略组织合作者之间关系中的个人品质；基于职能专业化的劳动分工；清晰的权力等级；定义组织中每个成员的权利和义务的规则体系；一种程序系统，用于确定组织运作中所有情况下的行动顺序；通过资格甄选和晋升员工。

就效率而言，官僚型组织具有优势，恰如机器生产方式与非机械化生产方式相比所得的优势。同时，根据韦伯的观点，组织是对人类自由的否定，而其自由本身就是目的，只有在组织外部才能实现。目标—理性的出发点不仅被简化为人类—机器，而且被简化为类似机器的组织。别尔捷耶夫（N. Berdyaev）指出，有机体与它的外部机械组织之间存在根本差异，而有机体中包含自我发展的内部目标。

工业社会中的机械论原则被投射到整个社会关系上，"对于机器系统而言有效的条件也适用于各种不同人类活动的结合……"[1]。

就像天体力学一样，这个人造空间的尘世力学是微调的钟表发条，一个庞大的工厂，一个被客观化的、周期性地再现的过程，其中人是像螺丝钉一样的一个小部分，同时也是一个功能。斯宾诺莎的自由出现在意料之外的情况下——是对某些角色的理性认识以及对这些角色进行追随的紧迫需求。

从现代的信息—交流革命可知，很明显，工业时代的传统官僚化组织已经走进了死胡同。交流实践技术的发明和改进对社会发展的各个方面都产生了巨大影响，它定义了全新的组织形式，其功能特征包括：结构、管理系统、信息流的方向和信息传递的方法以及组织文化等。在新

---

[1] Маркс 1969 Маркс К., Энгельс Ф. Сочинения / К. Маркс, Ф. Энгельс. – 2 - е изд. - М.：Изд - во политической литературы, 1969. – Т. 27., –644 с, 214с.

型组织形式中许多经典的管理问题也得到了不同程度的解决。但是，现代计算机通信技术会大量利用自己的活动来协调信息流和员工的工作，从而在大型的、复杂的组织中大大优化了这些流程。

可以将这种趋势设定为传统关系在各种不同的组织活动中的重大转化，其发展方向是通信—技术解决方案在其结构中的明显优势。福斯特（L. Foster）和福林（D. Flynn）写道："权力机构的传统等级已被取代，能力的等级来了……权力和资源越来越集中在专业知识中心，而不是形式化的等级层次上。"[1]

塔尔得（G. Tarde）曾经注意到了沟通与整个组织之间的紧密关系。按照他的理论，信息传递的主导性质决定了社会结构的种类，每种交流类型都对应于某种社会类型。那么，现代信息通信技术在这种类型学意义上起什么作用？

卡斯特斯（M. Castells）指出了社会发展与组织技术发展之间的直接联系，他写道："社会能否控制住技术、特别是战略技术的能力在很大程度上决定了社会的命运"[2]。

世界图景的"展开"过程非常模棱两可，并且在许多方面仍未得到充分控制。阿加齐（E. Agazzi）在谈到文明发展的新技术阶段时指出："技术系统的功能本质上与目标无关，它的特征是'内在'发展，它会在自己的根基上增长。正是对目标的无关性使它能够感知不同的目标和价值观。极端的复杂性、自给自足和普遍存在是技术系统和工业系统以及技术文明与工业文明之间的本质差异。技术文明是一种生活方式，交流和思考方式，它通常是支配一个人的一系列条件的总和"[3]。

似乎阿加齐（E. Agazzi）在谈到社会—技术进步的几乎绝对的独立性的时候夸张了太多。如他所说，如果技术文明是"一种生活方式，交流

---

[1] L. W. Foster, D. M. Flynn, "Management Information Technology: Its Effects on Organizational Form and Function", *Management Information Systems Quarterly*, 1984, No. 8, pp. 229 - 236, 231.

[2] Кастельс, М. Информационная эпоха: экономика, общество и культура / М. Кастельс. - М.: ГУ ВШЭ, 2000. -608 с, 30с.

[3] Агацци, Э. Моральное измерение науки и техники / Э. Агации. - М.: Моск. филос. фонд. -1998. -344 с, 90с.

和思考方式",那么就会出现一个相应的问题:一个人能够确定这些属于人本身的现象并对其产生影响吗?

系统工程是控制技术中的出发点和基础。在"人工智能的哲学和方法论问题"科学理论研讨会上,俄罗斯科学院哲学研究所教授格洛霍夫(A. G. Gorokhov)在其学术报告"从继电器开关系统到纳米技术"中对其实质、结构和机制进行了深入的研究。从比较—历史角度,他指出最初的领域之一是自动化控制系统。当时关于管理的控制论盛行,管理被看作管理行为对控制数值偏离计划结果的反应。这主要是因为工程师进入了这个行业。企业,乃至更大程度上的整个行业及其管理结构都是复杂的社会—经济系统,控制论的概念性规定不足以对其进行描述。完全使它们自动化是不可能的并且通常是不切实际的。在这里有必要设计或(更准确地说)重组生产和管理活动。因此,这样的系统不是自动控制的系统(SAC),而是控制的自动系统(ASC)。

从本质上讲,对于现代科学技术,重要的是科学家和工程师可以在其帮助下提前正确地计划和实施其活动,并获得理想的结果。当今纳米系统工程中正在开发的各种图形表达和模型都是在为实现此目标服务。因此,在科学理论和应用领域中,建立各种逻辑模型的作用都在增加,这些逻辑模型一方面是用来结合不同学科的科学知识;另一方面则是作为以实际应用为重点的未来发展的"项目"。

但是,尽管系统技术非常重要,它们只是组织—交流活动的前提条件。与所有其他社会现象相比,组织活动的特殊性在于它们具有交流理智或它们是"社会处理器"。这种理智是在作为社会文化一部分的广义知识的基础上来创建真实(和非真实)的对象、过程和现象的完美(或脑力)模型的能力。

哲学家和诗人图特切夫(Tyutchev)用以下的话语表达了我们行动结果的不确定性:"我们未被给予预测我们的话会得到怎样回应的能力。"但是理智不仅可以创建现存的事物的模型,还可以创建可能存在的未来的模型,这些模型作为管理的基础,从其最简单的历史形式开始,以现代战略管理结束。

管理本身及其不可分割的组成部分——计划,可以定义为一种社会活动,它以控制为基础和手段,以达到创建一种未来最优理想状态的结果，并以此建构其控制论的模型。这些模型在给定参数方面是最佳的，而且这些模型还具有可实现性。许多漂亮的模型都具有无法将它们转化为现实的缺点。从最一般的意义上讲，可实现性是从客观世界的结构中创建行为与模型同构系统的实际可能性。

术语"模型"和"建模"在不同的上下文中的使用非常广泛。施托夫（V. A. Shtoff）对这些概念的定义如下："模型被理解为一种心理上可想象的或物质上可实现的系统，它可以显示或复制研究对象，从而能够替代它，以便其研究为我们提供有关该对象的新信息"①。他的结论是："因此，模型与建模对象的关系不是一致的，而是类比的……类比是结构的相似性"②。因此，模型是通过关联关系与建模对象关联的系统理想构造，也就是说，它能够表示建模对象的某些属性和关系，以及它们的本质性的相互关系。

模型的系统性质是至关重要的，因为模型元素之间的关系及其交互作用必须与对象元素之间的关系相对应。系统的模型只能是系统。作为客观现实的反映，它由某些符号结构（描述理论的文本，包括数学符号）和能够解释这些文本和实验的人工制品系统组成，反之亦然——通过实验结果对理论的文本加以修改。

要实施计划，必须在交流意识中、在"社会处理器"中拥有我们要计划其未来状态的对象的模型，又要有它周围环境的模型，从而确保更改的对象或新创建的对象可以实现并可以存在于这个环境中。它是一个通过各种相互作用连接成的一个有机体的整体系统，它的主要目的是构建与描述对象相关的模型。该系统预测控制对象发展的各种选项的能力很重要。计划进行的时间越长，变更越密集，认知模型应该越详细，系统要素的模型和它们之间的关联规律也就应该越准确。

任何系统可能具有的建模可能性（创建反映外部对象的内部模型）都会受到其复杂性的限制。关键是如果要进行建模，任何认知系统都必

---

① Штофф, В. А. Моделирование и философия / В. А. Штофф. - Л. : Наука, 1966. - 301 с, 19с.

② Штофф, В. А. Моделирование и философия / В. А. Штофф. - Л. : Наука, 1966. - 301 с, 139с.

须创建其建模的事物或过程的内部模型。但是，它只能使用其内部元素进行建模。如果被建模系统中比建模系统中具有更多的元素和关系，则必须简化和粗化这个模型。

由于不仅需要预见外部世界的自身发展，还要确保包括本身就已经很复杂的竞争性自我复制系统的发展，这就使问题变得更加复杂。因此，所有预见都是近似的。然而，进化的管理是可行的，我们能够创建的未来模型越准确（不一定更复杂），它就具有更高的质量。

20世纪70年代以来，对复杂的系统和过程进行建模的需求（主要是在工业企业管理领域）引起了大家对于为这种建模创建专用软件（称为模仿建模）的问题的重视。在整个经济朝着使用计算机技术的新方向发展的条件下，企业需要对信息过程进行建模，因为任何企业都开始不仅被视为官僚结构，而且被视为处理信息的系统。这就强调了开发特殊编程语言（称为模仿模型算法语言）的必要性，这些语言已成为复杂系统的结构表达与对其用高级编程语言描述之间的一种桥梁。

建模包括方案规划所需的在线模型时，计划参与者应该能够在某些实施方案的假设下快速模拟事件的发展。理想情况下，有必要建立一个全过程的仿真模型，以预测其演变过程。

为了改进计划过程，必须创建对象或过程的永久信息模型，因为有序地收集和整理大量信息需要更多的时间和材料成本。先创建这样的管理模型，然后对其进行更新和完善，这样做将会带来更大的收益。这种逻辑势在必行地需要一种能够贯彻以下原则的全新类型的管理。

（1）反转原则。价值—语义学的"支点"是有必要从社会及其子系统变革的新局面出发——反转其进化逻辑：在所有先前的阶段里生存是发展的必要先决条件，但从现在开始，发展是生存的条件。坚持这一原则意味着需要"人与物"之间的增效协同关系——管理现代信息技术在其相互作用中的"综合主体"的认知和交流潜力。

（2）情景和战略计划统一的原则。如果我们不是教条主义地即以流行的意识形态学精神看待问题（最新说法将其称为"稳定发展"），而是从人类学的角度讲，也就是说看其实质，现代世界主要关注情境管理，而忽略了超前战略规划的问题。这与卡夫卡《城堡》中囚犯的情况相似：七年来，他费尽心思地偷偷挖了一条隧道想借以逃脱，当他终于看到了隧道尽头的灯光时，他听到了监狱长的声音："恭喜，您终于挖到隔壁的牢房里了"。

当然，这完全不意味着否认情境管理及其在短期（约一年）的"滑动"运营状态中的更正。因为此时交流型管理机制的作用很小。战略管理却是另外一桩事情，它需要长期的情景预测、建模和较长时间的计划。波普尔（K. Popper）在他的著作《进化认识论》中写道："从进化的观点来看，理论（像所有一般知识一样）是我们适应环境的尝试的一部分。这样的尝试就像期望和期待。……所有知识的职能是试图预测我们周围环境中将发生的事情"①。为此，有必要开发可能的信息交流方案。而且，用最粗的线条得出未来几个最可能的模型比起消耗有限的认知资源来建立单一情景、更差异化的模型更为正确。

（3）战略建模和规划涉及实施将受控系统与环境分离的原则。要"掌握"组织的这种状态，有必要：①强调其完整性，即了解其哪些部分对于组织的保存和复制并非必需，而哪些是必需的；②确定其集成结构级别，即了解该组织是将哪种集成级别的元素组织到系统中的；③突出用于组织运作的典型相互作用；④找出组织的再生方式及其动态稳定性；⑤最后确定其演化方式。

在这样一个完整而同时又构成差别特征的工作中，"最薄弱环节"的问题变得尤为重要。美国宇航员格伦（J. Glenn）精巧地证实了这一点，他是第一位人类绕月之旅的指挥官。当他的团队完成必要的任务并打算重返地球时，飞船的自动控制系统证明了这种操作的不可能性。似乎宇航员必须为最坏的情况做好准备，但是格伦及时发现了仪器的故障，最终宇航员离开了地球卫星——月球，并安全着陆。在这个历史性时刻，指挥官说出了一句非常有力的话："还是要依靠人啊！"

（4）人类行为学浮现（拉丁语 emergere：出现，浮出表面）原则。这是该原则令人印象深刻的胜利，即系统产生新事物的能力。系统论的浮现是指在任何系统中都存在一些特殊的属性，它们并不是该系统的子系统或组成部分所固有的，同时也不是那些并非由特别的系统形成关系

---

① Поппер, К. Реализм и цель науки / К. Поппер // Современная философия науки. – М. : Логос, 1996. – С. 92 – 106.

所联结的元素之和所固有的，是指系统的各种属性对系统各个组成成分的属性之和的不可约性。在生物学和生态学中，浮现的概念可以表达如下：一棵树并不是森林，多个单细胞的积累并不是生物。例如，物种或生物种群的特性并不代表单个个体的特性，诸如生育率或死亡率之类的概念并不适用于单个个体，而是整体上适用于整个种群或物种。

组织管理的浮现是技术和社会进步的必然要求，而知识资源管理的文化在其中起着决定性的作用。在我们这个时代，在工业、科学、社会等各个领域产生新事物、创新的能力正成为生存和发展的关键问题。因此，管理应该是动态的，也就是说，它不仅应是包含一组数据的集合，它还应具有现实性和可预测的特征，具体来说，它还应包含关于某些行动，以及这些行动所导致的将来会发生哪些变化的预测性结果信息，还有一些已经制订的计划，在实现后对各方面运作影响的信息，更重要的是要包含一些来自与计划有关的工作或人员提供的有根据的信息。管理模型应该是演进的，即反映组织的组成和结构的历史连续性及其有意识和有计划地进行组织重组的真实可能性。管理模型实际上是对管理过程的一种建构。在这个过程中，特别是在具体的管理活动中，必然会留下过程的运动轨迹，这如同行星系统的运转。实际上，无论是在抽象化的模型中，还是具体的管理实践中，依赖形成有效管理的基础是知识和经验，而不是全依赖技术或自动化本身，实际的管理控制主体应该是人，这就为内置于管理中的知识为主体的控制，奠定了基础。在这项活动中有必要根据尼采（F. Nietzsche）提出的标准来区分过程："我们正在成长，但没有发展"。为了确定产品和连续浮现（emergence）过程的可持续发展原则，必须在增长、进化与发展之间进行明确区分。这需要管理团队的综合（交流）智力和潜力。

（5）基于能力（competence-based）的方法原则。在现代管理中，"知识"与"信息"不同。能力是组织作为社会机构及其合作者以最佳方式进行某些活动的特征，是由知识、技能和才能的和谐集合组成的。管理活动的组织被认为是"知识处理器"[1]。管理的主体是能力不断建立、

---

[1] Amin, A., Cohendet P., Organisational Lefming and Governance Through Embedded Practices, *Journal Management and Governance*, No. 4, 2000, p. 93.

维持、保留和发展的机构，因此需要对知识进行连续处理（processing）。

需要强调的是，组织的能力既不能归结为各种个人能力，也不能归结为个人能力的总和，其应具有系统—协同的性质。

（6）该领域的一位著名专家彼得洛维奇（M. Petrovich）追踪了组织对该过程的逻辑和技术进行掌握的动态机制。他指出，在现代组织中，经济、政治和行政权力的符号和因素会随着时间而发生变化。17世纪或更早的时期是基于蛮力的权力时代。这时的政府行政效能及管理质量水平无疑是相对较低的。亚历山大大帝的父亲菲利普二世的格言是："我知道满身背负金子的骡子战无不胜"——这一说法在当今已不像往日那般充满哲理。一种基于信息生产及其传递、使用和影响人们行为技术的权力才是最有效、最高质量的权力形式。

如今，经济、管理和市场营销正在实现从大规模生产和分销到高度定制化、有个性化地生产和满足客户需求的巨大飞跃。正在真正地或以模仿的形式形成以个人为目标的"个体的管理—营销"。因此，为抽象的消费者设计的管理和经济不可避免地会失败。

彼得罗维奇提醒人们注意发展各种形式的参与式管理（participative management）的广泛需求，即让员工参与制订计划和采取决策的过程。这表现为对资本的股本（股份）参与、收入分配以及各种专业团体的活动。

要特别注意人员培训。目前的主要趋势是在工作场所外进行培训，例如，美国公司每年在工作场所外培训的花费约为500亿美元。在传统教育形式之外，最受欢迎的教育类型是视频和电视讲座、用于自学的计算机程序和互联网课程等。[1]

（7）不论其规模和发展方向如何，现代组织密切而稳定增长的兴趣是基于同步原则的活动。其实质在于作为生产和管理最重要因素的时间利用的合理化，在于确保内部和外部过程与制度的一致性。

在所有国家中，主要机构（企业、公共组织、政府官僚机构、立法机构、家庭、教育系统和国际组织）的同步极为重要。为了应对内部和

---

[1] Петрович, М. Новые тренды современных организаций / М. Петрович // Беларуская думка. – 2013. – №7. – C. 48–54.

外部的高度动态发展以及社会过程的不匹配现象，产生了联盟、同盟和国际间协议。

新的组织发展基于现代的内部和外部交流，社会技术交流和信息正在成为组织价值体系中最重要的需求。管理在现代信息社会中的作用的变化主要是由于它越来越依赖新的、有前途的知识形式这一事实。至于把知识运用于管理本身，美国管理学家德鲁克（P. Drucker）称其为"管理领域的革命"[1]。

20世纪末，托夫勒（E. Toffler）在思考信息文明形成的前景时，这样说道："……一场全球性的权力之战在等待着我们，但其基础不是暴力，不是金钱，而是知识……最高质量的权力是通过应用知识得到的"[2]。托夫勒认为人类社会此前的、各个层面上的权力体系正在瓦解，他认为这与旧式管理风格的失败紧密相连，[3] 与基于信息和知识的新经济传播紧密相连，这总体上标志着社会向文明发展新阶段的全球性过渡。"……如果没有计算机、没有新兴复杂的生产过程、没有集成的多种多样（且不断变化）的技术、没有阔步前进的市场非大众化趋势、没有必要的信息数量和质量——这些都是系统能够生产物质价值所必需的，那么发达经济连30秒都难以持续……这是理解未来权力变化的关键，这也解释了为什么控制知识和交流手段的竞争在整个世界空间中爆发。"[4]

如今，源于层级交流的过渡十分引人注目。在层级交流中，当信息的使用者在社会活动的范畴和可能性系统中选择信息的来源、内容和实现方式时，信息接收者的角色就被急骤地降低到社会—积极层面。这也是管理交流基础上的一个新转变，它使得协调民众与当局之间、国家与社会之间、企业与客户之间以及工厂与消费者之间的关系成为可能。

现代的预测方法，即所谓的"预测"（foresight），也是建立在管理的

---

[1] Дракер, П. Посткапиталистическое общество // Новая постиндустриальная волна на Западе: Антология / Под ред. В. Л. Иноземцева. - М. : Academia, 1999. - С. 67 - 100, 71с.

[2] Тоффлер, Э. Метаморфозы власти: Пер. с англ. / Э. Тоффлер. - М. : ООО «Издательство АСТ», 2001. -669 с, 36с.

[3] Тоффлер, Э. Метаморфозы власти: Пер. с англ. / Э. Тоффлер. - М. : ООО «Издательство АСТ», 2001. -669 с, 23с.

[4] Тоффлер, Э. Метаморфозы власти: Пер. с англ. / Э. Тоффлер. - М. : ООО «Издательство АСТ», 2001. -669 с, 19с.

交流原则基础上的。最初，它们专注于科学和技术规划领域，并且试图对其目的进行根本性的改变。如果早先此目标与特定科学或技术领域的发展的长期预测相关联，并考虑其状态的初始水平，则现代的前瞻性预测系统的重点将放在未来需求而不是在现有的可能性上，同时也放在旨在实现未来需求的可能性发展预测上面。如今，前瞻性预测已被越来越多地用作塑造未来的系统工具，它可以考虑到社会活动的所有领域（科学技术、经济、社会关系和文化）都可能发生的变化。

　　成功实现预测—计划的关键是企业、科学界和政府机构协调一致地工作——它们正在努力在信息和交流的基础上达成共识。重要的是要强调，预测是一个沟通—管理过程，可以让我们针对未来需求做出协调而有效的决策。

治理现代化与社会全面进步

当代中国社会治理发展历程与方位

朱 涛

中国社会科学院社会发展战略研究院副研究员

改革开放四十余年来，中国走出了一条中国特色的发展道路，不仅在经济领域的成就举世瞩目，成长为世界第二大经济体，而且在社会治理方面也进行了大量的探索和实践，积累了宝贵的经验。纵观我国社会治理的变迁历程，总结我国社会治理改革的基本经验，对于进一步加强和创新社会治理，推进社会治理体系和治理能力现代化建设具有重要意义。

一 社会治理的改革与探索（1978—2012年）

1978年12月，党的十一届三中全会宣告将党的工作重点转到社会主义现代化建设上来。随着市场化改革的深入，社会治理为适应市场化改革和对外开放的需要，从放松"管控"开始，逐步向现代社会"管理"接轨，社会管理体制机制等议题也不断进入改革进程中。

1. 基层社会管理体制改革

党的十一届三中全会之后，农村地区推行生产承包责任制，生产大队和生产小队自然解体，人民公社体制已不适应生产承包责任制的要求。1982年12月，《中华人民共和国宪法》明确规定改革农村人民公社政社合一的体制，并确立农村基层政权为乡（镇）。1983年10月，中共中央、国务院印发《关于实行政社分开建立乡政府的通知》,要求各地有步骤地实行农村政社分开的改革,恢复乡人民政府体制。在乡以下,将原来的生产大队、生产小队改建为村民委员会和村民小组,全国范围内的人民公社改制全面铺开。至1984年年底,全国各地建立了9.1万个乡(镇)政府,92.6万个村民委员会。① 人民公社制度在改革中退出了历史舞台。1987年11月,《中华人民共和国村民委员会组织法(试行)》肯定了各地自发组建村民委员会的做法,并将村民委员会规定为村民"自我管理、自我教育、自我服务"的群众性自治,将村民自治用法律形式予以确认。1998年11月,经过约十年的实际运作和经验总结,《中华人民共和国村民委员会组织法》正式颁布,进一步完善了村民自治制度,将村民自治的内容概括为"民主选举、民主决策、民主管理、民主监督"。同时,明确了村党组织对村民自治的支持和保障作用,规定村党组织在村级组织中处于领导核心地位。2006年1月1日起全面取消农业税后,意味着村级组织代表国家为村民提供基本公共服务和社会管理的责任更加明确了。

在城市,1980年,全国人大常委会重新公布了《城市街道办事处条例》和《居民委员会组织条例》,街道办事处、居民委员会的机构和职能得以恢复。在社区建设上,1986年民政部首次把"社区"概念引入城市管理,提出在城市中开展社区服务工作,标志着我国社区服务和建设工作的开始。1989年12月通过的《中华人民共和国城市居民委员会组织法》,重申居民委员会是居民"自我管理、自我教育、自我服务"的基层群众性自治组织。此后,我国各地在实践中不断完善居民委员会制度,城市居委会发挥着越来越多的功能。一是工作范围逐步拓宽,拓展到社区的方方面面,包括宣传法律、法规和国家政策、维护居民的合法权益、办理公共事务、调解民间纠纷等;二是居民自治水平不断提高,普及居委会直选,推动社区工作人员的专业化,将社区居民议事会等制度引入社区自治过程中;三是居委会动员居民和辖区单位普遍开展了便民利民的服务活动。2000年11月,中共中央办公厅和国务院办公厅转发民政部《关于在全国推进城市社区建设的意见》,指出大力推进社区建设,是新形势下坚持党的群众路线、做好群众工作和加强基层政权建设的重要内

---

① 卢汉龙:《新中国社会管理体制研究》,上海人民出版社2015年版,第87、287页。

容，是面向新世纪我国城市现代化建设的重要途径。这一文件标志着此前多年的试验探索阶段宣告结束，社区建设被作为加强基层政权建设、改革城市基层管理体制的重要思路和重大举措。社区建设的核心已经不是社区服务，而是管理体制的创新。[1]

2. 户籍管理改革

改革开放以来，严格限制人口流动的户籍管理制度开始松动，户籍制度在城市化进程中不断调整。1984年10月13日，国务院发布《关于农民进入集镇落户的通知》，规定："凡申请到集镇务工、经商、办服务业的农民和亲属，在集镇有固定住所，有经营能力，或在乡镇企事业单位长期务工的，公安部门应准予落常住户口，及时办理入户手续，发给《自理口粮户口簿》，统计为非农业人口"。这一规定明确了农民自理口粮入镇的条件、程序和待遇，标志着在户籍意义上原本紧闭的城乡人口流动大门开始打开。1985年7月13日，公安部颁布了《关于城镇暂住人口管理的暂行规定》，对流动人口实行《暂住证》制度，允许暂住人口在城镇居留，公民具有在非户籍地长期居住的合法性。

1992年8月，公安部发出《关于实行当地有效城镇居民户口的通知》，受此影响，全国各地兴起了户籍制度改革的实践。浙江、广东、山东等地先后开始试行"当地有效城镇居民户口"，即"蓝印户口"，"蓝印户口"介于正式户口和暂住户口之间，管理的基本思路是在当地有效，按常住人口管理，统计为"非农业人口"。当时全国各地出现了各种各样的地方性城镇户口，如上海市1994年2月颁布的《上海市蓝印户口管理暂行规定》指出，"在上海投资人民币100万元（或美元20万元）及以上、或购买一定面积的商品房、或在上海有固定住所及合法稳定工作者均可申请上海市蓝印户口，持蓝印户口一定期限后可转为常住户口"[2]。2001年3月，国务院批转公安部《关于推进小城镇户籍管理制度改革的意见》（以下简称《意见》），县以下放开户口限制，我国小城镇户籍制度改革全面展开。该《意见》进一步放宽了农村户口迁移到小城镇的条

---

[1] 夏建中：《从街居制到社区制：我国城市社区30年的变迁》，《黑龙江社会科学》2008年第5期。

[2] 卢汉龙：《新中国社会管理体制研究》，上海人民出版社2015年版，第219—220页。

件，将城乡户籍改革的权限下放到各地方政府，使地方政府有了一定的改革主动权。不过，小城镇户籍改革关注的还是那些已在小城镇工作、生活的人口，当时改革的目的还未定位在农村城镇化上。而2011年2月，国务院办公厅《关于积极稳妥推进户籍管理制度改革的通知》则指出，要引导非农产业和农村人口有序向中小城市和建制镇转移，逐步满足符合条件的农村人口落户需求，逐步实现城乡基本公共服务均等化。

3. 社会治安综合治理

加强社会治安工作，稳定社会秩序是改革开放之初社会治理的重点。1982年1月，中共中央在《关于加强政法工作的指示》中要求，为了争取治安情况根本好转，必须加强党的领导，全党动手，认真落实综合治理方针。[1] 1991年3月，中共中央决定成立中央社会治安综合治理委员会，协助中共中央、国务院领导全国社会治安综合治理工作，下设办公室，与中央政法委机关合署办公。同时，各级政府也按要求设立相应的社会治安综合治理领导机构，配备专人负责。这样，全国自上而下建立了体系化的社会治安综合治理机构，全国的社会治安工作进入了新的阶段。2001年9月，中共中央、国务院做出《关于进一步加强社会治安综合治理的意见》，提出要坚持"打防结合、预防为主"的方针，进一步把严打、严管、严防、严治有机结合起来，要坚决纠正"重打轻防"的错误倾向，切实把思想观念、工作重点、警力配置、经费投入、考核奖惩机制等真正落实到"预防为主"上来，深入开展矛盾纠纷排查调处工作，认真落实各项安全防范措施。[2] 2004年9月，党的十六届四中全会通过的《中共中央关于加强党的执政能力建设的决定》强调，坚持打防结合、预防为主、专群结合、依靠群众，加强和完善社会治安综合治理工作机制。这是在总结社会治安综合治理多年实践经验的基础上，对社会治安综合治理方针的重要补充。从此，"打防结合、预防为主，专群结合、依靠群众"的"16字方针"明确成为社会治安综合治理工作的指导方针。

---

[1] 卢汉龙：《新中国社会管理体制研究》，上海人民出版社2015年版，第305页。
[2] 倪小宇：《改革开放30年社会治安综合治理发展历程》，《福建警察学院学报》2008年第6期。

4. 社会管理的提出与发展

"社会管理"一词最早出现在1998年《关于国务院机构改革方案的说明》中，强调政府的基本职能在于宏观调控，社会管理和公共服务。2002年，党的十六大报告将社会管理明确为政府的四项主要职能之一。在第五部分"政治建设和政治体制改革"中指出，"要坚持打防结合、预防为主，落实社会治安综合治理的各项措施，改进社会管理，保持良好的社会秩序"。在这里，社会管理被列为维护社会稳定的具体途径。

2004年党的十六届四中全会在《中共中央关于加强党的执政能力建设的决定》中提到"加强社会建设和管理，推进社会管理体制创新。深入研究社会管理规律，完善社会管理体系和政策法规，整合社会管理资源，建立健全党委领导、政府负责、社会协同、公众参与的社会管理格局。"这是中央文件首次提出"社会建设"概念以及"党委领导、政府负责、社会协同、公众参与"的"16字方针"。社会管理的"16字方针"坚持党的领导，同时改变了以往强调单一政府管理的模式，突出政府、社会和公民的协同管理，标志着执政党对社会管理认识的深化。

2007年，党的十七大报告从实现全面建设小康社会新要求的角度提出了建设更加健全的社会管理体系的要求。在重申"健全党委领导、政府负责、社会协同、公众参与的社会管理格局"的同时，提出了"要最大限度激发社会创造活力，最大限度增加和谐因素，最大限度减少不和谐因素"的新要求。2011年7月，中共中央、国务院颁布《关于加强和创新社会管理的意见》，再次重申"党委领导、政府负责、社会协同、公众参与"的社会管理"16字方针"。

总体上，1978—2012年，随着人民公社制和单位制的不断瓦解，以村民委员会和居民委员会为代表的基层群众自治制度诞生并走向完善；户籍管理制度改革，人口在城乡之间的流动和迁居日益频繁。同时，在市场化改革的大潮下，社会矛盾和社会问题多发频发，社会治理改革的主要任务是应对和消解经济市场化所衍生的各种消极、负面后果，带有较强维稳色彩。[1] 在经济体制改革的同时，改革也进入社会领域，社会管

---

[1] 陈鹏：《中国社会治理40年：回顾与前瞻》，《北京师范大学学报》（社会科学版）2018年第6期。

理、社会建设等概念的提出,标志着党和国家意识到社会发展与经济发展的不协调,已经成为这一时期的主要矛盾。① 因此,统筹经济和社会发展,使经济和社会平衡协调发展,是时代向我们提出的重大课题。

二 新时代的社会治理(2012 年至今)

2012 年,党的十八大提出"要围绕构建中国特色社会主义社会管理体系,加快形成党委领导、政府负责、社会协同、公众参与、法治保障的社会管理体制"。这一表述首次提出了要构建中国特色社会主义社会管理体系,并增加了社会管理需要"法治保障",表明社会管理要与法治相结合,形成了社会管理体制的"20 字方针"。同时,党的十八大将社会管理和民生并列为社会建设的重要内容,提出要把社会管理和社会建设统一起来,以"创新社会管理"来促进社会建设,并要提高社会管理的科学化水平,积极鼓励社会主体参与到社会管理中来。

2013 年,中共十八届三中全会通过的《中共中央关于全面深化改革若干重大问题的决定》,在提法上首次将"社会管理"转化为"社会治理",并专列一章部署创新社会治理体制。这是中国共产党在党的正式文件中第一次提出"社会治理"概念,标志着我们党执政理念的新变化。习近平总书记强调:"加强和创新社会治理,关键在体制创新。"用"社会治理"来取代"社会管理",虽然是一字之差,背后其实是关于权力的属性、功能和运作方式,以及国家与社会之间关系的重新理解。社会治理中的"治理",意味着彻底放弃基于计划体制而来的国家(政府)包办单干的思路,并将"社会治理"作为国家治理体系和治理能力现代化的重要内容,② 实现了从"社会管理"向"社会治理"的理念新飞跃。

2017 年 10 月,党的十九大提出"打造共建共治共享的社会治理格局",在社会治理体制上,要求按"党委领导、政府负责、社会协同、公众参与、法治保障"的"20 字方针"继续完善,并首次系统提出了社会治理"四化",即提高社会治理社会化、法治化、智能化、专业化水平。

---

① 陆学艺:《当代中国社会建设》,社会科学文献出版社 2013 年版,第 1 页。
② 冯仕政:《社会治理新蓝图》,中国人民大学出版社 2017 年版,第 61—62 页。

2019年10月党的十九届四中全会提出坚持和完善共建共治共享的社会治理制度，明确提出了社会治理的"制度"建设。同时，将"民主协商""科技支撑"纳入社会治理体系要求，形成新"28字方针"，并将"社会治理共同体"的意义丰富为人人有责、人人尽责、人人享有。

可见，自党的十八大以来，社会治理在党和政府的各类表述中越来越受到重视，社会治理的理念、重点、内容也越来越明确，以"治理"为要求和特征的社会治理在社会主义建设事业中正发挥着越来越重要的作用。

1. 健全社区治理基本制度框架

2015年7月中共中央组织部、民政部等《关于进一步开展社区减负工作的通知》，2015年7月中办、国办《关于加强城乡社区协商的意见》，以及2017年6月中共中央、国务院《关于加强和完善城乡社区治理的意见》，成为党的十八大以来基层社会治理中三个标志性的社区政策文件。[①] 上述文件明确指出，城乡社区是社会治理的基本单元，完善社区治理体制，目标是要把城乡社区建设成为和谐有序、绿色文明、创新包容、共建共享的幸福家园。在具体措施上，上述文件要求各省（自治区、直辖市）按照条块结合、以块为主的原则，制定区县职能部门、街道办事处（乡镇政府）在社区治理方面的权责清单；依法厘清街道办事处（乡镇政府）和基层群众性自治组织权责边界，明确基层群众性自治组织承担的社区工作事项清单以及协助政府的社区工作事项清单；在社区工作事项之外的其他事项，街道办事处（乡镇政府）可通过向基层群众性自治组织等购买服务方式提供。同时，要求建立街道办事处（乡镇政府）和基层群众性自治组织履职履约双向评价机制。

2. 推动政府职能转变

党的十八大以来，国家不断推动政府职能转变，更加强调基层政府要在创新社会治理中发挥重要作用，各级地方政府开始深入探索以政府职能转变为核心的社会治理创新。例如上海市2014年取消了街道办事处的经济职能，基层管理的重心全面转移至公共服务、公共管理与公共安

---

① 陈鹏：《中国社会治理40年：回顾与前瞻》，《北京师范大学学报》（社会科学版）2018年第6期。

全领域，进而推动城市治理的精细化。① 2015年12月，中共中央、国务院印发《关于深入推进城市执法体制改革改进城市管理工作的指导意见》，提出构建权责明晰、服务为先、管理优化、执法规范、安全有序的城市管理体制，推动城市管理走向城市治理，促进城市运行高效有序。2017年2月，中办、国办印发了《关于加强乡镇政府服务能力建设的意见》，要求把握实现基本公共服务均等化的发展方向，以增强乡镇干部宗旨意识为关键，以强化乡镇政府服务功能为重点，以优化服务资源配置为手段，以创新服务供给方式为途径，有效提升乡镇政府服务水平。2018年2月，党的十九届三中全会做出了深化党和国家机构改革的决定，目标是构建系统完备、科学规范、运行高效的党和国家机构职能体系，形成总揽全局、协调各方的党的领导体系，职责明确、依法行政的政府治理体系，全面提高国家治理能力和治理水平。

3. 加强公共安全和矛盾化解

2015年4月，中办、国办印发《关于加强社会治安防控体系建设的意见》，要求以确保公共安全、提升人民群众安全感和满意度为目标，以突出治安问题为导向，以信息化为引领，以基础建设为支撑，加强信息资源互通共享和深度应用，加快公共安全视频监控系统建设，健全点线面结合、网上网下结合、人防物防技防结合、打防管控结合的立体化社会治安防控体系，形成党委领导、政府主导、综治协调、各部门齐抓共管、社会力量积极参与的社会治安防控体系建设工作格局，确保人民安居乐业、社会安定有序、国家长治久安。

2014年2月，中办、国办印发了《关于创新群众工作方法解决信访突出问题的意见》，强调通过加大保障和改善民生力度、提高科学民主决策水平、坚持依法办事等从源头上预防和减少信访问题；通过健全诉求表达和办理方式、突出领导干部接访下放重点、完善联合接访、发挥法定诉求表达渠道作用等方式，进一步畅通和规范诉求表达渠道。此后，2016年10月，中办、国办印发了《信访工作责任制实施办法》，按照"属地管理、分级负责，谁主管、谁负责，依法、及时、就地解决问题与疏导教育相结合"的工作原则，综合运用督查、考核、惩戒等措施，依

---

① 李友梅：《中国社会治理的新内涵与新作为》，《社会学研究》2017年第6期。

法规范各级党政机关履行信访工作职责。①

4. 引领社会组织健康发展

大力培育社会组织，激发社会活力是近年来我国社会治理模式转型中最引人注目的一条制度创新主线。② 2013 年 9 月国务院办公厅出台了《关于政府向社会力量购买服务的指导意见》，2015 年国务院办公厅转发了财政部、国家发展改革委、中国人民银行的《关于在公共服务领域推广政府和社会资本合作模式指导意见的通知》，改善了社会组织发展和参与社会治理的空间。在此基础上，地方政府以招投标、公益创投等形式的购买社会组织服务项目广泛发展。2015 年 9 月，中共中央办公厅印发了《关于加强社会组织党的建设工作的意见（试行）》，提出按照建设基层服务型党组织的要求，推进社会组织党的组织和党的工作有效覆盖，拓展社会组织党组织和党员发挥作用的途径，发挥党在社会组织中的战斗堡垒与政治核心作用。

2016 年 8 月，中共中央办公厅、国务院办公厅印发了《关于改革社会组织管理制度促进社会组织健康有序发展的意见》，提出坚持党的领导、改革创新、放管并重、积极稳妥推进，建立健全统一登记、各司其职、协调配合、分级负责、依法监管的中国特色社会组织管理体制，基本建立政社分开、权责明确、依法自治的社会组织制度，基本形成结构合理、功能完善、竞争有序、诚信自律、充满活力的社会组织发展格局。

5. 运用互联网提升社会治理

网络社会的兴起是当代社会治理面临的新挑战和新情境。党的十八大以来，运用互联网参与社会治理体现在：一是以"互联网＋"推动政府服务创新，全国各地创新出"最多跑一次""电子政务大厅"等跨部门数据共享、协同治理形式，政府信息公开明显提升，社会治理的智能化程度进展迅速。二是加强对网络空间的治理。截至 2020 年 3 月，我国网民规模达 9.04 亿，但网络空间并不是法外之地。2017 年 6 月《中华人民共和国网络安全法》开始实施，使得网络空间的治理有法可依，保障并促进了网络空间的健康发展。

---

① 张来明：《中国社会治理体制历史沿革与发展展望》，《社会治理》2018 年第 9 期。
② 李友梅：《中国社会治理的新内涵与新作为》，《社会学研究》2017 年第 6 期。

6. 创新社会治理的安全维度

党的十九大报告指出,"树立安全发展理念,弘扬生命至上、安全第一的思想,健全公共安全体系,完善安全生产责任制,坚决遏制重特大安全事故,提升防灾减灾救灾能力"。这就要求将"安全"作为社会治理的重要维度,有效抵御社会生活中的各类风险。同时,社会治理也与有效维护国家安全紧密相连。2014 年 4 月,中央国家安全委员会第一次会议正式提出"总体国家安全观"。2019 年 10 月党的十九届四中全会提出,坚持总体国家安全观,需以人民安全为宗旨,以政治安全为根本,以经济安全为基础,以军事、科技、文化、社会安全为保障,健全国家安全体系,增强国家安全能力。社会治理中贯彻总体国家安全观,就要坚持底线思维,着力防范化解重大风险。

总体上,自党的十八大以来,以习近平同志为核心的党中央大胆探索、勇于实践,全面创新社会治理体系,系统提升社会治理能力,迎来了和谐稳定良治的大好局面。[1] 在这一过程中,社会治理的内容和重点也在实践中不断发生着变化,社会治理的体系不断完善,走出了一条中国特色社会主义社会治理之路。

三 社会治理的基本经验

改革开放四十余年来,我国走出了一条有中国特色的社会治理之路,积累了适合中国国情的社会治理经验。

1. 坚持和完善党的领导

党的领导是中国特色社会主义制度的最大优势,中国共产党是社会治理的领导力量。由于文化、体制等因素的不同,世界范围内存在不同的政党政治模式,但就中国的社会治理而言,从革命走向建设,中国共产党始终扮演者领导核心的角色,对中国的发展和稳定发挥着不可替代的作用。中国共产党代表最广大人民的根本利益,最能够兼顾地区之间、部门之间、群体之间、公民之间的社会治理利益关系的协调发展,最能

---

[1] 张翼:《走中国特色社会主义社会治理之路》,《求是》2018 年第 6 期。

够动员整合各方面资源,推动社会治理创新发展。① 从社会治理体系的"28字方针"可以看出,社会治理要充分发挥党总揽全局协调各方的领导核心作用,牢牢把握党对社会治理的领导权。同时,加强党的自身建设,提高党的执政能力和水平,也是保持社会治理正确发展方向的保障。如果没有党自身的治理改革和自我革命,就不可能有中国社会治理的根本性变革。从这个角度而言,坚持党要管党、全面从严治党、坚决惩治腐败就是最大的社会治理。②

2. 因应形势推动治理模式转型

改革开放以来,随着各类生产要素的解放和适应对外开放的需要,社会治理逐渐放松管制,并开始引入"管理"理念,"加强政府的社会管理职能"成为市场化改革的重要保障。与此同时,改革涉及利益的调整分化,各类新社会问题、矛盾的相继出现,在经济体制改革的同时,改革也进入社会领域,社会管理、社会建设等概念的提出,标志着党和国家意识到社会发展与经济发展的不协调,亟须加强和创新社会治理。自党的十八大,特别是2013年党的十八届三中全会以来,社会治理改革不断推进,完善形成了"28字方针",社会治理的主体也走向多元化,正致力于打造"共建共治共享"的社会治理制度,走向制度之治。

3. 落脚基层不断创新社会治理

社会治理的基础在基层,城乡社区是社会治理的基本单元。"社会治理的重心必须落到城乡社区,社区服务和管理能力强了,社会治理的基础就实了。"③ 随着改革开放的不断深入,整个社会越来越以地域为基础,社区建设已成为社会治理的主要依托。近年来,全国各地涌现出诸多社区治理创新的典型,有的从增强居民参与能力入手,组织居民协商解决涉及公共利益的决策事项;有的引导各类主体参与社区建设,调动企业、社会组织等参与社区服务项目,提高了社区的服务供给能力;有的以社区治理法治化为抓手,制定修订社区治理的法律法规,推进公共法律服

---

① 张翼:《走中国特色社会主义社会治理之路》,《求是》2018年第6期。
② 魏礼群:《党的十八大以来社会治理的新进展》,《光明日报》2017年8月7日。
③ 习近平:《推动中国上海自由贸易试验区建设 加强和创新特大城市社会治理》,《人民日报》2014年3月6日。

务体系建设，增强了社区依法办事的能力。可见，社会治理只有落脚于基层，才有不断创新的动力，真正回应民众需求。

4. 回应人民呼声不断改革社会治理

从"为人民服务"到"以人民为中心"，社会治理的改革呼应了人民的需求，从而使社会治理始终有着强大的革新动力。例如，严格的户籍管理制度，曾极大限制了人民自由迁徙的权利，是造成城乡隔离、城乡差距的重要制度性障碍，而社会治理改革则不断放开户籍限制，允许城乡之间人员的自由流动，逐步实现城乡基本公共服务均等化。政府曾经包办社会生活，而居民自治、村民自治则鼓励发挥人民群众自身的治理活力。因此，推进任何一项改革，包括推进社会治理改革、社会体制改革，都需要站在人民立场上把握涉及改革的重大问题，从最广大人民利益出发谋划改革思路，制定各项改革措施。

5. 立足现实使社会治理符合国情

中国疆域辽阔，人口众多，同时又具有久远的历史文化传统，社会治理既不能简单沿用历史上的某些模式，也不能照搬某些"先进"的西方治理模式。当前，网络空间的迅速发展是社会治理面临的新现实，需根据互联网特点跟上并改进"虚拟"社会的治理方式，探索网上网下治理的协同与衔接。同时，自治、德治、法治等都是社会治理的可能路径，需根据不同地方的不同状况，结合实际综合应用，使社会治理从"单一"到"多元"，动员多种资源和多类主体共同参与，倡导源头治理,[1] 以实现良好的社会治理效果。

四 社会治理展望

回顾改革开放以来的发展历程，中国的社会治理发生了多维的变迁。社会治理已成为中国现代化发展经验的重要组成。展望未来，社会治理方式需不断创新，社会治理制度需不断完善。一是继续坚持党委领导、政府负责。在立足国情完善社会治理制度过程中，要把党的领导和我国

---

[1] 景天魁：《源头治理——社会治理有效性的基础和前提》，《北京工业大学学报》（社会科学版）2014年第3期。

社会主义制度优势转化为社会治理优势，政府负责不是政府要包揽一切，而是要负责激发社会活力，动员群众参与到社会治理的实践中来。只有培育更多的社会治理主体，并在相互之间构建完善的协商、互动、合作机制，才能有效满足人民群众的各种需求。二是不断提升社会治理的法治化水平。随着改革的不断深入，社会治理涉及利益协调、矛盾化解、社会稳定的情况将更为复杂，新时代提升社会治理法治化水平需遵循"科学立法、严格执法、公正司法、全民守法"，真正实现社会治理的良法善治。三是将社会治理与社会建设更好地统一起来，在改善民生中推进社会治理。形成有效的社会治理，目的不仅仅是形成良好的社会秩序，还要使人民获得感、幸福感、安全感更加充实、更有保障、更可持续。

构建更可持续的生态治理体系

Natalia Lazarevich

白俄罗斯国家科学院哲学研究所首席研究员

确保为社会发展提供有效的环境条件，是国家和公共行政管理部门的一项重要任务。在这方面，对生态系统的研究涉及生态系统与人类和社会的直接联系，生态系统本身被视为社会生态系统。任何社会生态系统都由两个主要子系统组成——自然子系统和社会组织子系统。人类在其生命（作为生物存在）和物质生产（作为社会存在）的过程中，只有在与环境不断相互作用的条件下才能生存。

人类对自然子系统的可持续性过程进行管理，分析其结构，认识到生态系统的稳定性不仅依赖于能量和物质的自然交换，也依赖其结构所形成的复杂性。

自然子系统可持续性过程的管理是通过分析其结构和了解以下事实来开展的，即稳定性不仅取决于能量和物质的自然交换，还取决于在演化过程中所形成的其结构的复杂性，以及系统内各种形式和关系的形成。这些进化过程决定了哪些是适应性更强的生物系统，从而确保这些生物系统保持稳定状态。

社会子系统包括人口、工业、工程、通信、能源和其他复杂对象，其运行和管理源于科学和社会经验、经济效益和社会规划。

整个社会生态系统的成功运行取决于考虑每个子系统的特点并建立它们之间的关系。社会生态危机通常是由于自然子系统和社会子系统之间缺乏和谐的关联而发生的。这通常是因为往往优先考虑社会和经济因素——企业数量增加、城市密度增加等,而社会生态系统的自然组成部分则根据残差原则而发展。最后,这种不平衡导致整个社会生态系统的危机和不稳定运行,这会影响人民的生活质量及其参与经济生产过程的效力。这就是为什么研究、预测和管理社会生态系统的发展过程是国家和公共行政管理部门的主要任务之一。

社会生态系统可以说是一种自我调节系统,其和谐发展由一系列措施来保证。在这方面,著名科学家巴钦斯基(Bachinsky G. A.)强调,这绝不意味着人类可以改变子系统中发生的自然规律和内部过程。然而,人类能够并且应该学会正确使用它们,以便对整个系统进行有针对性的管理。[1] 这种环境对象的正常运行状态是动态平衡状态,其中社会与自然之间的物质—能量交换有机地蕴含在物质和自然能量流动的自然循环中,物质和能量的整体平衡因此得以维持。如果由于不平衡的人为影响导致这种平衡被扰乱,社会生态系统就开始退化;同时,社会生态系统完全解体的可能性很高,由此产生各种环境和社会经济后果。

任何社会生态系统都是一个具有复杂层次结构的系统。例如,人们可以谈论全球国家社会生态系统,而这些系统又由区域级的、从地区到区域级的子系统等组成。所述各级子系统在正常条件下都是自然互联的。随着等级的提高,各子系统对相邻生态系统的依赖度降低,同时自我调节的自主性和能力提高。社会生态系统不同于自然系统本身,它们的特点不仅与人类和自然系统相互作用的水平相关,而且与人类感知、评估这些相互作用的结果,包括环境危机和冲突情况相关。社会生态系统可以说是将人口及其生活基础设施与各国、行政地区、城市和农业企业等自主管理行政单位内的环境相结合的区域系统。小型家庭农场也可以归于社会生态系统,视为微生态系统,应通过合理的自然管理来保证其动态平衡。[2]

应再次强调,社会生态系统属于动态系统范畴,其正常运行是通过

---

[1] G. A. Bachinsky, *Social Ecology: Theoretical and Applied Aspects*, Kyiv: Nauk. dumka, 1991, p. 22.

[2] G. A. Bachinsky, *Social Ecology: Theoretical and Applied Aspects*, Kyiv: Nauk. dumka, 1991, p. 23.

维持这样一种平衡来实现的：在这种平衡中，社会与自然之间的物质—能量交换有机地蕴含在自然进化之中。一个正常运行的社会—生态系统是这样一个系统：其主要结构要素是稳定的，内部所发生的进程不违反其完整性和质量确定性。因此，社会生态系统比纯粹的自然或社会系统复杂得多，预测此类系统的发展是一项非常紧迫的任务。

预测过程包括确定或制定可能的发展变量，以及评估实施某些发展变量的可能性。在进行社会自然预测时，很难用估计概率量化结果。这种对特定发展道路的可行性进行概率评估的程序通常只是相对于技术系统而言的。这就是之所以研究过程可能的发展选项清单的方式进行预测分析的原因。该清单作为选项清单，每个选项均附有有意义的描述（预测分析的主要结果），作为系统开发方案的基础。这一预测分析程序的目的是分析和描述执行已制订的计划草案的各种后果。对预测结果的后续分析可以评价计划行动的现实性和质量。

有三组供实际使用的预测和管理方法：外推法、专家评估法和逻辑建模。外推法基于对所研究过程发展结果的自觉简化、借助数学模型对所获得数据的描述以及以"模型"方式对未来时刻的进一步计算。用该方法可以在将来搜索系统状态的可接受估计值，但仅用于描述演化发展的过程。建模的内容和目的是设计适应性特性，分析社会在使生物圈达到均衡的过程中表现出必要的灵活性、执行自我调节功能的能力。在生物圈功能质量恶化的情况下，社会—自然建模应提供在不干扰自然界生物平衡的情况下维持人类作为生物物种存在的必要条件的方法。

众所周知，任何系统（包括社会生态系统）的发展过程都包含进化性变化和从一个状态突然转变到另一个状态这两个时期。突然转变是由自然和社会现实的重大变化造成的——世界人口状况的变化、环境污染的增加、各种自然和社会灾难。

21世纪也许是人类历史上环境最危险的世纪，全球能源危机、人口生物退化、自然资源缺乏和枯竭等问题明显恶化。环境退化导致自然生态系统自我调节机制遭到破坏，不断增长的工业过程对现代文明构成严重威胁。根据现有预测，21世纪也将是新疾病数量增长的世纪，新冠肺炎疫情已经证明了这一点。

社会—自然系统发展出现突然转变的一个例子是与使用工具有关的

人类自然史。物质文化的进步可以而且应该说是以工具，即人工器官来补充自然器官功能能力的过程。长期以来，人类所创造的工具只补充了一些对人类重要的功能。就这一点而言，自然选择的压力非常巨大，因此遗传转化的速度非常快。向生产性经济的转变成一种客观过程，它几乎同时决定了不同民族和文化之间与自然之间的一种新型关系。维尔纳茨基（V. I. Vernadsky）预见到，人类对周围自然的影响会迅速增加，以至于人类会很快变成构成地球表面的主要地质作用力量。①

基于进化发展模型的预测表明，在从某个时刻开始已使用技术的框架内，有必要引入越来越多的新能源能力，而且越来越多的资源用于满足工业本身的需求。如果说经济增长的特点是定量指标（产量增加、国内生产总值增长等），那么，为了分析经济发展，则使用教育和卫生等类别的定性特征。可持续经济增长是指数量特征变化的单向向上矢量，而经济发展则允许偏离这种动态，从而有利于确保定性的"非经济"特征（环境状态、公共卫生等）。

不同国家经济发展水平的标准是生产资源（劳动力、自然和人为资源，或人力、自然和人为资本）的利用效果。最重要的经济发展指标是人均国内生产总值（GDP），其增长表明国家利用生产资源的效率和该国公民平均福祉双双增长。因此出现了冲突情况，可以通过彻底改变能源生产和消耗技术加以解决。节能技术的出现、业内新技术流程的引入、数字控制和通信的发展是飞跃式发展，可以协调社会生态系统的进一步发展。

逻辑建模法涉及模型构建，不同现象之间可以进行类比，分析不同过程的关系，总结各种物理性过程的数据。人类自发或自觉地对自然过程、特别是人工选择进行建模，并执行与某些人群有关的选择性功能，促进巩固连续系列世代的某些标志并清除其他标志。因此，不仅本体自然（即物体和事物）开始为人类服务，而且动态自然，首先是进化原则和机制也开始为人类服务。②

---

① Vernadsky V. I. Philosophical thoughts of naturalist, V. I. Vernadsky. – M., 1988, p. 56.
② Vodopianov P. A. Strategy of being of humankind: from the apocalyptic to the noospheric age, P. A. Vodopianov, V. S. Krisachenko. – Minsk: Belaruskaya navuka, 2018, p. 124.

现代社会最重要的变化是那些能够引导最新技术模式的价值来解决积累的环境问题的变化。农业化学的发展已经将农业变成世界工业的最大分支。只有采用全新的技术和实用工艺，才能实现农业的进一步开发和有效应用。由于引入了生物技术方法，原材料、领土的利用更加全面了，可再生自然资源的培育和利用得以强化。同时，随着新产品的生产，还采用生物技术方法制造产品，这些产品的传统制造方法不太环保。一般来说，合理引入生物技术有助于提高国民经济的环境友好性，有助于形成更加和谐的社会与自然的关系。

预测管理方法可以预测特定活动领域的非标准方法和情况，找到最佳解决方案，在比较分析的基础上考虑所分析系统的实际改进前景。专家评估法也可以作为预测系统突然变化的建议方法。在这种情况下，通过处理一些专家的意见，可以总结进行预测分析所需的信息。因此，将各种情况考虑在内，就可以制订系统开发方案及其可能的变量。例如，通过政府间气候变化专门委员会，我们掌握了以下信息。1880年到2012年，世界平均气温上升了0.85摄氏度。而且，气温每升高1度，粮食产量就会下降约5%。如果我们不保证执行必要的发展方案，那么，考虑到目前大气中温室气体的浓度水平和持续排放，到21世纪末，世界气温的升高很可能超过1.5摄氏度。根据共同但有区别的责任和相关能力的原则，所有国家均应根据各种国情和《应对气候变化威胁的巴黎协定》采取行动，防止气候变化。

当今的环境安全不仅决定着文明发展的载体，而且也是人类生存的条件。生态社会可持续性日益被视为现代社会世界观体系的基本价值观。有效解决环境问题的工具应当与形成建设性的环境意识及人类和社会行为联系在一起。这是一个相当复杂的过程，涉及主流价值观的转换以及根据现代创新发展动态制定新的规范和规则。我们整个时代最重要的问题，由英国著名社会学家安东尼·吉登斯（A. Giddens）在"后传统社会"概念中确定，与我们生活在极端动态的世界有关，在这样的世界里，瞬息万变和不稳定占主导地位，一切都受到质疑，甚至被完全拒绝。所谓的"内置"元素——信仰、道德规范、行为模式和稳固的传统——从社会生活中消失。在这种情况下，国家和公共行政管理部门的组织和管理职能将提升，包括保护建设性的环境价值和制订建设性的社会政策计划。应通过预测和论证解决经济发展问题、社会和文化领域问题以及环境问题的有效工具，加强国家作为政治制度主要纽带、国家和公共组织活动协调者、社会进程调节主体的作用。这一切都应符合可持续发展的利益，同时应当通过改进环境立法、采用有效的经济管理方法、实行环境控制和保护来实施国家环境政策。

今天，文明面临着新的普世生态文化的形成问题，它提出了新的以生态为中心的环境意识和新的面向自然、环境友好型的组织生活和生产过程的类型和方法。在新的生态思想的框架下，人类和自然不是相互对立的自主实体，尤其是对抗性的实体。相反，积极行动、自我发展的人和人类可以说是自然的一部分，执行着作为整个自然自我发展基础的一般普遍法则。作为主体的人类并不对抗作为客体的自然。人类成为共同进化发展战略的主体，成为国家与公共行政管理部门相应政策的主体。

中国社会治理现代化与创新发展机制

马 峰

中国社会科学院社会发展战略研究院副研究员

一 新时代社会治理现代化的使命与任务

推进新时代社会治理现代化不但是实现国家治理现代化的题中之义，也是推动破解社会建设领域发展不平衡、不充分问题的重要制度建构。打造共建共治共享的社会治理格局和形成社会治理共同体，既是党中央的重要战略部署，也是时代发展之需，更是推进制度现代化的必然要求。新时代社会治理现代化对于保持社会稳定、维护国家安全、防范社会风险、提高社会运营能力具有重要意义，需要从全面加强和完善党委领导、强化政府职责和建设责任政府、强化社会协同和公众参与等方面推进新时代社会治理现代化。

习近平总书记在经济社会领域专家座谈会上指出："要完善共建共治共享的社会治理制度，实现政府治理同社会调节、居民自治良性互动，建设人人有责、人人尽责、人人享有的社会治理共同体。要加强和创新基层社会治理，使每个社会细胞都健康活跃，将矛盾纠纷化解在基层，将和谐稳定创建在基层。"[①]

社会治理体系与治理能力现代化建设是国家治理体系与治理能力现

---

① 习近平：《在经济社会领域专家座谈会上的讲话》，《人民日报》2020 年 8 月 25 日第 2 版。

代化建设的重要组成部分。党的十八届三中全会通过的《中共中央关于全面深化改革若干重大问题的决定》从创新社会治理体制的高度出发，将社会治理现代化作为全面深化改革的重要一环，提出"改进社会治理方式。坚持系统治理，加强党委领导，发挥政府主导作用，鼓励和支持社会各方面参与，实现政府治理和社会自我调节、居民自治良性互动"[①]。

党的十九大报告进一步指出："打造共建共治共享的社会治理格局。加强社会治理制度建设，完善党委领导、政府负责、社会协同、公众参与、法治保障的社会治理体制，提高社会治理社会化、法治化、智能化、专业化水平。"[②]

从改进社会治理方式到打造共建共治共享的社会治理格局，从全面深化改革的视角全面推进社会治理体系现代化，形成了新时代社会治理新格局。党委领导、政府负责、社会协同、公众参与、法治保障的社会治理体制日臻完善。

党的十九大以来，我国按照十九大的部署，持续深入推进社会治理体系和能力现代化，不断满足人民对美好生活的向往和发挥主人翁意识的时代需求。习近平总书记在2019年中央政法工作会议上提出"打造人人有责、人人尽责的社会治理共同体"的科学判断。总书记指出："要完善基层群众自治机制，调动城乡群众、企事业单位、社会组织自主自治的积极性，打造人人有责、人人尽责的社会治理共同体。"[③] 人人有责、人人尽责社会治理共同体科学概念的提出，进一步深化了新时代推进社会治理体系与治理能力现代化的新认识。

党的十九届四中全会通过的《中共中央关于坚持和完善中国特色社会主义制度 推进国家治理体系和治理能力现代化若干重大问题的决定》从坚持和完善中国特色社会主义制度、推进国家治理体系和治理能力现代化的高度提出要"坚持和完善共建共治共享的社会治理制度，保持社会

[①]《中共中央关于全面深化改革若干重大问题的决定》，《光明日报》2013年11月16日第1版。

[②] 习近平：《决胜全面建成小康社会 夺取新时代中国特色社会主义伟大胜利——在中国共产党第十九次全国代表大会上的报告》，《光明日报》2017年10月28日第1版。

[③]《全面深入做好新时代政法各项工作促进社会公平正义保障人民安居乐业》，《光明日报》2019年1月17日第1版。

稳定、维护国家安全"①，并进一步指出："社会治理是国家治理的重要方面。必须加强和创新社会治理，完善党委领导、政府负责、民主协商、社会协同、公众参与、法治保障、科技支撑的社会治理体系，建设人人有责、人人尽责、人人享有的社会治理共同体，确保人民安居乐业、社会安定有序，建设更高水平的平安中国。"②

党的十八大以来，我们不断推进国家治理体系和治理能力现代化，不断提高防范和化解重大风险的能力，政治、经济、文化、社会、生态文明建设皆取得历史性成就，在世界发展高度不确定的背景下，中国集中、统一、高效、民主、法治的治理体系，在后危机时代纷乱的各国治理变革中，更彰显传统与现代完美结合的创新治理体系所代表的中国智慧。

今天伴随着国家治理体系和治理能力现代化的推进，特别是党的十八大以来在新理念新思想新战略指导下进行的新的实践，我国新的社会治理体系机制架构基本形成，高效、集中、法治的社会治理能力基本建立，已基本建成党委领导、政府负责、社会协同、公众参与、法治保障的社会治理体系，提高了社会治理社会化、法治化、智能化、专业化水平，增强了全社会防范和抵御安全风险的能力。

建设人人有责、人人尽责、人人享有的社会治理共同体，完善党委领导、政府负责、民主协商、社会协同、公众参与、法治保障、科技支撑的社会治理体系，不但是全面建成小康社会后，开启社会主义现代化建设新征程的时代要求，也是坚持和完善中国特色社会主义制度、推进国家治理体系和治理能力现代化的客观要求，对于保持社会稳定、维护国家安全、防范化解重大风险、提高社会运营能力具有重要意义，也是有力的制度保障。

经济发展与社会发展总是同步而行的。经济发展的成果必然会反映到社会发展层面，社会发展层面越是实现稳定发展、高质量发展的局面，

---

① 《中共中央关于坚持和完善中国特色社会主义制度　推进国家治理体系和治理能力现代化若干重大问题的决定》，《光明日报》2019 年 11 月 6 日第 1 版。

② 《中共中央关于坚持和完善中国特色社会主义制度　推进国家治理体系和治理能力现代化若干重大问题的决定》，《光明日报》2019 年 11 月 6 日第 1 版。

越能更好地促进经济发展，为经济的发展、政治的稳定、文化的昌明、生态的优化提供社会的力量和战略的支撑。社会建设是"五位一体"的重要一环，而社会发展可以说是社会建设的核心要旨。一方面，人民对于经济发展成果的最直接的体验和感受，来自社会发展层面的反馈，包括就业、社保、公共卫生、社会治理等，涉及社会发展的方方面面。另一方面，社会发展的水平、程度，从另一个侧面讲，也是社会进步水平，更是一个国家、民族现代化水平的标志。我们常说一个社会是不是一个有希望、有吸引力、有魅力的社会，很大程度上指的是一个国家的社会发展水平，高水平的社会发展能力，是检验一个社会能不能促进人的全面发展和社会全面进步的标志。

中华人民共和国成立以来，我国社会发展事业发生了翻天覆地的变化，人民在社会发展领域的现实感受和获得感显著提高，民生福祉发生深刻变化。随着国家经济的发展、国力的增强，人民社会发展事业不断迈上新的发展台阶。随着社会发展事业的进步，为全国人民更加紧密地团结起来，同心戮力推进中国特色社会主义事业取得一个又一个胜利，奠定了坚实的基础。

二 新时代社会治理共同体建设的方位与作用

新时代的中国社会治理面临国内外多种社会发展风险因素的影响，新问题、新挑战不断。不确定性风险成为新时代中国社会治理面临的主要挑战，全球性的社会风险，即由全球风险外溢引入的社会风险和挑战，在全球一体化密切的背景下，成为新型社会风险的主要来源。"在充分肯定成绩的同时，必须清醒认识到，我国正处在转变发展方式、优化经济结构、转换增长动力的攻关期，结构性、体制性、周期性问题相互交织，'三期叠加'影响持续深化，经济下行压力加大。当前世界经济增长持续放缓，仍处在国际金融危机后的深度调整期，世界大变局加速演变的特征更趋明显，全球动荡源和风险点显著增多。我们要做好工作预案。"[①]

[①]《中央经济工作会议在北京举行》，《光明日报》2019年12月13日第1版。

国内外的发展形势，要求做好工作预案。2021年是"十四五"开局之年，也是实现第二个百年奋斗目标打好基础的关键之年。基本实现现代化，进而建成社会主义现代化强国是近代以来无数仁人志士为之奋斗的中华民族复兴之梦。新时代社会治理体系与能力现代化，必然成为新时代国家治理体系和治理能力现代化建设的重要组成部分。我们必须明确的是"治理是各种公共的或私人的个人和机构管理其共同事务的诸多方式的总和。它是使相互冲突的或不同的利益得以调和并且采取联合行动的持续的过程"①。

从国外情况来看，2008年国际金融危机后，西方社会一系列制度失序、国家治理失序导致的社会治理危机潜藏在社会运行的方方面面，正在向世人展示一个因内部社会冲突而导致的从国家到社会整体治理失序或制度崩塌而引发的高风险社会的到来，西方或这些已完成工业化或进入后工业化的国家和地区，正面临一种高风险社会下的"秩序危机"。事实上，"国际上的问题林林总总，归结起来就是要解决好治理体系和治理能力的问题"②。

2019年以来世界大变局演变的特征更趋明显，全球动荡源和风险点显著增多，因提高燃油税引发的"黄马甲"运动在法国已经延续多年，成为法国社会发展的常态社会现象，而且因为养老金改革引发的大罢工、大游行造成了法国社会的这个冬天持续动荡。社会发展"分蛋糕"与"切蛋糕"成为社会不同阶层难以调和的利益格局。"当前，新冠肺炎疫情全球大流行使这个大变局加速变化，保护主义、单边主义上升，世界经济低迷，全球产业链、供应链因非经济因素而面临冲击，国际经济、科技、文化、安全、政治等格局都在发生深刻调整，世界进入动荡变革期。"③

可以看到，尽管全球动荡源和风险点显著增多的原因是全方面、多方位的，但是从老牌资本主义国家到新兴市场国家，其引燃社会动荡的

---

① 俞可平：《全球治理引论》，《马克思主义与现实》2002年第1期。
② 《习近平会见联合国秘书长古特雷斯》，《光明日报》2019年4月9日第1版。
③ 习近平：《在经济社会领域专家座谈会上的讲话》，《人民日报》2020年8月25日第2版。

直接原因跟燃油税、养老金、地铁等公共交通价格紧密相连，民生难题、社会政策缺位成为深层次社会发展矛盾的主要外在表象。西方社会内部由此引发的社会动荡，进而反映到制度层面导致的从国家治理体系到社会治理体系的困境成为影响社会运行和运转的重大风险。

当今时代发展的不确定性风险远超以往，面对不确定的风险，没有一个现代化的治理体系作为基础，没有一个现代化的治理能力作为后盾，很难应对今天各种潜在和显在的风险因素。风险常在，而一套混乱、失序、冲突、崩塌的治理体系以及衍生的治理能力，不可能有效应对今天纷繁复杂社会带来的高风险因素的挑战。事实上，"社会运动既是实践性搏击的原初动力又是其表现形式，它不仅表现为社会运动，还包含建立积极的社会机制"[①]。

从国内发展的视角来看，我国社会发展事业不断取得重大成就，从人均收入到摆脱贫困，从税收改革到药品降价，从网络提速降费到垃圾分类引领的新时尚……人民群众的幸福感、获得感、安全感显著提高，人民在社会发展中感受国家稳定发展的成就。经济发展与社会发展的双轮驱动，促进发展中的不充分、不平衡问题得到不断破除。

从教育来看，2019年，全国学前教育毛入园率达83.4%，比2000年提高37%；义务教育巩固率94.8%，普及程度达到世界高收入国家平均水平；高中阶段毛入学率89.5%，是2000年的2倍；高等教育毛入学率51.6%，是2000年的4倍，迈入普及化发展阶段。2019年，新增劳动力平均受教育年限13.7年，比2010年增加1.29年，其中受过高等教育的比例达50.9%。[②]

从居民健康来看，截至2019年年底，城乡居民健康水平持续提高，居民人均预期寿命由2000年的71.4岁提高到2019年的77.3岁，婴儿死亡率从32.2‰下降到5.6‰。[③]

从社会保障来看，截至2019年年末，全国基本养老保险参保人数达

---

① ［德］斯科特·拉什：《风险社会与风险文化》，《马克思主义与现实》2002年第4期。
② 万东华：《从社会发展看全面建成小康社会成就》，《人民日报》2020年8月4日第11版。
③ 万东华：《从社会发展看全面建成小康社会成就》，《人民日报》2020年8月4日第11版。

到9.68亿人，是2000年的7.1倍，覆盖率超过90%。①

从居民收入来看，2019年，全国居民人均可支配收入30733元，首次跨入3万元大关，比2000年实际增长4.4倍，年均实际增长9.2%。②

人民享有的社会发展水平获得了显著的提高，党领导人民在社会发展领域取得了历史性的发展成就。根据联合国开发计划署编制的人类发展指数（HDI），2000年我国人类发展指数为0.591，低于0.641的世界平均水平，2018年上升至0.758，成为1990年有该指数以来，世界上唯一一个从"低人类发展水平"跃升到"高人类发展水平"的国家。③

虽然我国社会发展事业取得了历史性的成就，但是在即将全面建成小康社会，开启全面建设社会主义现代化国家新征程的时代背景下，处于新发展阶段的我国社会发展也面临新的发展任务、发展挑战、发展难题，补短板、强弱项，以更大的勇气、智慧破除影响社会发展的体制机制障碍，实现社会发展的现代化显得更加紧迫。发展起来以后的问题只能在发展中解决。面对我国社会结构正在发生深刻变化，社会观念、社会心理、社会行为正在发生的深刻变化。要统筹世界百年未有之大变局与中华民族伟大复兴的战略全局，根据新发展阶段的新特征新要求，以及发展过程中面对的新矛盾新挑战，辩证看待我国社会发展的阶段性特征和任务。

一方面，我国已进入高质量发展阶段，社会主要矛盾已经转化为人民日益增长的美好生活需要和不平衡不充分的发展之间的矛盾。随着我国社会发展形态发生深刻变革，社会利益关系日趋复杂，价值取向更加多元，利益诉求更加多样，经济形态与社会发展形态的影响相互促进，人民对更高水平的社会发展充满期待，对更高效的治理能力和治理水平提出更高的现代化要求。而且人民不仅对物质文化生活提出了更高要求，而且在民主、法治、公平、正义、安全、环境等方面的要求日益增长，

---

① 万东华：《从社会发展看全面建成小康社会成就》，《人民日报》2020年8月4日第11版。

② 方晓丹：《从居民收支看全面建成小康社会成就》，《人民日报》2020年7月27日第10版。

③ 方晓丹：《从居民收支看全面建成小康社会成就》，《人民日报》2020年7月27日第10版。

人民对公平正义的追求愿望更加强烈。

另一方面，我国社会结构正在发生深刻变化，社会整体的运行机制也在发生深刻变革，面向中长期的社会发展，受到国内外经济形势变化的牵动影响更加明显，各类矛盾风险交织叠加、社会治理面临复杂形势，而且各类利益诉求相互交织，要在发展中努力实现各类、各种诉求的平衡，达成更广泛的社会发展共识，实现社会利益调节更高水平的动态平衡，为中长期经济发展和现代化目标的实现，继续提供社会稳定的力量和社会发展的战略支撑。

"事实证明，发展起来以后的问题不比不发展时少。"[①] 在新时代社会主要矛盾发生转化的背景下，不平衡不充分的问题日渐突出，总体来看，主要是发展不平衡不充分的一些突出问题尚未解决，民生领域还有不少短板，城乡区域发展和收入分配差距依然较大，群众在就业、教育、医疗、居住、养老等方面面临不少难题……而且，"我国社会结构正在发生深刻变化，互联网深刻改变人类交往方式，社会观念、社会心理、社会行为发生深刻变化。'十四五'时期如何适应社会结构、社会关系、社会行为方式、社会心理等深刻变化，实现更加充分、更高质量的就业，健全全覆盖、可持续的社保体系，强化公共卫生和疾控体系，促进人口长期均衡发展，加强社会治理，化解社会矛盾，维护社会稳定，都需要认真研究并作出工作部署"[②]。新时代中国社会治理现代化，必然为破解发展的不平衡、不充分提供从制度到效能的保障。

在新时代中国社会治理体系和治理能力现代化建设过程中，我们还面临新型社会风险带来的新挑战。事实上，"新型社会风险对社会治理提出新问题、新挑战。当今世界，现代化的推进特别是新科技不断产生，在推动经济社会发展的同时，也使人类社会进入现代'风险社会'。现代风险不同于传统风险的最大特征就是不确定性和难以预测性，其迅速而

[①] 习近平：《在经济社会领域专家座谈会上的讲话》，《人民日报》2020年8月25日第2版。

[②] 习近平：《在经济社会领域专家座谈会上的讲话》，《人民日报》2020年8月25日第2版。

广泛的传播可能造成大范围社会恐慌"①。

在新时代社会治理体系和治理能力现代化建设过程中，我们既要应对传统社会风险的挑战，也要面对新型社会风险的挑战。在国际形势发展高度不确定，主要发达经济体内部民粹主义泛起、治理失序的情况下，中国的国家治理和社会治理现代体系构建在进入新时代背景下，其有效的应对力、高度发展的聚合力、结构性改革的推进力、强有力的组织力，成为后金融危机时代国际社会应对挑战、加快治理体系和治理能力重组和建构的重要参照系，"中国之治"正成为各国借鉴的重要制度供给和国际公共产品。

三 社会治理创新与形成新时代社会治理共同体

一个现代化的社会，应该既充满活力又拥有良好秩序，呈现出活力和秩序的有机统一。人的全面发展与社会的全面进步是高质量社会发展新局面的应有之义。今日中国之社会发展站在了新的历史起点。新发展格局正在加速发展，必将更加深刻地影响社会发展形态的演化，最直接的就是就业形态。新发展动能的快速发展，将会更直接地影响社会生活、社会心理、社会行为更微观和具体的层面，其所带动的微观社会发展变化将对治理能力提出更高的、更直观的要求，人们的生活将会向着更加高端、智能的方向转变。新发展活力的涌泉而出，将会更加激发社会创造、创新的活力，人民的社会发展参与水平将会进一步地提高，人民的首创精神将会得到更大的弘扬，人人都有通过辛勤劳动实现自身发展的机会。

站在"两个百年"梦想历史交汇的时间节点，时代发展的变革原点，时代课题是理论创新的驱动力。要不断拓展共建共治共享社会发展新局面，推动社会全面进步。

首先，要坚持稳中求进工作总基调，以稳促进、以稳促发展，不断

---

① 李培林：《用新思想指导新时代的社会治理创新》，《人民日报》2018年2月6日第7版。

满足人民对社会发展的新期待,对美好生活的新向往,对治理能力的新要求。既要掌握好度,维持发展的大局,又要善于抓住机遇,不失时机地促进发展。在保持"量"稳的同时,要谋"质"的变革,持续推动社会高质量发展,持续推动社会向着高质量发展的态势转变。实现从传统的社会发展模式向高质量社会发展模式的转变,过程是持续的,时代发展的背景、发展进程的阶段性特征、发展方向的长期化目标都要求我们坚持稳中求进推动社会发展。我国发展更加突出的是不平衡、不充分的问题,我国现在处于并将长期处于社会主义初级阶段的基本国情没有变,我国属于发展中国家的发展属性没有变。这都需要我们在新发展阶段,坚持稳中求进推动社会发展,保持社会发展的定力,在持续的发展中促进民生的改善和对人民美好生活的满足;在持续的发展进步中补齐民生短板,扩大民生红利;以持续的发展动力促进社会发展,增强社会发展事业的同步性、可持续性,增强人民对社会发展的未来预期,在稳中提质、在稳中增效。

其次,坚持以新时代全面深化改革促进社会发展。全面深化改革是我们这个时代发展的重要标志。全面深化改革的持续发力,让制度红利持续发挥效果,转化成发展的制度动力。全面深化改革不但解决了很多长期困扰、影响我们发展的体制机制问题,而且为进一步深入发展提供了新的制度动能。发展的根本目的是为人民谋幸福,我们坚持以经济建设为中心不动摇,持续将经济建设的成果转化为促进社会发展的动力,实现经济发展与社会发展的同步。改革开放已走过千山万水,但仍需跋山涉水,面对国内外的发展形势,新发展阶段要将全面深化改革推向纵深,释放制度活力,催动中国社会发展的活力和能量。

新时代促进社会发展,要继续坚持改革开放敢闯敢干的精神,要继续坚持全面深化改革敢于刀刃向内自我革命的精神,在就业优先、创新创业创造、户籍制度、公共服务均等化、用人制度改革、基层人员发展、贫困群体向上流动、教育优先发展、公平就业、强化社会救助、人民健康等涉及社会发展的具体方面"下一番绣花功夫"。每一个方面的改革,涉及人民群众的切身利益,要聚焦重点,敢于突破条条框框的束缚,敢于打破利益固化的藩篱,促进社会流动,让流动的中国更精彩。

时代发展到今天，人民对社会发展的需求和要求发生了根本性变化，顺应人民对社会发展的新要求、新变化，就是顺应人民对发展的新期待。发展是党执政兴国的第一要务，也是人民的第一期待。要以新发展阶段全面深化改革的纵深发展，形成发展的制度张力，引导个人发展融入国家富强、民族复兴进程，促进经济持续健康发展、社会公平正义、国家长治久安。

最后，坚持以全面建设现代化引领新时代社会发展。当前，世界发展面临大变革、大调整，国际经济、科技、文化、安全、政治等格局都在发生深刻调整，世界进入动荡变革期。今后一个时期，我们将面对更多逆风逆水的外部环境，必须做好应对一系列新的风险挑战的准备。但是中国经济长期向好的基本趋势，中华民族走向复兴与繁荣的历史发展态势是没有改变的，也不会发生改变。

全面建设现代化时期是一个必然要经历的崭新时代，实现现代化凝聚了中华民族共同的心愿。全面建设现代化时期的社会发展要聚焦现代化发展的时代要求，进一步适应高质量发展的时代要求，进一步深化与国家治理体系与治理能力现代化的同频共振，努力实现更高质量、更有效率、更加公平、更可持续、更为安全的发展。

要落实好"十四五"时期社会发展规划，满足人民发展新期待。要根据社会发展的新经验、新认识，针对内外部发展变化的新情况，充分发挥中国特色社会主义的制度优势。增强针对"十四五"时期及更长远时期社会发展特征的适应能力，既要增强宏观驾驭能力，又要增强微观治理能力，及时发现问题、解决问题，及时发现新方法、新经验，及时加以总结、加以提炼、加以推广，不断在与发展环境的短兵相接、斗争接触中，发挥制度优势，转化为促进社会发展的治理效能。

要增强新发展阶段社会发展政策的稳定性。要"稳"字当头，扎扎实实把基础工作、系统性工作做好，保持战略定力。尽力而为，量力而行，注重加强普惠性、基础性、兜底性民生建设，满足人民多层次多样化需求，使改革发展成果更多更公平惠及全体人民。要保持社会政策的稳定性、连续性、可持续性。既要兜住底线，又要挖掘社会发展的增长潜力，抓重点、补短板、强弱项，重点解决经济社会发展中存在的长期性、根本性问题，努力践行新时代枫桥经验。

改革开放不断催生发展活力。在新发展阶段，要更加坚持以习近平新时代中国特色社会主义思想为指导，不断深化对社会发展的新认识，以全面建设现代化引领新发展阶段社会发展，不断完善共建共治共享的社会治理制度，实现政府治理同社会调节、居民自治良性互动，建设人人有责、人人尽责、人人享有的社会治理共同体。不断加强和创新基层社会治理，使每个社会细胞都健康活跃，将矛盾纠纷化解在基层，将和谐稳定创建在基层。更加注重维护社会公平正义，促进人的全面发展和社会全面进步。

四 结语

中国特色的社会治理格局，正在成为一种中国方案和中国智慧，在世界各国应对高风险发展的危机中彰显出它的时代价值和制度优势。"相比过去，新时代改革开放具有许多新的内涵和特点，其中很重要的一点就是制度建设分量更重，改革更多面对的是深层次体制机制问题，对改革顶层设计的要求更高，对改革的系统性、整体性、协同性要求更强，相应地建章立制、构建体系的任务更重。"[①] 高效运转、核心稳固、协调有力、凝聚共识、积淀深厚、有效参与、积极应对成为中国特色社会治理格局的时代特色。

聚焦中国社会发展的新特征，中国社会建设的新特点，新时代我们必须推进社会治理现代化。中国社会发展的态势正在经历态势调整阶段，这一调整阶段与中国经济走势呈现同步性，新旧动能转换在经济领域转换态势，同样传导到社会发展领域。政府、市场、社会成为2008年金融危机后世界范围内实现有效发展的"三边机制"。看得见的手和看不见的手依然存在，其效能也在发挥，但是社会治理成为影响经济发展的新功能，社会的作用更加突出。一系列新经济新业态的出现，社会功能发挥了独特的作用。结构性就业矛盾的解决一部分要靠社区的转接，去过剩产能的下岗工人要靠基层治理为其搭建避风港，社会治安的强化、风险

[①] 习近平：《关于〈中共中央关于坚持和完善中国特色社会主义制度　推进国家治理体系和治理能力现代化若干重大问题的决定〉的说明》，《光明日报》2019年11月6日第4版。

防控的加强为经济发展提供了强有力的保障，为政府治理解决了"最后一公里"问题，弥补了发展死角，弥合了社会分歧，可以说社会治理也是生产力，也是满足人民美好生活需求，解决发展中不平衡、不充分的"利器"。

白俄罗斯社会治理与性别平等

Volha Davydzik

白俄罗斯国家科学院哲学研究所中白哲学与文化研究中心

白俄罗斯的社会政策首先旨在实现社会的可持续发展,[①] 其次是发展人力资本,[②] 最后是支持最弱势群体。[③] 明智的做法是,需假设社会转型的性质是逐点的、局部的、基于事物的实际状态,这种假设在实现社会和谐与可持续发展目标的过程中将是最有效的。此外,还必须为管理决策程序提供一种算法,该算法首先应建立在理性和人道主义方法的基础之上。

在白俄罗斯,围绕确保性别平等展开的讨论越来越重要,并成为实现国家政治和经济领域现代化的有效工具。各方面的代表都参与到这一问题的讨论中来,开展了许多活动、展览项目、公民行动,旨在加强研究兴趣,并吸引公众关注这些问题。《2017—2020 年保障性别平等国家行动计划》(以下简称《国家行动计划》)为性别发展注入了新的动力,该

[①] National Strategy for Sustainable Development (NSDS) for the period until 2020: – [Electronic resource]: Access mode: un. by. Access date: 08/01/2018.

[②] State program "Education and Youth Policy" for 2016 – 2020 – [Electronic resource]: Access mode: edu. gov. by. Access date: 08/01/2018.

[③] State program on social protection and promotion of employment for 2016 – 2020 – [Electronic resource]: Access mode: mintrud. gov. by. Access date: 08/01/2018.

计划于2017年2月根据白俄罗斯共和国部长理事会令批准。① 这是一份国家政策文件，旨在制定相关机制，在制定和实施社会各个领域公共政策措施的过程中采用性别办法。性别主流化的重点领域是，在社会经济参与、家庭关系、性别教育和启蒙等方面人人平等。

将上述方面纳入立法框架，对在国家政策中涵盖性别敏感问题发挥了重要作用。在这种情况下，我们首先讨论建立一个防止家庭暴力的立法框架，以及一个生殖健康的立法框架。因此，捐赠人和患者的年龄限制问题越来越重要（男性捐赠人40岁，女性捐赠人35岁，患者49岁）。专家认为，鉴于需要进行强制性体检，这种限制是过分的。"从女权主义议程的角度来看，生殖和性别是政治范畴，经常被纳入权力斗争，因为生殖是社会存在的必要条件。因此，首先受国家、社区、家庭、群体控制的是妇女。对父权制度的批判需要我们重新思考可以制定哪些反抗战略和克服这些权力战略的问题"②。

年龄限制适用于想要进行绝育手术的男性。该手术适用于至少有两个孩子的35岁以上的男性，但也有例外情形。"……已通过的立法规范表明，生殖自由在我国有具体的限制。特别值得一提的是，我们谈论的一切至少在某种程度上可以破坏一个活跃的有生育能力的身体的规范。被视为'生殖潜力'和'人口储备'的妇女被迫遵循'来自上级'的指示，不能够充分控制自己的生殖权"③。

将性别意识纳入社会主体和人道主义研究，与专业知识有着密切关系。性别的社会生产概念也是一个很有前途的现代社会哲学理论研究方向。现代社会哲学将此概念解释为融入社会主体的意识形态常数、社会分层的要素，把社会关系放在性别层面上。

社会实践领域的问题仍然十分紧迫，一是统计数据代表性差，统计

---

① National action plan for gender equality in Belarus for 2017 – 2020：Electronic source：Access mode：http：//www.government.by/upload/docs/file59fe04a05ce85ea9.PDF，Access Date：11/10/2018.

② Schurko, T. Female body between feminism, pro – life and state politics//［Electronic resource］：– – Access mode：www.n – europe.eu. Access date：11/12/2018.

③ Schurko, T. Female body between feminism, pro – life and state politics//［Electronic resource］：– – Access mode：www.n – europe.eu. Access date：11/12/2018.

数据不完整，一方面是因为参与冲突局势的个人的主观因素而无法获取客观信息，另一方面是政府机构的制度和立法框架不完善。二是仍然非常需要多学科研究，以便制定"歧视""暴力""家庭暴力""受害人""挑衅者"等常规概念领域的联合解决办法，澄清许多现象的本质，并分析国内立法，就遵守《国家计划》所通过的规定提出改革建议。应当指出，学术界在白俄罗斯落实性别平等理念、在国内法中执行国际惯例方面的跨部门合作中发挥了重要作用。白俄罗斯的性别研究有20年的历史，研究主题和对象、地方社区呈现多样性和碎片化。不过，某些论述仅停留在对这一问题的不同考虑层面，而现在则建立了一个全新的讨论领域——克服了传统社会的价值观。同时，这一领域既可能包含许多与人为因素相关的风险，又在跨学科研究方面高度以知识为基础。在这方面，必须了解在公共组织、政府和学术界的参与下扩大机构间合作的重要性，以便制定解决白俄罗斯性别不平等问题的最佳办法。从其与世界实践趋势的关联性和白俄罗斯社会现状的相关性来看，所有这些措施和决策将促进国家的可持续发展以及民族认同的现代化。

国家计划的某些细节对白俄罗斯的社会经济领域至关重要，因为需要将性别视角纳入社会项目的预算规划中。遵守这一方面的国家社会政策意味着男女平等获得社会支持资源，并考虑到男女在规划和批准项目方面的经验和需要。

许多欧洲国家以及一些独联体国家都实行了性别预算，提高了预算资金的支出效率，以支持和发展这一领域的重大举措。对国家机构工作的这种调整使得在考虑到性别因素的情况下，能够根据具体情况下的需要酌情调动财政资源并准确地进行分配。为此，有必要就需要政府援助的特定群体的利益进行性别分析。在对预算规划的这种认识中，从福利分配的角度考虑社会正义和社会团结问题。

把性别预算战略纳入支持白俄罗斯人民的社会项目的制定过程中，这种做法具有重要的战略性。这对于有效落实白俄罗斯共和国的整个性别政策十分重要，其中包括对《国家行动计划》的说明和调整；在实践中制定立法框架，防止一切形式的性别和年龄歧视，以及与性别和年龄有关的一切形式的暴力；为参与政治、经济、文化和其他领域的公共生活创造平等条件，无论这些方面的情况如何。在白俄罗斯制定和通过社会项目的过程中实行性别预算，将提高面向特定群体和当下社会存在阶段实际所需特定活动的预算资金的规划和支出效率。

性别预算的特殊性与特定群体的性别和年龄特点有关，并非完全用于"女性"筹资。其主要任务是观察所有参与者的平等性，研究社会经济因素如何影响不同的群体和参与者。性别分析作为这种规划的基础，旨在了解：第一，政治与社会实践直接相关；第二，规划社会项目直接取决于社会学数据和人文领域关于目标群体的研究以及其他项目的有效性。这种定位使人们认识到，科学方法需要与国家规划和管理过程密切融合。因此，在分析预算指标的有效性时考虑了性别方面，而在分析性别预算时必须确定两个领域：性别预算敏感性指标、预算指标对有效制定性别政策的影响。[1]

在实施性别政策的过程中，落实性别政策对于确保所有发展目标以及社会的和谐发展十分重要，在这种发展中，可成功实现自治和对现有地方群体的战略需求的管制，同时尊重每一位参与者的权利和自由。性别敏感预算需要取消有匿名需求的社会的一般代表，而制定有针对性的、旨在解决具体问题的项目。[2]

因此，可以注意到以下几点。性别敏感预算是组织透明支出过程的工具，可以由民间社会提出请求并进行有效监测。不仅欧洲，而且独联体的许多国家在社会政策中引入性别预算的做法使得相关国家能够优化支出，改善当地群体和参与者参与社会经济进程的社会气氛，取得明确

---

[1] Salosina L. G. Gender Approach in Budget Planning // News. Volgogr. state un. – Series 3. – 2008. – No 2（13）. – C. 185 – 190；Kambariddinova N. ，What is gender budgeting //［Electronic resource］：Access mode：http：//www.publicfinance.uz/upload/iblock/a7f/Gender_overview_NK.pdf. Access Date：02/27/2019.

[2] Gender Responsive Budgeting //［Electronic resource］：Access mode：https：//unwomen.org.au/our–work/focus–areas/what–is–gender–responsive–budgeting/. Access Date：25.02.2019；Gender Mainstreaming and a Human Rights Based Approach，Budapest，2017：[Electronic resource] / UN Food and Agriculture Organization. Access mode：http：//www.fao.org/3/a–i6808r.pdf. Access date：11/15/2018；Gender Mainstreaming：A Review, New York, 2002［Electronic Resource］/ Office of the Special Adviser on Gender Issues and Advancement of Women // UN. Access mode：http：//www.un.org/womenwatch/daw/public/gendermainstreaming/Russian%20Gender%20Mainstreaming_full.pdf. Access date：11/16/2018.

和有效的结果，而不是把钱花在匿名代理人身上。在实践中，性别敏感预算可以提高贫困和弱势群体的福利、教育、社会保障和保护水平；是支持和优化性别政策的有效工具。应在非政府组织、妇女运动、专家平台、与政府机构和国际组织平等合作的媒体等相关机构和民间社会参与者的帮助下，促进性别政策的目标和目的。

实施性别政策可提高国民经济水平，改善社会政治气氛，采用有效工具实现弱势群体的平等参与。白俄罗斯已经搭建了一个平台，开始有效执行性别政策，并在规划社会项目的过程中实行性别预算。然而，旷日持久的决策过程导致社会政治和经济增长领域缺乏有效性，以及国内人力资本的外流。

应当指出，及时评估某一特定社会项目的有效性可确保提高受益人群的生活质量。为了执行这项任务，白俄罗斯开发并改进了各种监测和评估系统，为社会政策的战略分析、修订和改正提供了机会。

可持续发展目标（以下简称 SDG)[1] 是一个全面了解社会政策领域、制定旨在改善社会气氛的项目和子项目的大型框架。白俄罗斯可持续发展目标的一个重要特点是其在各个不同层面的落实——从政府到青年领导人和非政府组织。因此，白俄罗斯创造了良好环境，便于那些与当地群体相互沟通并且属于社会需求的利益相关者的意见领袖直接参与社会项目的相关工作。为了最有效地开展工作以实现可持续发展目标，有必要采取一系列保障措施：（1）为民间领袖和相关计划提供获得国家资源的机会；（2）执行经济和社会现代化进程；（3）实现民间社会执行各级（从地方政府到国家代表）项目的潜力。例如，落实《国家行动计划》。通过众多行动主体的相互沟通可以做到这一点，包括政府代表、科学和专家界代表以及非政府组织和意见领袖代表。[2]

例如，在落实第 5 项可持续发展目标（性别平等）、第 8 项可持续发展目标（体面工作和经济增长）、第 10 项可持续发展目标（缩小差距）

---

[1] Belarus launched the Decade of Action to achieve the Sustainable Development Goals：[Electronic resource］．- Access mode：https：//un. by/novosti-oon/v-belarusi/. Access Date：02/10/2020.

[2] Artemenko, E. K. Results of a study of the situation in the field of gender discrimination in the labor market and in hiring / Mr. sociologist. sciences E. K. Artemenko. - Minsk：Businessofset LLC. - 2019. - 70c.

的框架内，白俄罗斯以"性别视角"为切入点开展了一项关于劳务市场和招聘中性别歧视的研究。[1] 作为实施本研究的一部分，确定了相关任务，旨在查明显性和隐性（有意识和无意识的）歧视案例，描述影响歧视和歧视性行为机制的因素。按照社会人口特征（受教育程度、居住地、年龄、性别等）以被调查者为对象，可以确定劳务市场上的歧视程度，查明白俄罗斯劳务市场的弱势群体和歧视类型。该研究表明，人们坚持自身的权利并反对劳动中的歧视，但是保护个人权利的意识与在现实中参加面试或职场工作中个人权利的伸张是有差异的。

如上文所述，性别预算是向真正需要额外资源和支持系统的人群分配资金的有效机制。定向资金和资源有助于高效制定民众援助项目和子项目的预算，监测效率并考虑群体的现实需要。因此，以当地群体为重点、扩大规模、制定评估和监测标准，有助于优化各种类型的资源并制定子项目，从而就白俄罗斯的社会政策形式制定最有效的战略。另外，通过向专家咨询、与相关人群直接沟通，最大限度地降低评估和监测社会项目工作的成本。这有助于调整现有项目，并预测新的趋势，瞄准新的群体和利益。[2]

例如，乌克兰和哈萨克斯坦采用性别敏感预算的经验表明，分析社会项目的财务费用既能够优化现有开支，又能够查明涵盖所有利益的缺点。分析表明，妇女会消费更多的医疗服务，更经常寻求医疗帮助，而男性人口消费医疗服务的次数则少得多，特别是那些与男性生殖健康直接相关的服务。因此，通过性别敏感预算查明哪些领域存在问题，以及资金不足还是过多，是按照决定利益的因素（比如：劳动分配在不同地

---

[1] Artemenko, E. K. Results of a study of the situation in the field of gender discrimination in the labor market and in hiring / Mr. sociologist. sciences E. K. Artemenko. – Minsk：Businessofset LLC. – 2019. – 70c.

[2] Shadrina, L. Yu. Sociological monitoring as a means of information support for assessing the effectiveness of social technologies：– [Electronic resource]：Access mode：https://cyberleninka.ru/article/n/sotsiologicheskiy-monitoring-kak-sredstvo-informatsionnogo-soprovozhdeniya-otsenki-effektivnosti-sotsialnyh-tehnologiy/viewer. Access Date：02/10/2020.

方的传统作用或男女人口的服务消费量）进行福利分配的有效社会机制。①

引入提高效率的新机制也适用于教育。白俄罗斯规定人人都享有平等受教育的权利（《白俄罗斯共和国宪法》第 32 条、第 49 条）。② 然而，不同人群需要不同的方法，应根据不同人群的需要，资助和设计教育项目。例如，白俄罗斯族群（比如：罗姆人）融入社会和社会化有其自身的具体情况，需要其他方法和办法。罗姆族群的女孩十几岁时经常因早婚和孕产以及需要与成年家庭成员平等履行家务而退学。另外，还有一些与外部环境和成见相关的障碍。因此，罗姆族群的少女在平等获得社会资源方面更加脆弱，最没有动力做出独立的职业选择。③ 这个例子清楚地说明了如何根据特定的社会现实来确定社会项目的重点、持续时间、目标和目的、财务成本额。以上例子和许多其他例子是制定创建社会项目的战略和方法的出发点，这些社会项目将侧重于当地社区，考虑具体需求，并将涵盖超出现有标准方法范围的那些小群体。特别值得一提的是，性别敏感方法是确定人口中需要不同方法的群体以及确定其实际需要和解决具体问题的方法的良好机制。总之，可以提供一系列的机会，根据目前所追求的目标，为这种改进创造有利的环境。

---

① Why gender budgeting is not "taken from men and given to women"？：–［Electronic resource］：– Access mode：https：//forbes. kz//process/expertise/pochemu_gendernoe_byudjetirovanie_eto_ne_otobrat_u_mujchin_i_otdat_jenschinam/. Access Date：02/12/2020.

② Constitution of the Republic of Belarus：［Electronic resource］：– Access mode：http：//pravo. by/pravovaya-informatsiya/normativnye-dokumenty/konstitutsiya-respubliki-belarus/. Access Date：02/12/2020.

③ Social integration of the Roma population in the Republic of Belarus：［Electronic resource］：– Access mode：http：//romaintegration. by/wp-content/uploads/2016/09/Roma _ socialintegration _ forsite. pdf. Access Date：02/26/2020.

治理现代化与治理创新发展

中国增值税改革的宏观经济效应与经济治理效能

娄 峰

中国社会科学院数量经济与技术经济研究所研究员

本文从经济系统论角度,根据最新投入产出表和财政税收的现实特征,编制了中国财政税收社会核算矩阵,构建出中国财政税收可计算一般均衡（CGE）模型,并模拟分析了降低企业增值税税率对宏观经济及其结构的影响。模拟结果显示：降低企业增值税税率有利于中国实际GDP增长,有利于降低通货膨胀压力；该政策对进出口影响显著,尤其是对出口的影响巨大；增值税税率每降低1%可以使得政府税收总收入下降1.5%；该政策可以提高社会总福利,从而有利于社会和谐发展。

一 引言

"十三五"时期是中国实现经济增长方式转换的关键时期,也是我国建设创新型国家、全面建设小康社会的决战阶段,为此,中央明确提出"供给侧结构性改革"的重大发展战略,习近平总书记也多次强调供给侧结构性改革一定要"降成本"。目前,从国内环境上看,中国企业综合税负偏高,负担过重,实体经济利润空间不断收窄,由此,企业、社会团体和学术界的"减税"呼声日渐高涨；从国际环境来看,美国特朗普总统任内,大幅降低企业所得税,使现行所得税从35%降至15%；英国2016年也公布下调企业所得税税率计划,从20%调低至15%以下；印度

2017年年初分别下调了个人所得税、消费税和服务税等税率,以刺激国内需求。因此,在这种国际国内大背景下,降低税负既是促进我国实体经济复苏的关键措施,也是减缓资本外流压力、激发经济体活力、提高我国企业竞争力的迫切需求。

本文结构如下:第二部分对已有文献进行综述,第三部分介绍本文构建的财政税收CGE模型,第四部分对模拟结果进行比较和分析,最后一部分根据分析结论提出本文的政策建议。

二 文献综述

在后经济危机时代,我国传统的货币工具和财政支出工具的有效性下降。一方面货币政策存在利率下调空间有限、指向性不强、传导渠道不畅等问题,另一方面财政支出的有效性面临融资困难、投资回报率下降、经济结构扭曲和腐败等障碍,[①] 因此税收政策成为中国降低企业负担、稳定经济增长的重要选项。理论上,减税不仅可以通过降低要素实际价格的方式促进企业投资并提高实际产出,还会对劳动力市场等方面产生系统性影响。既有研究对企业税负的下降的宏观经济效应主要围绕对投资和经济增长、劳动力市场和国际贸易这三个方面的影响展开。

首先是企业税负的下降与投资以及经济增长的关系。理论上,税率下降会降低租用资本的租金或者投资的必要报酬率,从而提高投资规模,并进而增加产出。大部分的经验研究也证实了企业会对税收激励做出积极反应。[②] 针对我国的研究大多将增值税转型作为降低增值税有效税率的一项拟自然实验,考察其政策效果。大部分此类研究利用计量方法确认

[①] 申广军、陈斌开、杨汝岱:《减税能否提振中国经济?——基于中国增值税改革的实证研究》,《经济研究》2016年第11期。

[②] Hall, R. E., Jorgenson, D. W., "Tax policy and investment behavior: Reply, and further results", *The American Economic Review*, Vol. 59, No. 3, 1969; Hassett, K. A., Hubbard, R. G., "Tax policy and business investment", *Handbook of Public Economics*, No. 3, 2002.

了增值税转型的减税效应对企业投资具有显著的正向作用。① 此外，李林木等（2017）发现降低税费有利于促进企业研发投资和创新能力，进而促进企业转型升级。

其次是对劳动力市场的影响。部分研究关注了税率变化对就业的政策效果，这些研究同样以增值税转型为背景，所得结论却并不一致。增值税转型导致资本要素价格相对劳动要素价格下降，企业会更多地用资本来替代劳动力的投入，从而对就业产生负面影响。聂辉华、方明月和李涛对东北地区的计量检验和陈烨等利用CGE的模拟验证了这一结论。② 陈烨等进一步指出，无歧视生产型增值税减税政策有利于同时促进就业和经济增长。③ 而申广军等认为增值税转型会导致资本对劳动的替代，但是单位产品的成本的降低促进企业扩大生产，也会提高对资本和劳动的引致需求。④ 因此，减税对劳动投入的影响取决于替代效应和规模效应的相对大小。该文通过计量模型发现，减税对就业的挤出主要集中于私营企业、中西部地区和非出口企业。总体上看，减税并未显著挤出就业，反而有提高就业的趋势。

另一部分研究关注了税率变化对居民收入的影响。这方面的研究大多利用CGE模型对"营改增"的减税效果进行模拟分析，结论也存在分歧。葛玉御等发现企业税负的降低可以通过促进经济增长、促进第二和第三产业以及中小企业的发展、降低消费品价格等方式提高居民的收入水平。⑤ 由于低收入者收入增长更快，因此减税可以缩小城乡内部以及城

---

① 聂辉华、方明月、李涛：《增值税转型对企业行为和绩效的影响》，《管理世界》2009年第5期；许伟、陈斌开：《税收激励和企业投资——基于2004—2009年增值税转型的自然实验》，《管理世界》2016年第5期；申广军、陈斌开、杨汝岱：《减税能否提振中国经济？——基于中国增值税改革的实证研究》，《经济研究》2016年第11期。

② 聂辉华、方明月、李涛：《增值税转型对企业行为和绩效的影响》，《管理世界》2009年第5期；陈烨、张欣、寇恩惠、刘明：《增值税转型对就业负面影响的CGE模拟分析》，《经济研究》2010年第9期。

③ 陈烨、张欣、寇恩惠、刘明：《增值税转型对就业负面影响的CGE模拟分析》，《经济研究》2010年第9期。

④ 申广军、陈斌开、杨汝岱：《减税能否提振中国经济？——基于中国增值税改革的实证研究》，《经济研究》2016年第11期。

⑤ 葛玉御、田志伟、胡怡建：《"营改增"的收入分配效应研究——基于收入和消费的双重视角》，《当代财经》2015年第4期。

乡之间的收入差距。而汪昊则认为，虽然"营改增"造成的平均税负下降有利于改善收入分配，但税制累退性的增加却恶化了收入分配差距。①因此两者的总效应虽然有利于改善全国以及城镇和农村内部的收入分配，但却导致城乡之间收入分配差距的上升。

最后是对国际贸易的影响。以增值税转型为背景的实证研究发现，减税可以通过降低企业更新技术成本和税收造成的价格扭曲等方式提升企业生产率，进而增加出口。②

综合已有研究来看，以增值税转型和"营改增"为背景的考察表明，税率的改变会对我国宏观经济会产生显著的系统性影响。不过尚未有文献在增值税已成为企业最主要的税负的背景下，直接对企业税率政策的改革方案进行模拟研究。而且也缺乏从系统论的角度基于统一的框架对减税的宏观经济效果进行的全面评估。同时，由于考察角度的差别，不同研究对某些问题，例如对劳动力市场影响的结论，具有显著的差异，因此得到全面的结论需要新的研究提供更多证据。此外现有研究注意到，由于竞争程度、融资约束以及资本成本敏感性等的不同，减税效果在不同行业、所有制企业及地区之间存在显著差异，③但是目前还缺乏对细分行业的减税效果的专门考察。因此本文基于 CGE 模型，利用其结构性和系统性的特点，针对我国增值税减税政策的宏观经济效果进行了模拟分析，并特别关注了税收变化对细分行业的影响，对现有的研究进行了补充。

三　中国财政税收 CGE 理论模型构建

（一）中国财政税收宏观社会核算矩阵（SAM）编制及数据说明

对中国财政税收进行政策模拟分析之前，需要构建中国财政税收社

---

① 汪昊：《"营改增"减税的收入分配效应》，《财政研究》2016 年第 10 期。
② Liu, Q., Lu, Y., "Firm investment and exporting: Evidence from China's value-added tax reform", *Journal of International Economics*, Vol. 97, No. 2, 2015. 汪小勤、曾瑜：《增值税转型对我国出口二元边际的影响——基于引力模型的实证分析》，《经济经纬》2016 年第 6 期。
③ Liu, Q., Lu, Y., "Firm investment and exporting: Evidence from China's value-added tax reform", *Journal of International Economics*, Vol. 97, No. 2, 2015. 申广军、陈斌开、杨汝岱：《减税能否提振中国经济？——基于中国增值税改革的实证研究》，《经济研究》2016 年第 11 期。

会核算矩阵（SAM 表）。SAM 表是对一国（或地区）一定时期（通常为一年）经济结构的全面系统描述，是以矩阵的形式表示国民经济核算账户间的交易及其关联，系统地反映了一定时期内社会经济各主体（企业、政府、居民、国外）之间的各种经济联系和交往。

本文以中国 2012 年投入产出表为数据基础，结合《中国税收年鉴》《中国海关年鉴》《中国财政年鉴》《中国经济统计年鉴》等，编制出中国财政税收社会核算矩阵（SAM）表。考虑了中国财政税收的主要特征，本模型构建的财政税收宏观 SAM 包括 16 个账户：生产、商品、劳动、资本、居民、企业、政府、国内增值税、营业税、其他间接税、关税、企业所得税、个人所得税、储蓄、存货和世界其他。并进一步把生产和商品细分为 42 个产业部门，[①] 中国财政税收宏观社会核算矩阵（SAM）表如表 1 所示。

表1　　　　中国财政税收宏观社会核算矩阵（SAM）表　　　　单位：百亿元

	生产	商品	劳动	资本	居民	企业	政府	国内增值税	营业税	其他间接税	关税	企业所得税	个人所得税	储蓄	存货	世界其他
生产		14650														1367
商品	10648				1985		732							2340	327	
劳动	2641															
资本	1991															
居民			2679			398	16									

---

① 具体包括：农林牧渔业，煤炭开采和洗选业，石油和天然气开采业，金属矿采选业，非金属矿及其他矿采选业，食品制造及烟草加工业，纺织业，纺织服装鞋帽皮革羽绒及其制品业，木材加工及家具制造业，造纸印刷及文教体育用品制造业，石油加工、炼焦及核燃料加工业，化学工业，非金属矿物制品业，金属冶炼及压延加工业，金属制品业，通用、专用设备制造业，交通运输设备制造业，电气、机械及器材制造业，通信设备、计算机及其他电子设备制造业，仪器仪表及文化办公用机械制造业，工艺品及其他制造业（含废品废料），电力、热力的生产和供应业，燃气生产和供应业，水的生产和供应业，建筑业，交通运输及仓储业，邮政业，信息传输、计算机服务和软件业，批发和零售贸易业，住宿和餐饮业，金融业，房地产业，租赁和商务服务业，研究与实验发展业，综合技术服务业，水利、环境和公共设施管理业，居民服务和其他服务业，教育业，卫生、社会保障和社会福利业，文化、体育和娱乐业，公共管理和社会组织业。

续表

	生产	商品	劳动	资本	居民	企业	政府	国内增值税	营业税	其他间接税	关税	企业所得税	个人所得税	储蓄	存货	世界其他
企业				1991			23									
政府								265	157	314	225	220	58			
国内增值税	265															
营业税	157															
其他间接税	314															
关税		225														
企业所得税						220										
个人所得税					58											
储蓄					1050	1319	444									−146
存货														327		
世界其他		1221														

（二）中国财政税收 CGE 理论模型框架及主要方程式

中国财政税收 CGE 模型共包括 42 个部门，根据国际惯例，模型假设企业是在规模收益不变的生产技术条件下按成本最小化或利润最大化原则进行生产决策。生产方程有两层嵌套的结构，即由中间投入品和增加值方程两部分构成，中间投入品按固定投入产出系数（Leontief 函数）关联；增加值方程由两种生产要素（劳动和资本）组成，并假设生产要素之间存在不完全替代性，采用常替代弹性 CES 方程形式进行复合。生产活动对要素的需求遵循企业利润最大化或成本最小化原则进行要素配置，因此，此时要素的边际成本（即要素的价格）等于产品的边际收益。中国财政税收 CGE 模型的市场商品流通框架如图1所示。

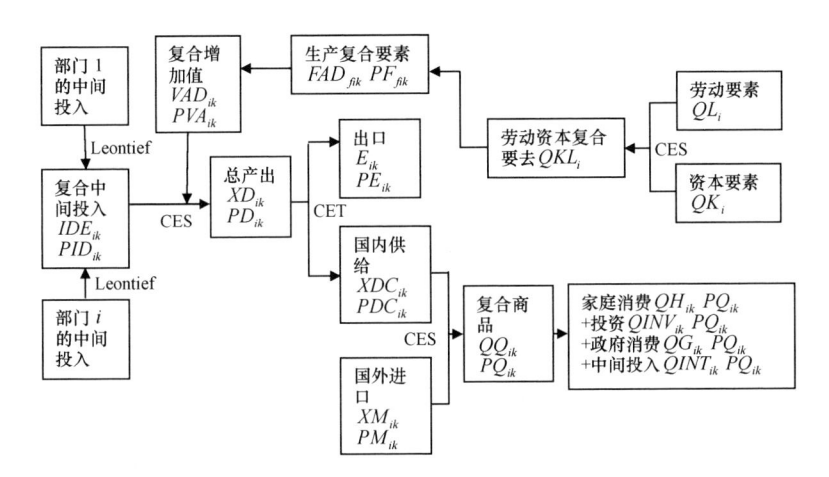

图1 中国财政税收 CGE 模型的市场商品流通框架

本文的财政税收 CGE 模型共包括八个模块：生产模块、消费模块、财政税收模块、收入模块、储蓄—投资模块、价格模块、国际贸易模块、均衡闭合模块。[①]

本文基于一般均衡理论和财政税收理论等推导的系统方程组，利用 GAMS 软件自主编写程序，并进行系统调试。经检验，该模型通过了可行性检验、一致性检验、齐次性检验、WALRAS 检验等，因此可以用该模型来进行相关政策模拟分析。

四 基于中国财政税收可计算一般均衡（CGE）模型政策模拟

为此，从经济系统论角度，根据中国最新的投入产出表和税收结构

[①] 八个模块的具体方程表达式在娄峰（2018）中有详细的推导和论证。

的现实特征，编制了中国财政税收社会核算矩阵，构建出中国财政税收可计算一般均衡（CGE）模型，并模拟分析了增值税税收制度改革。在全面"营改增"之后，增值税成为中国财税收入的主要构成之一，2017年增值税在国家财政税总收入中占比较大，因此，本文进行如下政策模拟。

（一）政策模拟 I

模拟假设：降低企业增值税税率，将现有四档增值税税率（17%、11%、6%、3%）全部下调到原来的13/17，即 $rvat(i) = 0.7647 * rvat0(i)$，$rvat0(i)$ 为行业原增值税税率，$rvat(i)$ 为变动后的行业增值税税率，其他条件不变，模拟对国内生产总值、产业结构、居民收入和居民消费、政府收入和政府消费、进出口、社会福利等宏观经济变量的影响，模拟结果如表2所示。

表2　政策模拟 I 中的主要宏观经济变量增长率

变量名称	增长率（%）	变量名称	增长率（%）
实际 GDP	0.4093	农村居民实际总收入	1.4769
名义 GDP	-1.0996	城镇居民实际总收入	0.4479
GDP 平减指数	-1.5027	农村居民总储蓄	-0.0484
第一产业增加值（名义值）	1.1497	城镇居民总储蓄	-1.0580
第二产业增加值（名义值）	0.4920	增值税	-21.1155
第三产业增加值（名义值）	-3.3912	营业税	-4.0421
总储蓄	-14.5901	消费税	-1.2512
固定资产总投资	-11.9886	其他间接税	-1.3971
总进口	-1.3987	关税	-1.8564
总出口	16.2820	城镇居民个人所得税	-0.0480
贸易顺差	83.5851	农村居民个人所得税	-1.0132
农村居民名义总收入	-0.0480	企业所得税	0.5658
城镇居民名义总收入	-1.0615	政府总收入	-5.8385
社会福利变量增长量（水平 Value 值）			
社会福利增加额	1110.1438		

表2显示在降低企业增值税税率，将增值税的普通税率从17%下调到13%，其他条件不变的假设条件下，中国实际GDP将提高0.4%，这说明该政策有利于提升GDP实际增长率，有利于经济增长。从产业上看，第一产业和第二产业的名义增加值分别提高1.1%和0.5%，但第三产业的名义增加值却下降3.4%，这说明该政策虽然会使得第三产业增速降低，从而减少第三产业在国名经济中的比重，但由于第一产业和第二产业主要由实体经济部门构成，因此该政策总体有利于实体经济发展，有利于巩固中长期经济发展的基础和动力。另外，GDP平减指数下降1.5%，由于该政策降低了企业生产成本，从而使得产品的销售价格下降，最终使得总体价格水平有所下降，这说明该政策有利于减缓和抑制中国通货膨胀压力。

从贸易上看，在该政策下，中国出口提高16.28%，进口下降1.4%，说明该政策可以有效提高产品的国际价格竞争力，促进出口显著提升；由于模型中设定汇率固定不变，因此随着出口水平的大幅提高和进口水平的略微下降，中国货物贸易顺差大幅提高83.6%。其原因在于随着企业增值税税率的下调，中国企业的生产成本减低，国内产品价格也随之下降，从而使得产品价格相对便宜，因此刺激了国内外市场对中国产品的需求，又由于国内外替代性产品的存在，因此使得中国出口增加、进口减少。

从居民收入上看，虽然由于物价总水平的降低使得农村居民和城镇居民的名义总收入分别下降0.05%和1.1%，但扣除价格因素，中国农村居民和城镇居民的实际总收入分别增加1.48%和0.45%，这说明该政策有利于居民的收入水平提高，有利于降低城乡居民收入差距。

从税收结构上看，在该政策下，政府的增值税收入大幅减少21.1%，并导致营业税、消费税、其他间接税、关税、城镇居民个人所得税和农村居民个人所得税分别下降4.04%、1.25%、1.40%、1.86%、0.05%和1.01%；而企业所得税反而增加0.57%，从而导致政府税收总收入下降约5.8%。说明该政策总体会使得政府收入下降，但是企业所得税的增加也侧面反映了该政策促进了企业利润增加，有利于企业的长期发展，符合国家供给侧结构性改革所倡导的"降成本"发展战略。

另外，在该政策下，社会福利水平增加了1110.14模拟值，说明该政策可以有效提高社会总福利，有利于社会和谐发展（见表3）。

表3　　　　政策模拟 I 中的主要经济变量分行业变化率　　　　单位：%

	国内总产出	总产出价格	资本形成	居民总消费	政府消费	出口	进口
农林牧渔业	1.27	-0.46	-12.91	-0.16	-5.41	3.15	0.31
煤炭开采和洗选业	0.52	-2.86	UNDF	2.42	UNDF	12.90	-5.28
石油和天然气开采业	2.88	-2.23	UNDF	UNDF	UNDF	12.58	-1.85
金属矿采选业	1.63	-1.80	UNDF	UNDF	UNDF	9.29	-2.08
非金属矿及其他矿采选业	-3.61	-1.47	UNDF	UNDF	UNDF	2.28	-6.70
食品制造及烟草加工业	1.50	-1.22	UNDF	0.47	UNDF	6.59	-1.53
纺织业	12.88	-1.63	UNDF	1.25	UNDF	20.56	5.13
纺织服装鞋帽皮革羽绒及其制品业	10.01	-2.05	UNDF	1.79	UNDF	19.50	0.28
木材加工及家具制造业	-2.06	-1.45	-11.79	0.81	UNDF	3.84	-6.76
造纸印刷及文教体育用品制造业	2.75	-1.65	-11.78	0.81	UNDF	9.83	-1.68
石油加工、炼焦及核燃料加工业	0.51	-2.05	UNDF	1.04	UNDF	9.19	-3.90
化学工业	4.28	-1.68	UNDF	1.01	UNDF	11.58	-0.39
非金属矿物制品业	-6.89	-1.70	UNDF	0.71	UNDF	-0.29	-10.15
金属冶炼及压延加工业	-0.06	-1.49	UNDF	UNDF	UNDF	6.11	-4.53
金属制品业	0.87	-1.75	-11.60	1.00	UNDF	8.25	-4.07
通用、专用设备制造业	-2.59	-1.87	-11.41	1.21	UNDF	5.04	-10.07
交通运输设备制造业	-4.50	-2.08	-11.48	1.30	UNDF	3.86	-9.59
电气、机械及器材制造业	-0.06	-1.83	-11.46	1.20	UNDF	7.61	-6.52
通信设备、计算机及其他电子设备制造业	31.93	-2.24	-10.83	2.12	UNDF	44.44	10.80
仪器仪表及文化办公用机械制造业	20.56	-1.93	-11.83	0.80	UNDF	30.31	1.53
工艺品及其他制造业（含废品废料）	0.61	-1.32	-12.27	0.26	UNDF	6.10	-3.20
电力、热力的生产和供应业	1.05	-2.21	UNDF	1.61	UNDF	10.95	-3.59

续表

	国内总产出	总产出价格	资本形成	居民总消费	政府消费	出口	进口
燃气生产和供应业	1.12	-1.65	UNDF	0.83	UNDF	8.09	-2.24
水的生产和供应业	1.90	-1.54	UNDF	0.83	UNDF	8.41	-2.51
建筑业	-11.73	-1.17	-12.28	0.11	UNDF	-7.49	-13.84
交通运输及仓储业	-1.50	-0.79	-12.61	0.07	-5.08	1.68	-3.25
邮政业	0.70	-0.95	UNDF	0.16	UNDF	4.62	-1.61
信息传输、计算机服务和软件业	-2.69	-0.58	-12.79	-0.13	UNDF	-0.42	-3.96
批发和零售贸易业	3.22	-3.01	-10.00	2.79	UNDF	16.66	-6.82
住宿和餐饮业	-0.12	-0.72	UNDF	-0.25	UNDF	2.82	-1.91
金融业	1.36	-0.09	UNDF	-0.93	-5.76	1.71	1.17
房地产业	-3.29	0.04	-13.35	-0.75	UNDF	-3.45	-3.20
租赁和商务服务业	2.81	-0.96	UNDF	0.04	-4.81	6.84	-0.87
研究与实验发展业	1.10	-0.95	UNDF	UNDF	-5.12	5.01	-0.92
综合技术服务业	-2.44	-0.59	-12.79	UNDF	-5.28	-0.10	-3.59
水利、环境和公共设施管理业	-2.66	-0.81	UNDF	-0.24	-5.07	0.56	-4.25
居民服务和其他服务业	0.15	-0.69	UNDF	-0.26	UNDF	2.97	-1.76
教育业	-3.91	-0.28	UNDF	-0.45	-5.57	-2.82	-4.45
卫生、社会保障和社会福利业	-1.69	-1.07	UNDF	0.14	-4.82	2.62	-3.79
文化、体育和娱乐业	-1.32	-0.65	UNDF	-0.26	-5.24	1.27	-2.96
公共管理和社会组织业	-5.40	-0.40	UNDF	UNDF	-5.46	-3.87	-6.17

注：UNDF 表示该行业初始值为零。

表 3 显示，从行业角度上看，该政策方案下，总体而言第一产业和第二产业的国内总产出普遍有所增加，而第三产业的总产出有所减少，其中通信设备、计算机及其他电子设备制造业，纺织业，纺织服装鞋帽皮革羽绒及其制品业的国内产出增幅最大，分别为 31.93%、12.88% 和 10.01%；几乎所有行业的产出价格水平均有所下降，其中，批发和零售贸易业，煤炭开采和洗选业，通信设备、计算机及其他电子设备制造业

的产出价格下降最多,分别下降3.01%、2.86%和2.24%;由于政府收入的减少,使得各行业原有的政府消费均有所减少,普遍下降约5%。

表3还显示,在该政策下,中国各行业出口大多均有所增加,其中通信设备、计算机及其他电子设备制造业,仪器仪表及文化办公用机械制造业,纺织业的出口增幅最大,分别为44.44%、30.31%和20.56%,说明该政策可以使得中国产品,尤其是通信设备、计算机及其他电子设备制造业、仪器仪表及文化办公用机械制造业、纺织业的国际竞争力水平提升,有利于中国企业参与国际竞争。从经济理论上看,进出口增幅主要取决于该行业的需求替代弹性系数,由于这些行业的替代弹性系数相对较大,因此在生产条件发生变化时,这些行业发生较大的变动。

(二)政策模拟Ⅱ

模拟假设:降低企业增值税税率,将现有四档增值税税率全部下调到原来的15/17、13/17、11/17、9/17,[分别 rvat(i)=15/17 * rvat0(i);rvat(i)=13/17 * rvat0(i);rvat(i)=11/17 * rvat0(i);rvat(i)=9/17 * rvat0(i),rvat0(i)为行业原增值税税率,rvat(i)为变动后的行业增值税税率]其他条件不变,模拟对国内生产总值、产业结构、居民收入和居民消费、政府收入和政府消费、进出口、社会福利等宏观经济变量的影响,模拟结果如表4所示。

表4　　　政策模拟Ⅱ中的主要宏观经济变量的变化率　　　单位:%

变量名称	增值税税率 rvat(i) =				平均弹性系数
	0.8824 * rvat0(i)	0.7647 * rvat0(i)	0.6471 * rvat0(i)	0.5294 * rvat0(i)	
实际GDP	0.20	0.41	0.66	0.85	0.10
名义GDP	-0.52	-1.10	-1.82	-2.72	-0.29
GDP平减指数	-0.72	-1.50	-2.46	-3.54	-0.40
第一产业增加值(名义值)	0.55	1.15	1.70	2.31	0.28
第二产业增加值(名义值)	0.15	0.49	1.45	3.04	0.20
第三产业增加值(名义值)	-1.50	-3.39	-6.29	-10.38	-0.99
总储蓄	-6.30	-14.59	-28.43	-48.76	-4.41

续表

变量名称	增值税税率 rvat（i）=				平均弹性系数
	0.8824 * rvat0（i）	0.7647 * rvat0（i）	0.6471 * rvat0（i）	0.5294 * rvat0（i）	
资本形成	-5.09	-11.99	-23.92	-41.78	-3.69
总进口	-0.80	-1.40	-1.13	0.40	-0.22
总出口	6.90	16.28	32.85	58.00	5.06
贸易顺差	36.20	83.59	162.22	277.26	25.17
农村居民名义收入	0.00	-0.05	-0.19	-0.49	-0.03
城镇居民名义收入	-0.51	-1.06	-1.68	-2.40	-0.28
增值税	-10.46	-21.12	-31.82	-42.76	-5.29
营业税	-1.77	-4.04	-7.68	-12.88	-1.20
消费税	-0.54	-1.25	-2.45	-4.23	-0.38
其他间接税	-0.60	-1.40	-2.82	-4.97	-0.43
居民所得税	-0.47	-0.97	-1.55	-2.23	-0.25
企业所得税	0.31	0.57	0.67	0.54	0.12
关税	-1.02	-1.86	-1.87	-0.59	-0.34
政府总收入	-2.84	-5.84	-9.16	-12.87	-1.50
社会福利变量增长量（水平 Value 值）					
社会福利增加额（亿元）	519.93	1110.14	1830.65	2672.72	

表4显示，该政策有利于中国实际 GDP 增长，有利于降低通货膨胀压力。从弹性系数上看，增值税税率每降低1%可以使得 GDP 实际增速提高约0.1%，而 GDP 平减指数（反映物价总水平）增加约0.4%；从产业结构上看，增值税税率每减少1%可以使得第一产业和第二产业名义增加值分别增加0.3%和0.2%，而第三产业名义增加值减少约1%。

从贸易上看，该政策对中国的进出口影响显著，尤其是对出口的影响巨大。平均弹性系数表明，在汇率保持不变的前提条件下，增值税税率每减少1%可以使得出口大幅增加5.1%，贸易顺差更是大幅提高约25%。当然在实际经济中，随着中国出口的快速提升和贸易顺差的大幅增加，肯定会使得人民币汇率升值压力骤增，甚至会激发国际贸易保护倾向进一步抬头，从而引起贸易摩擦和贸易制裁，进而削弱该政策的实际效果。

从政府的税收来源结构上看,增值税税率每降低1%可以使得中国增值税、营业税、消费税、其他间接税和居民所得税分别下降5.29%、1.20%、0.38%、0.43%和0.25%,而企业所得税反而上升0.12%。总体来说,增值税税率每降低1%可以使得中国政府税收总收入下降1.5%。

另外,在该政策下,社会福利水平分别增加519.93亿元、1110.14亿元、1830.65亿元和2672.72亿元,增值税税率每降低1%可以使得中国社会总福利增加约294亿元,说明该政策总体可以提高社会总福利,从而有利于社会和谐发展。

五 政策建议

(一) 以"稳增长"为目标,供给侧改革和扩大内需并重

首先需要明确当前积极财政政策的核心目标及其实现路径。经济理论表明,供给与需求是推动经济增长的两个基本力量。只有供给与需求彼此适应、协调均衡提升,长期的经济增长才能实现。因此,以"稳增长"为核心目标的积极财政政策,应着力对供给与需求两方面发挥其重要作用。在当下,支持供给侧改革与扩大内需是积极财政政策促进经济增长的两个主要实现途径。一方面,积极财政政策要大力支持供给侧改革,核心是为实体经济减轻税费负担和经济结构调整提供有力支撑。另一方面,积极财政政策要在扩大市场需求方面下功夫,努力改善企业发展的需求环境。企业发展的原动力在于市场需求,如果没有市场需求,企业就没有发展的空间和动力源泉。需要特别强调,在目前复杂的经济形势下,应有意识加强积极财政政策对扩大内需的作用,如何有效启动市场需求是至关重要的问题。

(二) 切实有效降低企业税费负担,适当降低增值税税率

2016年7月26日,中共中央政治局会议明确提出了降低宏观税负的要求。近几年实施的结构性减税政策对降低企业税负无疑起到了积极作用,中国税收占生产总值的比重呈现下降趋势;然而,总体上看,中国企业的宏观税负依然处于较高水平,具体体现在如下方面:非税收入快

速增长、个人所得税增长过快、企业增值税负担过重等。在经济增速减缓、企业利润增速下滑的形势下，当前积极财政政策的一个核心内容是减轻企业税费负担，降低企业税费负担有利于增强企业，尤其是中小企业恢复活力，从而促进企业增加投入、扩大生产、增加就业、刺激产业发展。政策模拟也显示，适当降低增值税税率有助于中国实际 GDP 增长、有利于降低通货膨胀水平、有利于出口和社会福利提高等。

"一带一路"倡议与白俄罗斯国家治理现代化

Dzmitry Smaliakou
白俄罗斯国立科学院哲学研究所哲学博士
岭南师范学院中白研究中心高级研究员

一 概述

随着两极体系在 20 世纪末逐步瓦解，国家治理问题变得越来越重要。在全球合作的新形势下，随着不同国家之间建立对一体化趋势产生巨大影响的新合作方式，各国关系发生了新变化，东欧和亚洲经济得以重组和重启。这体现为各国积极消除政治、经济、贸易和其他壁垒，并建立更紧密的经贸联系，国际合作大幅加速。已启动的世界政治和经济合作主要围绕区域一体化的方向进行，可以说区域一体化是当今世界的重要趋势，是在世界最终实现全球化之前全球发展达到的新水平。

然而，20 世纪末的和谐氛围在"9·11"恐怖袭击后出现动荡，这说明了世界矛盾的多源性。随着苏联的解体和中国的改革开放，区域发展和世界发展出现了新动态。21 世纪初恐怖活动及局部战争的增多表明全球化进程中还有很多问题要解决，例如全球化组织机制不健全，区域合作机制不完善。因此，应按照新的原则创新构建全球化，以便继续开展促进经济进一步增长所需的全球治理活动。经济全球化既要考虑区域不平衡问题，又要考虑各区域参与者加强区域和全球合作的意愿。

21世纪初恐怖主义问题更加严重，人们更加认为全球化是不公平的，全球化需要更加均衡、包容。

同时，中国经济快速增长，中国对世界发展的贡献越来越大。中国于2013年宣布实施"一带一路"倡议，这有助于推动新型全球化。对于中国而言，新的倡议是成功的改革开放政策的延续，它在许多方面确保了经济增长，使中国成为世界最大的经济体之一。

"一带一路"倡议很快获得了国际社会的广泛响应。2017年5月在北京举行了第一次"一带一路"国际合作高峰论坛。[①] 论坛汇聚了60多位国家元首以及众多政界人士、科学家和专家。与会代表表示需要重新思考和调整以前的全球化，因为许多穷国和发展中国家没有充分参与到全球化进程中，而欧洲—大西洋世界的富国却成为全球化的主要受益者。"一带一路"倡议将有助于促进实施新的全球一体化，促进欧亚大陆互联互通，形成更加均衡的全球化，这种全球化不仅对世界领先国家，还有其周边国家都将产生积极的影响。

"一带一路"有利于促进经济增长，实现合作共赢。人们期待"一带一路"倡议能够推动建立人类命运共同体。人们期待中国机遇以及新的增长点。

因此，"一带一路"倡议的重要方面是实现互联互通，而交通运输部门无疑是首要基础。就这一点而言，相关国家应该改革国家治理以适应新的合作可能性，这对于确保国际合作取得成功至关重要。

二 白俄罗斯的发展

随着白中关系的发展，白俄罗斯决定加强同中国的联系，并将其作为发展的优先方向。

白俄罗斯选择与中国合作的战略方针后，立即采取果断措施，加强白俄罗斯与中国的互动。白俄罗斯做了大量规划工作，到2013年"一带一路"倡议宣布之时，白俄罗斯已经制订了许多政府层面的计划，特别

---

① Official website of "One Belt, One Road" Forum, http://www.beltandroadforum.org/.

是在政治、经济、军事和社会等领域。[①] 2016 年 9 月白俄罗斯和中国在亚历山大·卢卡申科总统和习近平主席的见证下签署了共同促进"一带一路"建设的一揽子措施。[②] 这是白俄罗斯参与共建"一带一路"的起点。在共建"一带一路"背景下,双方同时签署了众多教育、科学、交通运输、投资、安全等领域的协议,[③] 推动白中双边合作与"一带一路"建设的衔接。随后,白俄罗斯将"一带一路"建设计划纳入 2016—2020 年国家社会经济发展规划,[④] 以此确认白俄罗斯作为独立国家的国家发展和可持续发展的重要性。

自上述文件签署以来,白俄罗斯和中国的合作显著增长,"建立了双边贸易和大型合资企业,扩大了物流联系,在实践中不仅有商业与政治的'结合',而且有科学与文化的'结合'过程"[⑤]。随着时间的推移,双方逐渐认识到,没有适当的科学支持,就无法成功和深入地开展合作。为此,白俄罗斯和中国建立了多个联合研究中心。中国还为白俄罗斯学生提供了更多的奖学金,举行了多次双边会议,中国向白俄罗斯提供了更多的财政援助。[⑥]

很快,白俄罗斯通过了在"一带一路"倡议框架内实现双边合作成

---

① 26. Смоляков, Д. А. Белорусско-китайское сотрудничество в области образования в контексте реализации инициативы "Один пояс, один путь" / Д. А. Смоляков // Вестник Минского государственного лингвистического университета: научно-методический журнал / Министерство образования Республики Беларусь. — 2017. - № 1. - С. 25 - 32.

② Итоги развития проекта «Один пояс — один путь» /СОНАР/ 23. 08. 2018. Available at: https://www.sonar2050.org/publications/pervyy-yubiley-puti/.

③ Ци Хуаньюань. Беларусь и Китай активизируют взаимовыгодное сотрудничество по всем направлениям концепции «Один пояс, один путь» Available at: https://rep.bntu.by/bitstream/handle/data/39623/Belarus_i_Kitaj_aktiviziruyut_vzaimovygodnoe_sotrudnichestvo_po_vsem_napravleniyam_koncepcii_Odin_poyas_i_odin_put.pdf?sequence=1&isAllowed=y.

④ Программа социально-экономического развития Республики Беларусь на 2016 - 2020 годы. Available at: http://www.government.by/upload/docs/program_ek2016-2020.pdf.

⑤ Итоги развития проекта «Один пояс — один путь» /СОНАР/23. 08. 2018. Available at: https://www.sonar2050.org/publications/pervyy-yubiley-puti/.

⑥ Smaliakou, D. Sino-Belarusian Cooperation in Sphere of Education Faced the Challenges of the Belt and Road Initiative Between China and Belarus // Zhang Yi; Wang Lei / China and Belarus: Forge Ahead Together in the "Belt and Road" Construction. : Beijing, China Social Sciences Press, 2019. pp. 201 - 215.

效的主要标准体系。① 中国在白俄罗斯合作建设的产业和项目首先为白俄罗斯国内市场提供货物与服务，还应提高进入欧亚经济联盟和欧盟国家市场的这些产业和服务的质量。在这个阶段，白俄罗斯不仅要生产本国消费市场需要的产品，还要开发出口到第三方市场的产品。白俄罗斯产品将蓄力进入中国市场，参与到更广阔的世界市场竞争之中，并吸引中国投资，促进白俄罗斯国内市场发展。

同时，"一带一路"倡议具有更广阔的国际合作意义。鉴于此，通过与中国的合作，白俄罗斯可以更好地改善民生，提高国家治理能力。在现实中，白俄罗斯国家治理的能力由外部投资和加强与中国的伙伴关系得以发展。换言之，白俄罗斯通过加强以商业规划为指导的发展，提高经济发展水平。

首先，在第一阶段的框架内，白俄罗斯的外汇外流加剧，每年有超过10亿美元外流，信贷条件造成了贸易赤字，增加了白俄罗斯的外债。② 白俄罗斯在财政资源方面没有完全的可持续性，长期需要外部支持来维持国家债务，因此，外汇流向国外对国民经济安全产生了强烈的负面影响。参与"一带一路"倡议，极大改善了白俄罗斯投资环境，促进了就业和社会发展。

5年内白俄罗斯外汇外流差额高达100亿美元。③ 贸易成交额的双边结构也发生了变化。由于白中关系的发展，中国对白俄罗斯的技术出口有所增加。早期中国主要向白俄罗斯供应食品，现在则供应电脑、车辆、加工设备等。白俄罗斯对中国的出口也在不断增加。传统的钾肥出口、粮食出口也持续增长。这些举措有力提升了白中双边贸易水平。

---

① Итоги развития проекта «Один пояс — один путь» /СОНАР/ 23.08.2018. Available at：https：//www.sonar2050.org/publications/pervyy-yubiley-puti/.

② Рудый, К. В. Беларусь-Китай：сдвиги в экономическом сотрудничестве // Белорусский экономический журнал. 2019 №2. С. 38 – 51. Available at：http：//bem.bseu.by/rus/archive/2.19/2 – 2019_rudy.pdf.

③ Итоги развития проекта «Один пояс — один путь» /СОНАР/23.08.2018. Available at：https：//www.sonar2050.org/publications/pervyy-yubiley-puti/.

三 经济特区——中国的发展路径

近年来，中国成为在国外建立经贸合作区的领导者之一。2016年，中国已在36个国家建立了77个工业园，总投资241.9亿美元。同时，园区入驻企业总数达1522家，总产值达702.8亿美元。[①]

在国外建立经贸合作区对东道国的可持续发展产生了积极影响，可以说，建立国家层面的这种合作被双方视为根据对公平全球化的理解而进行的互利合作。因此，经贸一体化并不在于建立超国家的政府机构、财政补贴或技术捐赠，而是在于创造就业机会和税收。

中国在白俄罗斯也建立了这种技术和经济合作区。白中"巨石"工业园"突出呈现出经贸合作区的优势特性"。[②] 该项目在白俄罗斯被称为"一带一路"倡议的明珠，也就是说，它是白俄罗斯参与新型全球化的基石，[③] 也是白中合作的典范。

在白俄罗斯和中国签署了关于相互支持和投资安全方面的协议之后，建立工业园区成为可能。双方同意在2010年3月建立一座白俄罗斯—中国工业园，建设工作于2014年开始，并有第一批企业入驻。2017年，白俄罗斯总统颁布了第166号令，确定了在该工业园营商的必要条件。园区的税收和法律条件对外国投资更加便利，独联体国家和波罗的海国家之间没有类似条件。为了强调工业园的独特性，以优惠待遇（自由经济区、高科技园区）区别该工业园和其他地区，明确了投资项目的优先领域：电子、电信、制药、精细化工、生物技术、工程、新材料、综合物流、电子商务、与处理和存储大量数据有关的活动、社会文化活动、研究和

[①] Яо Цзяхуэй. Беларусь и КНР: торгово-экономическое сотрудничество в контексте реализации стратегии «экономического пояса Шелкового пути» // Журнал международного права и международных отношений. 2017. № 1 – 2（80 – 81）. С. 122 – 129. Available at: http://elib.bsu.by/bitstream/123456789/183567/1/tsyahuey_Journal2017_1 – 2.pdf.

[②] Сазонов, С. Л. Экономическая парадигма формирования «пояса и пути» / С. Л. Сазонов // Стратегия Экономического пояса Шелкового пути и роль ШОС в ее реализации: материалы «круглого стола», 16 марта 2016 г. – М.: ИДВ РАН, 2016. – С. 131 – 148.

[③] «Великий Камень» — это «жемчужина» в китайском «Шелковом пути»? /REGNUM/ 13.08.2018. Available at: https://regnum.ru/news/2463458.html.

设计工作。①

"巨石"工业园早在"一带一路"倡议之前已列入计划,"一带一路"倡议使工业园高质量发展。该工业园除了经济和税收优惠政策,也具有地理因素的优势。"巨石"工业园坐落于白俄罗斯首都,靠近明斯克国际机场,依白俄罗斯的主要经济和交通大动脉而建。连接俄罗斯和波兰边境的奥尔撒—布列斯特(Orša-Brest)高速公路,以及连接立陶宛和乌克兰边境的高速公路。单就此而言,"巨石"园区建立了贸易和物流分园。该物流中心由中国招商局集团建设,计划投资 5 亿多美元。② 物流设施将包括展览中心、酒店、室内和室外仓库、零售空间、办公室和其他设施。未来会在该园区建立一个通往波罗的海国家的无水港,以及连接中国—白俄罗斯—欧洲走廊的高速铁路。

"巨石"工业园的物流设施应理解为泛欧亚基础设施的一部分。"巨石"工业园是欧亚互联互通的一部分,更是推进新型全球化的经典案例。建立从中国到欧洲的物流设施意味着建立铁路和公路连接网络,欧亚走廊的中国部分包括从中国东部和中南部各省到新疆维吾尔自治区的高速公路和铁路,这些网络可通往哈萨克斯坦边境并到达欧洲。现在,一座新的欧亚大陆桥从中国穿过哈萨克斯坦、俄罗斯和白俄罗斯到达波兰,然后进入欧洲国家,并通向欧洲北部和西部的海港。

从中国到欧洲已经拥有多条国际货运铁路线路,包括重庆—杜伊斯堡(德国)、武汉—帕尔杜比采(捷克共和国)、成都—罗兹(波兰)、郑州—汉堡(德国)、义乌—马德里(西班牙)。沿着这些铁路线,简化了货物报关手续和通关手续,从而加快了货物交付速度,降低了货物交付成本。

在该走廊内,白俄罗斯是中国和欧洲之间的物流枢纽。为了在

---

① «Великий камень»-самый большой индустриальный парк, построенный Китаем за рубежом » / СТВ/02. 07. 2019. Available at:https: //news. 21. by/other-news/2019/07/02/1831256. html.

② Торгово-логистический субпарк China Merchants Group в "Великом камне" обойдётся в $550 млн26 ноября 2015. Available at:http://www. logists. by/news/view/velikiy-kamen-obojdetsya-v–55–mln-doll.

2018年加强合作，杜伊斯堡港集团（德国）入驻"巨石"工业园。同时，中国积极发展丝绸之路沿线各国的基础设施。在白俄罗斯，中国已经为当地铁路系统的两个铁路段进行了电气化改造，两个项目总投资达1.571亿美元。2018年对第三个铁路段进行了电气化改造。必须指出，白俄罗斯铁路直接参与了欧盟与中国东西部之间运输设施发展的若干项目，这些项目使用从欧洲返回的空车，对当地运输稳定产生了积极影响。[①] 为此，白俄罗斯政府在"巨石"园区内设立了明斯克地区海关的通关点，优化办事流程。在新冠肺炎疫情肆虐期间，中欧交通线的价值变得更加明显。

四　结论

旨在改善欧亚之间物流基础设施是"一带一路"倡议的重要内容。改善交通设施的目的不仅在于加速货物运输，而且还在于填补双向交通流量。考虑到合作建立技术经济合作区的机会，白俄罗斯应更加积极地开展"一带一路"共建，更有效地利用中欧交通互动的增长。中国的这项倡议可推动白俄罗斯基础设施现代化阶段的需求和就业，带来与欧盟贸易的增长，而且来自中国的物资产品，可以通过税收减免和就业增长带来利润。

就这一点而言，白俄罗斯必须优化营商环境，以便加强白俄罗斯私营企业和中国民营企业的互动。与国家机构相比，白俄罗斯私营企业必须更多地参与白中商业互动，更积极地制定商业规划。当然，国家治理改革必须在必要时让白俄罗斯更加适应"一带一路"倡议的实施，在白俄罗斯和中国的双边贸易中更有效地进行国家层面的尝试。国民经济的

---

① Папковская, В. И. Развитие международного транспорта Республики Беларусь в рамках инициативы «Один пояс, один путь» //Устойчивое развитие экономики: международные и национальные аспекты［Электронный ресурс］: электронный сборник статей III Международной научно-практической online-конференции, Новополоцк, 18 – 19 апреля 2019 г. / Полоцкий государственный университет. – Новополоцк, 2019. Available at: http://elib.psu.by/bitstream/123456789/23655/1/%D0%9F%D0%B0%D0%BF%D0%BA%D0%BE%D0%B2%D1%81%D0%BA%D0%B0%D1%8F%20D0%92.%D0%98._%D1%81%1418 – 421. pdf.

增长及地方经济和法制的现代化、智力潜力的开发和社会领域的改善是白俄罗斯国家责任的一部分。因此，白俄罗斯政府必须关注国家和社会治理，因为商业互动应该主要由私营部门开展，政府要为它们提供好服务。

中国生态文明的制度和行动建构与生态环境领域治理现代化

林 红

中国社会科学院社会学研究所助理研究员

在风险社会中，任何人既是原因也是结果，系统的各组成部分存在一种总体的共谋。① 正是意识到这种风险，国际社会和各国正在采取多元的方式应对生态风险社会的到来。《全球环境展望 6》指出，导致地球不健康后果的驱动因素和压力源于人类社会长期以来未能将环境和健康影响内化于经济增长过程、技术革新和城市设计，包括人口、城市化、经济发展、技术创新、气候变化等因素，例如大量使用化学品（许多化学品对健康和环境具有毒性影响）、巨量废弃物（许多废弃物基本上未经管理）、被触发和加剧的气候变化影响、不平等导致的人口变化等。② 为应对这些挑战，该报告建议各国确立绿色、健康和包容性经济的发展理念，并系统性地反映在现有的国家政策中。

中国通过积极落实《变革我们的世界：2030 年可持续发展议程》和《巴黎协定》以及生态文明建设，在国际和国内层面践行保护全球生态环境的承诺。从 1978 年的《中华人民共和国宪法》确认环境保护是国家职能之一，到 2018 年把新发展理念、生态文明和建设美丽中国的要求写入

---

① ［德］乌尔里希·贝克：《风险社会》，何博闻译，译林出版社 2004 年版，第 28—34 页。
② UN Environment, *Global Environment Outlook-GEO-6*: *Healthy Planet, Healthy People*, 2019, Nairobi. DOI 10.1017/9781108627146. pp. xxix – xxx.

宪法修正案；从1974年成立国务院环境保护领导小组，到2018年重组生态环境部；从1979年制定《中华人民共和国环境保护法（试行）》、1989年修订并正式颁布《中华人民共和国环境保护法》，再到2014年修订通过被誉为"史上最严环保法"的新《中华人民共和国环境保护法》，中国在环境保护方面，走出了一条符合自身国情的生态文明建设之路。新时代中国坚持以习近平生态文明思想为指导，不断推进美丽中国建设，为美丽世界做出更多贡献。

一 中国生态文明的思想流变

自1949年以来，中国的环境治理体系从改革开放前工业污染防治的初步探索、改革开放初期的"预防为主、防治结合"，到20世纪90年代的"污染防治和生态保护并重"，进入21世纪的"在发展中保护、保护中发展"，再到中国共产党十八大以来的"坚持生态优先"，经历了从无到有、从起步构建到全面提升的多次重大战略转型，实现了从"污染防治观"到"生态文明观"的认知演变。[1]

20世纪70年代，以国际生态环境保护理念为背景，中国召开了第一次全国环境保护会议并通过了《关于保护和改善环境的若干规定》，提出需要从战略层面看待环境问题，这是1949年以来中国发布的第一个以环境保护为主题的文件。1981年，国务院颁布《关于在国民经济调整时期加强环境保护工作的决定》，明确指出"环境和自然资源，是人民赖以生存的基本条件，是发展生产、繁荣经济的物质源泉。管理好我国的环境，合理地开发和利用自然资源，是现代化建设的一项基本任务"[2]。1982年公布实施的《宪法》规定"国家保护和改善生活环境和生态环境，防治污染和其他公害"。在1983年12月举办的第二次全国环境保护大会上，时任国务院副总理李鹏提出"环境保护是中国现代化建设中的一项战略

---

[1] 张小筠、刘戒骄：《新中国70年环境规制政策变迁与取向观察》，《改革》2019年第10期。

[2] 中国网，国务院关于在国民经济调整时期加强环境保护工作的决定（一九八一年二月二十四日发布），2006年8月8日，http://www.china.com.cn/law/flfg/txt/2006-08/08/content_7058576.htm。

任务，是一项基本国策"。1990年，《国务院关于进一步加强环境保护工作的决定》正式以中央政府权威文件的形式确认了环境保护的基本国策地位，并以"保护和改善生产环境与生态环境、防治污染和其他公害，是中国的一项基本国策"的表述方式纳入1991年通过的《国民经济和社会发展十年规划和"八五"计划纲要》。随后，1992年中国共产党的十四大报告提出"认真执行控制人口增长和加强环境保护的基本国策"。1996年时任国家主席江泽民在第四次全国环境保护大会上强调"控制人口增长，保护生态环境，是全党全国人民必须长期坚持的基本国策"。这些国家顶层设计类的政策文本和领导人讲话，进一步确认了环境保护的基本国策地位。

继环境保护被确定为一项基本国策，在国家发展战略层面，可持续发展理念被视为国策意识的具象化。1992年6月在巴西里约热内卢举行的联合国环境与发展大会，通过了《环境与发展宣言》《21世纪议程》等重要文件，国际社会确立了可持续发展的核心理念。中国政府不仅积极参与了此次大会的相关活动、签署了上述文件，并于1994年率先批准了《中国21世纪议程：中国21世纪人口、资源、环境与发展白皮书》，提出了可持续发展总体战略与政策、社会可持续发展、经济可持续发展、资源的合理利用与环境保护的整体规划，确定了78个具体行动领域，不但反映了中国对可持续发展的内在需求，也表明了中国政府积极履行国际承诺、为全人类共同事业做出应有贡献的态度和决心。1995年，十四届五中全会通过了《中共中央关于制定国民经济和社会发展"九五"计划和2010年远景目标的建议》，提出促进"经济增长方式从粗放型向集约型转变"。2000年，十五届五中全会通过的《中共中央关于制定国民经济和社会发展第十个五年计划的建议》认为，"实施可持续发展战略，是关系中华民族生存和发展的长远大计"。2002年，党的十六大报告系统总结了过去的基本经验，把实施可持续发展战略，实现经济发展和人口、资源、环境相协调确认为党领导人民建设中国特色社会主义必须坚持的基本经验，强调实现全面建设小康社会的宏伟目标，必须使可持续发展能力不断增强，生态环境得到改善，资源利用效率显著提高，促进人与自然的和谐，推动整个社会走上生产发展、生活富裕、生态良好的文明发展道路。可持续发展正式成为中国实现社会主义现代化目标的重大战略。

进入21世纪，中国特色社会主义现代化进程面临承上启下、继往开来的全新局面，相当程度上，国家发展依然受制于传统现代化理念与模式。以胡锦涛同志为总书记的党中央提出"必须牢固树立和认真落实科学发展观，把科学发展观贯穿于发展的整个过程和各个方面"，以科学发展观来统领中国新一个十年（2002—2012）的社会主义现代化建设，而在生态环境领域则要求努力实现我国经济产业与技术结构的转型升级和建设一个"环境友好型、资源节约型"的社会（简称"两型社会"思想）。2003年6月25日由中共中央、国务院发布的关于加快林业发展的决定中提出"建设山川秀美的生态文明社会"，这是国家权威文件首次明确使用"生态文明"这一概念。随后，党的十六届三中全会提出的"科学发展观"和十六届四中全会提出的"构建和谐社会"，都包含生态文明理念及其政策意涵的国家论述。2005年，党的十六届五中全会明确提出，要加快建设资源节约型、环境友好型社会，大力发展循环经济，加大环境保护力度，切实保护好自然生态，认真解决影响经济社会发展特别是严重危害人民健康的突出的环境问题，在全社会形成资源节约的增长方式和健康文明的消费模式。2007年，党的十七大报告正式提出了"生态文明"这一概念，"建设生态文明，基本形成节约能源资源和保护生态环境的产业结构、增长方式、消费模式"。显然，这一时期的发展语境下，建设"两型社会"是"生态文明"的具象化内涵。

党的十八大以来，以习近平同志为核心的党中央站在中国特色社会主义现代化新的历史起点上，系统总结我国改革开放实践过程中经济社会现代化发展以及环境保护基本国策、可持续发展战略和"两型社会"建设的经验，着眼于从一种更高的政治哲学与战略视野层面系统性解决我国经济社会发展中渐趋突出的不全面、不充分、不均衡问题，以习近平总书记治国理政系列重要论述为基础逐渐形成"习近平新时代中国特色社会主义思想"，生态环境治理维度上表达为"习近平生态文明思想"。实际上，早在2003年时任浙江省委书记习近平就提出了"生态兴则文明兴、生态衰则文明衰"的重要论断。[①] 2012年11月党的十八大报告第一

---

① 习近平：《生态兴则文明兴：推进生态建设打造"绿色浙江"》，《求是》2003年第13期。

次明确把生态文明建设与经济、政治、文化和社会建设一起共同列为中国特色社会主义现代化建设总体布局的核心元素，并要求将其贯彻于"各个方面和全过程"。2013年11月，党的十八届三中全会确定了60项改革任务，主题之一是加快生态文明制度建设，实现国家生态环境治理体系与治理能力的现代化。2015年9月，中共中央、国务院印发《生态文明体制改革总体方案》，明确要求推进"健全自然资源资产产权制度、建立国土空间开发保护制度、建立空间规划体系、完善资源总量管理和全面节约制度、健全资源有偿使用和生态补偿制度、建立健全环境治理体系、健全环境治理和生态保护市场体系、完善生态文明绩效评价考核和责任追究制度"等生态文明"四梁八柱"制度框架体系的核心改革。2015年10月，党的十八届五中全会提出"创新、协调、绿色、开放、共享"五大新发展理念，并建议将其作为制定国民经济和社会发展第十三个五年计划的指导性原则。2017年10月，党的十九大报告第一次明确阐述了中国生态文明建设的阶段性目标，即于2020年之前"打好（赢）污染防治的攻坚战"，2020—2035年实现"生态环境根本好转、美丽中国目标基本实现"，2035—2049年实现"生态文明全面提升"。2017年10月24日通过的新《中国共产党章程》写道，"跨入新世纪，我国进入全面建设小康社会、加快推进社会主义现代化的新的发展阶段。必须按照中国特色社会主义事业'五位一体'总体布局和'四个全面'战略布局，统筹推进经济建设、政治建设、文化建设、社会建设、生态文明建设"。2018年3月，新修订的《宪法》序言的第七段表述为"推动物质文明、政治文明、精神文明、社会文明、生态文明协调发展，把我国建设成为富强民主文明和谐美丽的社会主义现代化强国，实现中华民族伟大复兴"，生态文明正式以国家基本法的形式得到确认。

1973年至2018年，中国共召开了八次全国环境保护会议。历次全国环境保护会议都有标志性成果，集中体现了中国环境保护事业与时俱进、不断开拓创新的发展历程。1973年国务院召开第一次全国环境保护会议，提出"全面规划、合理布局，综合利用、化害为利，依靠群众、大家动手，保护环境、造福人民"的环保工作32字方针。1983年召开的第二次全国环境保护会议，把环境保护确立为基本国策，制定了"经济建设、城乡建设和环境建设要同步规划、同步实施、同步发展，做到经济效益、社会效益、环境效益相统一"的指导方针，明确了"预防为主、防治结合"、"谁污染、谁治理"和"强化环境管理"的环境保护三大政策。1989年召开的第三次全国环境保护会议，提出"向环境污染宣战"，积极推行环境保护目标责任制、城市环境综合整治定量考核制、排放污染物许可证制、污染集中控制、限期治理、环境影响评价制度、"三同时"制度、排污收费制度八项环境管理制度。1996年召开的第四次全国环境保护会议，提出保护环境是实施可持续发展战略的关键，保护环境的实质是保护生产力，把实施主要污染物排放总量控制计划和跨世纪绿色工程规划作为改善环境质量的两大重要举措。2002年召开的第五次全国环境保护会议，要求把环境保护工作摆上同发展生产力同样重要的位置，按照经济规律发展环保事业，走市场化和产业化的路子。2006年召开的第六次全国环保大会，明确提出做好新形势下的环保工作，关键在于加快实现"三个转变"：从重经济增长轻环境保护转变为保护环境与经济增长并重，从环境保护滞后于经济发展转变为环境保护和经济发展同步推进，从主要用行政办法保护环境转变为综合运用法律、经济、技术和必要的行政办法解决环境问题。2011年召开的第七次全国环境保护大会，强调要坚持在发展中保护，在保护中发展，积极探索代价小、效益好、排放低、可持续的环境保护新道路，切实解决影响科学发展和损害群众健康的突出环境问题，努力开创环保工作新局面。2018年的第八次全国生态环境保护大会，习近平总书记在大会上讲话时强调，要加快构建生态文明体系，加快建立健全以生态价值观念为准则的生态文化体系，以产业生态化和生态产业化为主体的生态经济体系，以改善生态环境质量为核心的目标责任体系，以治理体系和治理能力现代化为保障的生态文明制度体系，以生态系统良性循环和环境风险有效防控为重点的生态安全体系，[①] 正式确立习近平生态文明思想。

从环境保护基本国策思想、可持续发展战略思想、"两型社会"建设思想，到生态文明思想，改革开放40多年来中国共产党及其领导的中国

---

① 新华网，《开创美丽中国建设新局面——习近平总书记在全国生态环境保护大会上的重要讲话引起热烈反响》，2019年5月20日，http：//www.xinhuanet.com//politics/2018 - 05/20/c_1122859915.htm。

政府在治国理政的实践中形成了一个理论架构上渐趋系统化、环境主义或生态主义意涵日益鲜明的绿色现代化观,而生态文明及其建设视域和语境下的"人与自然和谐共生的(社会主义)现代化"则是这一思想的最简明表述。①

二 中国生态文明的制度化建构

中国环境保护事业自20世纪70年代起步,经历了从无到有、从小到大、不断探索、逐步发展的过程,其制度化历程可以大体分为四个阶段。

第一阶段(1973—1993年):点源治理、制度建设

这一阶段,通过不断加强制度建设和开展重点地区污染治理,我国环境保护事业逐渐走上法制化轨道。1973年8月,第一次全国环境保护会议在北京召开。1978年12月,中共中央批转了国务院环境保护领导小组第四次会议通过的《环境保护工作汇报要点》。1979年9月,《中华人民共和国环境保护法(试行)》颁布,第一次从法律上要求各部门和各级政府在制定国民经济和社会发展计划时必须统筹考虑环境保护,为实现环境和经济社会协调发展提供了法律保障。《中华人民共和国水污染防治法》(1984年5月)、《中华人民共和国大气污染防治法》(1987年9月)、《中华人民共和国草原法》(1985年6月)、《中华人民共和国水法》(1988年1月)等环保单项法律法规相继制定颁布。1989年12月,《中华人民共和国环境保护法》正式颁布实施。从此,环境保护法律开始成为我国环境保护工作的重要保障,成为我国社会主义法律体系的重要组成部分。1990年,国务院印发《关于进一步加强环境保护工作的决定》,强调严格执行环境保护法律法规,依法采取有效措施防治工业污染,全面落实环境保护目标责任制、城市环境综合整治定量考核制、排放污染物许可证制、污染集中控制、限期治理、环境影响评价制度、"三同时"制度、排污收费制度八项环境管理制度。1993年3月,全国人大环境与资源保护委员会成立并提出"中国环境与资源保护法律体系框架"。以环

---

① 郇庆治:《改革开放四十年中国共产党绿色现代化话语的嬗变》,《云梦学刊》2019年第1期。

境保护是基本国策为核心的环境保护理论体系,以排污收费制度、"三同时"制度、环境影响评价制度为主体的环保制度和以《环境保护法》为基础的法制体系的相继建立,为下一阶段大规模环境治理奠定了基础。

第二阶段(1994—2004 年):流域整治、强化执法

20 世纪 90 年代初,我国进入第一轮重化工时代,城镇化进程加快,环境污染的结构型、复合型和压缩型特征开始形成,并促使这一阶段成为强化执法、全面治理污染和保护生态的重要时期。中国于 1992 年开始正式编制全国环境保护年度工作计划,并从"九五"时期正式开始编制国家环境保护五年规划,将环境保护规划纳入国民经济和社会发展总体规划中,从而使环境保护由单纯工业污染治理扩展到生活污染治理、生态保护、农村环境保护、核安全监管、突发环境事件应急等各个重要领域,并逐步参与到国民经济和社会发展的综合决策中。1998 年 4 月,作为国务院直属机构的国家环保局升格为国家环保总局。为了更好地协调有关部门共同推进环境保护,由国家环境保护总局牵头,分别建立了相关部际联席会议制度。2001 年 3 月,全国生态环境建设部际联席会议第一次会议召开;同年 7 月,国家环保总局建立全国环境保护部际联席会议制度。2003 年 8 月,经国务院批准,由国家环境保护总局牵头正式建立生物物种资源保护部际联席会议制度。

在这一阶段,国家层面的总体思路是污染防治抓重点流域区域、以重点带全面、推进全国环境保护工作。1994 年 6 月,国家环保局、水利部和沿淮河的河南、安徽、江苏、山东四省共同颁布我国大江大河水污染预防的第一个规章制度——《关于淮河流域防止河道突发性污染事故的决定(试行)》。1995 年 8 月,国务院颁布了我国历史上第一部流域性法规——《淮河流域水污染防治暂行条例》,明确了淮河流域水污染防治目标。在相关法律法规推动下,仅 1996 年,淮河全流域就有 4000 多家污染企业被关闭。1996 年开始实施的《中国跨世纪绿色工程规划》按照突出重点、技术经济可行和发挥综合效益的基本原则,对流域性水污染、区域性大气污染实施分期综合治理。到 2010 年,共实施项目 1591 个,投入资金 1880 亿元。先后确定了"九五"期间全国污染防治的重点地区,即"三河"(淮河、辽河、海河)、"三湖"(太湖、滇池、巢湖)、"两控区"(二氧化硫控制区和酸雨控制区)、"一市"(北京市)、"一海"(渤海），集中力量重点解决影响群众生活、危害身体健康、制约经济社会发展的环境问题。

1998年11月，国务院印发《全国生态环境建设规划》，启动了一系列生态保护重大工程。1999年开展退耕还林、还草工程试点，优先在生态敏感、生态安全地位重要区域开展退耕还林。2000年国家投资千亿元的天然林保护工程全面启动，重点保护长江上游、黄河中上游和东北天然林资源。2000年12月，国务院办公厅印发《全国生态环境保护纲要》。2002年3月，国务院批复《全国生态环境保护"十五"计划》。2003年5月，国家环境保护总局发布《生态县、生态市、生态省建设指标（试行）》，进一步深化生态示范区建设。

21世纪初，我国部分流域水污染从局部河段向全流域蔓延，加强防范突发环境事件成为这一阶段环境保护的重要内容。[1] 2002年3月，国家环保总局开始组建环境应急与事故调查中心。面对日益增多的突发环境事件，国家制定和完善了一系列涉及重点流域敏感水域水环境、大气环境、危险化学品（废弃化学品）应急预案以及核与辐射应急方案等一系列相关环境应急预案。2005年，我国政府制定《国家突发环境事件应急预案》，对突发环境事件信息接收、报告、处理、统计分析，以及预警信息监控、信息发布等提出明确要求。与此同时，我国环境保护投入迅速增加，环境保护投资占GDP比例不断提高。"九五"期间，我国环保投资是"八五"期间的2.7倍，达到3516.4亿元。1999年，环保投入占GDP比例首次突破1.0%，而"十五"期间，环保投资占同期GDP比例达1.19%。随着各级政府对污染防治工作重视程度的提高和环保投入不断增加，污染防治工作开始由工业领域逐渐转向城市，城市环境综合整治工作取得积极进展。

第三阶段（2005—2012年）：全防全控、优化增长

2005年以来，我国开始进入环境污染事件高发期。2005年至2009年，先后发生吉林松花江重大水污染、广东北江镉污染、江苏无锡太湖蓝藻暴发、云南阳宗海砷污染等一系列重大污染事件，对区域经济社会

---

[1] 中华人民共和国中央人民政府："环境保护状况"，2012年4月10日，http://www.gov.cn/guoqing/2012-04/10/content_2584066.htm，登录日期：2020年5月31日。

发展和公众生活造成严重影响。2005年12月，国务院发布《关于落实科学发展观加强环境保护的决定》，确立了以人为本、环保为民的环保宗旨，成为指导我国经济社会与环境协调发展的纲领性文件。"十一五"规划纲要针对我国资源环境压力不断加大的形势，提出了建设资源节约型、环境友好型社会的战略任务和具体措施。2006年4月，国务院召开第六次全国环保大会，提出"从重经济增长轻环境保护转变为保护环境与经济增长并重，从环境保护滞后于经济发展转变为环境保护和经济发展同步推进，从主要用行政办法保护环境转变为综合运用法律、经济、技术和必要的行政办法解决环境问题"的"三个转变"战略思想。从此，我国环境保护进入了以保护环境优化经济发展的全新阶段。2007年10月，党的十七大首次把生态文明建设作为一项战略任务和全面建设小康社会新目标明确下来。2009年，中国环境宏观战略研究提出了积极探索中国环保新道路的重大理论和实践命题。2011年，国务院召开第七次全国环境保护大会，印发《关于加强环境保护重点工作的意见》和《国家环境保护"十二五"规划》，为推进环境保护事业科学发展奠定了坚实基础。

第四阶段（2013年至今）：体制改革、整体转型

2013年以来，中国公众的生态环境意识日益提升，生态环境的主观感知成为中国人民定义美好生活的重要影响因素。党的十八届三中全会通过的《关于全面深化改革若干重大问题的决定》，进一步将生态文明建设提高到制度层面，更加明确提出了用制度保护生态环境的任务。党的十八届四中全会通过了《中共中央关于全面推进依法治国若干重大问题的决定》，对于生态文明建设从法治上提出了更高要求，规定"用严格的法律制度保护生态环境"，促进生态文明建设。2015年4月，中共中央、国务院发布了《关于加快推进生态文明建设的意见》，全面、系统地提出了生态文明建设的指导思想、基本原则、主要目标、主要任务和关键举措。同年9月，中共中央、国务院印发了《生态文明体制改革总体方案》，提出生态文明体制改革工作以"1+6"方式推进。这些纲领性文件从理念和战略、目标和任务、制度和体制三个层面形成了深化生态文明体制改革的战略部署和"四梁八柱"的制度框架；"1+6"方案在不同层面填补了生态文明建设基础性制度空白，并随着内容涵盖改革试验、空间规划、产权界定、职责分配、环境监测、环境损害、生态补偿、考核评价、责任承担等重要领域和关键环节的改革指向明确、实施主体明确、改革措施明确的专项方案逐步推进,开始在实践层面发挥重要作用。总体方案确定的2015—2017年要完成的79项改革任务均已完成;①"环保督察"极大地震慑了环境污染行为主体;"河长制""湖长制"实现了从水源到水龙头的全过程监管;"生态保护红线"推动全国范围的生态红线划定;"国家公园制度"推动着自然保护格局的形成;"领导干部自然资源资产离任审计"产生了强烈的警示作用;"生态文明建设目标评价考核"体现出对地区发展评价的崭新视野等。从顶层设计和整体部署,到分项领域和职能架构,中国系统性生态环境治理的制度构架正逐渐形成。

党的十九届三中全会以后,生态文明体制机制改革持续深化。一是国家层面的生态环境监管体制机制改革有序推进。整合相关部门分散的生态环保职责组建生态环境部,负责制定和实施生态环境规划、政策和标准,监测生态环境、开展污染防治和环保执法;整合有关部门的自然资源保护职责组建自然资源部,聚焦于对自然资产的产权界定、确权、分配、流转、保值与增值。生态环保机构改革强化了生态环境制度制定、监测评估、监督执法和督察问责职能,省以下环保机构监测监察执法垂直管理改革有序推进;生态环境领域"放管服"改革持续深化,推动着经济高质量发展和生态环境高水平保护;费改税、税额幅度提升以及环保税归地方政府所有三大创举推动环保税收制度精准落地;第三方治理机制向市场化运行方向发展;党政同责、责权明确的责任制度链条督促政府、企业和社会共担绿色发展职责;激励和约束并举的目标评价考核起到有力的导向和约束作用;组建生态环境综合执法队伍,统一实行生态环保执法,实行生态环保督察,对破坏生态环境的不法行为形成有力震慑。二是地方层面的制度配套和实践探索双管齐下。如生态红线制度方面,一些省份按照重要程度以分级形式对红线区实行差别化管理,一些省份探索建立起生态红线惩罚问责机制。又如,先行先试方面,贵州、福建、江西等首批国家生态文明试验区就《方案》提出的47项重点任务中的38项展开试验,探索不同发展阶段的生态文明建设的制度模式,形

---

① 杨伟民:《38次中央深改组会议中20次讨论生态文明体制改革相关议题》,人民网,2017年10月23日,http://cpc.people.com.cn/19th/n1/2017/1023/c414536-29604149.html。

成了富有成效的改革经验和制度成果。① 随着我国对生态文明体制系统性、整体性、重构性的改革不断推进，中国特色的环境治理体系正逐步现代化，为实现《生态文明体制改革总体方案》提出的"形成人与自然和谐发展的现代化建设新格局"② 目标奠定了坚实基础。

三 中国生态文明的行动化建构

2018年，中国生态环境保护进入新时代，地方政府以前所未有的决心和力度加强生态保护。③ 随着生态环境治理力度不断加码，中国生态环境质量持续改善，主要污染物排放总量和单位国内生产总值二氧化碳排放量进一步下降，国际生态文明发展指数排名大幅提升。④ 近年，从中央到地方，从环境要素（大气、水、土壤等）到生态系统，中国通过不同层面和不同类型的生态环境治理行动落实并深化生态文明的理念，主要体现在如下方面：⑤

全面推进蓝天保卫战。2018年7月，国务院印发《打赢蓝天保卫战三年行动计划》，明确了大气污染防治工作的总体思路、基本目标、主要任务和保障措施，提出了打赢蓝天保卫战的时间表和路线图。全国人大常委会组织开展大气污染防治法执法检查，强化区域联防联控，成立京津冀及周边地区大气污染防治领导小组，建立汾渭平原大气污染防治协作机制，完善长三角区域大气污染防治协作机制；开展蓝天保卫战重点区域强化监督，向地方政府新交办大气污染相关环境问题2.3万个，2017年交办的3.89万个问题整改完毕；全国实现超低排放的煤电机组约8.1

---

① 陈映：《中国生态文明体制改革历程回顾与未来取向》，《经济体制改革》2019年第6期。
② 新华网：《中共中央 国务院印发〈生态文明体制改革总体方案〉》，2015年9月21日，http：//www.xinhuanet.com//politics/2015-09/21/c_1116632159.htm。
③ 李培林、陈光金、王春光主编：《2020年中国社会形势分析与预测》（社会蓝皮书），社会科学文献出版社2020年版，第312页。
④ 陈佳、吴明红、严耕：《中国生态文明建设发展评价研究》，《中国行政管理》2016年第11期。
⑤ 中华人民共和国生态环境部：《2018中国生态环境状况公报》，2019年5月29日，http：//www.mee.gov.cn/hjzl/zghjzkgb/lnzghjzkgb/。

亿千瓦，占全国煤电总装机容量的80%，非石化能源消费比重达14.3%，北方地区冬季清洁取暖试点城市由12个增加到35个，完成散煤治理480万户以上；发布《柴油货车污染治理攻坚战行动计划》，制定重型柴油车国六标准，全面供应国六车用汽柴油，实现车用柴油、普通柴油、部分船舶用油"三油并轨"；推进大气重污染成因与治理攻关项目，在"2＋26"城市、汾渭平原和雄安新区推广"一市一策"驻点跟踪研究工作模式等，这些具体行动旨在实现"到2020年，二氧化硫、氮氧化物排放总量分别比2015年下降15%以上；PM2.5未达标地级及以上城市浓度比2015年下降18%以上，地级及以上城市空气质量优良天数比率达到80%，重度及以上污染天数比率比2015年下降25%以上"①。

着力推进碧水保卫战。2015年4月，国务院印发《水污染防治行动计划》，成为中国水污染防治工作的行动指南。2018年，中国出台《中央财政促进长江经济带生态保护修复奖励政策实施方案》，完成长江干线1361座非法码头整治，组建长江生态环境保护修复联合研究中心；发布实施城市黑臭水体治理、农业农村污染治理、长江保护修复、渤海综合治理、水源地保护攻坚战行动计划或实施方案，36个重点城市1062个黑臭水体中，1009个消除或基本消除黑臭，消除比例达95%，完成2.5万个建制村环境综合整治；推进全国集中式饮用水水源地环境整治，1586个水源地6251个问题整改完成率达99.9%；全国97.8%的省级及以上工业集聚区建成污水集中处理设施并安装自动在线监控装置；浙江省"千村示范、万村整治"荣获2018年联合国地球卫士奖等，这些行动旨在实现"到2020年，全国水环境质量得到阶段性改善，污染严重水体较大幅度减少，饮用水安全保障水平持续提升，地下水超采得到严格控制，地下水污染加剧趋势得到初步遏制，近岸海域环境质量稳中趋好，京津冀、长三角、珠三角等区域水生态环境状况有所好转。到2030年，力争全国水环境质量总体改善，水生态系统功能初步恢复。到本世纪中叶，生态

---

① 中华人民共和国中央人民政府，国务院印发《打赢蓝天保卫战三年行动计划》，2018年7月3日，http://www.gov.cn/xinwen/2018-07/03/content_5303212.htm，登录日期：2020年6月1日。

环境质量全面改善，生态系统实现良性循环。"①

稳步推进净土保卫战。2018年8月，全国人大常委会通过《中华人民共和国土壤污染防治法》，以专门法的形式为各种"因人为因素导致某种物质进入陆地表层土壤，引起土壤化学、物理、生物等方面特性的改变，影响土壤功能和有效利用，危害公众健康或者破坏生态环境的现象（土壤污染）"② 治理提供了法律支撑。2018年，中国31个省份和新疆生产建设兵团完成农用地土壤污染状况详查，26个省份建立污染地块联动监管机制；开展涉镉等重金属行业污染耕地风险排查整治，一些地区耕地土壤污染加重趋势得到初步遏制；开展耕地土壤环境质量类别划分试点和全国污染地块土壤环境管理信息系统应用，建成全国土壤环境信息管理平台，持续推进6大土壤污染防治综合先行区建设和200多个土壤污染治理与修复技术应用试点项目；推进生活垃圾分类处置和非正规垃圾堆放点整治，推进禁止洋垃圾进口工作，全国固体废物进口总量比2017年下降46.5%；严厉打击固体废物及危险废物非法转移和倾倒行为，"清废行动2018"挂牌督办的1308个突出问题中1304个完成整改，比例达99.7%等，这些行动成为《中华人民共和国土壤污染防治法》效力的实践例证。

开展生态保护和修复。中国于2012年1月启动"全国生态状况变化调查评估"，2016年发布《全国生态环境十年变化（2000—2010年）调查评估报告》后，于2017年2月又启动了全国生态状况变化（2010—2015年）调查评估，这项重大生态国情调查评估，范围包括全国31个省、自治区、直辖市和新疆生产建设兵团，旨在"摸清家底，发现问题，找出原因，提出对策"。2016年8月，中办、国办印发了《关于设立统一规范的国家生态文明试验区的意见》，选择生态基础较好、资源环境承载能力较强的福建省、江西省和贵州省作为首批试验区，开展生态文明体制改革综合试验，规范各类试点示范，为完善生态文明制度体

---

① 中华人民共和国中央人民政府：《国务院印发〈水污染防治行动计划〉》，2015年4月16日，http://www.gov.cn/xinwen/2015-04/16/content_2847709.htm，登录日期：2020年6月1日。

② 中国人大网：《中华人民共和国土壤污染防治法》，2018年8月31日，http://www.npc.gov.cn/npc/c30834/201808/13d193fc25734dee91da8d703e057edc.shtml，登录日期：2020年6月1日。

系探索路径、积累经验；① 2018年，全国范围内，国家级自然保护区增至474处，初步划定京津冀、长江经济带和宁夏等15个省份生态保护红线，山西等16个省份基本形成划定方案，启动生态保护红线勘界定标试点，推动国家生态保护红线监管平台建设；继续实施退耕还林还草、退牧还草工程，整体推进大规模国土绿化行动，完成造林绿化1.06亿亩；推进第三批山水林田湖草生态保护修复工程试点工作，恢复退化湿地107万亩，56处国际重要湿地生态状况总体良好；命名表彰第二批"绿水青山就是金山银山"实践创新基地和第二批国家生态文明建设示范市县等，这些行动，从实践层面回应了"全国生态状况变化调查评估"发现的问题。

强化生态环境保护督察执法。2018年，中国完成生态环境部组建工作，整合原部门相关职责，贯通污染防治和生态保护；印发《关于深化生态环境保护综合行政执法改革的指导意见》，整合生态环境保护领域执法职责和队伍，全面推行省以下生态环境机构监测监察执法垂直管理制度改革；出台《排污许可管理办法（试行）》，累计完成24个行业3.9万多家企业排污许可证核发，提前完成36个重点城市建成区污水处理厂排污许可证核发；全面落实《生态环境损害赔偿制度改革方案》，全面推行领导干部自然资源资产离任审计工作，开展自然资源资产负债表编制试点；空气质量排名范围扩至169个城市，定期发布空气质量及改善幅度相对较好和较差城市名单；2015—2018年，由环保部牵头成立，中纪委、中组部的相关领导参加的中央环保督察组掀起了多轮"督察风暴"，第一轮督察解决了共约15万个老百姓身边的问题，推动各地解决了2100多个比较大的生态环境问题；② 2019年6月，中共中央办公厅、国务院办公厅印发《中央生态环境保护督察工作规定》，并于同年7月正式启动第二轮"中央生态环境保护督察"，截至2020年1月5日，督察项目组已办结13319件，阶段办结2748件，责令整改企业8776家，立案查处3288家，

---

① 顾阳、熊丽：《我国首批3个生态文明试验区用来做什么?》,《经济日报》2017年10月3日，https://baijiahao.baidu.com/s?id=1580232816825073136&wfr=spider&for=pc。

② 中国新闻网：《生态环境部：第一轮环保督察共解决约15万个问题》，2019年9月29日，https://m.chinanews.com/wap/detail/sp/sp/shipin/cns-d/2019/09-29/news8968837.shtml。

处罚金额约25400.06万元，立案侦查169件，行政拘留38人，刑事拘留70人，约谈1935人，问责359人；其中，解决垃圾、扬尘、异味、噪声等城市公共环境管理问题8707件，解决污水直排及水体黑臭问题1559件，整改毁林毁草、围湖占湖、矿山开发等生态破坏问题1050件。①

推动社会力量参与生态文明建设。2018年，全国性"12369"环保举报平台共受理并按期办结公众举报71万余件；生态环境部牵头多部门联合发布《公民生态环境行为规范（试行）》，旨在"引领公民践行生态环境责任"，并启动"美丽中国，我是行动者"主题实践活动；制定《环境影响评价公众参与办法》，鼓励和规范公众参与环境影响评价；全国首批124家环保设施和城市污水垃圾处理设施向公众开放5218次。此外，社会组织也通过各自的优势路径参与生态文明建设，例如：WWF于2019年在全球发起的"净塑城市"倡议于2020年正式落地中国，三亚、扬州成为首批加入城市；② 2020年4月22日地球日，环保组织自然之友及其合作伙伴共同发起倡议，以"绿色办公"的方式，鼓励公众、企业在办公场景作出更环境友好的行为选择。

推动区域生态文明共建。"一带一路"建设正在为沿线国家和地区的可持续发展提供源源不断的动力，成为区域共建共治共享绿色可持续未来的优秀案例。③ 2015年，中国发布《推动共建丝绸之路经济带和21世纪海上丝绸之路的愿景与行动》，明确提出要突出生态文明理念，加强生态环境、生物多样性和应对气候变化合作，共建绿色丝绸之路。随后，中国又陆续发布《"十三五"生态环境保护规划》（2016年）、《关于推进绿色"一带一路"建设的指导意见》（2017年）、《"一带一路"生态环境保护合作规划》（2017年）④ 等政策性文本，为建设绿色"一带一路"

---

① 中华人民共和国生态环境部：《第二轮第一批中央生态环境保护督察群众举报问题办理进展》（截至2020年1月5日），2020年1月10日，http：//www.mee.gov.cn/home/ztbd/rdzl/msqhqzlywtzxzz/gzdt/202001/t20200110_758567.shtml。
② 中共江苏省委新闻网：《扬州成为中国首批"净塑城市"》，2020年4月22日，http：//zgjssw.jschina.com.cn/shixianchuanzhen/yangzhou/202004/t20200422_6612955.shtml。
③ 李培林、陈光金、王春光主编：《2020年中国社会形势分析与预测》（社会蓝皮书），社会科学文献出版社2020年版，第296—310页。
④ 中华人民共和国环境保护部：《关于印发〈一带一路生态环境保护合作规划〉的通知》，2017年5月12日，http：//www.mee.gov.cn/gkml/hbb/bwj/201705/t20170516_414102.htm。

奠定了坚实的政治和制度基础,从顶层角度明确了总体思路、目标和任务,并提出用3—5年时间,建成务实高效的生态环保合作交流体系、支撑与服务平台和产业技术合作基地,制定落实一系列生态环境风险防范政策和措施;用5—10年时间,建成较为完善的生态环保服务、支撑、保障体系,实施一批重要生态环保项目,并取得良好效果;[1]与沿线国家的生态环境保护部门以及有关国际组织共签订50多份合作文件,正式成立"一带一路"绿色发展国际联盟,合作机制不断健全完善;启动"一带一路"绿色供应链平台,成立了澜沧江—湄公河环境合作中心、中柬环境合作中心,积极筹建中非环境合作中心,不断搭建扩展合作平台,推动区域生态文明共建。

四 结语

中国正面临一种"压缩的现代化",这种"压缩性"特征既加强了风险的生产,又没有给风险的制度化预期和管理留下充裕的时间,[2]为应对这种从生态环境风险衍生而来的风险社会图景,中国通过制度和行动层面的努力,尝试通过生态文明建设"形成人与自然和谐发展的现代化建设新格局"[3]。"社会主义生态文明观"作为中国生态文明及其理论建设或话语体系的一个核心性概念或范畴,可以概括为如下四个内在关联的要素或环节:基于生态学思维的严格自然价值理念或人与自然关系观念;整体统筹与法治生态系统及其要素治理体系和生态环境保护制度体系;综合考量生产、生活与生态理性要求或目标的绿色生产生活方式和文明发展道路;主动兼顾美丽中国建设与全球生态安全的天下情怀。[4]从顶层

---

[1] 中华人民共和国中央人民政府:《四部门联合发布〈关于推进绿色"一带一路"建设的指导意见〉》,2017年5月27日,http://www.gov.cn/xinwen/2017-05/27/content_5197523.htm。

[2] 贝克、邓正来、沈国麟:《风险社会与中国——与德国社会学家乌尔里希·贝克的对话》,《社会学研究》2010年第5期。

[3] 新华网,《中共中央国务院印发〈生态文明体制改革总体方案〉》,2015年9月21日,http://www.xinhuanet.com//politics/2015-09/21/c_1116632159.htm。

[4] 郇庆治:《社会主义生态文明观阐发的三重视野》,《北京行政学院学报》2018年第4期。

设计到地方实践,从政策文本到个体行动,中国积极"迎接为加速向更公平、环境更可持续的经济和更健康的社会转型所必需的各种紧急性变革,通过自上而下的政策指导和自下而上的倡议巩固各国及其人民现在和将来的福祉和繁荣"①。《中共中央关于坚持和完善中国特色社会主义制度、推进国家治理体系和治理能力现代化若干重大问题的决定》明确提出要建设人人有责、人人尽责、人人享有的社会治理共同体;中共中央办公厅、国务院办公厅于 2020 年 3 月印发《关于构建现代环境治理体系的指导意见》提出"健全环境治理全民行动体系"②,进一步明确了公众(每一个人)对环境治理的行动责任。中国在"社会主义生态文明观"的指引下,正在"推动形成绿色发展方式和生活方式,是发展观的一场深刻革命"③。

---

① UN Environment (2019). Global Environment Outlook-GEO – 6: Healthy Planet, Healthy People. Nairobi. DOI 10. 1017/9781108627146. p. XXX.
② 中国政府网:《中共中央办公厅 国务院办公厅印发〈关于构建现代环境治理体系的指导意见〉》,2020 年 3 月 3 日,http://www.gov.cn/zhengce/2020 – 03/03/content_5486380.htm?trs =1。
③ 《习近平在主持中共十八届中央政治局第四十一次集体学习时讲话》,人民网,http://theory.people.com.cn/n1/2018/0103/c416126 – 29743660.html。

白俄罗斯治理现代化进程中的人格认同

E. V. Kuznetsova

白俄罗斯国家科学院哲学研究所

全球化、一体化与社会文化合作研究中心高级研究员

  哲学、社会学、心理学、人类学、人种学、文化研究等许多学科对认同过程进行了研究。这些学科各有自己的方法论原理，并从不同角度探索认同过程中的各种成分。研究人员彼此互动得越多，我们对这个问题的认识就越完整，因为认同感也是文化、民族、语言和其他层面不同互动的结果。本文将尽最大努力，研究人的自我认同问题。

  为了对受试者认同感问题得出结论，我们在调查中运用了比较类型学方法，对比了不同文明阶段不同类型的认同感。我们还使用了系统方法，因为这种方法有助于从不同角度对问题进行分析。

  首先我们来确定"认同感"和"认同"的概念。假设这两个概念之间的区别不重要，但语义上的区别很实用，因为它们的意思都是相同的现象学现实。通常，第一个概念表示结果，第二个概念表示过程。根据人类存在不同历史阶段的社会和文化条件，我们区分了以下在某一历史阶段形成的占支配地位的认同感类型，包括族群认同感、语言认同感、宗教认同感、民族认同感、文化认同感、先验认同感。

  族群认同感是基本的受试者认同感类型之一。因此，族群认同感是指受试者与其血缘关系、"根"的关系，当然也就是每个人的自决过程。

族群认同感概念的主要理论分析方法主要是通过心理学和社会哲学研究来实施的。从历史上来看，认同问题的主要方法之一以精神分析学创始人弗洛伊德的理论为基础。沙利文（人际精神分析学）、弗洛姆（人本主义精神分析学）、埃里克森（表观遗传分析学）也在精神分析学中研究了认同问题。

心理学中解释族群认同感的最新方法之一是由行为主义创立的。行为学家认为，认同过程是群体间冲突的结果。他们的研究证实，在某些情况下，一个人由于其外在相似性可以同时认同两个族群。但是，这些族群在外表上必须彼此相似，例如白俄罗斯人和俄罗斯人。如果族群彼此不相似，特别是如果它们属于不同的种族，那么混血家庭的孩子对于两个种族来说都是陌生人。

行为方法的代表认为，认同过程是由不同群体之间的行为决定的。族群认同感的形成是一个动态的过程，不同的因素可能会影响民族认同感的形成。任何变化都会导致认同感的转变，尤其是在住宅或环境发生变化的情况下。最近几十年，族群认同感已成为重点研究的对象。20世纪90年代的政治事件大大加快了俄罗斯及全世界基于人与人之间关系的进程。由于若干因素（全球化、融合、消除不同界限等）的影响，当代社会在个人层面和群体层面的民族状况需要对许多概念和类别进行负责任的深入分析。如果族群认同感是被其他种类的社会认同感（如公民认同感）逼出来的，那么这对于人的总体认同感可能非常危险，有可能破坏"自我"形象，使受试者失去与其在世界上的本土文化的联系。一个人可能失去在这个世界上的自己。这种认同感是人格形成以及人与人之间互相交流的关键。

在讨论受试者的认同感时，对于我们来说更重要的一个因素是语言。语言和人是彼此紧密相连的。洪保德（V. Humboldt）认为，沉思和民族心态在某种程度上形成了语言的结构。特别值得一提的是，他认为，对于走上"全神贯注沉思之路"的人来说，屈折变化的语言很典型。[1] 在"语言是人民的精神"的准则下，洪保德明白"精神和心理活动是一种特

---

[1] Humboldt, V. *Language and Philosophy of Culture*, V. Humboldt. – Moscow：Progress，2007，p. 78.

殊形式的合理物化，对于所有讲国家语言者来说都是特殊的"①。无论如何，个人对语言的解释总是由相关国家普遍存在的语言模式来界定。

在每一种语言里，我们都要谈到所谓的"自由"单位。因此，每个人的言语均包括"句式"和"自由"单位。但是，借助"句式"，可以清楚地了解相关国家的所有精神特性，"句式"不仅包括固定词组，而且包括各种短语单位。不了解人民的文化，就不可能理解短语单位。其实，所有语言单位都有不同程度的文化丰富度。洛谢夫（A. F Losev）恰当地指出："单词、特别是名字包括几个世纪以来积累的全部文化财富"。

受试者的认同感也是通过非语言工具形成的，它是一种副语言。副语言的形成是由和语言本身相同的因素所决定的，有国家文化和心态。所以副语言包括以下媒介：面部表情、手势、交流者之间的距离、各种特性的举止神态。所有这些媒介在不同国家都大不相同，表现也不同。我们举一个最有名的例子。在白俄罗斯，当我们点头时，意思是"是"，而在保加利亚意思却是"不"。因此，语言认同是一个与族群或民族认同一样复杂的过程。如果我们在沟通中谈到受试者说话的口头和非口头语言特征，必须考虑到所有的变化，识别某个受试者。语言认同与民族认同有关联，因为语言是决定受试者属于特定民族群体的最重要因素之一。

根据马克思主义理论，封建主义转变到资本主义导致形成了作为国家的人民共同体民族社会形式。许多研究强调国家是一种现代现象。在国外研究中，"国家"一词具有政治含义。科学家将属于一个（民族）国家的人定义为一个国家。在国内文献中，我们发现了对国家的另一种定义。白俄罗斯科学家认为经济因素在形成这种社会共同体方面是最重要的。但是，我们选择那些倾向于所谓的后现代概念、赋予"国家"概念政治内容的科学家的立场。白俄罗斯有许多不同的民族，本土文化是不同民族元素的复杂融合体。从这个角度来看，我们将在本作品中研究国家认同感问题。所以根据我们的理解，国家认同感等同于公民认同感。

许多研究人员（M. Semluk、S. Walker）恰当地指出，冷战的结束和最近几十年世界政治地图的变化导致许多国家出现了认同危机，因为所

---

① Kiselev, I. *Evolution of the Image of the State in International Relations*, I. Kiselev, L. Smirnova. – St. Petersburg: Publishing House of St. Petersburg University, 2006, p. 180.

有国家都被迫重新审视自己在国际舞台上的角色和地位。[①] 布鲁姆（W. Bloom）强调国家认同感与政治行为的影响有联系，并确定这些现象之间有三种关系。[②]

第一种：民族认同感是外交政策的一种资源。弥赛亚民族主义就是这种认同感的一个例子。弥赛亚世界观往往导致国家对其他国家采取侵略行动，"弥赛亚主义"宣传通常是帝国主义的核心所在。

第二种：外交政策是一个国家的建设工具。外交政策在确定国家的身份方面发挥着特殊作用。

第三种：通过非国家行为体形成的国家认同感决定着外交政策。当一些公共思想获得国家地位并影响国家的外交政策时，就会发生这种情况。

今天已经很明显的事实是，国家之间的经济边界遭到破坏，政治和文化争议得以消除。国家形象变了，国家公民的国家认同感也变了。

现在是一个持续不断变化、灾难、动乱和混乱的时代。许多观点不能描述这个时代了，包括那些传统认同感所基于的观点。今天的人类认同相当复杂，而且其发生主要是因为社会上的人际关系很复杂。职业活动、社会流动、社会隶属关系等因素开始影响认同过程。文化和社会的发展导致认同范围扩大，即在这一领域出现了新的认同种类和新的研究方式。

研究认同感问题的最著名的社会学人物之一是涂尔干（E. Durkheim）。根据大型人群的集体观点，他认为社会因素在受试者的认同过程中最重要。涂尔干将这种观点与观念、习俗、宗教信仰、道德态度、公共制度等整体体系联系起来。[③] 这些是在受试者的生命过程中用于认同的模型和要素。涂尔干认为我们每一个人身上都有两个生物，其中一个由心理定式组成。心理定式是指受试者（个体的"我"）的私人生活。社会的"我"是一个人身上的第二个生物，它是一系列的态度、情感和习

[①] Kiselev, I. *Evolution of the Image of the State in International Relations*, I. Kiselev, L. Smirnova. – St. Petersburg: Publishing House of St. Petersburg University, 2006, p. 42.

[②] Bloom, W. *Personal Identity, National Identity and International Relations*, W. Bloom. – Cambridge: Cambridge University Press, 1996, p. 89.

[③] Durkheim, E. *Sociology of Education*, E. Durkheim. – Moscow: Science, 1996, p. 57.

惯。涂尔干指出，必须为新生的自私、不合群的生物添加一个社会生物。"给个人优点添加这种内容、将个人优点连接到一个连贯单位内的过程就是个人认同过程"。

霍尼（K. Horney）在她的研究中分析了社会文化主宰者的作用，她认为文化条件对个人的发展和机能有深远影响。① 从她的视角来看，社会文化因素可以解释人与人之间的关系。美国科学家博厄斯（F. Boas）对生活在不同文化环境下的不同民族的成熟过程进行了比较研究，他确信年轻人的行为是由生物因素和特定文化的属性决定的。②

在著名哲学家、心理学家和方法论家舒德洛维茨基（G. Schedrovitsky）看来，自决对于任何人来说都是其一生中最重要的行为。他写道："情况是这样的：如果没有自决，那么人就永远不会成为一个有人格的人。"③ 他认为，对于一个人来说，在自决过程中最重要的事情是反思。舒德洛维茨基认为，一个人认为其原来的生活框架是其行为的主题，这是第一层次的反思。第二层次的反思是反思者对自己的定位。反思方式是一种智力方式，也就是语言表达。所以根据舒德洛维茨基的概念，沟通是反思和自决的基本条件。

其他一些学者也认为反思是文化认同的一种内部机制。斯洛博契科夫（V. Slobodchikov）和伊萨耶夫（E. Isaev）指出，反思是针对自决而言的，是由社会存在的多种现实和实际情况造成的，要求一个人有能力与他人沟通。④ 只有成为宇宙或世界文化的一部分，人们才能成为有人格的人。所以沉思或先验自我认同是终极个人自我认同方式。

舒德洛维茨基写道，沟通是实现个人自我认同的条件。现代人无法离开沟通，他们必须互相理解，渴望把新的东西传给别人。在巴赫金（Bakhtin）那里，活着就是要进行对话、提出问题并回答问题。现代世界

---

① Horney, K. *Our Internal Conflicts. Moscow*, K. Horney. – M.：. April – Press；Exmo – press, 2000. – 340c.

② Boas, F. *Some Problems of Methodology in the Social Sciences*, F. Boas. – Chicago：University of Chicago Press, 2002. – 238c.

③ Schedrovitsky, G. P. *On the Boards. Public lectures on Philosophy*, G. P. Schedrovitsky. – M.：School of Political Culture, 2004, p. 58.

④ Slobodchikov, V. I. *Foundations of Psychological Anthropology*, V. I. Slobodchikov, E. I. Isaev. – Moscow：School – Press, 2005, p. 94.

所有进程的主要目的都可以表述为在共同的文化和交流空间的建设性对话。瓦西连科（A. Vasilenko）将这种空间描述为"思想的共同空间"。它是在讨论过程中形成的一系列共同观念和概念，这些观念和概念不属于任何一方，超出了谈话者的主观意见，成为共同伙伴的身份。[1] 这种对话是形成新的政治和社会文化概念的艺术，可以解释一个共同的政治互动领域。

但是，这种对话的主要目标是伙伴的自我实现。在实际文化对话的背景下，这个问题成为现代世界交际领域每种文化的自我实现问题。各种沟通研究院帮助分析这种对话，确定互动的方式和手段。

沟通是个人在社会上存在的必要条件，因为正如亚里士多德所说，人是天生的政治动物。几个世纪以来，许多科学交叉点（比如：哲学、社会学、心理学、语言学）的科学家对沟通现象进行了研究。"互动"一词往往被许多学者替换为"沟通"一词。根据我们的观点，"沟通"一词比"互动"一词更广泛。我们来尝试区分这两个概念。

"沟通"一词来自拉丁语。沟通的意思就是分享、谈论、讨论。《现代西方社会学词典》（1990年）提供了沟通的以下定义：①物质和精神宁静的客体的沟通手段；②一个人向另一个人传递信息；③社会中的信息沟通和分享（社会沟通）。因而，"互动"一词包含在"沟通"一词之中。《韦氏新词词典》（1989年）给出了以下解释：①传递行为；②对话中的信息、信号和消息交换；③信息或消息；④以同情心为基础的亲密关系；⑤沟通手段。

柯尼茨卡雅（V. P. Konetskaya）强调了现代人对"沟通"一词的不同理解——认为它是一种沟通手段、互动概念的同义词，"社会上为了产生影响而进行的信息交换"[2]。这里我们必须输入一个词，比如社会沟通，也就是雅斯贝尔斯（K. Jaspers）、托夫勒（A. Toffler）、哈贝马斯（J. Habermas）、布伯（M. Buber）、米德（J. G. Mead）、贝尔（D. Bell）、

---

[1] I. Vasilenko, "I. About the Possibilities of Political Hermeneutics", *The Questions of Philosophy*, 1999, No. 6, p. 5.

[2] Konetskaya, *V. P. Sociology of Communication*, V. P. Konetskaya, Moscow: Science, 2007, p. 121.

希部塔尼（T. Shibutani）、沃森（D. Watson）的著作中所描述的理论方面。如果我们总结研究资料，就可以得出结论：社会沟通是一种常见的人类活动，是由具体情况、法规、沟通规则决定的，是社会上行为人之间的精神和信息交流。

今天，世界变成了一个交往空间，破坏了前人赖以生存的许多道德规范、价值观和道德指南。由于科技的发展以及新的沟通方式的出现，一个人得到了全新的机会，但同时他发现自己独自面对周围世界。重大变革涉及社会的所有领域。重建传统价值观、大规模沉思、管理中的新原则意味着一个社会的彻底变革。上述趋势是在沟通话语交流强化的背景下展开的。个人和民族之间的互动决定了当代文化世界的观点、其存在和发展状况。显然，我们不能把转型社会文化发展阶段受试者的认同感说成是永久不变的。一个现代人可以有几种相互竞争或相辅相成的认同感，但他的认同感现在处于危机之中，正在改变。对一些人来说，有丧失个人或群体层面（全部或部分）认同感的风险，认同感可能是虚假的，有可能破坏"我"的形象、失去人际关系、失去文化本身。一个受试者的真实认同感只能通过他参与文化和交流的过程而确定。沟通使我们能够确定人的真实认同感。行为人自身之间的互动越有意义、越丰富，对其进行认同的过程就越正确，但同时也就越复杂。

在所有类型的认同感（族群认同感、宗教认同感、语言认同感、国家认同感、先验认同感）中，先验认同感是终极的认同感形式，是当代社会文明阶段最重要的认同感。一方面，国际社会现在所处的转型时代开始需要基于理性化（科学）的知识。另一方面，如果一个人获得了巨大的人身自由，他就需要一种内心的自我道德调节机制，使这个人做出对社会负责任的道德行为（反思）。沟通可以成为这种机制，它可以提供国家与社会的联系，社会、国家与个人的联系。沟通形成了现代国际社会一种新的思想观念。反思沟通的现状，认可其新的结构是文化多元化发展的条件。

中国企业民主管理制度发展历程与新方位

孙兆阳

中国社会科学院社会发展战略研究院副研究员

一 起步的八十年代

改革开放放松了对企业的约束,通过建立市场机制、矫正要素价格扭曲、恢复个人劳动报酬等制度性改革,企业的活力得到释放,生产的效率和积极性得到提升,同时企业家、管理者对企业支配和控制的权力也得到极大的增强。1981年7月,中共中央、国务院转发了《国营企业职工代表大会暂行条例》,推广职工代表大会制度;1986年9月颁布了《全民所有制工业企业职工代表大会条例》(以下简称《职代会条例》),确立了职工代表大会的性质、职权、内容等;并在1988年4月通过了《中华人民共和国全民所有制工业企业法》(以下简称《企业法》),正式确定了职代会制度的法律地位。

基层民主制度是作为体现社会主义制度的优越性而提出来的,这一阶段的文章也主要是从企业的社会主义性质出发,强调企业民主制度,特别是职代会的必要性和必然性,比如,陈文渊,[1] 漆记成,[2] 田

---

[1] 陈文渊:《实现企业民主管理的基本形式——试谈职工代表大会制度》,《北京政法学院学报》1981年第3期,第63—69页。

[2] 漆记成:《企业民主管理浅见》,《江西财经学院学报》1981年第1期,第77—80页。

梅、周贵①等。但是，改革的首要目标是要建立和开放市场，发挥市场配置资源的主体作用，激发市场主体活力，提高生产效率和经济效益。为了激励企业的市场活力，政府逐渐撤出对企业经营活动的直接管理，实行厂长/经理负责制，企业的管理者被赋予了更大的权力。1984年，党的十二届三中全会制定《关于经济体制改革的决定》，指出："现代企业分工细密，生产具有高度的连续性，技术要求严格，协作关系复杂，必须建立统一的、强有力的、高效率的生产指挥和经营管理系统。只有实行厂长（经理）负责制，才能适应这种要求。"于是，更多的学者转向讨论厂长/经理负责制与企业民主管理制度的职权分布与权责关系，比如，刘忠耀，② 史探径，③ 桑维军、郭宏军，④ 张琨，⑤ 桉苗、崔义⑥等。在改革大潮的推动下，企业民主管理因对管理权力的监督和约束而被认为是影响效率的做法。

二　九十年代的发展

进入20世纪90年代后，随着国企改革速度的加快，除了在原国有企业和国有控股企业中还存在着职代会，很多新出现的外企、民营企业都拒绝了在组织内成立职工代表大会。特别是1998年以来对国有企业的"抓大放小"，在一些大型国有企业改组为股份制的同时，一大批中小型国有企业通过改组、承包、联合、兼并、租赁、拍卖等形式成为非公有制企业。在市场机制的推动下，盈利成为改制后企业和民营企业的主要生产目标，为了改变改革前国企人浮于事的状况，并提高生产效率，企业经营者和民企所有者大多建立了集中式的管理体制。

一些学者认为，企业民主管理制度具有监督管理者的职能，职工代

---

① 田梅、周贵：《浅谈企业民主管理问题》，《经济问题》1983年第4期，第40—41页。
② 刘忠耀：《关于实行厂长负责制的几个理论问题》，《财经问题研究》1984年第6期，第24—32页。
③ 史探径：《论劳动合同和劳动合同制》，《法学研究》1987年第4期，第71—78页。
④ 桑维军、郭宏军：《试论工会在促进企业民主管理中的作用》，《社科纵横》1989年第3期，第54—57页。
⑤ 张琨：《试论现阶段企业民主管理》，《兰州学刊》1989年第2期，第103—106页。
⑥ 桉苗、崔义：《工人阶级现状与职工代表大会制度研究》，辽宁人民出版社1990年版。

表大会等制度对提高企业绩效和改善收入分配应该能够发挥更大的作用。这一阶段，国外理论大量进入中国，在企业民主制度研究方面主要有三个来源：

一是经济民主或工业民主理论。这些理论强调在建立现代企业制度时体现职工的主体地位，强调"主人翁"精神，从而突出民主管理、民主参与的应然性。因为这时吸纳城镇就业的主力仍然是国有企业和集体企业，民营、外资等非公有制企业和个体经营刚刚兴起，还没有成为市场的主要力量，所以研究的重点还是国有企业管理中体现公有制前提下的职工地位。比如，职工作为企业的主体是区别社会主义企业与资本主义企业的关键，要体现职工的主体地位，就要实现劳动制度、产权制度、经营制度、分配制度、领导制度等方面的民主化，职工拥有发言权、参与管理、参与利润分配和其他民主权利。[1] 这种民主权利正如国际劳工组织（ILO）界定的工业民主那样，是一种能够促进劳动者参与企业管理决策的各项政策或措施，从而使劳动者的权益获得雇主或管理人员的尊重，破除雇主或管理人员垄断管理权。[2] 总的来看，企业内经济民主意味着员工要分享管理的权利，同时对经济利益也要有同样的支配权。

但是，工业民主的"主人论"受到了市场竞争的冲击，企业民主被认为不利于企业生产效率的提升和在激励竞争中快速找到并利用机会。所以，随着国有企业改制逐渐深入，"股东至上"的逻辑取代"主人论"而占据主导地位，即将所有者或股东利益最大化是衡量企业制度效率的标准。有的学者认为，这种"主人论"主要是单纯从政治角度提炼出的，已经脱离了改革开放后形成的市场经济实践，企业民主管理必须更加尊重这一经济规律和社会发展规律。[3] 然而，"股东至上"的逻辑在理论上和实践中都是站不住脚的，因为企业制度本质上是由资本

---

[1] 蒋一苇：《职工主体论》，《中国劳动科学》1991年第9期，第3—8页。杜漪、张彦纯：《西方国家企业的"经济参与"制度》，《外国经济与管理》1994年第10期，第20—24页。吴光炳：《论劳动者参与国有企业剩余价值分配》，《中国劳动科学》1995年第8期，第8—10页。冯同庆：《企业经济民主——顺应自然的选择》，《工会理论与实践》2001年第8期，第4—8页。

[2] 祁华清：《国外工业民主模式与我国职工参与制度选择》，《中州学刊》2002年第3期，第18—21页。

[3] 秦中忠、赵雪飞：《对企业民主管理理论的再认识》，《中国劳动关系学院学报》2005年第1期，第34—36页。

和劳动共同组成的,是为利益相关者服务,每个利益相关者应具有平等的机会参与分配企业所有权。学者从另外两个方面批判了这种"股东至上"的观点。

二是劳动力产权或人力资本产权理论。根据马克思主义剩余价值理论,劳动者的劳动创造价值,也是剩余价值的唯一源泉,剩余价值被资本家剥夺后成为其利润,所以作为劳动力产权的所有者,劳动者应该同资本一样分享利润,这就是企业民主的根源。20世纪50年代,舒尔茨、贝克尔提出了"人力资本"理论,即除了传统的土地、资本、资源等要素,人的因素对经济发展至关重要。在企业运营过程中,劳、资双方都对企业投入了专用性资产,企业投入的是土地、厂房、设备等物质资本,劳动者是投入生产的劳动力的所有者,双方都在承担企业的经营风险,他们的利益都受企业经营结果的影响,所以企业的所有权和收入分配权应该由双方共享,双方应该有相同的权利和地位。[1] 在国有企业中,资产归全民所有,政府受委托代为持有,管理者投入劳动进行经营,工人也投入劳动开展生产,双方同样投入劳动到企业的生产经营中,那么他们的人力资本与物质和金融资本一样享有平等的受益分配。同时,民营企业、外资企业的出现为企业民主提出了新的挑战,即企业资产不来自国家或政府,劳动者是否还能要求同样的民主权利。利益相关者理论为此提出了一些新的见解。

三是利益相关者理论。这一理论的基础是西方20世纪80年代兴起的利益相关者和共同治理理论,从人权的角度论述工业民主与员工参与。在许多现代企业中,股东和管理者只承担了有限责任,他们的风险一部分通过投资多元化进行转化,另一部分转移给企业债权人、员工、政府、供应商等利益相关者,所以不能独占利润剩余。[2] 而且,这些团体的利益都与公司的生存直接相关,如果没有他们的支持,公司的运营效率也将大大降低,这就决定了各类团体都要积极参与公司的业务决定。[3] 这就要

---

[1] 周其仁:《市场里的企业:一个人力资本与非人力资本的特别合约》,《经济研究》1996年第6期,第71—80页。

[2] [美]玛格丽特·布莱尔:《所有权与控制——面向21世纪的公司治理探索》,张荣刚译,中国社会科学出版社1999年版。

[3] 刘连煜:《公司治理与公司社会责任》,中国政法大学出版社2001年版。

求不仅要重视股东利益，还要关注员工、供应商、债权人等对企业管理与决策的参与，通过广大员工的忠诚支持、协力合作，企业才能取得成功。[①] 他们认为，这对国有企业同样奏效，因为企业的效率首先建立在利益相关者平等的基础上，所以要通过每个产权平等的参与企业决策，使国有企业原有的"单边治理"过渡到"共同治理"，并平等地相互监督，才能提高国有企业治理结构的效率。

虽然从理论上看，民主管理是现代企业制度的重要内容，是社会化大生产的需要，[②] 能在处理好产权问题的同时，调动员工积极性，提高经营效率，[③] 但是职代会作用弱化，职工与企业管理者冲突加剧的问题在改革中还是不可避免地发生了。为此，政府试图强化职代会适用范围，扩大企业民主的形式。比如，1991年9月，颁布《中华人民共和国城镇集体所有制企业条例》，对城镇集体所有制企业的职代会性质、职权、组织制度和工作制度作了具体规定。1993年12月，八届人大常委会第五次会议通过了《中华人民共和国公司法》（以下简称《公司法》），规定了公司制企业要坚持民主管理制度，提出实行董事会和监事会中的职工代表制，增添了以监督权为主要目标的厂务公开和职工董事、监事等企业民主管理新内容。1994年出台的《劳动法》对不同所有制企业的民主管理的形式和内容作出规定。《公司法》和《劳动法》的出台极大地刺激了学者对企业民主制度的关注，所以1994年期刊文章数达到76篇，为整个90年代最高。

自改革开放以来，虽然国有企业和集体企业占城镇就业比例不断下降，从1978年的99.8%下降到1996年的71.6%，但到改制前仍是容纳非农就业的主体力量。所以在这一阶段，学者最为关注的问题仍主要与国有企业问题相关：

一是国有企业委托代理问题。国有企业改革在逐步明晰产权的过程

---

① 杨瑞龙、周业安：《论利益相关者合作逻辑下的企业共同治理机制》，《中国工业经济》1998年第1期，第38—45页。

② 郑显华：《对职工（代表）大会的法律思考》，《现代法学》1997年第2期，第64—67页。

③ 张海军、王旺盛：《建立现代企业制度必须重视和加强企业民主管理》，《华中师范大学学报》（哲学社会科学版）1995年第2期，第13—16页。

中，不断建立完善内部管理制度，但是委托代理关系以随之产生的委托代理问题却没有很好地解决，例如，一些国企业厂长经理的恶意经营时有发生。关于如何解决代理人问题，有的学者认为必须建立起国有企业"善良代理人"的机制，才能有效解决经营中存在的恶意侵占问题，来保证国家和人民的财产安全，这种机制产生的根本保障就是经济民主。① 一些更为激进的观点认为，必须将人民大众的意识法制化，通过制定法律使政府授权企业管理者，再以民主决策的方式制约其行为；② 或者在国有企业实行"社会化"和"民主化"改革，通过后福特主义生产方式和更广泛范围的民主参与和监督，消除少数管理者和特殊利益群体得利的情况。③ 这些观点在国有企业改制后逐渐消散。

二是国有企业利益分配和公司管理规范化问题。劳动者权益在国有企业改制过程中没有得到有效保障，主要原因之一是缺乏商业化民主管理制度传统，从而形成了高度的内部人控制，国有资产利益分配集中到管理者手中。在20世纪90年代中后期，随着国有企业改制势在必行，支持私有化的观点认为"谁投资、谁所有、谁受益"，且将投资定义为物质资本，从而将企业员工排除在受益群体之外。许多学者批评了这种观点。有的学者认为人力资本（包括经营者）应该与物质资本一样参与国有企业利润分配，这是贯彻劳动价值理论，实现国家富裕的必要途径。④ 从另一方面看，改革初期资本缺乏而劳动力过剩，资本收益占据企业利润绝大部分也无可厚非。但是随着资本累积的不断增加，人力资本的重要性日益凸显，科学技术的发展提高了劳动力的知识含量，劳动者对企业利润的贡献率不断提高，应该在更大范围内得到确认人力资本的收益权。⑤ 但是，如果忽视企业员工的利益，就会导致国有企业所有权配置出现扭曲，管理者掌

---

① 任碧云：《经济民主制度：寻求国有企业"单良代理人"的根本保证》，《山西大学学报》（哲学社会科学版）2000年第1期，第62—65页。

② 乔新生：《国有企业是职工自己的吗——关于产权与民主的思考》，《法人》2005年第1期，第29—30页。

③ 崔之元：《经济民主的两层含义》，《读书》1997年第4期，第79—82页。

④ 吴光炳：《论劳动者参与国有企业剩余价值分配》，《中国劳动科学》1995年第8期，第8—10页。

⑤ 李淑云：《论劳动者参与剩余价值分配》，《内蒙古财经学院学报》2002年第2期，第10—13页。

握实际上的控制权，导致员工失去剩余控制权和剩余索取权。①

委托代理与国有企业职工权益受损是相互关联的两个问题。由全民所有制和国营企业到国有企业的改变并不仅仅是名称的变化，更重要的是企业、资源、资本等资产处置权的变化。《宪法》第六条规定，"中华人民共和国的社会主义经济制度的基础是生产资料的社会主义公有制，即全民所有制和劳动群众集体所有制。"在这种情况下，国家受全民委托代为管理全民所有制资产，这是第一重委托代理。因为国家是一个抽象概念，在实际执行中，就需要依靠其具现代化载体，即中央和各级政府授权董事长、总经理代为经营资产的具体形式，即各类国有经济，这是第二重委托代理。《宪法》第七条规定，"国有经济，即社会主义全民所有制经济，是国民经济中的主导力量。"在这里，全民所有转化为国家所有，第一重委托代理关系进一步虚化，强调个体劳动获得收入，不再提及"主人翁"的说法和委托收益分配，而第二重委托代理则成为实在的权利义务关系。比如，现代企业制度的建立要求公司制企业的法人代表由资产所有者决定，国家成为国有独资公司和国有投资公司的投资主体，即拥有了作为"股东"任命企业领导者的权利，而职代会的选举权也就失去了存在的基础。②而在国有企业内部，管理者向委托授予方，即政府负责，在第一重委托代理缺位无法监督的情况下，职工缺乏监督制衡管理者权力的渠道。

三是协调"老三会"和"新三会"的问题。在《公司法》出台后，一些学者将研究的重点转向现代企业制度的建立，以及"老三会"与"新三会"在公司治理结构中的设计和关系上来。"老三会"是指党委会、工会、职工代表大会，"新三会"则指《公司法》规定的董事会、监事会、股东大会。有的学者认为公司在法律上的最高权力机构是股东大会，过度拔高职代会容易引起公司组织混乱。③从利益相关者角度考虑，国有

---

① 陈忠炼、赵学清：《劳动者参与治理：国有企业制度创新的基本途径》，《南京政治学院学报》2004年第3期，第49—52页。

② 刘元文：《相容与相悖——当代中国的职工民主参与研究》，中国劳动社会保障出版社2004年版。

③ 杨瑞龙、周业安：《论利益相关者合作逻辑下的企业共同治理机制》，《中国工业经济》1998年第1期，第38—45页。

企业处于激烈的市场竞争中，又同时受诸多法律、社会和政治条件约束，"新老三会"混杂在一起的模式对企业的约束太多，必然会降低企业的运营效率。① 但大多数学者不认可这类观点。冯同庆认为，改革开放以来，重建职工代表大会制度成为国有企业发展的重要选择，职工董事、监事制度是市场经济条件下公司发展的产物，也是职代会制度的延伸和发展。两者之间不是矛盾冲突的关系，而是不同发展阶段相互交叉的制度。② 卢崇昌也认为党委与"新三会"不存在冲突，从企业组织制度和激励机制角度看，职代会、工会与新三会及管理者存在对立统一的矛盾关系，但可以通过建立职工、经营者和股东物质利益趋同的机制来协调三者之间的关系。③ 在一些企业中，"新老三会"出现矛盾不是本质上的原因，而是制度在执行中有了偏差。比如，简新华认为"老三会"与"新三会"也不是简单叠加关系，否则就会形成两种领导体制和组织管理制度并存导致经营管理发生混乱，而应该合理分工与合作，在董事会、监事会中吸收党委委员和职工代表，职代会主要职能是选举这些代表，并选举建立工会组织。④ 更具体地说，是要处理好"三个关系"：一是理顺董事会领导下的经理负责制与发挥党委政治核心作用的关系；二是理顺职工代表大会与股东大会、董事会、监事会的关系；三是理顺公司监事会与纪检委的关系。⑤

在整个90年代，中国处于经济体制转型、产业结构调整、劳动关系充足、利益格局变化的特殊时期，在劳动者面临诸多困境的情况下，传统意识形态所坚持的工人阶级主人问地位空心化，造成民主管理和职工

---

① 郑海航、熊小彤：《基于不同理论框架下的公司治理——兼论我国国有企业治理》，《中国工业经济》2005年第6期，第105—111页。
② 冯同庆：《试论职工董事、监事制度与职工代表大会制度的关系》，《工会理论与实践》2000年第4期，第7—11页。
③ 卢崇昌：《公司治理机构与新、老三会关系论》，《经济研究》1994年第11期，第10—17页。
④ 简新华：《委托代理风险与国有企业改革》，《经济研究》1998年第9期，第44—49页。
⑤ 徐慧兰：《理顺"新三会"与"老三会"关系建立中国式企业领导体制》，《财贸研究》1995年第3期，第49—51页。王全兴：《职工参与制度探微》，《中国劳动科学》1995年第7期，第12—15页。

合法权利的缺失。① 这一阶段的研究主要是围绕国有企业改制和"新老三会"衔接问题,在全力加速改革开放的推动下,全国范围内形成了向 GDP 看齐、向效率看齐、向效益看齐的氛围。

三 拼搏的前十年

2001 年,中国加入世界贸易组织,进一步融入国际劳动分工,在外向型经济政策的刺激下,民营经济和个体经济得到极大发展,数以亿计的农村劳动力流向城镇、流向东南沿海,企业民主管理制度受到前所未有的挑战,这在学术领域表现为两个方面。

一是人力资源管理和员工参与的冲击。21 世纪初,人力资源管理理论以强调绩效的管理本质和更为新颖时尚的概念,受到政府和企业的欢迎,在中国迅速普及开来。企业纷纷把人事处改为人力资源部,大学里开设人力资源管理专业。人力资源管理理论中员工参与的概念及实践特征引起学者们关注。有的学者认为民主管理与员工参与本质不同,不能混用。比如,陈向聪认为我国民主管理是指企业职工以生产资料所有者、企业主人的身份参加管理本企业事务的制度,含有人民当家作主的意思,这与员工参与中员工的劳动者身份、产权清晰所有制、劳资之间的民主具有根本不同。② 但是,大部分学者认为民主管理与员工参与在机制与规则上没有实质性区别,概念的不同主要是学科的理论框架和表述方式相异,管理学,特别是人力资源管理是用员工参与,而社会学、政治学,特别是劳动关系学科更多采用工业民主、民主参与、企业民主、职工民主等。从内容、目的、程序、方法等方面看,我国企业民主管理与西方国家员工参与的机制和规则相同,是从不同角度描述了职工在企业管理

---

① 赵丽江、张远凤:《论发展工作场所的民主参与》,《北京行政学院学报》2007 年第 6 期,第 63—67 页。
② 陈向聪:《职工参与概念探析》,《福建政法管理干部学院学报》2002 年第 1 期,第 22—23 页。

中的地位和作用，其内涵和外延没有实质性区别。① 还有一些学者通过国别比较或历史比较的方法，分析了企业民主管理和员工参与表现形式的异同，认为两者有互相借鉴的意义。②

企业民主管理理论对员工参与概念的容纳和接受更多是一种现实的无奈。虽然中央政府不断强调企业民主管理的积极作用，但现实中这一制度使用范围日益萎缩。比如：2001年的《工会法》强调了工会的职能和解释了职代会与工会的职责关系，2006年全总颁布《企业工会工作条例》，把职代会作为企业工会的工作机制和制度来规范，2007年《劳动合同法》明确了职工代表大会是所有企业民主管理基本形式的制度基础。原因有两方面：其一是企业不愿意支持企业民主对管理权力的监督和约束；其二是人力资源管理和员工参与本质上加强了管理权力，且具有易操作性的优点。如果过于强调两者的不同，企业民主的生存空间会被进一步压缩，2002—2007年期刊文章数量逐年降低就是对这一问题的展示。

二是企业民主管理制度立法问题。虽然我国企业民主管理无论从内容上还是形式上都在发展和提高，但是学者注意到立法的缺失导致了民主管理的被动局面。具体来看，其一是立法层次不高、法律规定不明确、法律责任薄弱刚性不足，涉及民主管理内容的国家级法律规定有十多部，但没有一部系统全面的专门法，《职工代表大会条例》和《企业民主管理规定》又因为上下位法的问题会产生冲突；其二是法律规定不明确，规定过于原则，适用范围狭窄，《刑法》《民事诉讼法》等有关法律没有关于保护职工参与企业民主管理的可操作性条款；其三是法律责任不明，

---

① 程延园：《对企业民主管理立法的几点思考》，《北京市工会干部学院学报》2006年第3期，第14—16页。胡放之：《员工参与与工资决定——基于企业工资集体协商的实证分析》，《科学决策》2010年第9期，第35—45页。谢增毅：《职代会的定位与功能重塑》，《法学研究》2013年第3期，第110—121页。

② 刘元文：《村务公开、厂务公开与民主政治建设》，《工会理论与实践》2000年第6期，第40—44页。祁华清：《国外工业民主模式与我国职工参与制度选择》，《中州学刊》2002年第3期，第18—21页。苏晓红、侯朝轩：《中外员工参与企业管理的比较分析》，《河南师范大学学报》（哲学社会科学版）2004年第5期，第94—97页。高玉林：《企业治理中的劳动者参与研究——一个西方经济学和马克思主义经济学的综述》，《财经理论与实践》2005年第4期，第11—16页。谢玉华、何包钢：《工业民主和员工参与：一个永恒的话题——中国工业民主和员工参与研究述评》，《社会主义研究》2008年第3期，第86—93页。

刚性不足，《劳动法》《工会法》《劳动合同法》《公司法》也仅规定了职工、工会举报，政府调查处理，而没有对违法民主管理规定的行为设定法律责任和处罚；其四是工会独立性不强，会费由企业拨付，工会主席由管理层兼任，工会职责形式化；其五是对职工董事的比例或数量没有硬性规定，对职工监事的比例规定得比较低，对职工董事、监事产生和罢免的程序、任职资格条件不明确。[1] 面对企业民主管理的法律缺陷，许多学者提出了建议，主要包括提高立法层次、拓展覆盖范围、完善法律内容、明确法律责任等方面。

作为现代管理制度的一个方面，民主管理必然会随着企业和市场改革的深入而发挥更多的作用。一般认为，企业民主管理能够提供制度化的、常规化的渠道让员工在不同环节和层面进行参与，使劳资双方进行相互的利益表达、沟通和协调，[2] 有利于形成利益共同体，增强企业凝聚力，提高员工公平感和满足感。[3] 不论在外资企业，[4] 还是在民营企业，[5] 工会、职代会等制度都表现出稳定员工队伍，促进和谐人际关系、劳动关系建设的作用。

---

[1] 罗培新：《我国职工参与管理之立法缺漏及其完善》，《上海大学学报》（社会科学版）2000年第4期，第73—78页。张荣芳：《浅论我国职工民主管理制度的法律完善》，《法学评论》2000年第2期，第108—112页。王一程、负杰：《改革开放以来的中国基层民主建设》，《政治学研究》2004年第2期，第26—33页。寿继国：《关于企业民主管理制度建设的实证研究》，《中国劳动关系学院学报》2006年第2期，第40—43页。陈外华：《论公司治理中的职工参与制——以经济民主的视角》，《政法学刊》2008年第4期，第97—101页。刘元文：《论民主参与法与职工代表大会制度建设》，《工会理论研究》2011年第6期，第7—9页。吴亚平：《完善企业民主管理立法的几个问题》，《中国劳动关系学院学报》2013年第1期，第72—76页。刘文华、赵磊：《企业民主管理法律规制研究》，《中国劳动》2017年第10期，第4—10页。

[2] 吴建平、陈紫葳：《企业民主管理的实证基础——以员工参与与员工满意度相关关系为视角》，《中国劳动关系学院学报》2010年第4期，第71—75页。

[3] 林育芳：《企业民主管理与劳动关系和谐》，《中共云南省委党校学报》2009年第2期，第115—117页。

[4] 赵炜：《新型劳动关系下的工人与工会——对一家外国独资企业工人和工会状况的实证调查》，《中国党政干部论坛》2003年第6期，第24—27页。

[5] 杨勇、高汝熹：《论私营企业和谐劳动关系的构建》，《中国人力资源开发》2007年第3期，第34—37页。谢玉华：《中国工业民主和员工参与制度及功能：国企民企外企的比较——来自湖南的调查》，《经济社会体制比较》2009年第1期，第129—135页。

四　新时代和新发展

2012年4月，国资委、全总等六部委联合发布《企业民主管理规定》，对民主管理的指导思想、基本原则、组织制度作了规定，并设专章对职代会制度、厂务公开制度以及职工董事职工监事制度做出了规定。党的十八大报告也将职代会等企事业单位民主管理制度作为基层民主的重要组成部分，指出："全心全意依靠工人阶级，健全以职工代表大会为基本形式的企事业单位民主管理制度，保障职工参与管理和监督的民主权利。"

在世界经济增长乏力和国内深化改革的压力双重作用下，中国经济呈现增长速度换挡期、结构调整阵痛期、前期刺激政策消化期的"三期叠加"的阶段性特征。以习近平同志为核心的党中央大力深化改革，深入实施创新驱动发展战略，持续推动大众创业、万众创新；大力推进供给侧结构性改革，大力推动产业结构升级，逐步淘汰劳动密集型加工企业，着力发展装备制造业和高技术制造业；实施"中国制造2025""互联网+"等规划和行动，平台经济、分享经济、协同经济等新模式快速增长。2014—2016年，全国新登记市场主体超过4400万户，其中新登记企业1362万户，年均增长30%。面对经济下行的压力，如何淘汰落后产能实现产业升级换代、给企业减轻税负、激发经济活力成为当前最主要的问题。

五　总结

改革开放早期，政府为了激发企业经营者的生产积极性，一方面通过激励机制让管理者从企业经营中获得利益，另一方面在建立完善市场机制的同时，逐步放开对管理权限的限制。从党委领导下的厂长负责制，到厂长（经理）负责制，到承包责任制，再到推行股份制和现在的企业制度。

我国企业民主管理制度在继承传统的基础上，不断吸收先进管理经验，逐步探索出适合中国国情的企业民主管理制度。习近平总书记在党的十九大报告中指出,"完善政府、工会、企业共同参与的协商协调机制,构建和谐劳动关系"。学界要以习近平新时代中国特色社会主义思想为指导,深入贯彻党的十九大精神,强化企业党组织建设,加强企业民主制度建设,加强对企业民主管理的研究,提高民主管理在企业管理结构中的地位,为企业更健康的发展、员工更好的利益作出贡献。

治理现代化与民心相通

中国文化产业发展的特征与文化领域治理现代化

祖春明

中国社会科学院哲学研究所副研究员

自 2000 年"文化产业"概念首次出现在中国政府最高文件时开始，中国文化产业发展已经走过近 20 年的时间。在这 20 年中，文化产业从最初争取合法性存在到被国家确定为支柱性产业，其中经历了初始阶段时期、逆势增长时期和进入新常态的时期三个主要发展阶段。进入新时代以来，随着数字技术不断实现市场化，中国文化产业从规模扩张型增长转向创新驱动型增长，并逐渐呈现与中国国民经济和社会发展各领域融合发展的新态势。

一 "文化产业"概念解析

"文化"本身就是一个极其复杂的概念，其定义就有上百种之多。但在如此之多的"文化"定义中，却很难与"产业"概念联系在一起。为了厘清"文化产业"概念，有必要先梳理文化与产业的关系。我们可以沿着从经济到文化以及从文化到经济两条逻辑线索对其进行梳理。

（一）从经济到文化的逻辑线索

综合经济学家、社会学家和未来学家的观点，前现代以来的经济发展可以归结为五个阶段：以农业为基础的阶段、以工业为基础的阶段、以服务业为基础的阶段、以知识性服务业为基础的阶段、以艺术和文化知识服务业为基础的阶段。前三个经济发展阶段与本文主题关系不大，在此重点讨论第四个和第五个发展阶段。

20世纪七八十年代，随着新兴信息产业的发展，在服务业中把专门从事信息商品和劳务服务的产业部门称为"以知识为基础的经济部门"。20世纪90年代经济合作与发展组织（OECD）对其成员国的经济发展状况进行统计时发现，上述部门的产值占国民经济的比例达到70%以上，由此判断这些国家已经进入"知识经济"时代。

进入21世纪以后，在知识性服务业中专门满足人们精神文化需求的产品和服务日益突出，人们的消费注意力从物质需要转移到精神需要，从科学技术转移到心理和情感的满足，因此，可以说人类的经济发展正在持续经历从经济走向文化的阶段。

（二）从文化到经济的逻辑线索

与经济到文化的五个发展阶段相适应，从文化到经济也可以划分为五个阶段，并呈现出与经济生活不断融合的态势。第一阶段是以脱离大众的精英文化为标志，与农业为基础的经济发展阶段相适应；第二阶段是从传统文化走向商业文化，并以现代传媒技术的发展和文化市场的形成作为中介，与工业为基础的经济发展阶段相适应；第三阶段是从商业文化到文化产业，将商业文化建立在大众传媒的基础上，与服务业为基础的经济阶段相适应；第四阶段是从文化产业到内容产业，传媒汇流引发产业重组和整体格局的变化，与以知识性服务业为基础的经济发展阶段相适应；第五阶段是从内容产业到创意产业，国民经济从总体上转向以文化附加值为标志的经济，并与以艺术和文化知识服务业为基础的经济阶段相适应。

这里需要重点说明的是从第三阶段到第五阶段。在从商业文化到文化产业的发展过程中，电报的发明具有划时代意义。1876年，亚历山大·贝尔发明了电报，这实现了从纸媒到电子媒体的跨越式转变，随之又出现了广播和电视。这类面向大众播出的电子媒介的出现使各类文化的创作和保存具有了产业的规模，为文化产业的建立奠定了基础。

第四阶段被称为从文化产业到内容产业，主要是因为在数码技术和计算机网络技术出现以后，实现了所有媒体的汇流和统一。媒体汇流改变了传统媒体和整个文化产业的结构，乃至改变了整个经济生活的面貌。当所有媒体在互联网上实现汇流之后，传媒手段就会过剩，传播的内容就会成为决定媒体资源生存的关键因素，也就是所谓的"内容为王"时代到来了。

创意产业是内容产业的进一步升级。在数字化网络时代，内容产业向创意产业的进一步衍生表现为三种趋势：第一是强大的数字媒体技术可以实现对传统文化遗产的数字化处理，并在全世界进行传播。第二是数字技术又使我们的生活日益"传媒化"，越来越多的消费品成为有意义文化符号的载体，并构成这些消费品的价值主体。举个大家都熟悉的例子，迪士尼的唐老鸭就是具有较高品牌价值的文化符号，所有与之相关的商品都会因此获得较高的市场价格。第三是网络化趋势。在全球网络的冲击下，复制和传播的作用和成本都在下降，创新部分就成为最有价值的环节。因此，市场经济体就会以创意创新作为自己战略转型的中心。

（三）"文化产业"概念的内涵

由此可见，文化产业是文化与经济历史发展相互融合而形成的概念，但处于不同历史发展阶段的国家对文化产业的理解并不相同。例如，在美国这样完全实现市场经济的国家，文化市场充分发展，因此，文化产业被定义为"可商品化的信息内容产品业"，突出以"产品"为基点的完全市场化趋势。在欧盟，尽管在技术层面上已经与美国同步，但由于欧盟内部民族文化的多样性，因此，欧洲人对新兴文化产业的定义突出"意义内容"的特殊性，将其定义为"基于意义内容的生产活动"。韩国是文化产业中异军突起的力量，它正处于从文化产业向内容产业的升级之中，因此，文化产业被定义为"内容产业"。

综上所述，我们可以形成对文化产业的整体理解。文化产业是存在于现代社会物质生产活动之上的生产文化符号的产业，而以负载文化意义的文化符号的积累、生产、交换和消费为主线，按照产业发展链条的不同环节，可以将其区分为"文化意义本身的生产和再生产"，"以负载文化意义的产品的复制与传播"，以及"赋予一切生产活动和产品以文化标记"三重圆圈。

基于此，我们可以区分出"文化产业"概念的三个层次：第一个层次最狭义的概念是指"文化内容的创作、积累和展示"。它所指向的是"产业基础层"，包括文学艺术创作、音乐创作、摄影、舞蹈、工业设计与建筑设计以及其他各种创造性艺术活动领域。

第二个层次是扩展性概念，文化产业是指"文化制作与传播业"。它所指向的是"核心产业层"，文化产业可包括新闻出版业、广播业、影视业、音像业、电信业、网络业等。

第三个层次是最一般的概念，文化产业是指以文化意义为基础的产业。这个定义已经接近人类学的概念，即人类一切精神和物质的活动都具有传达社会意义的"符号"作用，它所指向的是"延伸产业层"，涵盖所有具有文化标记的产品，从服装业、建筑业到具有现代商标的一切产品。对于像中国这样尚处于工业化时代的国家来说，目前我们对于文化产业的理解仍处于第一层次和第二层次之间。

二 中国文化产业兴起的背景

2000 年对于中国文化领域来说具有重要的划时代意义。在这一年 10 月召开的中国共产党十五届五中全会上，"文化产业"这一概念第一次出现在中国"最高政策文件"之中，并由此开启了中国的文化体制改革历程。

关于中国的文化产业发展兴起的时间划分一直存在分歧：如果以 1978 年实行改革开放对文化事业单位普遍实行收费服务开始计算，可以说中国文化产业发展贯穿整个改革开放过程。如果以有关部门开始在政府文件中使用"文化产业"作为政策性语言来看，可以追溯到"八五"期间的 1992 年，在《中共中央国务院关于加快发展第三产业的决定》中第一次使用了"文化产业"的概念。如果从出现在党中央全会文件这一"最高政策文件"中来看，应该从 2000 年 10 月中共中央十五届五中全会通过的《中共中央关于"十五"规划的建议》开始，至今有 20 多年时间。以上标志性事件可以作为中国文化产业三种分期的依据。我们将选取第三种分期。

世纪之交，中国的文化产业在全球异军突起，这既是在中国改革开放推动下现代化进程的必然结果,也是新一轮全球化发展的必然趋势,更是中国政府应对"入世"全球化挑战的主动措施。

首先,从国内发展趋势看,文化产业的兴起是中国经济社会发展水平提高,居民收入水平提高和消费结构变化的结果。改革开放是中国经济社会发展的历史性起点。根据权威部门统计,从国民经济"六五"计划的20世纪80年代初到国民经济"九五"计划完成的1999年,中国的人均GDP已经接近1000美元,由此导致居民消费结构发生根本性变化。

消费结构变化的突出特征是显示出了"脱物"的倾向,即居民消费结构中用于文化教育部分的消费越来越大,增长速度越来越快。在这个转变过程中,生活必需品支出继续稳步下降,而服务性消费支出比重全面上升和加速,娱乐文教支出首次超过用品类支出,将中国居民消费次序从"吃、穿、用"改变为"吃、穿、娱乐文教"。相当一部分居民群体开始向教育、科技、旅游及精神产品消费等领域转变。总之,收入水平的提高和消费结构的变化,及其对文化类消费品的强烈需求,成为我国文化产业兴起的一个起决定作用的内在动因。

其次,从国际趋势看,知识经济的发展带动了新兴服务业的全面提升,到了20世纪80—90年代后,经济全球化向文化全球化进展的趋势明显,文化产业再一次在全球范围内蓬勃兴起,重塑了全球化的整体面貌。

知识经济的主要推动力来自数字化信息技术,以及由数字技术引发的现代传媒汇流,这就将知识经济的发展大潮引向了"文化经济"的方向。美国作为数字化信息技术的先行国家,主导了这个进程。美国国会1996年通过了新的《电信法案》。该法案为美国传媒业松绑,开启了美国的传媒业巨头走向世界的大门。

1998年,美国的消费类视听技术文化产品出口达到600亿美元,取代航空航天工业的位置,成为第一大出口产品。这标志着美国已经完成了新一轮产业结构调整,再一次抢占了国际性产业升级运动的制高点,将全球化推进到了新的阶段,并以美国特色塑造了新一轮全球化,所谓"麦当劳化"。

最后,从直接起因上看,中国文化产业是为了应对加入WTO的挑战,由中国政府在未完成工业化的情况下,主动出台的政策。

文化产业是发达国家从整体上进入"后工业化"发展阶段的产物,

发展文化产业是先行进入后工业化发展阶段的欧美等发达国家对全球经济文化发展的一次重塑。在全球性的产业升级和重组的形势下，完成工业化是中国的首要任务，加入WTO为中国提供了承接全球性产业转移的重大发展机遇，但是也面临开放文化类服务贸易的挑战。

对于中国的文化机构来说，加入WTO虽然面临文化产业竞争、文化资本冲击，以及文化价值观冲突等多重挑战，但也是一次千载难逢的机遇：可以有力地推动中国国内文化领域改革与发展的历史性进程，并进而以文化产业的发展作为支点推动整体经济结构的转型。权衡利弊，中国政府做出了发展文化产业的重大政策选择。

三 中国文化产业发展的特征

（一）初始阶段特征：产业启动与改革试点

在2000年10月11日中国共产党第十五届中央委员会第五次全体会议上，通过了《中共中央关于制定"十五"计划的建议》，提到了"推动信息产业与有关文化产业结合"；在第十五节"加强社会主义精神文明建设"中，提出了要"完善文化产业政策，加强文化市场建设和管理，推动有关文化产业发展"。

2001年3月，在九届人大四次会议朱镕基总理所做的"关于国民经济和社会发展第十个五年计划纲要的报告"中，党的十五届五中全会有关建议被表述为："深化文化体制改革，完善文化经济政策，推动有关文化产业发展"。发展"文化产业"的建议出现在中国最高政策文件——党中央全会决议和全国人大五年计划中，标志着文化产业在中国"合法化进程"的完成，是中国文化产业历史性的起点，具有重大的战略意义。

在2002年党的十六大报告中，关于文化体制改革的表述已经具体化为"抓紧制定文化体制改革的总体方案"这样一个紧急工作安排。根据这一要求，2003年开始启动"文化体制改革试点"。改革试点总共有35个试点单位和9个综合试点省市，行业遍及新闻媒体、出版单位、图书馆、博物馆、文化馆、文艺院团、影视制作企业、印刷、发行、放映公司等。试点单位分为"公益性事业"和"经营性产业"两种，分别提出了改革的目标和方法，并制定了相应的政策。试点于2005年基本结束后在全国展开。

（二）逆势增长阶段特征："逆势增长"与"支柱产业"

自 2000 年以来，中国的文化产业发展一路高歌猛进。2003 年文化体制改革试点开始后出台了配套政策，对改革企业加以优惠，刺激了产业发展速度的提升。2005 年改革在全国铺开，优惠政策实施面扩大，进一步刺激了产业扩张。

特别要说明的是，入世以来中国经济承接了开放红利，一路高速增长，到 2007 年达到了 13% 这一峰值，2008 年国际金融危机骤然来袭，经济增长速度在一年间下挫至 9% 以下。这时，文化产业却在影视和新媒体等领域出现了超常增长，成为国民经济中罕见的亮点，被称为"逆势增长"和"口红效应"。

这引起了综合经济管理部门的注意，2009 年 9 月国务院常务会议审议通过了《文化产业振兴规划》，将文化产业列为第十一个国家产业振兴规划。次年 10 月，在十七届五中全会通过的"十二五规划建议"中，又提出在十二五期间"推动文化产业成为国民经济的支柱性产业"，文化产业正式位列国家战略性支柱产业之中。

（三）新常态阶段特征："拐点"与"换挡"

将文化产业建设成为国民经济支柱产业，作为一个发展目标，在中国这样一个文化产品供应长期处于短缺状态的国家来说，是有市场需求空间的，问题只是在于产业的发展方式是否合理，以及文化管理体制和政策能否激励文化企业进行有效的生产创造。在这一点上说，中国文化产业并没有做好准备。

进入"十二五"以来，宏观经济开始从"高速"转向"中高速"，进入"新常态"，发展方式转型和经济结构调整终于实质性地启动，体制和政策的转变日益明显。文化产业本来属于宏观经济的组成部分，经济形势的变化从长期来看将改善消费环境，有利于文化产业的发展，但是在中短期时间里必定会有不利影响。此外，这个阶段也恰逢文化体制改革告一段落，与改革相关的政策效应逐渐衰减，文化产业的发展速度因此逐年下降。因此，中国文化产业 10 多年来发展的"热运行"态势在

"十二五"期间进入了"拐点"：2011年增长21.96%、2012年增长16.5%、2013年增长11.1%、2014年增长12.1%、2015年增长11%。

"拐点"的实质是"换挡"。在党的十八届三中全会通过的《中共中央关于全面深化改革若干重大问题的决定》中，出现了"使市场在资源配置中起决定性作用"的重大政策性表述，在有关文化政策的一节中，将第一主题词从"文化产业"换成了"文化市场"——建立健全现代文化市场体系。这说明，中国文化产业的发展正在从政府主导的启动阶段走向依靠市场内生动力发展的新阶段。

四　推进文化领域治理现代化

根据2004年、2008年、2013年三次经济普查中包含的文化产业数据，2004年，中国文化产业法人单位31.8万户，从业人员873万人，增加值3440亿元，占GDP的比重为2.15%。2013年法人单位91.85万户，从业人员1759万人，增加值20081亿元，占DGP比重为3.42%。10年间，法人单位增加了近2倍，从业人员增加了1倍，增加值增加了4.8倍。但是，放在改革开放的宏观形势中看，并从国际比较中衡量，中国文化产业还只是发展的初期阶段。

（一）发展动力从政府投资走向社会投资

中国的文化产业曾经是一个极度短缺的产业。经过大概3个五年计划的时间，持续年均20%以上的高速发展，文化产业供给短缺的局面得到极大缓解，在一些领域甚至出现了投资过度和泡沫化情形（如"动漫产业"），文化市场整体上进入了一个短缺与过剩并存的新时期。

关于"短缺与过剩并存"还可以进一步定义为：在相对较低发展水平基础上的，以及在有限开放的市场中的短缺与过剩并存。首先，从总体上说，我国文化消费水平还大大低于国际上相同国家平均水平，因此，所谓过剩还仅仅是在文化消费没有得到真正满足情况下的"相对过剩"。

其次，之所以出现短缺与过剩并存，就是因为文化市场开放程度有限，导致已经开放的市场投资和竞争过度，未开放的市场投资不足因而供给不足。此外，在市场开放不足而导致供给短缺的领域由于过于依赖财政扶持，还产生了大量的无效投资，出现了虚假繁荣。

走出短缺与过剩并存现状是必然的趋势。可以说，中国文化产业经过 10 多年的发展，以政府主导的投资高峰期已过，发展的动力将从政府投资走向社会投资，从投资推动转向消费拉动，发展方式将从数量规模型走向质量效益型。在正在到来的新的发展阶段，突破性的进展将集中在市场比较开放自由，文化科技融合创新比较活跃的新兴文化产业领域，因此将出现由技术创新驱动的大规模结构调整和优化升级。

（二）推动文化领域治理的现代化

世纪之交以来，表现在 GDP 增长数据上，中国的文化产业发展速度是令人印象深刻的，但是分析其原因，主要归因于体制性释放（文化体制改革）和政策性推动（文化体制改革的配套优惠政策），政府在发展中唱了主角，真正因大众收入水平提高而自发产生的，文化消费需求本身对文化产业发展的拉动作用还很不充分。

中国文化产业的发展是与文化体制改革并行的，属于"边改革边发展"。在新形势下，文化产业需要实现转型，而这个转型的实现有赖于国家宏观文化管理体制的改革——重构政府与市场的关系。

从文化体制改革的逻辑来看也在指向这个目标。2003 年以来改革的主线是"打造市场主体"，主要内容是"事业和企业分开"，这一目标已经取得了阶段性成果。接下来需要做的是，如何构建一个"现代文化市场体系"，使得转制后的企业有一个公平公开和自由竞争的市场环境。这一任务构成了党的十八届三中全会报告中提出的"建立健全现代文化市场体系"这一总任务的基础。

（三）新发展阶段中国文化产业领域治理现代化展望

展望中国文化产业的发展，可以看出中国文化产业发展存在五大市场空间。

第一，文化产业作为消费性服务业，将呈现巨大的发展空间。新发展阶段随着宏观经济发展方式转型实质性推进，消费环境的进一步改善，文化消费将会实质性启动，文化产业作为满足人民群众精神文化消费需求的产业，将呈现巨大的发展空间。

第二，文化产业作为生产性服务业，将成为国民经济转型和经济结构调整的重大支点。中国宏观经济领域发展方式转型和经济结构调整升级将带动相关产业发展，对文化产业作为生产性服务业的需求将呈现爆发式的增长，文化产业与实体经济出现大规模融合发展的趋势，国民经济越来越多的领域都会出现文化产业的身影。

第三，文化产业也是新技术产业，文化科技融合将成为最重要的发展动力，技术革命将推动文化产业出现重大结构调整和优化。现在已经可以看得很清楚，今后5—10年将是技术进步给文化发展带来根本性变革的时期。

第四，现代文化产业是城市化的产业，新型城镇化建设继续为文化发展带来巨大机遇。中国城市化进一步深化，还有大量人口要从农村转入城市。因此，已建城市有巨大存量的提升需要，新建城市有巨大增量的新生需要，都为文化发展开辟出了巨大的空间。

第五，文化贸易全面提升将推动全球文化发展进入"中国主场"新阶段。过去的十几年，随着文化产业的发展和文化体制的改革，中国国际文化贸易大幅提升。这一发展势头越来越强大，以至于今后5—10年可能是我国国际文化贸易出现根本性转变的时期。中国将从一个"进口版权，出口制成品"的国家转变为一个"出口版权，进口制成品"的国家，以大规模的文化消费对国际文化市场做出新的贡献。

"一带一路"框架下中白旅游
合作前景与治理创新

张艳璐

中国社会科学院俄罗斯东欧中亚研究所副研究员

在当今世界经济中，旅游业是发展最快、对全球GDP贡献较大的产业之一，已成为世界经济增长的重要动力。而旅游合作正在成为国家间双边及地区多边合作的重要方向。在《2030年前白俄罗斯社会经济稳定发展战略》中，旅游业已被白俄罗斯确定为国家经济发展的主要动力之一。尽管在基础设施、发展资金等方面还存在诸多困难，并且白俄罗斯旅游业在国民经济贡献度、市场受欢迎程度、服务形式与水平等方面还存在诸多不足，但是白俄罗斯旅游业发展在资源、旅游基础设施建设、政策支持等方面已具备较好的发展基础，发展潜力巨大、前景广阔。在中白旅游合作方面，虽然依然存在阻碍，但在资源、政策、市场等方面已经具备了较好的合作条件。通过实施第三方市场联合开发、区域旅游集群建设、消费支付手段便利化以及创新产品宣传手段等措施，未来中白旅游合作有潜力成为继中白工业园之后中白间务实合作的又一亮点，进而成为"一带一路"合作框架下的新典范。

近几十年间，世界旅游业持续快速发展，特别是国际游客的数量始终保持逐年递增的态势，截至2017年旅游业已成为世界经济发展最快的产业之一。根据联合国世界旅游组织（UNWTO）的评估，2018年全球国际游客的出游量增长了 6%，已达 14 亿人次。① 在过去的数十年间，旅游业及围绕其所形成的经济体系已成为世界经济增长的重要动力，对全球国内生产总值（GDP）的贡献率超过了 10%，约每十个工作岗位中就有一个产生于旅游业。② 作为公认的资源消耗低、创造就业岗位多、综合效益高的产业，旅游业被许多国家确定为产业结构调整的重点方向以及增强国家综合竞争力的重要途径，在国民经济中的占比日益增加。与此同时，旅游业在促进各国人民相互了解上的作用也进一步凸显。它已不仅仅是一种表示游客关系集合的经济学概念，还是一种当代国家（地区）间关系中的社会现象，更是不同国家间的一种积极文化合作方式以及加强国家（地区）间相互关系总体趋势的自然结果，在人文交流、文化传播上扮演着重要角色。旅游合作正日益成为国家间双边以及地区多边合作的重要方向。

2017 年 12 月 1 日中国和白俄罗斯两国总理在俄罗斯索契举行会晤，其间，时任白俄罗斯总理安德烈·科比亚科夫正式向中方提出建议，将 2018 年定为中国"白俄罗斯旅游年"。李克强总理代表中方表示支持该提议，并表示中方将认真考虑白方提出的所有建议。根据新华社 2017 年 12 月 23 日的报道，中国与白俄罗斯就在 2018 年互办旅游年协商一致。2018 年 1 月 10 日，中国"白俄罗斯旅游年"率先在中国重庆举行隆重的开幕式，同时举办了"白俄罗斯中华亲"旅游论坛。在论坛上，时任白俄罗斯驻华大使鲁德指出，人文联系和旅游在中白双边关系中占据特殊的地位。它拉近了两国人民的关系，增强了相互之间的信任，为国家间关系建构了良好的基础。③ 1 月 12 日，中国国家旅游局副局长杜江与白俄罗斯体育和旅游部副部长波特诺在北京签署了 2018 年中国"白俄罗斯旅游年"合作备忘录。中白两国间的旅游合作自 2015 年 5 月开通直航航线后

---

① World Tourism Organization of UN, World Tourism Barometer, Volume 17, Issue 1, January 2019. http://cf.cdn.unwto.org/sites/all/files/pdf/unwto_barom19_01_january_excerpt.pdf.

② Cheryl Martin, Richard Samans, Preface in The Travel & Tourism Competitiveness Report 2017.

③ Торжественная церемония открытия Года туризма Беларуси в Китае состоялась в Чунцине, http://www.belta.by/society/view/torzhestvennaja-tseremonija-otkrytija-goda-turizma-belarusi-v-kitae-sostojalas-v-chuntsine – 283842 – 2018/.

迈上一个新的发展台阶，成为中白两国经济合作中继"中白工业园"之后的又一亮点。在第二届"一带一路"高峰论坛期间，中白两国领导人在会晤时将旅游与经贸、投资、教育和地方合作并列作为两国未来合作的重点。[①] 伴随着中白关系的不断提升与加强，中白间旅游合作持续升温，但是有关中白旅游合作的基础、问题以及发展前景等一系列问题依然需要进一步的探讨、研究。[②]

一 中白旅游合作的条件与基础

虽然位于太平洋东岸、亚洲东部的中国与地处欧洲腹地、中欧平原的白俄罗斯相距遥远，自然风貌与风土人情存在巨大差异，但两国间的旅游合作已具备一定的基础。

首先，中白关系为双方的旅游业合作及相关的人文交流营造了良好的政治环境。中白间稳定、友好的双边关系也为两国开展旅游合作奠定了坚实的基础。

中国是最早承认白俄罗斯独立的国家之一。自1992年1月20日中白建立外交关系以来，两国关系始终保持平稳发展。两国于2005年签署联合声明，宣布中白关系进入全面发展和战略合作的新阶段。此后，特别是2013年后中白关系持续升温。白俄罗斯总统卢卡申科于2013年访华，中白两国签署《中华人民共和国和白俄罗斯共和国关于建立全面战略伙伴关系的联合声明》；中国国家主席习近平于2015年访问白俄罗斯，双方签署《中华人民共和国和白俄罗斯共和国友好合作和约》《中华人民共和国和白俄罗斯共和国关于进一步发展和深化全面战略伙伴关系的联合声明》；2016年卢卡申科总统再度访华期间，两国签署《中华人民共和国和白俄罗斯共和国关于建立相互信任、合作共赢的全面战略伙伴关系的

---

① 《习近平会见白俄罗斯总统卢卡申科》，中国政府网，2019年4月25日，www.gov.cn/xinwen/2019-04/25/content_5386303.htm。

② 目前国内对于白俄罗斯旅游发展状况以及中白旅游合作现状与前景的研究成果较为匮乏，主要有Nahi-ZadaSabina的《白俄罗斯旅游贸易的ABC–XYZ及影响因素的分析》（华东师范大学2016年硕士毕业论文）、赵会荣的《对中国与白俄罗斯关系的分析与思考》（载《国外理论动态》2017年第11期）等文章对相关问题有所论述。

联合声明》,并宣布发展全天候友谊。

其次,中国和白俄罗斯政府都致力于发展本国旅游业,为此制定并实施了相关的发展规划和政策,取得了阶段性成效,为两国旅游合作奠定了物质基础。

独立以来,特别是在进入 21 世纪后,白俄罗斯政府重视并支持本国旅游业的发展,不仅于 1999 年 11 月 25 日颁布并实行了《白俄罗斯共和国旅游法》以规范旅游业相关活动,还自 2001 年至今制订并实施了四个国家级旅游业发展计划。对于最新版的《2016—2020 年白俄罗斯国家旅游业发展规划》,白俄罗斯前总理安德烈·科比亚科夫指出,在当前的白俄罗斯旅游发展综合规划中不仅是将旅游作为产业来发展,更将其作为白俄罗斯国家经济发展的主要推动力。[1] 在 2017 年 5 月出台的《2030 年前白俄罗斯共和国经济社会发展战略》中,旅游业也被列为白俄罗斯服务业发展的重点领域,确立了较高的目标:要在 2030 年前使白俄罗斯成为世界旅游前五十强国家,并将旅游服务出口额在国家服务出口总额中的占比提升至 3.5%。根据白俄罗斯体育与旅游部所公布的《2018 年度"好客白俄罗斯"国家规划实施成果报告》,白俄罗斯旅游业在 2018 年度超额完成了《2016—2020 年白俄罗斯国家旅游业发展规划》所规定的任务目标(详见表1),实现旅游服务贸易出口 2.305 亿美元,并为推介白俄罗斯旅游累计完成 39 次市场推广活动。此外,白俄罗斯政府还在 2012 年制定并批准了《"白俄罗斯城堡"国家规划》,对白境内 30 多处历史文化建筑进行了大规模整修。

表1　2018 年度"好客白俄罗斯"国家规划进度完成情况表

	完成量	计划量	超出额
新增持证导游数量(人)	138		
其中:讲解员	106	—	—
导游翻译	32		
新增和更新旅游线路数量(条)	11	—	—

---

[1] Годом туризма Беларуси в Китае будет объявлен 2018 - й, http://www.belta.by/society/view/godom-turizma-belarusi-v-kitae-budet-objjavlen - 2018 - j - 278487 - 2017.

续表

	完成量	计划量	超出额
外国游客到访量（千人次）	4781.9	4654	127.9
2018 年旅游服务出口额（百万美元）	230.5	208	22.5

资料来源：Информация о реализации в 2018 году Государственной программы "Беларусь гостеприимная" на 2016–2020 годы。

除国家层面的旅游发展规划外，白俄罗斯各地方政府还根据本地区情况制订相应的旅游业发展计划。例如，明斯克市议会于 2005 年 12 月 31 日批准通过了《2006—2010 年明斯克市旅游发展规划》。市政府期望通过该规划能够最有效地挖掘明斯克市的旅游业潜力，发展旅游基础设施，提高旅游业对该市经济发展的贡献，并创造条件使旅游业成为明斯克市经济的关键行业。格罗德诺州议会也曾于 2002 年批准了《2002—2005 年格罗德诺州旅游发展地方规划》。

同时，白俄罗斯还颁布一系列总统令。例如：第 371 号总统令《关于在白俄罗斯国家支持旅游业发展的若干措施》、第 372 号总统令《关于在白俄罗斯发展农业生态旅游的若干措施》以及第 462 号总统令《关于外国人出入境免签手续的规定》等。正是得益于国家的重视，白俄罗斯旅游业在近年发生很大变化，得以快速发展。特别是 2016 年，白俄罗斯在世界旅游理事会（WTTC）当年旅游行业投资增长排名中位于较快国家之列。根据 WTTC 评估，白俄罗斯 2016 年在旅游行业的投资增长达 12%，在 185 个被评估国家中排名第六位，远高于世界（4.7%）和欧洲（4.1%）的平均水平，大幅超过其邻近的立陶宛（160 位）、波兰（171 位）、俄罗斯（180 位）、乌克兰（183 位）等国。

在中国，2009 年 12 月 1 日出台《国务院关于加快发展旅游业的意见》（国发〔2009〕41 号），提出要把旅游业培育成为国民经济战略性支柱产业和人民群众更加满意的现代服务业的目标。中华人民共和国国务院于 2011 年将 5 月 19 日确定为"中国旅游日"。根据国家旅游局数据中心发布的统计数据，中国国内旅游增速超过预期，出入境旅游实现稳步增长。截至 2018 年上半年，中国的入境旅游人数达 6923 万人次。其中，入境外籍游客 1482 万人次，增长 4%。国际旅游收入达 618 亿美元，比上年同期增长2.8%。中国公民出境旅游人数为7131万人次，比上年同期增长15%[1]。另据《2018年旅游市场基本情况》，国内旅游市场持续高速增长，国内旅游人数55.39亿人次，同比增长10.8%；出入境旅游总人数2.91亿人次，同比增长7.8%；全年实现旅游业总收入5.97万亿元人民币，同比增长10.5%。全年全国旅游业对GDP的综合贡献为9.94万亿元人民币，占GDP总量的11.04%。旅游业直接就业人数达2826万人，共为7991万人提供了直接和间接就业岗位，占全国就业总人口的10.29%。在出境旅游方面，中国公民出境人数达1.4972亿人次，比上年同期增长14.7%。[2]

最后，中国和白俄罗斯的旅游资源各具特色，彼此之间存在较大的差异，为两国的旅游合作提供了空间与潜力。

与中国相似，白俄罗斯也拥有丰富的旅游资源。白俄罗斯是地处东欧平原的内陆国家，东部及北部与俄罗斯为邻，南部与乌克兰接壤，西部同波兰、立陶宛和拉脱维亚毗邻。国土面积20.76万平方千米，居欧洲第13位，人口950万。白俄罗斯地势平坦，多湿地，属温带大陆性气候，气候温润，气温舒适。白俄罗斯境内的湖泊、河流资源丰富。此外，白俄罗斯境内保存有较为完整的自然地貌景观，别洛韦日国家森林公园和斯特鲁维地理探测弧线等两处遗迹入选世界自然遗产名录。除自然资源外，白俄罗斯还拥有丰富独特的历史文化资源。白俄罗斯的文明史最早可以追溯到石器时代，在其境内曾出土过属于石器时代的石板、陶器等文物。公元7—8世纪，在斯拉夫传统与波罗的海诸部族文化传统的基础上开始逐渐形成白俄罗斯民族文化。白俄罗斯境内留存有圣索菲亚大教堂、圣叶夫罗西尼娅教堂、波罗欧克的鲍里斯—格列布修道院（别列奇茨修道院）、维捷布斯克的报喜教堂、格罗德诺的鲍里斯—格列布教堂（克洛日教堂）等一批宗教建筑艺术精品，其中建造于11世纪的白俄罗斯第一座石头教堂——圣索菲亚大教堂更是成为白俄罗斯的国家象征

---

[1]《2018年上半年旅游统计数据报告》，中华人民共和国文化和旅游部网站，2018年8月22日，http：//zwgk.mct.gov.cn/ceshi/lysj/201808/t20180822_834337.html? keywords=.

[2]《2018年旅游市场基本情况》，中华人民共和国文化和旅游部网站，2019年2月12日，http：//zwgk.mct.gov.cn/auto255/201902/t20190212_837271.html? keywords=.

之一。

与此同时，中国与白俄罗斯两国所具备的旅游资源在种类、类型、功能等方面存在着较大差异。在自然资源方面，素有"万湖之国"美誉的白俄罗斯以丰富的动植物资源见长；中国的自然旅游资源则因辽阔的地域以及大纬向跨度而以雄奇多变的地理风景和气候奇景为特色。在人文资源方面，白俄罗斯的相关旅游资源带有鲜明的东斯拉夫文明和苏联文化特色；而中国则是东亚文明圈的中心，相关旅游资源带有儒家文化的鲜明特点。此外，从功能角度看，白俄罗斯所具备的资源使其在开发跨境旅游、生态健康旅游、体育和商务旅游上具有优势；① 而中国则得益于旅游资源的全面性而适合开发各种现代旅游产品。正是旅游资源的差异性使得中国和白俄罗斯在旅游业发展过程中彼此之间的竞争较低，能实现优势互补，从而为两国间开展旅游合作提供了较为广阔的空间。

二 不断挖掘中白旅游合作潜力

目前，中国与白俄罗斯的旅游合作已初现成效。例如，在签证便利化方面，2018年8月10日已实现中国公民持因私护照免签入境白俄罗斯；而根据经中华人民共和国国务院批准、由中国出入境管理局出台的《部分国家外国人144小时过境免签政策》，白俄罗斯公民可以从上海浦东国际机场等15个口岸中的任一口岸入境或出境，并可在上海市、江苏省、浙江省、北京市、天津市、河北省和辽宁省七个行政区域免签停留144小时。在具体的旅游项目开发方面，中国旅游集团已将白俄罗斯旅游项目列为"一带一路"倡议框架下的2017年度重点开发项目。同时，由中国国际旅行社总社有限公司研发的"白俄罗斯7天初体验"独家特色旅游产品业已正式上线，首发团于2017年9月成行。此外，根据中国旅

---

① Национальная туристическая индустрия. Обеспечение доступности услуг по организации внутреннего туризма для Белорусских граждан. Безвизовый порядок въезда в Беларусь. http: // oshmiany. gov. by/uploads/files/IPG/IPG-ijun – 2017 – material-s-dopolnenijami-upravlenija-sporta-i-turizma – . pdf.

游研究院和携程集团联合发布的《2017年中欧旅游市场数据报告》显示，白俄罗斯已成为中国游客旅游人次增量最多的欧洲目的地国家之一，列第七位。尽管已经取得了一些成果，但是中白两国间的旅游合作依然处于起步阶段，还存在进一步拓展的空间。

第一，中白两国的旅游业发展水平存在一定差距，旅游合作潜力需深入挖掘。尽管欧洲是世界最大的国际旅游目的地，几乎占据了世界旅游业的半壁江山，旅游经济也是欧洲经济的支柱行业之一，在全球旅游市场中占据领导地位，但作为欧洲大家庭的一员，白俄罗斯旅游业的发展却低于欧洲国家的平均水平，没有在本国经济中占据重要位置，在全球旅游市场的地位处于较低水平。根据世界旅游理事会公布的统计数据，白俄罗斯旅游业2017年的直接产值为22亿白俄罗斯卢布（约合11.108亿美元），总产值为68亿白俄罗斯卢布（约合34.082亿美元），分别占白俄罗斯当年国内生产总值（GDP）的2%和6.2%。在创造就业机会方面，白俄罗斯旅游业2017年的直接就业岗位约8.6万个。在旅游服务出口方面，白俄罗斯在2017年实现21亿白俄罗斯卢布的旅游服务出口，约合10.423亿美元，占其2017年出口总额的3.0%。此外，在旅游业投资方面，白俄罗斯2017年的投资共计6亿白俄罗斯卢布（约合3.128亿美元），占其当年投资总额的2%。尽管白俄罗斯旅游业各项指标均实现增长，但主要指标值仍远低于世界和所在地区的平均水平（见表2），并呈现投入与产出增长双放缓的趋势。[1]

表2　　　　2017年白俄罗斯旅游业主要发展指标与世界及
地区平均水平对照表

	白俄罗斯	世界平均水平	欧洲平均水平
旅游业对GDP的直接贡献	11亿美元	215亿美元	59亿美元
旅游业对GDP的总贡献	34亿美元	629亿美元	195亿美元
直接就业数量	85900人	937500人	158500人

---

[1] World Travel and Tourism Council. Travel and Tourism Economic Impact 2018 – Belarus. https：// www.wttc.org/-/media/files/reports/economic-impact-research/countries – 2018/belarus2018.pdf.

续表

	白俄罗斯	世界平均水平	欧洲平均水平
就业总量	259200 人	2341000 人	582100 人
旅游业投资额	3 亿美元	48 亿美元	26 亿美元
旅客出口额	1 亿美元	81 亿美元	57 亿美元

资料来源：World Travel and Tourism Council. Travel and Tourism Economic Impact 2018 – Belarus. https：// www. wttc. org/ – /media/files/reports/economic-impact-research/countries – 2018/belarus2018. pdf。

如表3所示，除了旅游业投资的相对低水平，中白两国旅游业在竞争力、对国民经济和就业的贡献度、旅游服务出口、旅游投资的绝对值、出入境人员数量以及消费能力等旅游业发展情况的主要参考指标上都存在较大差距。

表3　　　　中白旅游业主要指标对比简表（以2017年的数据为准）

	白俄罗斯	中国
旅游业竞争力排名（在136个国家中）	未上榜	第15位
旅游业贡献度排名（在185个国家中）	第97位（绝对贡献排名）；第146位（相对贡献排名）	第2位（绝对贡献排名）；第75位（相对贡献排名）
对GDP的直接贡献	11.108亿美元，占GDP总量的2%	4023亿美元，占GDP总量的3.3%
对GDP的综合贡献	34.052亿美元，占GDP总量的6.2%	13493亿美元，占GDP总量的11%
直接就业贡献	8.6万个，占就业岗位总数的1.9%	2825万个，占就业岗位总数的3.6%
综合就业贡献	25.9万个，占就业岗位总数的5.8%	7990万个，占就业岗位总数的10.3%
游客出口额	10.423亿美元，占出口总额的3%	1253亿美元，占出口总额的5.2%

续表

	白俄罗斯	中国
旅游业投资额	3.128亿美元，占投资总额的2%	1547亿美元，占投资总额的2%
入境外国游客数量	28.27万人次	13948万人次
本国公民出境人数	72.7536万人次	13051万人次
本国公民出境旅游花费	6.124亿白俄罗斯卢布（约2.88亿美元）	1152.9亿美元

资料来源：根据中华人民共和国文化和旅游部、白俄罗斯统计委员会、世界经济论坛以及世界旅游理事会等机构公布的2017年相关数据自行编制。

第二，中白两国的旅游产品在彼此的旅游市场中吸引力有待提高。赴白俄罗斯旅游的外国游客以商务和体育休闲为主，缺乏有个性的团队游。此外，提供综合性的旅游服务是当代白俄罗斯旅游业的特点之一。但由旅行社完全负责组织旅游活动的形式却增加了旅行者的费用开支。与时下流行的强调个性、追求自主性和节省费用为特色的旅游理念存在差异。

此外，中国和白俄罗斯不是彼此主要的客源市场和旅游目的地。尽管得益于较为宽松的签证制度，中国游客赴白俄罗斯旅游的人数出现增长。根据白俄罗斯国家统计委员会的统计数字，2018年中国赴白游客数量为3277人，较2016年增加了1698人，但相较俄罗斯的20.74万人（2018年）存在太大的差距。而在2018年独联体以外国家赴白游客数量排行中居于立陶宛、波兰、拉脱维亚和德国之后仅位列第5位。[①] 白俄罗斯旅游产品的受众较为固定，主要集中在苏联加盟共和国地区和一些中东欧国家，在其他国家和地区的市场占有率虽有所增长，但仍处于较低水平。与此同时，对于白俄罗斯游客而言，中国也非其首选旅游目的地。根据白俄罗斯国家统计委员会的统计，2018年赴中国旅游的白俄罗斯团队游客共计1411人，与2017年持平，中国在被统计的27个非独联体国家中排名第25位，仅略高于英国和以色列。

① Национальный статистический комитет РБ. Туризм и туристические ресурсы в Республике Беларуси（статистический сборник）. Минск, 2019 г., 30с.

三 深化中白旅游合作

两国要将潜力转化为成果，切实推动两国在旅游领域的务实合作发展。

首先，在"一带一路"倡议等多边框架下推动中白两国联合开发国际旅游的第三方市场。市场是掣肘中白旅游合作的重要因素之一。白俄罗斯入境游的主要客源来自俄罗斯等独联体国家以及邻近的波兰、拉脱维亚、立陶宛等国家。白俄罗斯旅游产品在中国国际旅游市场中的竞争力偏弱，对中国出境游消费群体缺乏吸引力。尽管自2018年8月10日起，白俄罗斯对中国公民赴白旅游实行免签政策，但是赴白俄罗斯旅游的中国游客数量并没有出现巨幅增长。市场动能的缺乏以及未来盈利能力偏低的预期直接导致中白旅游合作项目的投资吸引力偏弱。在此情况下，根据白俄罗斯旅游业的自身发展条件以及旅游产品受众的特点，在推动开发彼此市场的同时，依托"一带一路"倡议以及欧亚经济联盟等多边机制加强中白两国针对国际旅游产品第三方市场的联合开发将是拓宽中白旅游合作市场渠道、增加合作项目投资吸引力的有效途径。

其次，利用白俄罗斯的地理位置优势，推动跨境、跨区域旅游合作的发展，构建独具特色的区域旅游集群。白俄罗斯地处东西交通枢纽的地理位置以及"过境之地""中转国"的地缘属性可为其发展跨境、跨地区旅游合作项目提供有利条件。同时，白俄罗斯境内分布着包括别洛韦日国家森林公园和斯特鲁维地理探测弧线等世界自然遗产在内的多处跨境旅游资源，为白俄罗斯与邻国一同开发区域旅游集群提供了可依托的天然载体，并使其在所处地区发展跨境、跨区域旅游合作成为可能。通过跨境、跨地区的旅游项目开发不仅可以部分抵消白俄罗斯与俄罗斯及立陶宛、拉脱维亚等中东欧国家间存在的旅游资源同质化问题，更重要的是还可以减少同类项目的重复建设，可在一定程度上降低国际旅游成本，提高旅游产品性价比，减少甚至避免白俄罗斯与邻国之间的恶性竞争，进而推动地区经济合作深化。

再次，引入第三方支付平台，推广互联网支付，实现旅游消费支付的便利化。旅游是一个集食、住、行、娱乐于一体的综合性经济活动，消费支付是其中最重要的一个环节。目前，虽然银联国际已于 2017 年与白俄罗斯最大的商业银行白俄罗斯银行签署全面合作协议，并且白俄罗斯银行在当年就实现了旗下全部自动取款机和商户受理银联卡业务，但是服务范围依然有限，并且对于早已习惯手机支付的中国消费者来说，无法满足消费支付的便利化需求。在中白开展旅游合作时可加强金融领域，特别是互联网支付方面的协作，将支付宝、微信支付等第三方支付平台引入白俄罗斯，推广更为便利的移动支付方式，间接激发游客的消费力。

最后，注重市场推广，采取新媒体以及热门电视秀等新途径推介彼此的旅游产品。中国和白俄罗斯各自的旅游产品在彼此的旅游市场中均较缺乏吸引力和竞争力。一方面是旅游产品不适应市场需求所致；另一方面也是最直接的原因则是产品宣传途径相对传统、力度不足且形式没有针对性，使潜在的消费者对产品缺乏认知和了解。对此，可以更多地尝试采用互联网、手机应用软件等新媒体对彼此的旅游产品进行推介。同时，还可以利用热门综艺秀、影视剧来让中白两国潜在旅游产品消费者对彼此的文化、景点有一个初步的了解，带动旅游产品消费。

"一带一路"倡议背景下中白社会体育人文合作与展望

方正威

白俄罗斯科学院哲学研究所博士

一 白俄罗斯与中国体育文化交流的意义

随着中国与白俄罗斯经济、文化交流的全面开展，如何进行下一步的交流与发展是一个重要的问题。社会体育活动作为文化交流的一部分，是可以回答这一问题的。

社会体育文化活动是多种交流的载体，它不仅是思想文化的交流，更是国家经济发展、社会思想等方面的交流与展示，这种特殊的载体，使得体育文化交流在中国的对外交流中占有重要的地位。

可以说，现代国家之间，除了正常的政治经济交流，最主要的就是体育文化交流，而且以奥运会及其他锦标赛为基础，正是这种交流形式促进了国家之间的了解与合作。所以，体育文化交流对于白俄罗斯与中国有着重大的意义。[1]

---

[1] 俞大伟、袁雷、朱景宏：《20世纪80年代中国体育外交的回顾与启示》，《南京体育学院学报》2017年第1期，第24—28页。

二 白俄罗斯与中国体育文化交流历程

白俄罗斯与中国的体育文化交流在两国建交之初就已经开始。1991年8月25日,白俄罗斯宣布独立,中国是首批承认白俄罗斯的国家之一。1992年1月19日至24日,时任白俄罗斯部长会议主席(政府总理)克比奇对中国进行正式访问。1月20日,两国正式建交。

1993年1月,时任白俄罗斯最高苏维埃主席舒什克维奇对中国进行正式访问,双方签署中白联合声明等文件。这是白俄罗斯国家元首第一次访华。

1995年1月,白俄罗斯总统卢卡申科对中国进行正式访问。中国是卢卡申科当选总统后出访的除原苏联地区以外的第一个国家。在同年的6月,时任国务院总理李鹏对白俄罗斯进行正式访问。在这两次两国国家领导人会见的同时,两国声明,表示将进一步加强中国与白俄罗斯在体育人文等方面的合作。

2001年4月,白俄罗斯总统卢卡申科对中国进行国事访问。两国国家领导人签署了《中白联合声明》。两国还签署了《中白政府关于保护知识产权的协定》《中国人民银行与白俄罗斯国民银行合作协议》《中白司法部合作协议》等文件。同年7月,时任中国国家主席江泽民对白俄罗斯进行国事访问。这是中国国家元首首次访问白俄罗斯。通过一系列的文件的签署,表明两国在经济、政治、科技、体育、人文等方面有明确的发展方向。

在2005年12月,白俄罗斯总统卢卡申科对中国进行国事访问。访华期间,两国元首共同签署了《中华人民共和国和白俄罗斯共和国联合声明》,宣布中白关系进入全面发展和战略合作的新阶段。两国元首还出席了两国经济技术合作等方面12项文件的签字仪式。同年两国签署两国工作会议议定书,表明中白双方同意继续与各国体育管理机构负责人举行定期会议和磋商以协调联合行动的做法。不久之后,时任中国国家体育总局局长、中国奥委会主席刘鹏会见了来华访问的白俄罗斯体育及旅游部长格利高罗夫一行,双方就加强两国间的体育交流与合作进行了会谈。通过这些会议的举行,再次表明中国重视与白俄罗斯发展友好体育合作关系，两国将进一步加强体育交流与合作，共同提高两国运动水平，促进两国运动员和人民之间的相互了解和友谊。

2007年11月，时任国务院总理温家宝对白俄罗斯进行正式访问。访问期间，双方签署了一系列双边合作文件。再次申明两国对于在政治、经济、科学、社会、体育人文等方面的展望。并且在此次访问中，对白俄罗斯派运动员参加2008年北京奥运会表示热情欢迎，并预祝白俄罗斯选手在北京奥运会上取得好成绩。

2008年7月2日，白俄罗斯国家奥委会和白俄罗斯体育记者协会在明斯克举行仪式，向白俄罗斯体育记者颁发采访北京奥运会的资格证书。白总统助理阿列克谢延科说，白俄罗斯人民将通过白新闻记者的报道了解北京奥运会的盛况，希望33名白方赴华记者客观、全面、深入地报道北京奥运会。格里戈罗夫部长说，白体育代表团约200名运动员将参加北京奥运会的26项比赛。这是1991年独立以来白俄罗斯参加奥运会人数最多、参加比赛项目最多的一次。希望记者们能忠实履行职责，将最精彩的比赛和东道国的社会生活全貌奉献给白俄罗斯观众。

2010年3月，时任中国国家副主席习近平对白俄罗斯进行正式访问。同年10月，白俄罗斯总统卢卡申科来华出席上海世博会，参加白俄罗斯国家馆日并进行访华活动。在活动中，双方国家领导人多次重申两国之间的友谊，并指出将进一步加强两国在社会人文等方面的交流与发展。

2017年6月，应白俄罗斯拳击协会邀请，中国拳击队派出6名女子选手出访参赛，并获得佳绩。通过此次实战热身，中国队女子选手验证了此前的专项训练效果，也发现了相应的不足与问题。

2017年11月，明斯克首届国际电竞锦标赛在白俄罗斯首都明斯克举办，布列斯特迪纳摩足球俱乐部在白俄罗斯电竞协会的支持下，举行多项国际电子竞技比赛。中国派出五个队伍参加这次比赛，同时中国的多个直播平台对这次比赛进行了全方位的直播。

2018年1月，第十四届白俄罗斯总统杯圣诞冰球锦标赛如期于白俄罗斯首都明斯克盛大开幕。这是白俄罗斯一年一度的国际性冰球传统盛会。白俄罗斯代表队由总统卢卡申科亲自领衔，历届参赛队伍大多来自欧洲及北美洲的冰球强国。白俄罗斯总统办公室及白俄罗斯冰球协会通过中国国际文化传播中心邀请其旗下的昆仑鸿星国家冰球俱乐部代表中国组队前往参加本次锦标赛。

2018年7月,白俄罗斯体育与旅游部部长谢尔盖·科瓦利丘克在明斯克举行的重庆文化和体育日活动的开幕式上表示,白俄罗斯和中国积极发展体育合作,并按照两国元首确定的合作方向,进一步建立两国间互信关系。

2019年"欧洲孔子学院杯"白俄罗斯国际武术公开赛在白国立体育大学正式开幕,这一赛事由白俄罗斯武术发展中心、白武术协会和白国立体育大学孔子课堂联合举办,共吸引了来自白俄罗斯、俄罗斯、乌克兰、拉脱维亚、波兰、意大利和中国的600多名运动员及体育爱好者参加。比赛分为武术套路和散打两大部分。武术公开赛期间活动主办方还将举办中国茶艺、书法及汉语推广等文化体验活动。

2019年4月25日,在第二届"一带一路"国际合作高峰论坛期间,国家主席习近平在人民大会堂会见白俄罗斯总统卢卡申科,并为援白俄罗斯国家足球体育场及国际标准游泳馆项目模型揭幕。仪式上,习近平主席与卢卡申科总统对模型进行了交流,并称赞方案具有白俄特色的设计理念。白俄罗斯国家足球体育场位于首都明斯克市中心地带,占地12.43公顷,总建筑面积4.8万平方米,总容量3.3万座。该项目不仅填补了中国专业足球体育场设计的空白,还开创了国内设计机构完整设计一座地处欧洲的欧足联标准体育场的先河,对中国体育建筑设计来讲都将是一个里程碑式的项目。

三 现代国际社会体育文化交流的重要性

当今世界,体育文化活动已经成为社会发展和人类文明进步的重要标志,在国际社会扮演着越来越重要的角色,发挥着越来越重要的作用。同时体育文化交流也是当代国际关系和文化交流的重要内容,是传播和平与友谊的使者,是化解矛盾与争端的重要方法。在一定的条件下,体育文化活动特别是竞技体育可以超越国家政治,实现公平竞争,因此也最容易打破界限,超越制度、信仰、观念的差异而进行交流合作。它对双方的和解有着积极推动作用,尤其是在竞技体育面向世界的今天,这种作用尤为明显。而造成这一结果的原因,正是体育文化活动的自身特性。

体育文化活动与其他文化活动是相互结合与共同发展的。首先，体育文化活动与教育相互结合，可以弥补教育教学的不足。在体育活动中的体能锻炼、组织纪律、竞争合作等实践活动能对人体身心和谐、社会适应、理想道德、意志品质等多个方面起着塑造、完善的作用，这些是其他教育方式和途径无法替代和弥补的。其次，体育活动与艺术活动相互结合，使静态与动态的美融合展现。由于体育活动具有动感美、人体美等，使得体育活动极具观赏性。而体育活动与艺术的结合还可从体育场馆等方面得到展现，北京奥运会所建鸟巢、水立方等是建筑艺术的珍品，中国援助建设的白俄罗斯国家体育足球场更是这一珍品的完美体现，有展现出超越政治的白俄罗斯与中国国家友谊。这些都说明，通过体育这一载体，艺术的表达更加丰富和全面，同时通过这种结合与现代科技的融入，关于体育活动的新闻报道、赛事直播、电影艺术等，使体育文化的交流更加直接和具有吸引力。人们通过这些内容丰富的文化形式，直接或间接地了解了彼此文化的内涵、特点和价值取向，缩小隔阂，从而达到文化交流的目的。[①]

首先，体育文化活动容易被社会大众接受，因为肢体语言是最简单与最直观的表现形式，而这种表现形式没有过多的其他因素影响，通过一定的传播与交流途径，对这种变现形式有所了解的人，都会接受并认可这种形式，这正是体育文化活动的重要特点。其次，现代社会的发展使得体育文化活动更容易被人接受与认可，在物质科技发达的现在社会中，体育所传达的精神思想是共同存在于每一个人的思想中的，休闲体育活动中，对身心健康的向往，对人与人之间情感交流的向往，对休闲舒适生活的向往是每个人的普遍需求；而竞技体育中，对人体极限的追求，对获胜目标的追求，在比赛中人性的表现，也是每个人都能感受到和接受的。而大众体育活动简单的活动规则与动作要求，和现代社会体育场地及器械的普及程度，使得每一个人都能参与到社会体育文化活动中去；对于竞技体育的赛事报到，电视直播等方式，也使得每一个人都

[①] 张海利、刘晓海、张海军：《论体育是中国文化对外交流的重要载体》，《体育文化导刊》2018年第10期，第11—14页。

能关注到这种体育形式，通过观赏体育运动促使自己精神的愉悦，从而加入到这种运动形式中。而信息技术的发达，更使得国家与国家之间，文化与文化之间，不再出现隔阂，都可以进行相同的观赏与参与。这些，使现代体育文化活动更加容易融入社会生活当中，也使体育文化活动可以作为一种文化交流的手段。

体育文化活动是不同文化特性的表达。也正是因为这一点，体育文化活动的交流，是对国际交流的重要补充与先行者。由于自然环境与国家历史等特点，造就不同的国家与社会，形成不同的文化与体育活动。更重要的在于，对于体育文化的精神内核不同的理解与发展，是东西方文化交流中的一个重要方面，对待休闲体育与竞技体育的不同态度，对待国家体育及社会体育的不同政策，都与每个国家及每个民族的自身特点有关系。体育文化活动交流与发展，正是了解这些不同的桥梁与纽带，而了解这些，也是为了促进发展国家及民族文化，更好地开展国际交流活动。当今国际的一大趋势是多元化的共同发展，民族的文化及体育活动也成为国际交流的一种趋势。这是因为，通过这些非奥运会项目，民族体育文化活动更能使得国家与社会大众之间相互了解与融合。在白俄罗斯明斯克多次举行的中国传统体育文化活动，以及十分重要的"欧洲孔子学院杯"白俄罗斯武术公开赛，都说明体育文化活动作为对外交流的一种手段，是先于政治及经济交流存在的。通过举办这种体育文化交流活动及比赛，首先激发社会大众的求知兴趣，对之后开展的社会文化交流有着积极的导向作用。也正是体育文化交流的存在，使得国家与国家之间，在此基础上进行更加完善的政治经济交流与合作。

体育文化活动是当前国家发展的重要展现，文化是社会的产物，而体育文化更是当前社会及经济发展的重要产物。通过对体育文化活动的开展与表现，能更好地了解国家在政治及经济方面的发展方向。现代的中国在政治与经济全面发展的同时，也在加快对体育产业、联赛制度、体育教育、社会体育等方面的完善与发展。中国在1994年开始足球职业联赛改革。2016年，中国国家体育总局关于体育发展"十三五"规划正式出台，标志着我国由体育大国向体育强国进发进入具体实施阶段，也是中国体育重点由竞技体育向学校体育和群众体育转变的开始。而在体育产业方面，中国向体育科学技术、体育文化等方向发展，在场馆建设、体育器械、赛事举办等方面取得全面的发展与成功。这些都是今后国际间体育文化交流的重要方向，也是国家间经济合作与发展的重要方向。

四　白俄罗斯与中国体育文化交流展望

首先，针对白俄罗斯与中国体育文化交流的现状，希望能进一步巩固和加强两国之间的体育交流，不断扩大两国体育文化领域的交流范围和交流群体。继续在白俄罗斯与中国体育合作框架协议的基础上加强沟通和联系，加大两国高校体育教育、体育科学研究的交流，加强友好城市的体育文化活动交流，扩大青少年体育文化活动交流范围，在此基础上促进两国的政治经济交流。[①]

其次，希望加强白俄罗斯与中国之间在竞技体育方面的合作与交流。之前通过白俄罗斯对中国在拳击、冰球等项目的邀请赛等方式，使中国认识到在当今全面的体育项目中自身的不足，为了弥补和加强竞技体育的发展，十分有必要开展白俄罗斯与中国的合作与交流。

最后，希望加强白俄罗斯与中国在体育文化活动之外的交流与合作。在体育信息媒体方面的合作，促进和加强两国体育新闻信息的共享，媒体报道信息的相互沟通，在此基础形成良好的社会舆论。在体育产业及体育衍生经济方面，也存在极大的交流与合作空间，通过两国间在场馆建设方面的合作与体育赛事举办等形式，可以进一步促进交流。这些交流与合作的出现与发展，对白俄罗斯与中国在当今国际社会中政治与经济地位有重要的影响，也是国家之间友好双赢的最佳表现。

---

① 韩小兰：《中俄体育交流研究》，《体育文化导刊》2014年第8期，第12—15页。

中国人才发展与治理新格局

戈艳霞
中国社会科学院社会发展战略研究院副研究员

改革开放四十多年来，中国人力资源素质和质量显著提高，进入人才发展新格局的时代。初步形成全国一盘棋的人才工作战略体系，提高人才政策与产业、经济社会发展战略规划的精准对接；强化区域比较优势理念；加强地区间高效协同、开放共享、互利共赢的人才合作关系。树立既立足国内又放眼全球的招才引智理念。

人才是驱动创新的第一资源。[1] 从党的十八大提出"广开进贤之路，广纳天下英才"到党的十九大确立"人才强国战略"，以习近平同志为核心的党中央持续释放加强人才工作的强劲信号。[2]

近年来，在劳动力供给减少和产业转型升级压力下，吸引和留住人才已经成为提升城市核心竞争力的关键所在。当前中国各大城市都加强了对人才的重视程度。各级各地政府都提出将人才作为科学发展最宝贵的资源，把人才的引进、培养作为各自工作的重要抓手，充分体现出各地政府对人才工作前所未有的高度重视。

单看2018年，至少有35个城市发布了40多次人才引进政策。众多城市出台的人才优惠政策都极具吸引力。例如，天津出台了"海河英才"

---

[1] 中共中央文献研究室（编）：《习近平关于科技创新论述摘编》，中央文献出版社2016年版。

[2] 程祥：《识才聚才用才——习近平开创人才工作新风》，人民网，2018年7月17日，http://politics.people.com.cn/n1/2018/0717/c100130152708.html。

行动计划，40 周岁以下本科毕业生即可直接落户，全年引进约 13 万人。①成都自 2017 年发布《成都实施人才优先发展战略行动计划》，宣布本科及以上学历青年人才凭毕业证即可办理落户手续，并对毕业 5 年内在蓉创业的大学生给予最高 50 万元、最长 3 年贷款期限和全额贴息支持，吸引了 13 万名本科以上人才来蓉落户发展。②武汉自 2017 年启动"百万大学生留汉创业就业计划"，大学毕业生凭学历即可落户武汉，有 70 多万名大学毕业生留在武汉创业、就业。③西安在 2018 年提出"面向全国在校大学生仅凭学生证和身份证即可在线落户"的举措，单日落户最高达 8050 人，全年新落户人数已经突破 30 万人。④无论东部一线城市，还是中西部二三线城市，都大幅降低落户门槛，并给予住房补贴或奖金津贴等优惠政策吸引人才，形成了人才发展新格局，随着改革开放格局的进一步加深，中国的人才引进也将呈现进一步扩大的趋势。

一 中国人才发展新格局出现的背景原因

(一) 经济发展模式转变、产业转型升级催生对人才的强劲需要

近代以来世界科学技术发展史表明，人才对于国家科技创新和经济社会发展具有极端重要性。党的十八大以来，党中央要求中国经济实现转型升级，其实现路径就是科技创新及其全方位的创新驱动。而创新驱动最核心的资源是人力资源，特别是高层次人才资源。党的十九大提出要实现经济从高速增长向高质量增长发展的目标，进一步强化了各地人才要新发展、要新增长的意识。

(二) 党的十八大以来地方主政官员自身强烈的求才意识

正如习近平总书记多次强调的，中国现在比历史上任何时期都更加需要人才。而真正有深切的认知、行动上采取务实重视人才举措的就是

---

① 数据来自天津市人民政府《2019 年天津市政府工作报告》，2019 年 1 月 14 日。
② 数据来自四川新闻网《出台人才新政十二条 成都去年吸引 13 万余名本科以上人才落户发展》，2018 年 2 月 25 日。
③ 数据来自武汉市人民政府《我市为武汉高校大学生发放市民卡》，2018 年 9 月 30 日。
④ 数据来自陕西省统计局《2018 年陕西省常住人口发展概况》，2019 年 5 月 15 日。

目前当政的各级官员，因为他们绝大多数都在改革开放后接受过高等教育，对知识有着本能的渴望，对人才的重要性有着真切的认识和认同。所以他们必然更加重视人才，对大学生自然有着特殊的认同感。

（三）城市发展质量提升的必然要求

改革开放以来，中国城市体量规模取得了长足的发展，而党的十八大以来城市发展的重心开始转向质量型效益型提升。城市发展已经不仅仅是简单的城市体量、单一的经济规模的粗放式扩大，更要求产业聚集、创新能力、高新科技、人口素质等内涵式特质化的发展。而这一切城市发展质量的综合提升都离不开人才的支撑与引领，从而进一步催化了城市及城市管理者对人才的极度渴求。

（四）二线城市向新一线城市晋级出位的需要

国家统计局数据显示，继天津、重庆、苏州后，2014—2017年杭州、成都、武汉、南京、青岛、长沙、无锡等二线城市经济总量相继进入"万亿俱乐部"[①]，经济增速长期高于全国平均水平，有望晋级为新一线城市。因此，这些二线城市有加快发展速度的强烈需求，同时也具备了招揽天下英才的实力。以杭州市为例，2017年常住人口比上一年增长了28万，创下历史新高。2017年国家确定的"国家中心城市"名单中，除了之前的北京、天津、上海、广州、重庆，新增加了杭州、成都、武汉、南京、郑州、青岛、西安等城市。这无疑加速了这些城市的再发展动力和相互竞争压力。

二　中国人才发展新格局的影响

在贯彻落实习近平总书记人才观要求和党的十九大精神的过程中，中国一些地方政府纷纷出台了各自人才引进的相关政策。

人才引进对提升创新能力、推动社会经济发展具有重要贡献作用。人才的来源既可以是本土人才，也可以是国际人才。在美国、德国等科

---

① 数据来自国家统计局出版的《2014—2017年中国统计年鉴》。

创强国，国际人才在人才引进中都占有非常重要的比重。《世界移民报告2018》数据显示，美国截至 2015 年引进的人才和其他移民总数约 4600 万人；[①] 德国截至 2018 年外来移民人数约 1350 万人。[②] 而《2013 国际移民报告》显示，居住在中国境内的外籍人员仅 84.85 万人，占总人口的 0.06%，基本上为全世界最低水平，远低于发达国家和地区的平均水平 10.8%，低于世界平均水平 3.2%。[③]

人力资本流动理论认为，人力资本流动是迅速增加人力资本投资的方式之一。在开放的市场经济条件下，人才的价值实现是通过市场机制进行流动配置的。人才通过流动获得良好的就业机会、更多的经济收益，以及非金钱性的满足。人才的培养不仅需要付出个人成本，而且需要投入社会成本。其中，个人成本是指由个人或家庭承担的教育费用等，而社会成本是指由全社会承担的教育公共设施费用等。

国际国内大城市的发展经验表明，一个城市要想吸引人才、留住人才，首先要解决好就业机会、生活质量和公共服务供给的问题。[④] 高素质劳动者和技能人才都是中国特色社会主义建设急需的人才。[⑤] 无论全国层面还是地方层面，人才需求都是多元化的，我们必须提倡多元化的人才观，最大限度地激发全国各个民族、各个阶层、各个方面的人才，为实现中华民族伟大复兴的中国梦汇聚成磅礴力量。

三 全面构建中国人才发展新格局

根据"科学、高效、精简"的原则，建立健全"效率优先，兼顾公平"的新型人才制度，加强人才的宏观调控，完善人才福利政策，促进效能提升。

[①] 数据来自《世界移民报告 2018》。
[②] 数据来自德国联邦统计局 2019 年 8 月公布的数据。
[③] 数据来自《中国国际移民报告（2015）》。
[④] Shari Garmise, *People and the Competitive Advantage of Place: Builiing a Workforce for the 21st Century*, New York: Routledge, 2006.
[⑤] 本书编写组编：《聚天下英才而用之——学习习近平关于人才工作重要论述的体会》，中国社会科学出版社 2017 年版，第 34 页。

构建全国一体化的人才工作体系。人才资源是国家发展的重要资源，人才政策的制定与实施必须始终坚持由中央统筹的基本原则，自觉践行习近平新时代中国特色社会主义思想的人才观，从"五位一体"总体布局、"四个全面"战略布局和实现"三步走"战略目标的高度谋划人才工作的方向和任务；必须始终坚持党管人才原则，聚天下英才而用之，加快建设人才强国；必须深刻理解"人才是第一资源"和"创新驱动实质上是人才驱动"的科学内涵和重大意义；必须构建全国一体化的人才工作战略体系，强化顶层设计和系统谋划，明确人才工作的总体思路。

提高人才政策与产业、经济社会发展战略规划的精准对接。人才是第一资源，是国家社会经济发展急需的稀缺性资源，因此在人才的使用上要着力提高精准性，避免人才资源错配带来的浪费问题。建议从"五位一体"总体布局、"四个全面"战略布局和实现"三步走"战略目标的高度谋划人才政策的制定原则，实现人才政策与区域发展战略规划的精准对接，促进人才资源发挥更加高效的作用。[①] 党的十九大提出的"七大战略"，各自有不同的区域性、产业性。而每一个战略的有效实施，都必然要有相匹配的人才资源支撑。比如粤港澳大湾区战略格局中需要的人才一定与京津冀一体化战略中的有所不同。因此，制定战略与制定人才政策时分别要有相应的考虑，无论中央政府还是地方政府，都要有战略谋划与战略实施的人才精准匹配对接理念。如果只有战略没有人才支撑的安排，那这种战略不仅难以实现而且难以持续。

充分发挥市场在人才配置中的作用，促进人才顺畅有序流动。市场是人才流动的主渠道，完善市场机制是确保人才顺畅有序流动的重要基础。我们应该充分尊重市场经济的发展规律和人才培养流动的规律，充分发挥市场在人才配置中的作用。认真落实中央《关于深化人才发展体制机制改革的意见》的决策部署，围绕实施人才强国战略和创新驱动发展战略，健全人才流动市场机制，规范人才流动秩序、完善人才流动服务体系，激活市场机制，破除妨碍人才流动的制度藩篱和其他各类障碍，不断促进人才顺畅有序流动、激发人才创新创业创造活力。

---

① 马子量：《西北地区产业集聚与城市人口集聚：交互协同及地理耦合——基于演化视角的空间统计分析》，《西南民族大学学报》（人文社科版）2016年第5期。

加强地区之间高效协同、开放共享、互利共赢的人才合作关系。不均衡发展是中国经济社会较长时间面临的问题，也是党的十九大系列重大判断中的一条。地方政府首先要牢固树立"四个意识"，深入贯彻落实《中共中央办公厅关于鼓励引导人才向艰苦边远地区和基层一线流动的意见》，加强对艰苦边远地区和基层一线的人才帮扶项目，促进地区之间高效协同、开放共享、互利共赢的人才合作关系，推进地区之间经济社会的协调发展。

强化区域比较优势理念。党的十八大以来，党中央特别注重区域经济一体化和地区经济发展优势。因此有关地方的产业发展、社会经济发展规划和人才规划都要坚持因地制宜的原则。按照党中央对各地的发展定位制定相适应的人才政策，实施与地方条件相匹配的吸引人才举措，促进各地产业与人才配置效率的提升，从而在全国层面上实现人才的最优配置效率。

招才引智既立足国内也要放眼全球。40多年来，中国经济发展之所以取得举世瞩目的成就，开放是前提条件。搞经济建设要打开国门，人才工作也要打开国门，广开门路招揽天下英才。人才工作既要立足于国内，也要有放眼全球的意识。全球化时代的一个特点必然是资源的全球化，对作为第一资源的人才，中国也应该从全球去审视。

在制订地方人才政策和实施人才工作中要深入贯彻落实"精准"理念。因为不同的地区、不同的城市在不同的发展阶段需要不同的人才，只有贯彻这一思想，才能实现人才精准，达到产业精准、事业发展精准的目标，否则就会造成低层次、同质化、碎片化的城市竞争，以及人才资源的闲置浪费和错配低效。

在制定地方人才政策和实施人才工作中要树立分层、分类、分步的理念和方法论。一个城市对人才的需要必然有高中低不同层次；对人才需要也分不同领域和不同产业；对人才的需要还会因发展进程不同而分不同阶段；因此必须树立这种差异化的意识，只有这样才会避免由于盲目引进而造成的户口、编制等资源的浪费，才会避免由于一哄而起地引进人才造成城市管理上的新短板、新问题。

在制订地方人才政策和实施人才工作中要放眼地区长期发展规划。中国各地在人才政策的制定与实施中可以从中借鉴经验，掌握产业发展的特点与规律，把营造产业链、生态链作为人才政策制定与实施的有机目标，因而使得政策制定具有一定的关联性和周期性。

要落实"尊重知识，尊重人才"的方针政策，积极实施科教兴国和人才发展战略，营造"尊重人才、尊重知识"的社会氛围，逐步提高人才待遇，改善其工作生活条件，促使其才智得到充分释放。针对艰苦边远地区和基层一线人才匮乏的难题，必须从制度上破解当前人才流动的难题，实施好对艰苦边远地区和基层一线的人才支持项目，健全人才帮扶协作机制，积极创造条件培养、吸引、用好各方面人才，为实现中华民族的伟大复兴打好人才基础。

Modernization of Governance and All-round Development of People

China's Population Changes and Future Governance Policy Framework

Zhang Yi

Director and Professor of National Institute of Social Development, CASS

Due to its huge base, China's population, which has long accounted for about 20%–25% of the world's total throughout history, has maintained an upward trend since the Opium War despite of the disturbance caused by wars. The founding of the People's Republic of China in 1949 marked an end to wars. Since then, peasants had access to arable land, workers had access to employment opportunities, and the general public had access to food and clothing, which paved the way for rapid population growth. While the improved medical and health conditions and effective control of infectious diseases made it possible to massively eliminate digestive diseases and respiratory diseases, and to reduce the mortality rate amid the rapid increase in the birth rate, thus creating a condition for "population explosion".

Ⅰ. Population Changes from 1949 to 1957

During the early years of the People's Republic of China, the foundation of the national economy was weak. However, due to the establishment of grassroots governments, the stable prices, and the reform of rural and urban economic systems, new vitality was injected into Chinese society. With the advancement of the land reform, poor peasants who had no or little land were allocated land. Under the guidance of the "Party's general line for the transition period"①, the primary agricultural cooperatives (pooling of land as shares) and advanced agricultural cooperatives (public ownership of land) were established based on mutual aid groups, marking the completion of the socialist transformation of agriculture, and transformation from a small-scale peasant economy involving more than 500 million peasants to a socialist collective ownership economy. ②Meanwhile, a series of reforms were conducted in cities, to confiscate bureaucratic capital to establish a state-operated economy, protect national industry and commerce, stabilize employment, abolish the feudal butler system, as well as establish trade unions, youth and women's organizations in enterprises so as to protect the basic rights and interests of workers and to improve the income of residents. The subsequent agricultural cooperative movements advanced the socialist transformation of handicrafts and capitalist industry and commerce. The transformation of rural and urban economic ownership led to fundamental changes in the structure and nature of China's social economy. The basic completion of the socialist transformation laid

---

① At the outreach session of the Political Bureau of the CPC Central Committee on June 15, 1953, Chairman Mao Zedong laid down the "Party's general line for the transition period", which was later formally expressed as: "The period from the founding of the People's Republic of China to the completion of socialist transformation is a transition period, during which, the Party's general line and general task is to gradually achieve the socialist industrialization of the country, and gradually complete the socialist transformation of agriculture, handicrafts and capitalist industry and commerce over a fairly long period of time". This general line, abbreviated as "one industrialization, three transformations" or "one body, two wings" was approved at the the fourth plenary session of the seventh CPC Central Committee in February 1954.

② As at the end of the year 1956, the number of peasants joining the agricultural cooperatives accounted for 96.3% of the total number in the country, of which, 87.8% joined the advanced agricultural cooperatives. This means that the agricultural cooperation, which was expected to be completed in 18 years, was completed at an accelerated speed in just seven years. Of course, there were also dissatisfactions among some peasants.

the economic foundation for the convening of the 8th National Congress of the CPC in 1956, at which, it was pointed out that "the principal contradiction in our country is already the contradiction between the people's requirements for the establishment of an advanced industrial country and a backward agricultural country, and the contradiction resulted from the need of the people for rapid economic and cultural development which fell short of their requirements". The new distribution policy brought out by the new institutional structure improved people's livelihood, so the overall fertility rate increased.

Table 1 Birth Rate, Mortality Rate and Natural Growth Rate of the Population During the Early Years of the People's Republic of China

Unit:‰

Year	Nationwide Birth rate	Nationwide Mortality rate	Nationwide Natural growth rate	Town Birth rate	Town Mortality rate	Town Natural growth rate	County Birth rate	County Mortality rate	County Natural growth rate
1949	36.00	20.00	16.00	—	—	—	—	—	—
1950	37.00	18.00	19.00	—	—	—	—	—	—
1951	37.80	17.80	20.00	—	—	—	—	—	—
1952	37.00	17.00	20.00	—	—	—	—	—	—
1953	37.00	14.00	23.00	—	—	—	—	—	—
1954	37.97	13.18	24.79	42.45	8.07	34.38	37.51	13.71	23.80
1955	32.60	12.28	20.32	40.67	9.30	31.37	31.74	12.60	19.14
1956	31.90	11.40	20.50	37.87	7.43	30.44	31.25	11.84	19.40
1957	34.03	10.80	23.23	44.48	8.47	36.01	32.81	11.07	21.74

Source: *China Statistical Yearbook 1987*, China Statistics Press, 1987, p. 90.

Table 1 shows that although the birth rate in 1949 was as high as 36‰, due to the high mortality rate of 20‰ in the same year, the natural growth rate still had a lower level of only 16‰. During the period from 1950 to 1954, the birth rate stabilized at around 37‰, while the mortality rate dropped from 18‰ in 1950 to 13.18‰ in 1954, so the natural growth rate rose from 19‰ to 24.79‰. Currently there are no data about the birth rate, mortality rate, and natural growth rate of the rural and urban populations before the year

1953. However, data in 1954 showed that during this period, cities and towns had a much higher birth rate and a much lower mortality rate than rural areas, suggesting a faster population growth in cities and towns than in rural areas. For instance, in 1954, the natural growth rate in cities and towns was as high as 34.38‰, while that in rural areas was only 23.80‰. In 1955, the natural growth rate was 31.37‰ in cities and towns and 19.14‰ in rural areas, suggesting that the post-war compensatory childbearing faded. Why did the population grow so rapidly? There are several reasons.

Firstly, a birth encouraging policy was introduced to meet people's need to lead a stable and peaceful life after war. Following the founding of the People's Republic of China, peasants had access to land and employment, so they had a strong desire to get married and have children.

Secondly, people married young. Although the *Marriage Law of the People's Republic of China* promulgated on May 1, 1950 stipulated that the legal age for marriage was 18 for women and 20 for men, it took time for the marriage law to become binding upon the parties to marriage. In fact, early marriage still existed in rural areas at that time, for both men and women. ①

Thirdly, the medical, health and epidemic prevention systems were established, which resulted in a quick decrease in the mortality rate of infants and young children, and an increase in the survival rate of the newborn population.

According to the first census conducted in 1953, the total population of the Chinese mainland was 594 million, which was largely different from the number of 480 million frequently cited in 1949. In fact, the total population in 1950 was

---

① According to the *Sample Survey on the Fertility Rate of One-thousandth Population Nationwide* organized by the former National Health and Family Planning Commission in 1982, the average age of women at first marriage rose from 18.57 in 1949 to 19.57 in 1960, and to 23.05 in 1980. The age declined slightly to 22.82 in 1981. According to the finding of Wang Yuesheng from data about the fifth census, among the people who got married during the period from 1950 to 1954, 30% of men and 25% of women got married below the legal marriage age. Wang Yuesheng, "The First Marriage of People Below the Age Prescribed by Laws and Policies", *Chinese Journal of Population Science*, Issue 6, 2005.

finally determined to be 550 million using the deduction method and based on the census data and the annual birth rate. ①China's total population reached 610 million in 1955 after a few years of growth.

The birth rate of China's population decreased to 32.60‰ in 1955, to 31.90‰ in 1956, and to 34.03‰ in 1957. The comparison between cities and towns and rural areas shows that cities and towns had a higher birth rate and a higher natural growth rate over a long period of time.

From 1949 to 1957, this period was characterized by restorative childbirth. Thanks to the better living, medical and health conditions, the growth rate of population in cities and towns was greater than that in rural areas.

II. Population Changes from 1958 to 1976

Seen from the overall growth trend of China's population, during the period from the 1960s to the mid to late 1970s, the population had been on a fast decline. Of course, from 1959 to 1961, the decline in China's population was mainly due to the declined growth rate of rural population (declined birth rate in counties). The "Great Leap Forward" movement and the "steel fever" occupied massive rural labor force. Table 2 shows that the population loss during these years was caused by the decreased birth rate and the increased mortality rate in counties. In 1960, the mortality rate dropped to 28.58‰, while the birth rate was only 19.35‰, resulting in a negative population growth rate of −9.23‰. After one-year gradual recovery, the population growth rate in counties in 1961 was only 2.41‰.

The year 1962 was a vital turning point in the history of China's population growth. Before this year, the birth rate and the natural growth rate in cities and

---

① In 1950, the Ministry of Internal Affairs announced that China's total population (including Taiwan) was about 480 million, while the figure announced by the Ministry of Finance was about 483 million. According to the opening speech given by Chairman Mao Zedong at the first session of the Chinese People's Political Consultative Conference, China's total population was 475 million.

towns were higher than those of counties, and after this year, the trend reversed. In 1962, the birth rate and the natural growth rate were 35.46‰ and 27.18‰ in cities and towns, and were 37.27‰ and 26.95‰ in counties. So the counties had a higher birth rate than cities and towns. After 1962, China saw a new round of compensatory childbearing, but the birth rate nationwide was declining. It dropped from 43.37‰ in 1963 to 19.91‰ in 1976. Therefore, from the decline in the birth rate to its subsequent increase caused by compensatory childbearing, and to its gradual decrease, China completed its historic demographic transition. In 1962, the CPC Central Committee and the State Council issued the *Instructions on Seriously Promoting Family Planning*; in 1971, the State Council forwarded the *Report on Implementing Family Planning* issued by the Military Control Commission of the Ministry of Health, the Ministry of Commerce, and the Ministry of Fuel and Chemical Industries to implement family planning and advocate late marriage and late childbirth.

In retrospect, the rapid population growth during the early days of this period was due to, on one hand, the rapid decline in the mortality rate, and on the other hand, the implementation of the "barefoot doctor" system, which controlled the spread of infectious diseases and gradually extended the average life expectancy of Chinese people. The population growth of China began to shift from the pattern of an agricultural society to that of an industrial society.

Table 2   Birth Rate, Mortality Rate and Natural Growth Rate from 1959 to 1976 in China   Unit:‰

Year	Nationwide Birth rate	Nationwide Mortality rate	Nationwide Natural growth rate	Town Birth rate	Town Mortality rate	Town Natural growth rate	County Birth rate	County Mortality rate	County Natural growth rate
1959	24.78	14.59	10.19	29.43	10.92	18.51	23.78	14.61	9.17
1960	20.86	25.43	-4.57	28.03	13.77	14.26	19.35	28.58	-9.23
1961	18.02	14.24	3.78	21.63	11.39	10.24	16.99	14.58	2.41

(Contd.)

Year	Nationwide Birth rate	Nationwide Mortality rate	Nationwide Natural growth rate	Town Birth rate	Town Mortality rate	Town Natural growth rate	County Birth rate	County Mortality rate	County Natural growth rate
1962	37.01	10.02	26.99	35.46	8.28	27.18	37.27	10.32	26.95
1963	43.37	10.04	33.33	33.33	7.13	37.37	43.19	10.49	32.70
1964	39.14	11.50	27.64	32.17	7.27	24.90	40.27	12.17	28.10
1965	37.88	9.50	28.38	26.59	5.69	20.90	39.53	10.06	29.47
1966	35.05	8.83	26.22	20.85	5.59	15.26	36.71	9.47	27.24
1967	33.96	8.43	25.53	—	—	—	—	—	—
1968	35.59	8.21	27.38	—	—	—	—	—	—
1969	34.11	8.03	26.08	—	—	—	—	—	—
1970	33.43	7.60	25.83	—	—	—	—	—	—
1971	30.65	7.32	23.33	21.3	5.35	15.95	31.86	7.57	24.29
1972	29.77	7.61	22.16	19.3	5.29	14.01	31.19	7.93	23.26
1973	27.93	7.04	20.89	17.35	4.96	12.39	29.36	7.33	22.03
1974	24.82	7.34	17.48	14.50	5.24	9.26	26.23	7.63	18.60
1975	23.01	7.32	15.69	14.71	5.39	9.32	24.17	7.59	16.58
1976	19.91	7.25	12.66	13.12	6.60	6.52	20.85	7.35	13.50

Source: *China Statistical Yearbook 1987*, China Statistics Press, 1987, p. 90.

The effective control over the population growth during the later days of this period was mainly contributed by the following factors.

Firstly, the grassroots organizations excised effective control. Under the "three-level" organizations in the grassroots society, i.e., the People's Commune, the production brigade and the production team, the population growth was effectively controlled through measures including the door-to-door visits.

Secondly, in the movement of "Chinese educated youth going and working in the countryside and the mountainous areas", a large number of young people of marriageable age in cities flowed to the countryside (involving 18 million to

30 million people in total) . ①This movement was initially intended to address the employment issue of urban youth, but later developed into a political movement. In this movement, some educated youths got married in the countryside, but most of them desired to get married after they got back to the city. This flow reduced the marriage rate and the fertility rate to some extent.

Thirdly, a late marriage and late childbirth policy was implemented. The "late marriage and late childbirth" policy broke the legal marriage age limit of 20 for men and 18 for women as described in the *Marriage Law* 1950. It encouraged young men and women to respond to the Party's and government's call to marry and give birth at a later time and devote themselves to socialist modernization. The actual age of marriage registration at that time was around 25 for men and 23 for women. In some places, a late marriage policy that the total age was around 50 was implemented for couples who had a great age difference. In municipalities such as Beijing, Shanghai and Tianjin, the age of marriage was even later.

Fourthly, the population control targets were proposed for the period of the 4th Five-Year Plan. The "4th Five-Year Plan" (1970 – 1975) clearly stated that efforts should be made to reduce the natural growth rate of urban population to around 10‰ and that of the rural population to around 15‰. It was the first time that the population control targets had been proposed in the official document of the government. At the first national family planning work report meeting held at the office of the Family Planning Leading Group under the State

---

① In 1953, the *People's Daily* published an editorial titled "Organizing Young College Graduates to Participate in Rural Work". In 1955, Chairman Mao Zedong made a remark that "The countryside is a vast world, where people can develop their skill to full." In 1966, the "Cultural Revolution" began, and the enrollment of colleges and universities suspended. In 1968, many high school graduates became idle as they could neither pursue higher education, nor were they able to find jobs in cities. In 1968, the *People's Daily* published an article titled "We also Have Two Hands, So We Should Not Stay Idle in Cities". In 1969, a greater number of educated youth moved to and settled down in the countryside. It was not until the end of the "Cultural Revolution" and resumption of the college entrance examination that they gradually returned to cities. The movement of Chinese educated youth going and working in the countryside and the mountainous areas came to an end after 1980.

Council, which was established in 1973, a birth policy promoting "late marriage, big birth spacing, and only two children" was proposed. In fact, by 1976, the population growth rate in cities and towns across the country had been reduced to 6.52‰, and that in counties had been reduced to 13.5‰, exceeding the planned targets.

III. Population Changes from 1978 to 2000

After the "Cultural Revolution" was over, China continued with its population control policy. In order to expedite economic development and reduce the negative impact of population growth on per capita indexes, the 5th Five-Year Plan proposed to reduce the natural growth rate of population in cities and towns to 6‰ and that in counties to 10‰. Since 1978, the government started to advocate couples to have one child, or at most, two children. ①The focus of the birth policy advocating "late marriage, big birth spacing, and only two children" as implemented during the "Cultural Revolution" was then shifted to "only two children".

Following the end of the "Cultural Revolution", three major events that had a profound impact on people's childbearing occurred one after another. One was the release of the new *Marriage Law of the People's Republic of China*, which was passed at the 3rd Session of the 5th National People's Congress in September 1980, and became effective on January 1, 1981. This law changed the legal age of marriage from the original 20 for men and 18 for women, to 22 for men and 20 for women. Although from a legal point of view, the legal age of marriage was postponed by the second marriage law, it was still earlier than the marriage age of 25 for men and 23 for women as advocated during the "Cultural Revolution" when the late marriage and late childbirth policy was implemented. The second was the implementation of the household contract

---

① See the "Report on the First Meeting of the Family Planning Leading Group under the State Council" endorsed by the central government in October, 1978.

responsibility system nationwide in 1982. Under the system, the collective farmland owned by original People's Communes, production brigades and production teams was contracted to households. This expanded peasants' autonomy in production and boosted social mobility. ①The third was the issuance of the *Notice on Separation of Governments from Social Organizations and Establishment of Township Government* by the CPC Central Committee and State Council in October 1983. According to the notice, governments were separated from social organizations, and the People's Communes were cancelled and replaced with township governments, and townships were defined as the rural grassroots administrative units. This led to weakened restraint of grassroots organizations.

Due to the implementation of the New Marriage Law, the number of couples getting married in China increased in the following years. The household contract responsibility system led to deconstruction of the rural grassroots production teams and production brigades, and stimulated the return of the traditional idea that families with more children were stronger and happier. In order to strengthen family planning, the Constitution amended in 1982 stated that "the state promotes family planning to enable the population growth to be compatible with the economic and social development plans" and "each couple has the obligation to implement family planning". At the 12th National Congress of the CPC, the family planning was defined as a basic state policy, and the *Instructions on Further Implementing Family Planning* was issued in the name of the CPC Central Committee and the State Council, reiterating that the population should be controlled within 1.2 billion by the end of the 20th century.

---

① The core of the "contracting production quotas to individual households" policy in rural reform was that "peasants may keep the rest grain for themselves after having submitting grain as a tax payment to the granary of the state and the collectives". This institutional reform boosted peasants' enthusiasm for production, which had long been suppressed by the "egalitarian practice of everyone taking food from the same big pot" and "egalitarianism", and solved the food problem that had plagued China for thousands of years.

Table 3 shows that the natural growth rate was 12‰ in 1978, 11.61‰ in 1979, and 11.87‰ in 1980. It surprisingly increased to 14.55‰ in 1981 when the family planning policy became a basic state policy. The rebound was seen in cities, towns and counties: the birth rate in counties was 21.55‰ in 1981 and 21.97‰ in 1982. The birth rate in cities and towns was 16.45‰ in 1981 and 18.24‰ in 1982. Thanks to the subsequent hard efforts, the birth rate in counties slightly decreased, but in 1986, it rebounded to 21.94‰ and that in cities and downs rebounded to 17.39‰.

In 1986, the total population control target by the end of this century (2000) was changed to around 1.2 billion. In 1987, it was changed to around 1.25 billion. In the implementation of the family planning policy, the work abide by the principles of "three un-changes" (that is, the overall responsibility for family planning remains unchanged in the hands of leaders of the Party and governments at all levels; the current family planning policy remains unchanged; and the established population control targets remain unchanged), "three priorities" (that is, in implementing the family planning policy, priorities should be given to publicity and education, contraception and regular work) and "three combines" (that is, to combine the family planning work with economic development, with the goal of helping peasants get rich through hard work, and the goal of building civilized and happy families).

Although the exploration of the "three priorities" system started in early 1980s, the system had not been satisfactorily implemented nationwide until around 2000. The family planning target was relaxed to around 1.25 billion in 1987, and was further relaxed to 1.3 billion. Through these institutional reforms, "two transformations" of the work mechanism were realized, i.e., transformation from focusing on family planning only to focusing on comprehensive management of population, and transformation from only utilizing social constraints, to combining social constraints with benefits while integrating publicity, education, comprehensive services and scientific management. With these efforts, the birth rate started to decline.

Table 3   The Birth Rate, Mortality Rate and Natural Growth Rate of China's Population   Unit: ‰

Year	Nationwide Birth rate	Nationwide Mortality rate	Nationwide Natural growth rate	Town Birth rate	Town Mortality rate	Town Natural growth rate	County Birth rate	County Mortality rate	County Natural growth rate
1977	18.93	6.87	12.06	13.38	5.51	7.87	19.70	7.06	12.64
1978	18.25	6.25	12.00	13.56	5.12	8.44	18.91	6.42	12.49
1979	17.82	6.21	11.61	13.67	5.07	8.60	18.43	6.39	12.04
1980	18.21	6.34	11.87	14.17	5.48	8.69	18.82	6.47	12.35
1981	20.91	6.36	14.55	16.45	5.14	11.31	21.55	6.53	15.02
1982	22.28	6.60	15.68	18.24	5.28	12.96	21.97	7.00	14.97
1983	20.19	6.90	13.29	15.99	5.92	10.07	19.89	7.69	12.20
1984	19.90	6.82	13.08	15.00	5.86	9.14	17.90	6.73	11.17
1985	21.04	6.78	14.26	14.02	5.96	8.06	19.17	6.66	12.51
1986	22.43	6.86	15.57	17.39	5.75	11.64	21.94	6.74	15.20
1987	23.33	6.72	16.61	—	—	—	—	—	—
1988	22.37	6.64	15.73	—	—	—	—	—	—
1989	21.58	6.54	15.04	16.73	5.78	10.95	23.27	6.81	16.46
1990	21.06	6.67	14.39	16.14	5.71	10.43	22.80	7.01	15.79
1991	19.68	6.70	12.98	15.49	5.50	9.99	21.17	7.13	14.04
1992	18.24	6.64	11.60	15.47	5.77	9.70	19.09	6.91	12.18
1993	18.09	6.64	11.45	15.37	5.99	9.38	19.06	6.89	12.17
1994	17.70	6.49	11.21	15.13	5.53	9.60	18.84	6.80	12.04
1995	17.12	6.57	10.55	14.76	5.53	9.23	18.08	6.99	11.09
1996	16.98	6.56	10.42	14.47	5.65	8.82	18.02	6.94	11.08
1997	16.57	6.51	10.06	14.52	5.58	8.94	17.43	6.90	10.53
1998	15.64	6.50	9.14	13.67	5.31	8.36	17.05	7.01	10.04
1999	14.64	6.46	8.18	13.18	5.51	7.76	16.13	6.88	9.25
2000	14.03	6.45	7.58	—	—	—	—	—	—

Note: Data about cities, towns and counties in 1987, 1988 and 2000 are not available.

Due to the hard work, the high birth rate, mortality rate and natural growth rate of China's population gradually declined. After 1990, the birth rate nationwide saw a consecutive decrease from 19.68‰ in 1991, to 18.24‰ in 1992, to 17.7‰ in 1994, to 16.98‰ in 1996, to 15.64‰ in 1998, and to 14.64‰ in 1999. Meanwhile, the natural growth rate of China's population also dropped to 11.6‰ in 1992, to 10.55‰ in 1995, to 9.14‰ in 1998, to 8.18‰ in 1999, and to 7.58‰ in 2000.

China's total population reached 1.267 billion in 2000. Although it was above 1.2 billion, it did not reach 1.3 billion. China then ushered in a low birth rate period. Census 2000 showed that China's total fertility rate had dropped to about 1.4, including 0.9 in cities, 1.2 in towns, and 1.6 in counties. Seen from the total fertility rate by regions, Beijing and Shanghai had the lowest rate of 0.7. [1]

IV. Population Changes from 2001 to 2008

The *Family Planning Law of the People's Republic of China* was enacted in December 2001. During the implementation of this law, some flexibility was introduced based on the consideration of density of registered population in cities, towns and rural areas and the special conditions of minority areas: in urban areas across the country, and rural areas in the four municipalities directly under the Central Government and in Jiangsu and Sichuan Provinces, the one-child policy was applied to Han residents; in rural areas other than the above provinces and cities, if the first-born child was a girl, couples were allowed to have another child five years later; in some areas of the five provinces and autonomous regions, couples were allowed to have a second child; if both husband and wife are only child, they were allowed to have a

---

[1] Development Planning Department of the National Population, Family Planning Commission and China Population and Development Research Center, *Population and Family Planning Datasheet*, China Population Publishing House, 2006, p. 105.

second child; and a more relaxed birth policy was applied to ethnic minorities with a relatively small population. The family planning policy was not implemented in Tibet and other regions.

Table 4　　China's Total Fertility Rate During the Period from 1960 to 2017 (person)

Year	The World Bank	National Bureau of Statistics	Year	The World Bank	National Bureau of Statistics	Year	The World Bank	National Bureau of Statistics
1960	5.748	—	1980	2.63	—	2000	1.497	1.22
1961	5.919	—	1981	2.57	—	2001	1.508	—
1962	6.089	—	1982	2.56	—	2002	1.524	—
1963	6.237	—	1983	2.582	—	2003	1.54	—
1964	6.346	—	1984	2.623	—	2004	1.554	—
1965	6.396	—	1985	2.661	—	2005	1.565	1.34
1966	6.375	—	1986	2.675	—	2006	1.572	—
1967	6.286	—	1987	2.654	—	2007	1.577	—
1968	6.133	—	1988	2.593	—	2008	1.581	—
1969	5.92	—	1989	2.489	—	2009	1.586	—
1970	5.648	—	1990	2.35	2.3	2010	1.59	1.18
1971	5.322	—	1991	2.187	—	2011	1.594	—
1972	4.956	—	1992	2.021	—	2012	1.599	—
1973	4.57	—	1993	1.868	—	2013	1.604	—
1974	4.181	—	1994	1.739	—	2014	1.61	—
1975	3.809	—	1995	1.639	1.56	2015	1.617	1.047
1976	3.472	—	1996	1.571	—	2016	1.624	—
1977	3.18	—	1997	1.527	—	2017	1.631	—
1978	2.938	—	1998	1.503	—			
1979	2.753	—	1999	1.494	—			

Source: https://data.worldbank.org/indicator/SP.DYN.TFRT.IN?locations=CN, compiled by the National Bureau of Statistics of China based on data from previous censuses or the 1% population sample survey.

Actually data from census 2000 had a high quality. The total fertility rate of 1.22 it obtained was consistent with the rate of 1% determined by the National Bureau of Statistics in 1995 based on the population sample survey.

The 1% population sample survey in 2005 showed that the total fertility rate was 1.34. Data from the sixth census in 2010 showed the total fertility rate in that year was only 1.18, including 0.88 in cities, 1.15 in towns, and 1.43 in rural areas. In the two influential journals—*Population Research* and *Chinese Journal of Population Science*, there were more and more articles discussing the rationality of the original family planning policy, and the split of opinion among different groups was widening. ①The 1% population sample survey in 2015 once again showed that China's total fertility rate was only 1.047, the lowest level in the world.

At the 3rd Plenary Session of the 18th CPC Central Committee in November 2013, the *Decision on Several Major Issues Concerning Deepening Reform* was passed, stipulating that "Families may have two children if one parent is an only child". In early 2014, new family planning regulations were passed at provincial people's congresses successively, and a new population policy was implemented. Table 5 shows that the number of births in 2014 reached 16.92 million (the number released by the National Bureau of Statistics was 16.87 million), higher than the number of 16.44 million in 2013. The number of births in 2015 fell below the record of 2014 to 16.55 million. The dividend of the "selective two-child policy" was released only for one year. At the 5th Plenary Session of the 18th CPC Central Committee convened at the end of 2015, the CPC Central Committee made a decision to adhere to the basic state policy of family planning, improve the population growth strategy, fully implement the policy that one couple may have two children and actively cope with population aging. In December 2015, the Standing Committee of the National People's Congress reviewed the draft amendment to the Population and

---

① Guo Zhigang, "What Caused the Low Fertility Rate of China's Population", *Chinese Journal of Population Science*, Issue 2, 2013.

Family Planning Law. In January 2016, the CPC Central Committee clearly pointed out that no approval was needed to give birth to a second child, and families could make a birth decision on their own.

The number of births in China rose to 17.91 million in 2015 (the number announced by the National Bureau of Statistics was 17.86 million), an increase of 1.31 million over 2015. In 2017, the number of births dropped to 17.28 million (the number released by the National Bureau of Statistics was 17.23 million). The number of births in 2018 saw a decline of only 15.27 million (the number released by the National Bureau of Statistics was 15.23 million).

Why was that? The main reasons were as follows.

Firstly, the number of couples getting married per year continued to decrease. That is, women born during the one-child policy period in 1980 reached the marriageable and childbearing age. The annual number of births stabilized at about 23 million throughout the 1980s but started to drop to between 19 million and 21 million during and after the 1990s, and the downward trend was continuing. When the "post 85s" and "post 90s" started to get married, the number of first-marriage couples each year started to plummet. For instance, the number of first-marriage couples in 2013 was 13.4113 million, and it dropped to 13.0204 million in 2014, to 12.2059 million in 2015, to 11.3861 million in 2016 and to 10.5904 million in 2017. In 2018, the number of married couples, including remarried couples, was only about 10.10 million, including less than 10 million first-marriage couples. [1] The decrease in the number of first-marriage couples would not only reduce the birth rate after first marriage, but also reduce the birth rate of the entire society in the long-term.

Secondly, the number of women entering the childbearing period each year was decreasing. Women of childbearing age in the current fertile period were born during the period when the original family planning policy was strictly

---

[1] Source: *China Statistical Yearbook 2018*, Table 22 – 24.

implemented. Due to the increased sex ratio at birth resulted from the one-child policy, i. e. , the fast increase in the number of males for every 100 females at birth, the original balance was broken down. ①The increase in the sex ratio at birth after the 1980s resulted in insufficient number of women of marriageable age, so some men could not find a wife to get married and to have children. According to the 1 ‰ population change sample survey in 2017, the sex ratio was 117. 70 for the age group 15 – 19, 110. 98 for the age group 20 – 24, and 104. 47 for the age group 25 – 29. ②When people in the age group 15 – 19 reach the marriageable age, it will be more difficult and expensive for them to get married. The decrease in the number of women of marriageable age would bring more serious impact: on one hand, there would be marriage squeeze caused by the marriage pressure of men of marriageable age, and on the other hand, the birth rate would decrease, thus leading to the decrease in the number of first births per year. In the entire newly-born population, second children given birth by existing women of childbearing age accounted for more than 50%.

Thirdly, the divorce rate increased and the age of first marriage was delayed. Due to the urbanization, popularization of higher education, post-industrialization, growth of women's income and regular population mobility, the divorce rate soared up, and the age of first marriage for the female population was delayed. During the process of reform and opening up, China firstly popularized compulsory education, and then exempted the tuition for all primary and junior high school students. In the 21st century, most regions have a high enrollment rate of senior high schools and a fast increasing gross enrollment rate of universities. ③The gross enrollment rate in higher education

---

① The normal sex ratio at birth is between 103 and 107. Any ratio above 107 is considered a high ratio, and that below 103, a low ratio. For a sex ratio at birth between 103 and 107, due to the higher mortality rate of male infants or boys and lower morality rate of female infants or girls, the sex ratio at the marriageable age will tend to balance.

② Source: *China's Population and Labor Statistical Yearbook 2018*, Table 2 – 3.

③ The gross enrollment rate of high schools in 2018 reached 88. 8%.

was only 1.55% in 1978, and 3.7% in 1988. After the expansion of university enrollment in 1999, it rose to 15% in 2002, 23% in 2007, 26.5% in 2010, 48.1% in 2018, and more than 50% in 2019, marking China's transition from the mass education stage to the education popularization stage. These factors quickly resulted in the delay in the age of first marriage for women. The average age of first marriage for women was delayed from 21.4 in 1990 to 25.7 in 2017. The average age at first childbirth increased from 23.4 to 26.8. In some big cities, megacities or megacity behemoths such as Shanghai and Beijing, the age of first marriage for women was delayed to a later time, and even to 29 – 30. The delay in the age of first marriage consequently led to a later age of first childbearing, a shortened child-bearing period of women of marriageable age, and a reduced birth rate of the whole society.

Table 5   Number of Births, Deaths and Net Increase of Population in China over the Past Years Since the Reform and Opening Up

(Unit:‰, 10,000 people)

Year	Birth rate	Mortality rate	Natural growth rate	Total population	Births	Deaths	Net population increase
1978	18.25	6.25	12.00	96259	1757	602	1155
1979	17.82	6.21	11.61	97542	1738	606	1132
1980	18.21	6.34	11.87	98705	1797	626	1172
1981	20.91	6.36	14.55	100072	2093	636	1456
1982	22.28	6.60	15.68	101654	2265	671	1594
1983	20.19	6.90	13.29	103008	2080	711	1369
1984	19.90	6.82	13.08	104357	2077	712	1365
1985	21.04	6.78	14.26	105851	2227	718	1509
1986	22.43	6.86	15.57	107507	2411	737	1674
1987	23.33	6.72	16.61	109300	2550	734	1815
1988	22.37	6.64	15.73	111026	2484	737	1746
1989	21.58	6.54	15.04	112704	2432	737	1695
1990	21.06	6.67	14.39	114333	2408	763	1645
1991	19.68	6.70	12.98	115823	2279	776	1503

(Contd.)

Year	Birth rate	Mortality rate	Natural growth rate	Total population	Births	Deaths	Net population increase
1992	18.24	6.64	11.60	117171	2137	778	1359
1993	18.09	6.64	11.45	118517	2144	787	1357
1994	17.70	6.49	11.21	119850	2121	778	1344
1995	17.12	6.57	10.55	121121	2074	796	1278
1996	16.98	6.56	10.42	122389	2078	803	1275
1997	16.57	6.51	10.06	123626	2048	805	1244
1998	15.64	6.50	9.14	124761	1951	811	1140
1999	14.64	6.46	8.18	125786	1842	813	1029
2000	14.03	6.45	7.58	126743	1778	817	961
2001	13.38	6.43	6.95	127627	1708	821	887
2002	12.86	6.41	6.45	128453	1652	823	829
2003	12.41	6.40	6.01	129227	1604	827	777
2004	12.29	6.42	5.87	129988	1598	835	763
2005	12.40	6.51	5.89	130756	1621	851	770
2006	12.09	6.81	5.28	131448	1589	895	694
2007	12.10	6.93	5.17	132129	1599	916	683
2008	12.14	7.06	5.08	132802	1612	938	675
2009	11.95	7.08	4.87	133450	1595	945	650
2010	11.90	7.11	4.79	134091	1596	953	642
2011	11.93	7.14	4.79	134735	1607	962	645
2012	12.10	7.15	4.95	135404	1638	968	670
2013	12.08	7.16	4.92	136072	1644	974	669
2014	12.37	7.16	5.21	136782	1692	979	713
2015	12.07	7.11	4.96	137462	1659	977	682
2016	12.95	7.09	5.86	138271	1791	980	810
2017	12.43	7.11	5.32	139000	1728	988	739
2018	10.94	7.13	3.81	139540	1527	995	532

Source: Data about 1978 – 2015 are from *China's Population and Labor Statistics Yearbook 2016*; data about 2016 – 2018 are from the *Statistical Communique of the People's Republic of China National Economic and Social Development* each year; data about births, deaths and net population increase are calculations based on the total population and the corresponding birth rate, mortality rate and natural growth rate. As data published by the National Bureau of Statistics were rounded up, the calculations here are slightly different from the exact data published by the Bureau.

Fourthly, the rising living costs reduced people's desire to have children. Since the reform and opening up, China has been on the rapid track of urbanization. China's urbanization level was only 17.9% in 1978, which quickly rose to around 59.6% by the end of 2018. Urbanization does not unselectively move all age groups into cities, but firstly and selectively absorbs young and competitive people, who are at the same time at the marriageable and childbearing age. These young people need to, on one hand, take care of their elderly parents in the hometown (due to the family planning policy, they have fewer siblings and a heavier burden in supporting parents), and on the other hand, earn money to raise their own children and afford the daily consumptions. However, due to the rocketing housing prices and expensive goods, they have a low willingness to give birth. The diversified and convenient contraceptive methods and the low wiliness to give birth directly result in a low birth rate.

Fifthly, the unsatisfactory childbearing environment restrains the desire of the entire society to give birth. Although the "universal two-child policy" was switched to "universal two-child policy", it is still hard to produce continuous dividend. One important reason lies in the inadequate and unaffordable access to child care, education, employment, medical care and other services. Due to the miniaturization and mobility of families and change of concepts of post − 80s about family and life, fewer couples rely on their parents to take care of their children. Hiring a baby-sitter to take care of their children is also costly for ordinary young couples. With high social competition pressure and extended working hours, the younger generation has less leisure time and less time to take care of their children. The costs of raising a child from birth to graduation from university are rising. Parents also need to buy a house or give a dowry for their children when they get married. Although migrant workers work or do business in cities, they have not been completely transformed into urban citizens. As the household registration system has not yet had its function returned to population information registration, migrant workers have unequal access to urban public services. Therefore, continued efforts are needed to build a family-friendly society that is conducive to childbearing in both workplace and family life.

Affected by the above factors, the actual fertility rate is still far below the policy fertility rate. A country or society would fall into the low-fertility trap when its total fertility rate has long been lower than 1.5 or 1.4, and would remain in the trap for a long time to come. This will affect the age structure and the elderly support structure of the population, and lead to accelerated aging of the population and a reduced size of the labor force that supports the entire society, as well as create an extremely high pension debt pressure, thus causing the society to transit from the population dividend stage to the population debt stage, and forming a demographic structure that is likely to cause a middle-income trap which will prevent people from getting rich before they get old. In fact, the population trap and the middle-income trap are common in developing countries. These two traps influence each other to form a predicament where no development is made but low-level growths.

V. The Future Governance Policy Structure

From the initial birth control, to advocating "one child is fine, two children were perfect and three children are too many", to "only-child policy" in the 1980s, and to the current "universal two-child policy", China's family planning policy has experienced a socially reflective regression process. This process has been accompanied by the contradiction between the supply of means of subsistence and the pressure from the number and structure of the population at different stages of economic development, and the contradiction between the basic state policy of family planning and family preferences. The evolvement of these contradictions shaped the population growth and structural change as a link between such family behaviors as marriage and childbirth, and the fertility rate, a government's control indicator.

The institution is designed to ease the pressure of population growth upon development of the national economy. The contradictions between the production and reproduction of the population and between the production and reproduction of subsistence material were the main social contradictions faced by all countries in the world after World War II. The "population explosion" after World War II was also the largest population "explosion" occurred within a short period of time in the world population history. Restricted by the growth of productivity and the economic and social development back then, China took the measure of controlling population growth to solve the problem of population pressure.

In fact, through these measures, China effectively controlled the population growth, eased the pressure from existing and incremental population upon the supply of subsistence materials, improved people's living standards, transformed itself from an agricultural country into an industrial country and established an industrial system with Chinese characteristics, as well as completed the transformation of GDP from agriculture-dominated to industry-dominated and then to post industry-dominated. Family planning reduced the family size and pressure of families on child raising, thus enabling families to spend more funds on their children. It boosted the nine-year compulsory education, and increased the enrollment rate of high schools and universities, as well as transformed China from a country with a large population to a country with strong human resources. The implementation of the family planning and one-child policy also dispelled the prejudice that men were superior to women prevailing throughout the entire feudal period, and increased the enrollment rate of girls and young women at all ages, and thereby increased the human capital of women and narrowed the gender gap in education, employment and occupation. By reducing the birth rate, family planning greatly reduced the children dependency coefficient of the entire society and children raising costs, and promoted social development. Thanks to family planning and pregnancy examinations, the mortality among pregnant and postpartum women was greatly lowered, the health of fetus was ensured, and the rate of birth defects was reduced. Family planning also prolonged women's employment time, improved women's family and social status, and greatly promoted social progress and development. Due to the difference of family planning policy between urban and rural areas, aging in cities accelerated, thus creating demand for migrant workers to work in cities following the reform and opening up, and speeding up China's urbanization. In conclusion, family planning gradually revealed its positive effects in the later stage, and continuously provided demographic dividend during the rapid economic development period. During the transition period of China's economy and society—especially the transition from high-speed growth to quality growth, it cut down the country's governance costs. By causing the demographic transition to occur when the aging degree of the population was still low, it also helped reduce the costs of the transition, and thus made an indelible contribution to China's modernization.

While exerting positive effects, the demographic transition or change also showed negative effects, which are becoming increasingly apparent. Demographic practice showed that the faster the positive effects of the demographic transition are exhibited, the faster the negative effects are seen. The demographic transition occurred as a result of social development and family planning. When developing population policies, the government and the academic community gave too much attention to the role of the government, but to some extent, ignored the role of the market and the society. Due to the constants efforts to suppress the population growth since the 1980s, the labor force has been on a decline. Since 2000, there has been a consecutive net decrease in the labor force, and since 2018, there has been a consecutive net decrease in the working population. The population aging today is resulted from the decreasing births since the 1980s and 1990s, which makes China the fastest aging country in the world, with the bottom of the population pyramid shrinking faster than that of all other developing countries. The contradiction between the government-promoted family planning and the family's demand for boys also resulted in a high sex ratio at birth, the negative effects of which were amplified through population migration and caused the present marriage squeeze. During the process of family miniaturization, the traditional family network and kinship network support system weakened, which forced the society to construct a new support system to alleviate the impact. The only reliable conclusion drawn from the population interventions by all countries in the world is that the government can effectively reduce the fertility rate but cannot effectively increase the fertility rate through incentives. Because implementing a birth-encouraging policy is far more expensive than implementing a birth control policy. In 2000, people aged 65 and above already accounted for about 7% of the total population. In 2018 the number reached 11.9% (people aged over 60 accounted for up to 17.9%). In some big cities, megacities and megacity behemoths where the family planning policy was strictly implemented, the registered population has already entered the aging stage (people aged 65 and above account for more than 14% of the total population). In 2018, the aging level of the registered population in Beijing already exceeded 25%. For cities like it, without the floating labor force, the normal production and reproduction would paralyze. At present and in the near future, with the population during the high-fertility period reaching the retirement age, aging will accelerate. Aging caused by the shrinkage of the top and bottom of the population pyramid will exert more serious negative effects. China is expected to see a faster aging speed during the 14th Five-Year Plan period. Against this backdrop, provincial capital cities and first-tier cities except Beijing and Shanghai competed with each other in attracting talents. Starting from about 2012, amid the reform of household registration system, the points-based household registration policy was introduced in many places to attract talents. From 2018, local governments started to lower the threshold for defining "talents" in policy, thus changing the competition for talents to competition for "population". By 2019, under the downward economic pressure, cities such as Shijiazhuang and Xi'an had substantially transformed the competition for talents to competition for "population". In short, the population reservoir in rural areas constantly supplying labor force has dried up. China can no longer depend on the net growth of its labor force to maintain lower labor costs. Megacity behemoths, megacities and large cities are drawing away the population of medium-sized and small cities. The resource flow accompanying the population flow will, after having hollowed out rural areas, hollow out towns and small cities. The demographic transition is now forcing the economic transition to occur to form new growth drivers. But the most reliable driver is the technological progress. After the disappearance of demographic dividend, China will start a long-term race against the population aging through technological progress. If the technological progress outpaces the population aging, China will see a smooth development;① otherwise, China needs to adjust the the development strategy in a long term.

The effect of improved production relations and other institutional facilities on productivity emancipation was observed during the reform and opening up process. For thousands of years, China has been in the Malthusian trap, or the risk of hunger caused by fast population growth. However, thanks to the social development since the reform and opening up, China has completely satisfied people's need for food and improved people's food structure, thus lifting people out of the survival crisis and nudging them toward high-end consumption. The pressure faced by China has now transformed from the total population to the age structure. The pressure from risks formed and accumulated at this stage is heavier than that imposed by total population. The issue of elderly care today becomes more important than ever.

Under this circumstance, the following substantial adjustments should be made to the population policy in the future.

Firstly, the *Family Planning Law* should be abolished in due course. Along with abolishment of the *Family Planning Law*, the social support fee shall be cancelled. All provisions restricting childbearing shall be deleted from the laws, regulations and government documents, and all policies restricting or selectively restricting childbearing shall be replaced with free childbearing policies. Although the fertility rate of human beings will decline with the increase of the level of modernization, there are still some couples having a preference for children. This will, to some extent, help slow down the fast decline in fertility rate and curb the population decline trend.

---

① Cai Fang, "Demographic Transition, Demographic Dividend and Lewisian Turning Point", *Economic Research*, Issue 4, 2010.

Secondly, the *Regulations on the Protection of Families Losing their Only Child* should be timely released. Humanitarian support, from materials to physiological services, should be provided for fragile families who claimed the one-child certificate, and whose only child died accidently. For families who have lost their only child and are entering the stage of losing their self-care ability, support consistent with the development level of the society should be provided.

Thirdly, a childbirth-friendly society should be established. Efforts should be made to improve social public services, provide equal access to basic public services, improve modern community governance systems and governance capabilities and earnestly answer the call of the 19th National Congress of the CPC for establishment of a family-friendly society or a childbirth-friendly society, including ensuring universal access to childcare, education, employment, medical services, elderly care, housing, and social welfare assistance. The fertility rate cannot be raised if the childcare and education are too expensive, the income gap is large, or the medical services, elderly care, housing and social welfare assistance are inaccessible and unaffordable. The younger generation is under the pressure of taking care of their parents and raising children, and is therefore reluctant to give birth. This is why the actual fertility rate is much lower than the policy fertility rate.

Fourthly, free public kindergartens should be established throughout the country. Efforts should be made to popularize public kindergartens and encourage private enterprises to set up nurseries or kindergartens to be purchased by the local government. Different admission fees may be set for families with different income levels, that is, families with lower income are exempted or partially exempted from the admission fee. When the national strength is strong enough, the public kindergartens will become completely free to reduce the pressure of families on raising children.

Fifthly, a family-based individual income tax collection system should be established. The individual income tax, when paid in the name of a couple or a family with one child, may be reduced or the threshold may be enhanced. For families with a second child, the tax may be further reduced. For families with three or more children, a negative income tax system is implemented, that is, for families with many children whose per capita disposable income does not meet a certain standard, their income will be supplemented to the certified standard.

Sixthly, local governments should be encouraged to introduce birth-encouraging policies. Experiments may be conducted before scaling up. In megacities and megacity behemoths where the aging of the registered residents is very serious, birth-encouraging policies may be introduced first, such as providing living allowances for newborns. As the country is in the primary stage of socialism, a fixed amount of living allowance may be provided for families with a second child.

Seventhly, the development of artificial intelligence and robots should be promoted. Efforts should be made to improve production efficiency, shorten working hours, reduce manpower consumption in laboring, extend holidays and improve the quality of life. The practice in developed countries shows that even if a costly birth-encouraging policy is introduced, the total fertility rate still cannot rise to the replacement level of 2.1. Under this circumstance, in order to ensure long-term smooth development of the national economy, vigorous efforts should be made to develop robots and various skills to enable robots to replace humans, and to, through human-machine interaction or construction of a human-machine society, reduce the pressure of aggravated aging of population on elderly care and add new growth drivers, so as to fulfill the Chinese dream of great national renewal.

In summary, above suggestions may be implemented in "three steps": the first step is to abolish the original birth control policy following completion of the construction of a well-off society in 2020; the second step is to construct a family-friendly society during the period from 2021 to 2025, to gradually but effectively reduce the child-raising costs and the third step is to implement a birth-encouraging policy after 2026, which may start with providing living allowances and other possible social services to families with a second child, to stimulate childbirth of existing and incremental women of childbearing age.

Interpersonal Information Interaction and Modern Governance Mechanism

Anatoly Lazarevich

Director and Professor of the Institute of Philosophy,
National Academy of Sciences of Belarus

The management issue is multifaceted in nature and can be differentiated depending on the area of application. At one time, assessing the fundamental shifts in the structure of social production method, Karl Marx wrote that "…a combination of social activities acts as a producer"[①]. In such management activity, two levels are clearly traced: firstly, participation in the management of technological processes, as transformed and controlled natural processes; secondly, participation in the management of the cooperation process and the division of functionally specific forms of employee activity.

General civilizational achievements in the fields of science, engineering and technology play a noticeable role in solving management issues. In the 1960s, the outstanding American economist and sociologist J. Galbraith introduced the concept of technostructure. A technostructure is a hierarchical organization that mainly unites specialists—from ordinary engineers to professional managers and directors. J. Galbraith believed that the

---

[①] Из неопубликованных рукописей К. Маркса. – Большевик. – 1939. – №11, с. 64.

technostructure is a kind of ruling elite concentrated in the large corporate sector of economy. Since large organizations play a leading role, the representatives of the technostructure occupy commanding posts in society.

One of the variants of the concept of technocracy is the theory of "elitist cybernetics" of K. Steinbuch. In his opinion, power in modern society should belong to mathematicians, economists and programmers, who can determine the effectiveness of management decisions better than others.

This article will try to discuss the mechanism of governance modernization from the perspective of distinguishing culture as an organism and civilization as a mechanism. The unity of organism and civilization is clearly manifested in the phenomenon of modern organization (from the Greek word: ὄργανον—tool). It is the purpose of the production, exchange, distribution and consumption of social wealth, the realization of specialized information communication structure and functional structure, and effective management of this process. Knowledge about organization, as a structural-procedural enzyme of control, is an essential component of praxeology (from ancient Greek πρᾶξις—activity, and λογια—science, teaching; namely about the organizational effectiveness of human activity).

The fact that social life is essentially practical was written by Karl Marx in his *Theses on Feuerbach*. But the term "praxeology" was first used in 1890 by A. Espinas. The development of praxeology was continued by the prominent economist L. von Mises. In his monograph *Human Action*, he created a new scientific direction—praxeology, the science of human behavior. [1]

From a praxeological standpoint, it is paramount to consider the management function of organizations and its role in the management of modern informational-communicative processes. By definition, organization is a system of people, structures and processes. Just like the "combined aggregate worker", there is also the "aggregate manager". The complexity of technology

---

[1] Мизес, Л. Человеческая деятельность: Трактат по экономической теории. – 2 – е испр. изд. / Л. Мизес. – Челябинск: Социум, 2005. – 878 с.

and economics, social and spiritual life is constantly increasing. This requires the division and cooperation of labor, including managerial labor, and above all, its support on the "sum of technologies", about which S. Lem wrote.

In principle, the organizational effect is an eternal companion and enzyme of human activities, starting from its primitive forms (division of labor during hunting in primitive communities), then to the great ancient civilizations (the construction of Egyptian pyramids, the eastern irrigation facilities). F. Engels convincingly showed the effectiveness of organizational synergy using a simple example. During the colonization years of Africa, there were constant clashes between French cavalry and Arab Mamelukes (slave cavalry). It is characteristic that 200 Mamelukes always defeated 200 Frenchmen. Troops of 500 horsemen from both sides fought with varying success. But 1000 French horsemen always defeated 1000 Mamelukes because of their higher level of organizational readiness.

It is by no means a paradox that more efficient organization is characterized by a higher level of organizational readiness. Systems, especially complex ones, are characterized by a hierarchical structure, that is, a certain sequence of inclusion of lower-level systems into higher-level systems. In a complex organization, especially anthropic systems, the processes of organization and management are distinguished as a specific feature, and these processes have changed from one mode of social production to another.

Industrial society is a machine-like Leviathan that requires rigidly centered, linear, and hierarchical governance. In his theory of "bureaucratic organization", M. Weber expressed this feature, which is capable of ensuring effective human activity in society. "Technical intelligence" endowed it with the following features: ignoring personal qualities in relationships between cooperators of organization; division of labor based on functional specialization; clear hierarchy of power; a system of rules defining the rights and obligations of each member of the organization; a system of procedures that determine the order of actions in all situations of the organization's functioning; selection and promotion of employees by qualification.

In terms of efficiency, a bureaucratic organization has the same advantages as a machine over non-mechanized methods of production. At the same time, according to Weber, organization is a denial of human freedom, and the freedom, as a final purpose, can be realized only outside the organization. The goal-rationality start is reduced not only to human-machine, but also to a machine-like organization. N. Berdyaev noted that there is a fundamental difference between the external mechanical organization and the organism, which contains the internal goal of self-development.

Mechanistic principles in an industrial society are projected onto the entire social relations. "What is valid for a system of machines is also true for the combination of various types of human activity…". ①

Like "celestial" mechanics, the earthly mechanics of this man-made space is a fine-tuned clockwork, an immense factory, an objectified, cyclically reproduced process, in which a person is also a small part and a function. Spinoza's freedom appeared in an unexpected light—as a rational knowledge of certain roles and a rigid necessity to follow them.

In the light of modern informational-communicative revolution, it has become obvious that the traditional bureaucratic organization of the industrial era has reached a dead end. The invention and improvement of technologies of communication practices has a huge impact on all aspects of social development, defining completely new forms of organization, features of its functioning, including aspects such as structure, management system, direction of information flow and method of information transfer, organizational culture. In new types of organization a number of classic management problems are also solved differently. However, modern computer communication technologies draw on themselves a significant amount of activities to coordinate information flow and staff work, significantly optimizing these processes in the case of large and complex organizations.

---

① Маркс 1969 Маркс К., Энгельс Ф. Сочинения / К. Маркс, Ф. Энгельс. - 2 - е изд. - М. : Изд-во политической литературы, 1969. - Т. 27., -644 с, 214с.

This trend can be designated as a significant transformation of traditional relations in the activities of various organizations in the direction of clear dominance of communicational-technological solutions in its structure. "The traditional hierarchy of plenary power is being replaced," write L. Foster and D. Flynn, " by a hierarchy of competences ⋯ Power and resources are increasingly concentrated in centers of experts, and not at formal hierarchical levels."[①]

G. Tarde once noted the close relationships between communication and organization as a whole. In accordance with his theory, the dominant nature of the transmission of information determines the method of social structure: each type of communication is corresponded to a certain type of society. What role do modern information communication technologies play in this typology?

M. Castells pointed out the direct connection between the development of society and that of organization technologies, noting that " the ability or inability of society to control technology, especially strategic technologies, to a large extent shapes the fate of society".[②]

The process of "deployment" of the world is extremely ambiguous and in many ways is still insufficiently controlled. E. Agazzi, speaking about the new technological phase of civilization development, notes, "The functioning of the technological system is essentially indifferent to the goals, it is characterized by 'immanent' development, growth on its own roots. It is the indifference to goals that allows the system to perceive different goals and values. Extreme complexity, self-sufficiency and ubiquity are the qualitative difference between a technological system and an industrial one—also between a technological civilization and an industrial civilization. Technological civilization is a way of life, communication and thinking, and it is a set of conditions that generally

---

① L. W. Foster, D. M. Flynn, "Management Information Technology: Its Effects on Organizational Form and Function", *Management Information Systems Quarterly*, No. 8, 1984, pp. 229 – 236, 231.

② Кастельс, М. Информационная эпоха: экономика, общество и культура / М. Кастельс. – М. : ГУ ВШЭ, 2000. – 608 с, 30с.

dominate human, especially since they are not subject to his control". ①

It seems that E. Agazzi exaggerates too much, speaking about the virtually absolute independence of socio-technological progress. If a technological civilization, as he claims, "is a way of life, communication and thinking", a counter question arises that is a person capable of determining these actually human phenomena and influencing them?

Systematic engineering is the initial and basic moment among control technologies. Its essence, structure and dynamics were substantively considered at the scientific and theoretical seminar of "philosophical and methodological problems of artificial intelligence" in the report of Professor A. G. Gorokhov "Logic and technology: from relay-switching systems to nanotechnology". In a comparative historical vein, he noted that initially one of the areas was automated control systems. At that time, the cybernetic concept about management prevailed as a reaction of control action to deviations of the controlled value from the planned result. This was due to the fact that mainly engineers came to this industry. Enterprises, and to an even greater extent industries and their management structures, are complex socio-economic systems, the conceptual provisions of cybernetics were not enough to describe them. It is impossible and often simply impractical to fully automate them. Here it is necessary to design—or rather reorganize—production and management activities. Therefore, such systems were not called systems of automatic control (SAC), but automated systems of control (ASC).

In essence, for modern science and technology, it is important that scientists and engineers—with its help—can correctly plan and implement their activities in advance and get the desired results. This goal is served by a variety of graphical representations and models that are developing today—in nanosystem engineering. Thus, both in scientific theories and in applied fields, the role of building various kinds of logical models is increasing. On the one

---

① Агацци, Э. Моральное измерение науки и техники / Э. Агации. – М. : Моск. филос. фонд. – 1998. – 344 с, 90с.

hand, these logical models are used to unite disparate disciplinary scientific knowledge, and on the other hand, to serve as a kind of "project" of future developments focused on practical application.

However, for all the importance of system technologies, they are only prerequisites for organizational-communicative activities. The peculiarity of organization, in comparison with all other social phenomena, is that it has a communicative intellect or "social processor". It is the organization, not a single person. Such intellect is the ability to create ideal (intellective) models of real (and unreal) objects, processes, phenomena on the basis of generalized knowledge that is a part of the culture of society.

The philosopher and poet Tyutchev expressed the uncertainty of the results of our actions in the following words, "we are not gifted to predict how our word will be responded". But intellect is able to create models of not only the existing, but also the probabilistic future, which serves as the basis of management, starting with their simplest historical types and ending with modern strategic management.

Management itself and its integral component—planning—can be defined as a social activity to create optimal, in terms of given parameters, and ideal ("mental") models of the future state of management process—the models that have the property of realizability. Many beautiful models have the disadvantage that they cannot be translated into reality. In the most general sense, realizability is a practical possibility to create a system—that is isomorphic in its behavior of a model from the structures of the objective world.

The terms "model" and "modeling" are used very widely in different contexts. V. A. Shtoff defined these concepts as follows: "A model is understood as such a mentally imagined or materially realized system, which while displaying or reproducing an object of research, is capable of replacing it in such a way that its study gives us new information about this object". [1]His

---

① Штофф, В. А. Моделирование и философия / В. А. Штофф. - Л. : Наука, 1966. - 301 с, 139с.

summary is that "the relationship between the model and the modeling doject is not a consistent relationship, but an analogy … analogy is the similarity of structures". ① Thus, a model is an ideal systemic construct associated with the modeled object by relevance relations, that is, it is capable of representing certain properties and relationships of the modeled object and their essential interconnections.

The systemic nature of the models is of a fundamental importance, because the relations and interactions between the elements of the model must correspond to the relations between the elements of the object. Only a system can be a system's model. As a reflection of objective reality, it consists of certain sign structures (texts describing the theory, including mathematical ones) and a system of artifacts capable of interpreting these texts and experiments, and inversely revising the text of the theory through experimental results.

To plan, one must have both a model of the object we want to plan for its future state, and a model of its environment in the communicative consciousness and the "social processor" to make sure that the changed or newly created object is realizable and can exist in this environment. It is an integral system connected by various interactions into a single organism. Its main purpose is to construct a model that is relevant to the displayable object. For planning, the ability of this system to predict various options of development of the managed object is important. The longer the period of time during which planning is carried out and the more intensive the changes, the more detailed the cognitive model should be, the more accurate the models of system elements and the regularity of connection between them should be.

The modeling probability (creating internal models that reflect external objects) that any system can have are limited by its complexity. The point is that for modeling any cognitive system we must create an internal model of the thing or process that it models. However, it can use only its internal elements

---

① Штофф, В. А. Моделирование и философия / В. А. Штофф. – Л. : Наука, 1966. – 301 с, 139с.

for modeling. If the modeled system has more elements and connections than the modeling system, it is necessary to simplify and coarsen the model.

The problem is significantly complicated by the fact that it is necessary to foresee not only its own development of the external world, including the development of competing self-reproducing systems, which are also very complex. Therefore, all foresight is approximate. Nevertheless, the management of evolution is possible, and the more accurate (and not necessarily more complex) model of the future we are able to create, the higher its quality.

Already in the 1970s, the need for modeling complex systems and processes (primarily in the field of industrial enterprise management) aroused people's attention to the problem of creating special software for this kind of modeling, which was called imitational modeling. It was about modeling information processes at an enterprise in the context of a new orientation of the economy towards the use of computer technology, since any enterprise began to be viewed not just as a bureaucratic structure, but as a system for processing information. This highlighted the need to develop special programming languages, which are called algorithmic languages of imitational modeling, and have become a kind of intermediaries between the structural representation of complex systems and their description in high-level programming languages.

The modeling includes on-line accessible models required for scenario planning. Planners should be able to quickly model the development of events in the assumption of certain options of their implementation. Ideally, it is necessary to build a simulation model of the entire process that allows predicting its evolution.

To improve the planning process, it is necessary to create a permanent information model of an object or process, since collecting and organizing large amounts of information in an orderly manner requires a lot of time and material costs. It is much more profitable to create such a management model and then update and refine it. Such logic imperatively requires a qualitatively new type of management capable of implementing the following principles.

Firstly, the principle of inversion. The value-semantic "fulcrum" is that it is necessary to proceed from a fundamentally new situation in the transformation of society and its subsystems—an inversion in the logic of its evolution: at all previous stages, survival was a necessary prerequisite for development, but from now on, development is a condition for survival. Following this principle means the need for a synergistic relationship between "people and things" — the cognitive and communicative potential of the "aggregate subject" of management and modern information technologies in their interaction.

Secondly, the principle of unity of situation and strategic planning. If we consider the problem not in a doctrinaire way, namely in the spirit of popular ideologemes (in their latest edition it is called "stable development"), but from an anthropological point of view, the modern world is predominantly concerned with situational management, leaving aside the problem of advanced strategic planning. This is a reminiscent of the situation with the prisoner from Kafkaesque's novel *Castle*. For seven years he conscientiously and secretly dug a tunnel to escape, and when he literally saw the light in the end of the tunnel, he heard the loud voice of the warden, "Congratulations, you are in the neighboring cell".

Of course, this does not mean at all a denial of situational management and its correction in the mode of operational, "sliding" planning for short periods (about a year). At this time, the role of communicative management mechanisms is minimal. Strategic management is a different thing, it requires long-term scenario forecasting, modeling and planning for longer periods. K. Popper wrote in his work "Evolutionary Epistemology", "From an evolutionary point of view, theories (like any knowledge in general) are a part of our attempts to adapt to the environment. Such attempts are like expectations and anticipations. This is their function, ···the function of all knowledge is an attempt to anticipate what will happen in the environment around us". [1]For this, it is necessary to develop probabilistic informational-communicative

---

[1] Поппер, К. Реализм и цель науки / К. Поппер // Современная философия науки. - М. : Логос, 1996. - С. 92 – 106.

scenarios. And it would be more correct to have several most probable models of the future, worked out in the most general terms, than to spend limited cognitive resources for a more differentiated modeling of one scenario.

Thirdly, strategic modeling and planning involves the implementation of the principle of separating controlled systems from the environment. To "grasp" this state of the organization, it is needed to: ① highlight its integrity, that is to understand which parts of it are not necessary for the preservation and reproduction of organization and which are necessary; ② determine its integrative structural level, that is to understand which integration level elements of the organization are organized into systems; ③ highlight the interactions typical for the functioning of the organization; ④ find out the way of reproduction of the organization and its dynamic stability; ⑤ finally, determine the ways of its evolution.

In such an integral and at the same time differentiated work, the problem of the "weakest link" acquires special significance. This was brilliantly confirmed by the American astronaut J. Glenn, the first commander of the man's odyssey to the moon. When his team completed the necessary tasks and intended to start back to earth, the automated control system of the space ship showed the impossibility of this operation. It would seem that the astronauts had to prepare for the worst, but Glenn detected a malfunction in the instruments in time, and, ultimately, the astronauts left the earth's satellite, the moon, and landed safely. At this historic moment, the commander said these overwhelmingly convincing words, "Next in line is Man!"

Fourthly, it was an impressive triumph of the praxeological principle of emergence (from the Latin word "emergere") as the ability of system to generate something new. Emergence in systems theory is the presence of special properties in any system that are not inherent in its subsystems and blocks, as well as the sum of elements that are not connected by special system-forming connections; of the properties of system to the sum of properties of its components. In biology and ecology, the concept of emergence can be expressed as follows: one tree is not yet a forest, an accumulation of individual cells is not yet an organism. For example, the properties of a species or biological population do not represent the properties of separate individuals, and concepts such as fertility or mortality do not apply to a separate individual, but apply to any population or species as a whole.

The emergence of organizational management is an imperative of technological and social progress, and the culture of intellectual resources management plays a decisive role in it. In our time, the ability to generate new things, the innovation ability in all areas—production, science, society—is becoming a critical issue of survival and development. Therefore, management should be dynamic, that is, it should include not just a set of data, but comprehensively well-grounded ideas about what changes will occur in the future as a result of certain actions, and how the process will function after the implementation of the plan. The management model should be evolutionary, namely, it should reflect the historical continuity of the composition and structure of organization and the real possibility of its conscious and planned reorganization. The management model is actually a construction of the management process. In this process, especially in specific management activities, the trajectory of the process will inevitably be left, which is like the operation of a planetary system. In fact, whether in an abstract model or in specific management practices, the basis for effective management is knowledge and experience, rather than technology or automation itself. The actual management control subject should be people, which lays the foundation for knowledge-based control built into management. In this activity, it is essential to distinguish processes according to the criterion proposed by F. Nietzsche, "We are growing, but not developing." A clear distinction must be made between growth, evolution and development in order to define the principle of sustainability as both a product and a process of continuous emergence. This requires the combined (communicative) intellectual potential of the management groups.

Fifthly, one of the leading principles of modern management is based on a competent approach. In this case, "knowledge" is known to differ from "information" . Competence is the property of organization as a social institution and its collaborators to conduct certain activities in the best possible way, and it is created by a harmonious set of knowledge, abilities and talents. The management organization is considered as a "knowledge processor" . ①The subjects of management are an institution in which competence is constantly created, maintained, preserved and developed, for which continuous processing of knowledge is required.

It makes sense to emphasize that the competence of organization is not reducible either to individual competencies, or even to their sum, but is their systemic and synergistic quality.

Sixthly, a well-known expert in this area, M. Petrovich, traces the dynamics of assimilation of the logic and technologies of this process by organizations. In modern organizations, he notes, there is a change in the symbols and factors of economic, political and administrative power over time. The 17th century and earlier is a time of power based on brute force. At this time, the level of government administrative efficiency and management quality is undoubtedly relatively low. The saying of Philip II, father of Alexander the Great, that "I don't know such a fortress that a mule laden with gold would not take" —is not as relevant now as it used to be. The most effective, high-quality form of power is becoming power based on the production of information, and its transmission, use and influence on people's behavior technology.

Today economics, management and marketing are taking a giant leap from mass production and distribution to highly individualized, targeted production and customer satisfaction. Formed "management-marketing individuals", in reality or with a share of mimicry, focused on the individual. Therefore, management and economics designed for the abstract consumer will inevitably fail.

---

① Amin, A., Cohendet P. Organisational Lefming and Governance Through Embedded Practices / A. Amin, P. Cohendet // Journal Management and Governance. −2000. − №4. − P. 93 −116, p93.

M. Petrovich draws attention to the general demand in the development of various forms of participative management, i. e. involving employees in the process of developing and making decisions. This is expressed in equity (share) participation in capital, distribution of income, and activities of various professional groups.

Special attention should be paid to personnel training. The main trend is training outside the workplace, on which, for example, American companies spend about 50 billion USD a year. Along with the traditional, the most popular types of education are lectures on video and on television, self-education programs, Internet courses, etc. ①

Seventhly, the subject of close and steadily increasing interest of modern organizations, regardless of their size and focus, is the activity based on the principle of synchronization. Its essence lies in the rationalization of the use of time as the most important factor of production and management, in ensuring the consistency of internal and external processes and institutions.

In all countries in the world, it is extremely important to synchronize the main institutions—business, political structures, public organizations, government bureaucracy, legislative institutions, families, educational system and international organizations. As a response to high internal and external dynamics and mismatch of social processes, alliances, unions and agreements are created.

The development of organizations is based on modern internal and external communications. Socio-technological communications and information are becoming the most important need in the system of organizational values. The change in the role of management in the modern information society is largely due to the fact that it increasingly depends on new and promising forms of knowledge. As for the application of knowledge to the sphere of knowledge and management itself, one of the most popular American theorists in the field of

---

① Петрович, М. Новые тренды современных организаций / М. Петрович // Беларуская думка. −2013. − №7. − С. 48 − 54.

management P. Drucker regards it as the "revolution in the field of management". ①But P. Drucker is not a pioneer of such an approach to the issue of the role of knowledge in management and the role of management itself in society.

By the end of the 20th century, E. Toffler, in the context of understanding the prospects for the formation of an information civilization, carries out the same idea, "…we are waiting for a global battle for power, but its basis is not violence, not money, but knowledge…The highest-quality power comes from the application of knowledge". ②Arguing that the former system of power at all levels of human society is falling apart, Toffler associates this with the collapse of the old management style③and the spread of a new economy based on information and knowledge, which, in general, marks a global transition of society to a new stage of civilizational development. "…A developed economy would not have lasted even 30 seconds without computers, new complex industries, the integration of many diverse (and constantly changing) technologies, the demassification of markets which continues to go by leaps and bounds, or the amount and quality of information that are necessary to the system to produce material values…This is the key to understanding the future metamorphoses of power, and this explains why the battle for control over knowledge and means of communication flares up throughout the entire world space". ④

Today the transition from a hierarchical communication is quite noticeable, when the consumer of information himself chooses its source, content and ways of implementing of social activity in the system of norms and possibilities. This is

---

① Дракер, П. Посткапиталистическое общество // Новая постиндустриальная волна на Западе: Антология / Под ред. В. Л. Иноземцева. - М. : Academia, 1999. - С. 67 - 100, 71с

② Тоффлер, Э. Метаморфозы власти: Пер. с англ. / Э. Тоффлер. - М. : ООО «Издательство АСТ», 2001. - 669 с, 36с.

③ Тоффлер, Э. Метаморфозы власти: Пер. с англ. / Э. Тоффлер. - М. : ООО «Издательство АСТ», 2001. - 669 с, 23с.

④ Тоффлер, Э. Метаморфозы власти: Пер. с англ. / Э. Тоффлер. - М. : ООО «Издательство АСТ», 2001. - 669 с, 19с.

also a new turn in the communicative foundations of management, which makes it possible to establish a relation between the population and the authorities, between the country and society, between the firm and the client, between the factory and the consumer.

Modern approaches to forecasting, the so-called "foresight", are also built on the basis of communicative principles of management. Initially they were focused on the field of scientific and technical planning and consisted in a radical change in its purpose. If earlier this goal was associated with long-term prediction of the development of a particular field of science or technology, taking into account the initial level of their state, then the modern forecasting system focuses on future needs, and not on the existing opportunities; it also focuses on forecasting the development of opportunities for the implementation of future needs. Today, forecasting is increasingly used as a systematic tool for shaping the future, allowing for possible changes in all spheres of social activity—science and technology, economics, social relations and culture.

The key to the successful implementation of the foresight-programs is the well-coordinated work of business, the scientific community, government authorities and civil society, which are trying to reach a consensus on an informational-communicative basis. It is important to emphasize that foresight is a communicative-management process that allows us to make coordinated and competent decisions on future needs.

Modernization of Governance and All-round Progress of Society

Changes of Social Governance in Modern Society in China

Zhu Tao

Associate Professor, National Institute of Social Development, CASS

For more than 40 years since the reform and opening up, China has made great economic achievements attracting worldwide attention on its development path with Chinese characteristics, becoming the world's second largest economy. In the meantime, China has also carried out a lot of exploration and practice in social governance and accumulated valuable experience. It is of great significance to summarize China's basic experience in social governance reform from the history in this regard for further strengthening and innovating social governance and promoting the modernization of social governance system and governance capacity.

I. Reform and Exploration in Social Governance (1978–2012)

In December 1978, the 3rd Plenary Session of the 11th CPC Central Committee declared the shift of work focus of the Party to socialist modernization. With the deepening of market-oriented reform, to meet the needs of market-oriented reform and opening up to the outside world, social governance began to gradually shift from releasing "control" to "management" in the modern society, and issues such as social management system and mechanism also entered the reform process.

1. Reform of the Grass-roots Social Management System

After the 3rd Plenary Session of the 11th CPC Central Committee, the production contract responsibility system was carried out in rural areas. With the natural disintegration of production brigades and teams, the people's commune system could not meet the requirements of the production contract responsibility system. In December 1982, the *Constitution of the People's Republic of China* clearly stipulated that the system of government-commune mixture in rural people's communes must be reformed, and that the rural grass-roots political power is the township (town). In October 1983, the CPC Central Committee and the State Council jointly released the *Notice on Separating Government and Commune and Establishing Township Governments*, requiring localities to implement the reform of separating rural governments from communes step by step and restore the system of township people's government. The original production brigades and production teams below the township level were transformed into villagers' committees and villagers' groups. The nationwide reform of people's communes was started. By the end of 1984, 91,000 township (town) governments and 926,000 villagers' committees had been established across China. [1] The people's commune system withdrew from the historical stage in the reform. In November 1987, the *Law of Organizing the Villagers' Committees of the People's Republic of China (For Trial Implementation)* affirmed the practice of spontaneously setting up villagers' committees in various places, and defined the villagers' committee as a form of mass self-governance involving "self-management, self-education and self-service", thus legally

---

[1] Lu Hanlong, *Research on the Social Management System of New China*, Shanghai People's Publishing House, 2015, p. 87, 287.

confirming villagers' self-governance. In November 1998, after about ten years of practical operation and experience, the *Law of Organizing the Villagers' Committees of the People's Republic of China* was officially promulgated, which further improved the system of villagers' self-governance and summarized the contents of villagers' self-governance as "democratic election, democratic decision-making, democratic management and democratic supervision". In the meantime, it clarifies the support and guarantee role of village Party organizations in villagers' self-governance, and stipulates that the village Party organization is in the core position of leadership in village-level organizations. The abolishment of the agricultural tax in January 1, 2006 further confirmed the responsibility of village-level organizations providing basic public services and social management for villagers on behalf of the state.

In cities, in 1980, the Standing Committee of the National People's Congress re-promulgated the *Regulations on Organizing Urban Sub-district Offices* and the *Regulations on Organizing Residents' Committees*, and thus the institutions and functions of sub-district offices and residents' committees were restored. In community construction, the Ministry of Civil Affairs introduced the concept of "community" into urban management for the first time in 1986, and proposed to carry out community service in cities, which marked the beginning of community service and construction in China. The *Organic Law of the Urban Residents Committees of the People's Republic of China*, passed in December 1989, reaffirms that residents' committees are grass-roots mass self-governing organizations with residents' "self-management, self-education and self-service". Since then, the system of residents' committees has been continuously improved in practice in all parts of China, and urban residents' committees have played more and more functions. First, the scope of work has been gradually expanded to all aspects of the community, including publicizing laws, regulations and national policies, safeguarding the legitimate rights and interests of residents, handling public affairs, and mediating civil disputes. Second, the level of residents' self-governance has been continuously improved. For example, the direct election of residents' committees has been widely implemented, the professionalization of community workers has been promoted, and the system of community residents' councils has been introduced into the process of community self-governance. Third, the residents' committees mobilized residents and units in their jurisdictions to generally carry out service activities to facilitate the people and benefit the people. In November 2000, the General Office of the CPC Central Committee and the General Office of the State Council forwarded the *Opinions of the Ministry of Civil Affairs on Promoting Urban Community Construction in China*, pointing out that vigorously promoting community construction is an important content of adhering to the Party's mass line, doing a good job in mass work and strengthening the construction of grass-roots political power under the new situation, and an important way for China's urban modernization in the new century. This document marks the end of the previous years' experimental exploration stage. Community construction began to be regarded as an important idea and major measure to strengthen the construction of grass-roots political power and reform the urban grass-roots management system. The core of community construction is not community service, but the innovation of management system. [1]

2. Reform of Household Registration Management

Since the reform and opening up, the household registration management system, which strictly restricts population mobility, has been loosened, and the household registration system constantly adjusted in urbanization. On October 13, 1984, the State Council issued the *Notice on Farmers Settling Down in Market Towns*, which stipulated that: "For farmers and their family who apply to work, do business and run service industries in market towns, have a fixed residence in market towns, and have operation capacity, or work in township enterprises and institutions for a long time, the public security department

---

[1] Xia Jianzhong, "From Subdistrict Office and Residents' Committee System to Community System: Changes of China's Urban Communities in the Past 30 Years", *Heilongjiang Social Sciences*, No. 5, 2008.

should grant them permanent residence, review and pass their household registration formalities in time, issue them the *Household Registration Booklet for Families with Self-Care Rations*, and count them as non-agricultural population". This regulation clarifies the conditions, procedures and treatment for farmers with self-care rations settling down in the town, which marks the accessibility of urban-rural population mobility in the sense of household registration. On July 13, 1985, the Ministry of Public Security promulgated the *Interim Provisions on the Administration of Temporary Residents in Cities and Towns*, stipulating the implementation of the *Temporary Residence Permit* system for the floating population, which allows temporary residents to live in cities and towns, and citizens' legality of long-term living in places without their household registration.

In August 1992, the Ministry of Public Security issued the *Notice on Implementing Local Effective Urban Residents' Household Registration.* As a result, the practice of household registration system reform rose all over the country. Zhejiang, Guangdong, and Shandong started to try out the "local effective urban resident accounts", that is, "blue-stamped accounts", which is between official accounts and temporary accounts. Its basic idea of management is that such resident accounts are effective in the local area, managed as permanent resident population and counted as "non-agricultural population". At that time, many kinds of local urban resident accounts appeared across China. For example, the *Interim Provisions on the Administration of Blue-Stamped Resident Accounts in Shanghai* promulgated by Shanghai in February 1994 pointed out that "whoever has invested 1 million yuan (or 200,000 USD) or above in Shanghai, or bought a certain area of commercial housing, or had a fixed residence in Shanghai and a legal stable job can apply for the Blue-Stamped Resident Account in Shanghai, which can be converted into permanent resident account after a certain period of time". [1] In

---

[1] Lu Hanlong, *Research on the Social Management System of New China*, Shanghai People's Publishing House, 2015, pp. 219 – 220.

March 2001, the State Council approved and forwarded the Ministry of Public Security's *Opinions on Promoting the Reform of Household Registration Management System in Small Towns*. The household registration restrictions below the county level were lifted, and the reform of household registration system in China's small towns was in full swing. The *Opinions* further relaxed the conditions for the migration of rural household registration to small towns, and delegated the authority of urban and rural household registration reform to local governments, giving local governments a certain initiative in reform. However, the household registration reform in small towns just pays attention to people who have already worked and lived in small towns, and the purpose of the reform at that time was not yet oriented at rural urbanization. In February 2011, the *Notice of the General Office of the State Council on Actively and Steadily Promoting the Reform of Household Registration Management System* pointed out that it is necessary to guide the orderly transfer of non-agricultural industries and rural population to small and medium-sized cities and designated towns, gradually meet the needs of eligible rural population to settle down, and gradually realize the equalization of basic public services between urban and rural areas.

3. Comprehensive Management of Public Security

Strengthening social security and stabilizing social order were the key points of social governance at the beginning of the reform and opening up. In January 1982, the CPC Central Committee stated in the *Instructions on Strengthening Political and Legal Work* that to strive for a fundamental improvement in the public security situation, it is necessary to strengthen the leadership of the Party, and that the whole Party should take measures to conscientiously implement the comprehensive management policies.[1] In March 1991, the CPC Central Committee decided to set up the Central Committee for Comprehensive

---

[1] Lu Hanlong, *Research on the Social Management System of New China*, Shanghai People's Publishing House, 2015, p. 305.

Management of Public Security to assist the CPC Central Committee and the State Council in leading the comprehensive management of social security in the whole country. It has an office and works together with organs of the Central Political and Legal Committee as one office while keeping separate identities. At the same time, governments at all levels also set up corresponding leading institutions for comprehensive management of public security as required, with special personnel in charge. In this way, a systematic institution of comprehensive management of public security from top to bottom was established across the country, and the public security work of the whole country entered a new stage. In September 2001, the CPC Central Committee and the State Council issued the *Opinions on Further Strengthening the Comprehensive Management of Public Security*, requiring adhering to the principle of "putting prevention first while taking firm action", further integrating severe crackdown, strict management, strict prevention and strict governance, resolutely correcting the wrong tendency of "valuing crackdown and neglecting prevention", earnestly implementing the principle of "prevention first" in ideological concepts, work priorities, police force allocation, financial investment, and mechanisms for assessment, reward, and punishment, thoroughly investigating and dealing with conflicts and disputes, and conscientiously implementing all safety measures.[1] In September 2004, the *Decision of the CPC Central Committee on Strengthening the Construction of the Party's Ruling Ability*, adopted by the Fourth Plenary Session of the 16th CPC Central Committee, emphasized that we should adhere to the principle of putting prevention first while taking firm action, combining the efforts of both professionals and the masses, and relying on the masses, so as to strengthen and improve the working mechanism of comprehensive management of public security. This is an important supplement to the policy of comprehensive management of public security on the basis of summing up the practical

---

[1] Ni Xiaoyu, "Development History of Comprehensive Management of Public Security in the 30 Years since the Reform and Opening Up", *Journal of Fujian Police College*, No. 6, 2008.

experience in this regard for many years. From then on, the principle of "putting prevention first while taking firm action, combining the efforts of both professionals and the masses, and relying on the masses" was confirmed as the guiding principle for the comprehensive management of public security.

4. Proposal and Development of Social Management

The term "social management" first appeared in the *Notes on the Institutional Reform Plan of the State Council* in 1998, which emphasized that the basic functions of the government are macro-control, social management and public services. In 2002, the report of the 16th National Congress of the Party made social management one of the four main functions of the government. In the fifth part, "political construction and political system reform", it is pointed out that we should adhere to "putting prevention first while taking firm action", and implement various measures for comprehensive management of public security, so as to improve social management and maintain a good social order". Here, social management is listed as a specific way to maintain social stability.

In 2004, the 4th Plenary Session of the 16th CPC Central Committee stated in the *Decision of the CPC Central Committee on Strengthening the Construction of the Party's Ruling Ability* that "we should strengthen social construction and management and promoting the innovation of social management system, make in-depth study of social management laws, improve social management systems, policies and regulations, integrate social management resources, and establish a social management pattern featuring Party committee leadership, government execution, nongovernmental support and public participation. This is the first time that the Central Document has put forward the concept of "social construction" and the principle featuring "Party committee leadership, government execution, nongovernmental support and public participation". While upholding the Party's leadership, this principle of social management changes the previous mode of emphasizing single government management, and highlights the collaborative management of government, society and citizens, which marks the deepening of the ruling party's understanding of social management.

In 2007, the report of the 17th National Congress of the CPC put forward the requirement for building a better social management system from the perspective of realizing the new requirement for building a well-off society in an all-round way. While reaffirming the idea of "perfecting the social management pattern featuring Party committee leadership, government execution, nongovernmental support and public participation", it puts forward the new requirement of "maximizing the vitality of social creation, maximizing the harmonious factors and minimizing the disharmonious factors". In July 2011, the CPC Central Committee and the State Council promulgated the *Opinions on Strengthening and Innovating Social Management*, which reiterated the principle of social management featuring "Party committee leadership, government execution, nongovernmental support and public participation".

Generally speaking, from 1978 to 2012, with the disintegration of the people's commune system and the unit system, the grassroots mass self-governance system represented by the villagers' committee and residents' committee was born and improved. With the reform of household registration management system, the flow and migration of population between urban and rural areas became more frequent. At the same time, in the context of the market-oriented reform, social contradictions and social problems occurred frequently. The main task of social governance reform was to deal with and eliminate all kinds of negative consequences derived from economic marketization, with a strong intention for maintaining stability. [1] Besides the economic sector, the reform also entered the social field. Putting forward the concepts of social management and social construction indicated that the Party and the state were aware of the disharmony between social development and economic development became the main contradiction in this period. [2]

---

[1] Chen Peng, "Forty Years of Social Governance in China: Review and Prospect", *Journal of Beijing Normal University* (*Social Science Edition*), No. 6, 2018.

[2] Lu Xueyi, *Society Building of Contemporary China*, Social Sciences Academic Press, 2013, p. 1.

Therefore, making economic and social development balanced and coordinated is a major issue that the times put forward to us.

II. Social Governance in the New Era (Since 2012)

In 2012, the 18th National Congress of the CPC put forward that "with the aim of establishing a socialist system of social management with Chinese characteristics, we should quicken the pace of building a law-based social management system featuring Party committee leadership, government execution, nongovernmental support and public participation". This statement put forward for the first time that it is necessary to establish a socialist system of social management with Chinese characteristics, and added "law-based" to the social management system, indicating that social management should be combined with the rule of law, upgrading the original principle of the social management system. At the same time, the 18th National Congress of the CPC listed social management and people's livelihood as important contents of social construction, and proposed to unify social management and social construction, promote social construction by "innovating social management", improve the scientific level of social management, and actively encourage social subjects to participate in social management.

In 2013, the 3rd Plenary Session of the 18th Central Committee of the CPC adopted the *Decision of the CPC Central Committee on Several Important Issues of Comprehensively Deepening Reform*, which firstly transformed "social management" into "social governance", and devoted a special chapter to deploy the innovation of the social governance system. This is the first time that the Communist Party of China put forward the concept of "social governance" in its official documents, which marks a new change in our Party's governance philosophy. General Secretary Xi Jinping emphasized: "The key to strengthening and innovating social governance lies in institutional innovation." Replacing "social management" with "social governance", although it is a difference with one word, is actually the re-understanding of the attribute, function and operation mode of power, and the relationship between the state and society. "Governance" in social governance means completely abandoning the idea, which is based on the planned system, that the state (government) takes care of everything. By taking "social governance" as an important part of the modernization of the national governance system and governance capacity,[①] China has realized a new leap in concept from "social management" to "social governance".

In October 2017, the 19th National Congress of the CPC put forward "establishing a social governance model based on collaboration, participation, and common interests". In terms of the social governance system, it is required to improve the law-based social governance model under which Party committees exercise leadership, government assumes responsibility, non-governmental actors provide assistance, and the public get involved, and for the first time, it systematically proposed to strengthen public participation and rule of law in social governance, and make such governance smarter and more specialized. In October 2019, the 4th Plenary Session of the 19th CPC Central Committee proposed to uphold and improve the social governance system based on collaboration, participation, and common interests, and clearly put forward the "system" construction of social governance. At the same time, "democratic consultation" and "scientific and technological support" are brought into the requirements of the social governance system, forming a new principle. It also proposed to build a "social governance community" in which everyone enjoys it by shouldering their own responsibility well.

It can be seen that since the 18th National Congress of the CPC, more and more priority has been given to social governance in various expressions of the Party and the government, and the concept, key points and contents of social governance have become increasingly clear. Social governance with "governance"

---

① Feng Shizheng, *New Blueprint of Social Governance*, China Renmin University Press, 2017, pp. 61 – 62.

as its requirement and characteristic is playing an increasingly important role in the cause of socialist construction.

1. Improvement of the Basic Institutional Framework of Community Governance

The *Notice on Further Carrying out Community Burden Reduction Work* released by the Organization Department of the Central Committee of the CPC and the Ministry of Civil Affairs in July 2015, the *Opinions on Strengthening Consultation between Urban and Rural Communities* issued by the General Office of the CPC Central Committee and the General Office of the State Council in July 2015, and the *Opinions on Strengthening and Perfecting Urban and Rural Community Governance* released by the CPC Central Committee and the State Council in June 2017 have become three landmark community policy documents in grassroots social governance since the 18th National Congress of the CPC. [1] The above documents clearly point out that urban and rural communities are the basic units of social governance, and that the goal of improving the community governance system is to build harmonious, orderly, green, civilized, innovative and inclusive urban and rural communities based on collaboration and common interests. In terms of specific measures, the above documents require all provinces (autonomous regions and municipalities directly under the Central Government) to formulate a list of powers and responsibilities of district and county functional departments and sub-district offices (township governments) in community governance in accordance with the principle of principally local leadership, linear and local leadership combined, to be clear about the boundaries of powers and responsibilities between sub-district offices (township governments) and grassroots mass self-governing organizations according to law, and be clear about the list of community work undertaken by grassroots mass self-governing organizations and the list of community work that

---

[1] Chen Peng, "Forty Years of Social Governance in China: Review and Prospect", *Journal of Beijing Normal University (Social Science Edition)*, No. 6, 2018.

assists the government. For matters other than the community work, sub-district offices (township governments) can provide services by purchasing services from grassroots mass autonomous organizations. At the same time, it is required to establish a two-way evaluation mechanism for sub-district offices (township governments) and grassroots mass self-governing organizations to perform their duties.

2. Promotion of the Transformation of Government Functions

Since the 18th National Congress of the CPC, the state has continuously promoted the transformation of government functions, and emphasized that grassroots governments should play an important role in innovating social governance. Local governments at all levels have begun to explore the innovation of social governance with the transformation of government functions as the core. For example, in 2014, Shanghai abolished the economic functions of sub-district offices, and the focus of grassroots management shifted to the fields of public service, public management and public safety, thus promoting the thoughtfully-designed urban governance. [1] In December 2015, the CPC Central Committee and the State Council issued the *Guiding Opinions on Deepening the Reform of Urban Law Enforcement System and Improving Urban Management*, proposing to build a safe and orderly urban management system with clear rights and responsibilities, service first, optimized management, and standardized law enforcement, so as to promote the transformation from urban management to urban governance and make cities operate in a more efficient and orderly way. In February, 2017, the General Office of the CPC Central Committee and the General Office of the State Council issued the *Opinions on Strengthening the Service Capacity Building of Township Governments*, demanding that the development direction of realizing the equalization of basic public services should be grasped, and that the service level of township governments should be

---

[1] Li Youmei, "New Connotation and New Action of Social Governance in China", *Sociological Studies*, No. 6, 2017.

effectively improved by enhancing township cadres' awareness of serving the people, strengthening township governments' service functions, optimizing the allocation of service resources, and creating new service supply ways. In February, 2018, the 3rd Plenary Session of the 19th CPC Central Committee made a decision to deepen the reform of the Party and state institutions, with the goals of building a systematic, scientific, standardized and efficient functional system of the Party and state institutions, forming a Party leadership system that provides overall leadership and coordinates all parties, a government governance system with clear responsibilities and law-based administration, and comprehensively improving China's capacity for governance.

3. Strengthening Public Safety and Conflict Resolving

In April 2015, the General Office of the CPC Central Committee and the General Office of the State Council issued the *Opinions on Strengthening the Construction of Public Security Prevention and Control System*. It requires that, with the goal of ensuring public safety and enhancing people's sense of security and satisfaction, we should highlight public security issues. With the IT-based application and taking infrastructure as the support, we should strengthen the sharing and deep application of information resources, and speed up the construction of public security video surveillance system. We should improve the comprehensive social security prevention and control system, which adopts point-lines-plane integrated ways, online-offline integrated ways, human-equipment-technology integrated ways, and crackdown-prevention-control integrated ways. We should form a working pattern of social security prevention and control system led by the Party Committee, implemented by the government, coordinated by comprehensive management, managed by all departments, and actively participated by nongovernmental forces, so as to ensure that the people live and work in peace and contentment, the society is stable and orderly, and the country enjoys long-term stability.

In February 2014, the General Office of the CPC Central Committee and the General Office of the State Council issued the *Opinions on Innovating the Methods of Masses-Related Work to Solve Prominent Problems of Public Complaints*. It emphasizes the prevention and reduction of public complaints from the source by increasing security and improving people's livelihood, improving the level of scientific and democratic decision-making, and acting by law. It also emphasizes further open and standardize expression channels by improving the way of expressing and handling complaints, leading cadres handling key complaints delegated from the upper level, improving joint efforts for handling visits, and giving play to the role of statutory channels of expressing complaints. In October 2016, the General Office of the CPC Central Committee and the General Office of the State Council issued the *Measures for the Implementation of the Responsibility System for Public Complaints*. The working principles are that "the complaints should be managed by places within their jurisdiction, different levels hold corresponding responsibilities, those in charge assume full responsibility, problems should be timely solved in situ pursuant to the law, and that counseling and education measures should be taken". Measures such as supervision, assessment and punishment should be comprehensively applied to legally regulate the Party and government organs at all levels in performing their duties related to public complaints. ①

4. Leading the Healthy Development of Social Organizations

Vigorously cultivating social organizations and stimulating social vitality is the most striking main line of institutional innovation in the transformation of China's social governance model in recent years. ②In September 2013, the General Office of the State Council issued the *Guiding Opinions on the Government's Purchase of Services from Social Forces*, and in 2015, the General

---

① Zhang Laiming, "Historical Evolution and Development Prospects of China's Social Governance System", *Social Governance Review*, No. 9, 2018.

② Li Youmei, "New Connotation and New Action of Social Governance in China", *Sociological Studies*, No. 6, 2017.

Office of the State Council forwarded the *Notice on the Guiding Opinions on Promoting the Cooperation Mode between Governments and Social Capital in Public Services* by the Ministry of Finance, the National Development and Reform Commission and the People's Bank of China. They improved the space for social organizations to develop and participate in social governance. On this basis, local governments purchase social organization services in the forms such as bidding and venture philanthropy. In September 2015, the General Office of the CPC Central Committee issued the *Opinions on Strengthening Party Building in Social Organizations (for Trial Implementation)*, proposing to, in accordance with the requirements for building grassroots service-oriented Party organizations, promote the effective coverage of Party-related work and organizations in social organizations, expand the ways for Party organizations and Party members to play their roles in social organizations, and give full play to the Party's key role as the political core in social organizations.

In August 2016, the General Office of the CPC Central Committee and the General Office of the State Council issued the *Opinions on Reforming the Management System of Social Organizations to Promote Their Healthy and Orderly Development*. The *Opinions* requires that we should uphold the Party's leadership, reform and create new ways, keep a right balance between delegation and the exercise of control, and actively and steadily promote its development. We should establish and improve a social organization management system with Chinese characteristics in which registration is unified, all sides at different levels perform their corresponding duties in a coordinated way, and supervision is carried out according to the law, thus basically establishing a system for social organizations with separate and clear rights and responsibilities of the government and the society and with law-based governance, and basically forming a development pattern for social organizations with a sound structure, complete functions, orderly competition, integrity, self-discipline, and full of vitality.

5. Using the Internet to Improve Social Governance

The rise of network society is a new challenge and new situation for contemporary social governance. Since the 18th National Congress of the CPC, the Internet has been used in the participation in social governance. First, the Internet Plus has promoted the innovation of government services. Cross-departmental data sharing and collaborative governance forms such as "running at most once" and "e-government hall" have been innovated throughout the country. The openness of government information has been significantly improved, and the intelligent degree of social governance has made rapid progress. Second, the governance of cyberspace has been strengthened. As of March 2020, the number of Internet users in China has reached 904 million. However, cyberspace is not a place beyond the rule of law. The *Cyber Security Law of the People's Republic of China*, which came into effect in June 2017, has made the governance of cyberspace have a law to abide by, and ensured and promoted the healthy development of cyberspace.

6. Innovation in the Security Dimension of Social Governance

As the report of the 19th National Congress of the CPC pointed out, "We will promote safe development, and raise public awareness that life matters most and that safety comes first; we will improve the public safety system and the responsibility system for workplace safety; we will take resolute measures to prevent serious and major accidents, and build up our capacity for disaster prevention, mitigation, and relief." This requires taking "safety" as an important dimension of social governance to effectively resist various risks in social life. At the same time, social governance is also closely linked with the effective maintenance of national security. In April 2014, the National Security Commission of the Communist Party of China formally put forward the "holistic view of national security" at its first meeting. In October 2019, the 4th Plenary Session of the 19th CPC Central Committee put forward that to uphold the holistic view of national security, we should take people's security as the purpose, political security as the foundation, economic security as the basis, and military, scientific, technological, cultural and social security as the guarantee, so as to improve the national security system and enhance the national security capability. To implement the holistic view of national security in social governance, we must be ready for worst-case scenarios and focus on preventing and resolving major risks.

Generally speaking, since the 18th National Congress of the CPC in 2012, the CPC Central Committee with Comrade Xi Jinping as the core has boldly explored and practiced, comprehensively innovated the social governance system, and systematically improved the social governance capacity, so that China has seen a good situation of harmonious, stable and good governance.[1] In this process, the content and focus of social governance have been changing in practice, and the system of social governance improving. Therefore, we have taken a path of socialist social governance with Chinese characteristics.

III. Basic Experience of Social Governance

For more than 40 years since the reform and opening up, China has taken a path of social governance with Chinese characteristics and accumulated experience in social governance suited to China's national conditions.

1. Upholding and Improving the Leadership of the Party

The leadership of the Party is the greatest advantage of the socialist system with Chinese characteristics, and the Communist Party of China is the leading force of social governance. Due to differences in culture, system and other factors, there are different models of party politics in the world. However, as far as China's social governance is concerned, from the revolutionary times to

---

[1] Zhang Yi, "Taking the Path of Socialist Social Governance with Chinese Characteristics", *QIUSHI*, No. 6, 2018.

the construction of the People's Republic of China, the Communist Party of China has always been the leading core that played an irreplaceable role in China's development and stability. Representing the fundamental interests of the overwhelming majority of the people, the Communist Party of China can best coordinate the development of social governance interests among regions, departments, groups and citizens, and can best mobilize and integrate various resources to promote the innovative development of social governance. ①The principle of the social governance system shows that, for social governance, we should give full play to the Party's leading core role in overall coordination, and the Party should firmly grasp its leadership over social governance. At the same time, strengthening Party building and improving the Party's ruling ability and level are also the guarantee for maintaining the correct development direction of social governance. Without the Party's own governance reform and self-revolution, there could be no fundamental change in China's social governance. From this perspective, the greatest social governance is to insist that the Party should exercise effective self-supervision, practice strict self-governance in every respect, and crack down on corruption. ②

2. Transformation of Governance Model in Response to the Situation

Since the reform and opening up, with the freeing of various production factors, to meet the need of opening up, social governance has gradually seen deregulation and the concept of "management" began to be introduced. "Strengthening the government's function of social management" has become an important guarantee for market-oriented reform. As the reform involves the adjustment and differentiation of interests, various new social problems and contradictions appeared one after another. In addition to the economic sector,

---

① Zhang Yi, "Taking the Path of Socialist Social Governance with Chinese Characteristics", *QIUSHI*, No. 6, 2018.

② Wei Liqun, "New Progress in Social Governance since the 18th CPC National Congress", *Guangming Daily*, August 7, 2017.

the reform also entered the social field. The concepts of social management and social construction indicate that the Party and the state were aware of the disharmony between social development and economic development, and it was urgent to strengthen and innovate social governance. Since the 18th National Congress of the CPC in 2012, especially since the 3rd Plenary Session of the 18th CPC Central Committee in 2013, the reform of social governance has been continuously promoted, and the principle of social governance has been perfected. The subjects of social governance have also become diversified. We are committed to building a social governance system of based on "collaboration, participation, and common interests" and moving towards institutional governance.

3. Constant Innovation of Social Governance at the Grassroots Level

The foundation of social governance lies at the grassroots level, and urban and rural communities are the basic units of social governance. "The focus of social governance must get down to urban and rural communities. If the service and management ability at the community level gets strong, social governance will have a solid foundation."[①] With the deepening of the reform and opening up, the whole society is increasingly based on regions, and community building has become the main support of social governance. In recent years, many typical examples of community governance innovation have emerged throughout China. Some enhance residents' participation ability and organize residents to negotiate and solve decision-making matters involving public interests. Some guide various subjects' participation in community construction, and mobilize enterprises and social organizations to participate in community service projects, thus improving the service supply capacity of the community. Some focus on the legalization of community governance, including formulating or revising laws and regulations of community governance,

---

① Xi Jinping, "Promoting the Construction of Shanghai Pilot Free Trade Zone, Strengthening and Innovating the Social Governance of Megacities", *People's Daily*, March 6, 2014.

promoting the construction of public legal service system, and enhancing the community's ability to act according to the law. It can be seen that only when social governance at the grassroots level is carried out well, can it have the motive force for continuous innovation and truly respond to the needs of the people.

4. Constant Reform of Social Governance in Response to People's Needs

From " serving the people " to " the people-centered development philosophy", the reform of social governance has echoed the needs of the people, thus making social governance always have a strong driving force for innovation. For example, the strict household registration management system seriously restricted the people's right of free migration. It was an important institutional obstacle that caused urban-rural segregation and urban-rural gap. However, the social governance reform has continuously lifted household registration restrictions, allowing the free flow of people between urban and rural areas, and gradually realizing the equalization of basic public services between urban and rural areas. The government used to manage people's social life, while residents' self-governance and villagers' self-governance encourage the people to exert their own governance vitality. Therefore, to promote any reform, including reforms in social governance and social system, it is necessary to view the major issues involved in reform from the people's standpoint, plan reform ideas and formulate various reform measures in the interests of the overwhelming majority of the people.

5. Adjustment of Social Governance in line with National Conditions

In China, a country with a vast territory, a large population, a long history and rich cultural traditions, we can neither simply follow some historical models nor copy some "advanced" western governance models in social governance. At present, the rapid development of cyberspace is a new reality faced by social governance. It is necessary to keep up with and improve the governance mode of "virtual" society according to the characteristics of the

Internet, and explore the coordination and convergence of online and offline governance. At the same time, self-governance, rule of virtue, and rule of law are all possible paths of social governance. We need to comprehensively apply to it according to the different conditions in different places. To make social governance have more than one subject, we should mobilize the participation of various resources. We should also advocate source governance,[①] so as to achieve good social governance effects.

IV. Prospects for Social Governance

Looking back on the development process since the reform and opening up, we can see China's social governance has undergone multidimensional changes. Social governance has become an important component of China's experience in modernization. In the future, more methods of social governance need to be created, and the system of social governance needs to be constantly improved. First, we need to insist the principle that Party committees exercise leadership, and government assumes responsibility. In perfecting the social governance system based on the national conditions, it is necessary to transform the advantages of the Party's leadership and China's socialist system into the advantages of social governance. That government assumes responsibility does not mean government takes care of everything. Instead, we should stimulate social vitality and mobilize the public's participation in the practice of social governance. Only by cultivating more subjects of social governance and building a perfect mechanism of consultation, interaction and cooperation among them can we effectively meet the various needs of the people. Second, we must constantly improve the legalization of social governance. With the deepening of reform, we will face more complicated situations in social governance, including interest coordination, conflict resolution and social stability. To

---

① Jing Tiankui, "Source Governance: Foundation and Premise of Social Governance Effectiveness", *Journal of Beijing University of Technology (Social Science Edition)*, No. 3, 2014.

improve the legalization of social governance in the new era, we need to follow the guideline of "scientific legislation, strict law enforcement, fair justice and law-abiding by the whole people", so as to truly achieve good results of social governance by law. Third, to better integrate social governance and social construction, we need to promote social governance in improving people's livelihood. The purpose of effective social governance is not only to have a good social order, but also to guarantee people a fuller, more secure and more sustainable sense of gain, happiness and security.

Build a More Sustainable Ecological Governance System

Natalia Lazarevich

Leading Researcher, Institute of philosophy,

National Academy of Sciences of Belarus

Ensuring effective environmental conditions for development of society is an important task of national and public administration. In this regard, the study of ecological systems involves their direct connection with human and society; ecological systems themselves are considered as socioecosystems. Any socioecosystem consists of two main subsystems-natural and socially organized ones. Human cannot exist otherwise than in conditions of continuous interaction with the environment in the process of their life (as a biological being) and material production (as a social being).

Management of the processes of sustainability of natural subsystem is carried out by analyzing its structure and understanding that stability depends not only on the natural exchange of energy and matter, but also on the complexity of its structure formed during evolution, on the emergence of diverse forms and relationships within the system. These evolutionary processes determine more adapted biological systems, which guarantees preservation of their stable state.

Social subsystem includes the population, industrial, engineering, communication, energy and other complex objects, the functioning and management of which takes place due to scientific and social experience, economic effectiveness, and social planning.

Successful functioning of the entire socioecosystem depends on taking into account the features of each subsystem and establishing the relationships between them. Socioecological crises usually occur because of the lack of harmonious correlation between the natural and social subsystems. This usually happens because the preference is often given to social and economic factors-increase of the number of enterprises, increase of urban density, etc., while the natural component of the socioecosystem develops according to the residual principle. In the end, this imbalance leads to the crisis and unstable functioning of the entire socio-ecological system, which affects the quality of life of people and the effectiveness of their participation in the processes of economic production. That is why the study, prediction, and management of the processes of development of socioecosystems is one of the main tasks of national and public administration.

The socioecosystem can be considered as a self-regulating system, the harmonious development of which is ensured by a set of measures. The famous scientist Bachinsky G. A., in this regard, emphasizes that this in no way means that human can change the laws of nature and internal processes that occur in subsystems. However, human can and should learn to use them correctly and direct their action for the purposeful management of the entire system. [1]The normally functioning state of such environmental object is the state of dynamic equilibrium, in which the material-energy exchange between society and nature is organically inscribed in the natural cycle of substances and natural energy flows. As a result, the overall balance of substances and energy is maintained. If as a result of unbalanced anthropogenic influences this equilibrium is disturbed, socioecosystems begin to degrade; at the same time,

---

[1] G. A. Bachinsky, *Social Ecology: Theoretical and Applied Aspects*, Kyiv: Nauk dumka, 1991, p. 22.

there is a high probability of their complete disintegration with all the resulting environmental and socio-economic consequences.

Any socioecosystem is a system with a complex hierarchical structure. For example, one can talk about global-state socioecosystems that, in turn, consist of subsystems of the regional level, regional-from the district level, etc. All mentioned levels in normal condition are naturally interconnected; with increase of the rank, their dependence on the neighboring ecosystems decreases, while autonomy and the ability to self-regulation at the same time increases. Socioecosystems differ from natural systems themselves: they have the features that are associated not only with the level of anthropogenic interactions with natural systems, but also with the opportunity of human to perceive, evaluate the results of these interactions, including the situations of environmental crises and conflicts. Socioecosystems can be considered as territorial systems that combine human populations and the infrastructure of their life with the environment within autonomously managed administrative units of various ranks-states, administrative regions, cities and agricultural enterprises, etc. Small household farms can also be attributed to them, considering them microsocioecosystems, the dynamic equilibrium of which should be ensured by rational nature management. [1]

Let us emphasize once again that socioecosystems belong to the category of dynamic systems, the normal functioning of which is achieved by maintaining such an equilibrium, in which the material-energy exchange between society and nature is organically inscribed in natural evolution. A normally functioning socio-ecological system is the one, in which its main structural elements are stable, and the processes that take place inside it do not violate its integrity and qualitative certainty. Therefore, socioecosystems are much more complex than purely natural or social systems, and prediction of the development of such systems is a very urgent task.

---

[1] G. A. Bachinsky, *Social Ecology: Theoretical and Applied Aspects*, Kyiv: Nauk dumka, 1991, p. 23.

The process of prediction includes identification or formation of possible variants of development, as well as evaluation of the likelihood of implementation of certain variants of development. When making social-natural predictions, the result is difficult to quantify using probability estimates. Such a procedure of probabilistic assessment of the feasibility of a particular development path is typical, as a rule, for technical systems only. That is why the prognosis is made in the form of the list of possible options of development of the studied processes. This list acts as a list of options, each of which is accompanied by its meaningful description-the main result of prognosis-as the base of the scenario of development of the system. The purpose of this prognostic procedure is to analyze and characterize various consequences of implementation of the developed draft plan. Subsequent analysis of the results of prediction lets to evaluate the realism and quality of the planned actions.

There are three groups of methods of prediction and management offered for practical use: extrapolation methods, expert assessment methods, and logical modeling. The extrapolation method is based on conscious simplification of the results obtained in analyzing the development of the studied processes, description of the obtained data with the help of mathematical models, and their further calculation in the form of "models" for future moments of time. This method lets to search for acceptable estimates of the state of the system in the future, but its use is justified only for describing the processes of evolutionary development. The content and purpose of modeling is to design adaptive properties, to analyze the ability of society to show the necessary flexibility, to perform the function of self-regulation in the process of bringing the biosphere processes into equilibrium. In conditions of deterioration of the quality of biosphere functioning, social-natural modeling should offer ways to maintain the necessary conditions for the existence of humankind as a biological species without disturbing the biological balance in nature.

It is known that the processes of development of any system (including socioecological systems) involve both the periods of evolutionary change and abrupt transitions from one state to another one. Abrupt transitions are caused by significant changes in the natural and social reality-change of the demographic situation in the world, increase of environmental pollution, various natural and social disasters.

The 21st century turned out to be perhaps the most environmentally dangerous in human history, when the problems of the global energy crisis, biological degradation of the human population, depletion and lack of natural resources etc. have clearly worsened. Environmental degradation, which leads to disruption of the mechanisms of self-regulation of natural ecosystems, growing industrial press represent a serious threat to modern civilization. According to the existing predictions, the 21st century will also be the century of the growth of the number of new diseases, which is already evidenced by the COVID – 19.

An example of the presence of abrupt transitions in the development of socio-natural systems is the natural history of humankind associated with the use of tools. The progress of material culture can and should be considered as the process of supplementing the functional capabilities of natural organs with tools, that is, with artificial organs. For a long time, the created tools made up only some of the functions important to humans. In this regard, the pressure of natural selection was very significant, hence the high speed of genetic transformations. Transition to productive economy became that objective process, which determined a new type of relationship with nature almost simultaneously among different peoples and cultures. V. I. Vernadsky foresaw that the impact of human on the surrounding nature would increase so quickly that soon would come the time when human would turn into the main geological force, which forms the face of the Earth. [1]

Predictions based on the models of evolutionary development show that within the framework of the used technologies, from the certain moment of time, it is necessary to introduce more and more new energy capacities, moreover, an increasing part of the resources is used to meet the needs of the industry itself. If economic growth is characterized by quantitative indicators

---

[1] Vernadsky V. I. Philosophical thoughts of naturalist, V. I. Vernadsky. – M. , 1988, p. 56.

(increase of production, GDP growth, etc.), then, to analyze economic development, qualitative characteristics are used, for example, such categories as education and health. Sustainable economic growth means a one-directional upward vector of change of quantitative characteristics, while economic development allows the deviation from such dynamics in favor of ensuring the qualitative "non-economic" characteristics (state of the environment, public health, etc.).

The criterion of the level of economic development of different countries is the effectiveness of use of production resources-labor, natural and human-made resources, or human, natural and human-made capital. The most important indicator of economic development is GDP per capita, the increase of which indicates both the increase of the efficiency of use of productive resources of the country and the increase of the average well-being of its citizens. Consequently, there is a conflict situation, which can be resolved through radical changes in the technology of production and consumption of energy resources. Emergence of energy-saving technologies, introduction of new technological processes in the industry, development of digital controls and communication is that leap in development, which can harmonize further development of socio-ecological systems.

Logical modeling methods involve construction of models, in which the analogies are drawn between different phenomena, the relationship of separate processes is analyzed, the data on the processes of various physical nature are summarized. Human, spontaneously or consciously, models natural processes, in particular artificial selection, and performs the selective function in relation to some populations, contributing to consolidation of some signs in the sequential series of generations and removal of other ones. Therefore, not only object nature (i.e. objects and things) began to serve human, but also dynamic nature, first of all, evolutionary principles and mechanisms. ①

---

① P. A. Vodopianov, V. S. Krisachenko., Strategy of being of humankind: from the apocalyptic to the noospheric age, Minsk: Belaruskaya navuka, 2018, p. 124.

The most important changes for modern society are those that let to direct the values of the latest technological modes to solving the accumulated environmental problems. Development of agricultural chemistry has turned agriculture into the largest branch of the world industry. Its further development and effective application are possible only when using fundamentally new technologies and practical techniques. As a result of the introduction of biotechnological methods, there takes place more complete utilization of raw materials, territories, intensification of cultivation and use of renewable natural resources. At the same time, along with production of new products, biotechnological methods are also used to make products, traditional methods of creation of which are less environmentally friendly. In general, reasonable introduction of biotechnology can contribute to increase of environmental friendliness of the national economy, emergence of more harmonious relations between society and nature.

Methods of predictive management let to predict non-standard methods and situations in a particular field of activity, find the best solutions, take into account the real prospects of improvement of the analyzed systems on the base of their comparative analysis. The method of expert assessment can also be the recommended method for predicting abrupt changes in the systems. The information necessary to form a prognosis is summarized in this case by processing the opinions of a number of experts. As a result, there is developed a scenario of development of the system, as well as its possible variants, taking into account various circumstances. For example, thanks to the Intergovernmental Panel on Climate Change, we have the following information. In the period from 1880 to 2012, the average world temperature rose by 0.85 degrees Celsius. Moreover, each increase of temperature by 1 degree leads to decrease of the grain yield by about 5 percent. If we do not ensure implementation of the necessary scenario of development, then, taking into account the current level of concentration of greenhouse gases in the atmosphere and continued emissions, the increase of the world temperature is likely to exceed 1.5 degrees Celsius by the end of this century. In accordance with the principle of common but differentiated responsibilities and related capabilities, all countries should take action to prevent climate change, taking into account various national circumstances and the *Paris Agreement* to combat the climate change threat.

Environmental safety today not only determines the vector of development of civilization, but it is also a condition of survival of humankind. Ecosocial sustainability is increasingly seen as a fundamental value in the worldview system of modern society. Instruments of effective resolution of environmental problems should be associated with the formation of constructive environmental awareness and behavior of human and society. This is a rather complicated process connected with the transformation of the prevailing values and making new norms and rules imposed by the modern dynamics of innovative development. The most important problem of our time, fixed by the famous British sociologist A. Giddens in the concept of "post-traditional society", is connected with the fact that we live in the archdynamic world, where transience and instability dominates, everything is being questioned and even completely rejected. The so-called "built-in" elements-beliefs, ethical norms, behavioral stereotypes, and stable traditions-disappear from social life. In such circumstances, the organizational and regulatory function of national and public administration will increase, including preservation of constructive environmental values and development of constructive programs of social policy. Strengthening the role of the state as the main link of the political system, coordinator of the activities of the state and public organizations, subject of regulation of social processes should be carried out through prediction and justifying the effective tools of solving the problems of economic development, social and cultural sphere in conjunction with the solution of environmental problems. All this should meet the interests of sustainable development and should be coupled with implementation of the state environmental policy through improvement of environmental legislation, introduction of effective economic methods of management, environmental control and protection.

Today, civilization faces the problem of formation of the new universal ecological culture, which suggests the new ecocentric environmental consciousness and new nature-oriented, environment-friendly types and methods of organizing life and production processes. In the framework of the new ecoideology, human and nature are not opposed to each other as autonomous, especially antagonistic entities. On the contrary, human and humankind are considered as such an actively acting, self-developing part of nature, which implements the general universal laws that are at the base of self-development of nature as a whole. Human as a subject does not oppose nature as an object; human becomes the subject of coevolutionary strategy of development and the corresponding policy of national and public administration.

China's Social Governance Modernization and Innovative Development Mechanism

Ma Feng

Associate Professor, National Institute of Social Development, CASS

I. Mission and Task of Social Governance Modernization in the New Era

Advancing social governance modernization in the new era is not only the key to China's governance modernization, but also a crucial system to address the imbalance and inadequacy in social progress when China is about to finish the building of a moderately prosperous society in all respects and embark on a new journey towards a modern socialist country. To build a community of social governance and a social governance model based on collaboration, participation and common interests is the Party Central Committee's primary strategic decision, the need for the development, and the inevitable requirement for promoting system modernization. The social governance modernization in the new era is of great significance for maintaining social stability and national security, forestalling social risks and improving social governance capacity. In this regard, efforts should be made to comprehensively strengthen and perfect the leadership of the Party committees, consolidate the duties of the government and make it accountable, as well as reinforce social coordination and public participation.

General Secretary Xi Jinping highlighted at the symposium on economic and social work, "It is necessary to improve the social governance system based on collaboration, participation and common interests, thus realizing a positive interplay of government governance, social regulation and residents' self-governance, and building a community of social governance under which everyone performs their duties and shares in the benefits; besides, it is urgent to strengthen and innovate the social governance at grassroots level to make each part of the society vital and resolve conflicts and disputes in harmony."①

The modernization of social system and capacity for governance is an important part of the modernization of China's system and capacity for governance. In order to innovate the social governance system, the 3rd Plenary Session of the 18th CPC Central Committee upheld the social governance modernization as a critical part of deepening the reform in all respects and thus adopted the *Decision of the Central Committee of the Communist Party of China on Major Issues Concerning Deepening the Reform in All Respects*, emphasizing the need to "perfect the mode of social governance by adhering to systematic governance, strengthening the leadership of the Party committees and carrying forward the leading role of governmental departments, so as to achieve public participation and a positive interplay of government governance, social regulation and residents' self-governance."②

It was further stressed in the report delivered at the 19th National Congress of the Communist Party of China to "establish a social governance model based on collaboration, participation and common interests by stepping up institution building in social governance and improving the law-based social governance model under which Party committees exercise leadership, government assumes

---

① Xi Jinping, "Speech at the Symposium on Economic and Social Work", *People's Daily*, Page 2, Aug. 25, 2020.

② "Decision of the Central Committee of the Communist Party of China on Major Issues Concerning Deepening the Reform in All Respects", *Guangming Daily*, Page 1, Nov. 16, 2013.

responsibility, non-governmental actors provide assistance, and the public get involved, coupled with strengthening public participation and rule of law in social governance, and making such governance smarter and more specialized."[1]

A new social governance model in the new era is established thereby by improving the mode of social governance, building a social governance model based on collaboration, participation and common interests, as well as deepening the reform and advancing the modernization of social governance system in all respects. The law-based social governance system under which Party committees exercise leadership, government assumes responsibility, non-governmental actors provide assistance and the public get involved has been polished day by day.

Efforts have been made to advance the modernization of social system and capacity for governance continuously and deeply in line with the decisions made at the 19th National Congress of the Communist Party of China, so as to constantly meet people's yearning for a better life and the call for the sense of ownership. General Secretary Xi Jinping put forward the scientific proposal for "building a community of social governance under which everyone performs their duties" at the 2019 central conference on political and legal work. General Secretary Xi stated to "build a community of social governance under which everyone performs their duties by perfecting the community-level self-governance system and mobilizing the initiative of the urban and rural masses, enterprises, public institutions and social organizations on self-governance".[2] The scientific concept of the community of social governance under which everyone performs

---

[1] Xi Jinping, "Secure a Decisive Victory in Building a Moderately Prosperous Society in All Respects and Strive for the Great Success of Socialism with Chinese Characteristics for a New Era Delivered at the 19th National Congress of the Communist Party of China", *Guangming Daily*, Page 1, Oct. 28, 2017.

[2] "Do a Good Political and Legal Job in All Respects in the New Era Thoroughly to Promote Social Equality and Justice and Ensure People's Living and Working in Peace and Contentment", *Guangming Daily*, Page 1, Jan. 17, 2019.

their duties further contributed to the novel understanding of the modernization of social system and capacity for governance in the new era.

In order to uphold and improve the system of socialism with Chinese characteristics and advance the modernization of China's system and capacity for governance, the Fourth Third Plenary Session of the 18th CPC Central Committee adopted the *Decision of the Central Committee of the Communist Party of China on Major Issues Concerning Upholding and Improving the System of Socialism with Chinese Characteristics and Advancing the Modernization of China's System and Capacity for Governance*, emphasizing the need to "uphold and improve the social governance system based on collaboration, participation and common interests, as well as maintain social stability and defend national security";① it was further pointed out, "Social governance is important to national governance. Hence it is critical to reinforce and innovate social governance, perfect the science and technology backed and law based social governance system under which Party committees exercise leadership, government assumes responsibility, democratic consultation comes into play, non-governmental actors provide assistance and the public get involved, as well as build a community of social governance under which everyone performs their duties and shares in the benefits, so as to ensure people's living and working in peace and contentment, realize stable and orderly society, and carry out the Peaceful China initiative more effectively."②

The modernization of China's system and capacity for governance has been advanced and approaches to forestall and defuse major risks have been upgraded constantly since the 18th National Congress of the Communist Party of China, contributing to historic achievements in political, economic, cultural, social

---

① *Decision of the Central Committee of the Communist Party of China on Major Issues Concerning Upholding and Improving the System of Socialism with Chinese Characteristics and Advancing the Modernization of China's System and Capacity for Governance*, Guangming Daily, Page 1, Nov. 6, 2019

② *Decision of the Central Committee of the Communist Party of China on Major Issues Concerning Upholding and Improving the System of Socialism with Chinese Characteristics and Advancing the Modernization of China's System and Capacity for Governance*, Guangming Daily, Page 1, Nov. 6, 2019

and ecological civilization sectors. Regardless of considerable uncertainties in global development, China's centralized, unified, efficient, democratic and legal governance system embraces the Chinese wisdom represented by the innovative governance system that perfectly combines tradition and modernity in the post-crisis era full of chaotic governance changes in various countries.

Alongside modernizing China's system and capacity for governance, the framework of China's new social governance system has been built fundamentally especially under the guidance of new ideas, thoughts and strategies since the 18th National Congress of the Communist Party of China, contributing to efficient, centralized and legal social governance capacity, and the law-based social governance system under which Party committees exercise leadership, government assumes responsibility, non-governmental actors provide assistance and the public get involved; furthermore, the capability to forestall and defuse security risks is enhanced because the public participation and rule of law in social governance are strengthened, and such governance is made smarter and more specialized.

Building a community of social governance under which everyone performs their duties and shares in the benefits and improving the science and technology backed and law based social governance system under which Party committees exercise leadership, government assumes responsibility, democratic consultation comes into play, non-governmental actors provide assistance and the public get involved are the call for embarking on a new journey towards a modern socialist country after the building of a moderately prosperous society in all respects; they, as reliable institutional guarantees, are also the objective requirements of upholding and improving the system of socialism with Chinese characteristics and advancing the modernization of China's system and capacity for governance, which is of great significance for maintaining social stability and national security, forestalling and defusing major risks and improving social governance capacity.

Economic growth and social progress always coincide. Social progress will inevitably usher in economic achievements, while stabler and better social progress can better boost economic growth and back economic growth, political stability, cultural prosperity and ecological optimization. Social construction, a momentous part of the five-sphere integrated plan, takes social progress as the core. On the one hand, people enjoy the economic achievements directly in employment, social insurance, public health, social governance and other aspects of social progress; the level of social development, on the other hand, represents the level of social progress, especially the level of modernization of a country or nation. Whether or not a country is promising, attractive and charming as we have often said depends more on the level of social progress of a country. High-level social progress is a sign to the well-rounded human development.

Great changes have taken place in China's social development since the founding of the People's Republic of China, contributing to concrete fruits, a significantly enhanced sense of gain and profound changes in people's livelihood. Social progress has continuously embraced new heights alongside the economic growth nationwide and the increase in national strength, thus laying a solid foundation to unite the Chinese people more closely to win more and more victories in advancing the socialism with Chinese characteristics.

II. Orientation and Function of Building the Community of Social Governance in the New Era

New problems and challenges emerge in China's social governance in the new era due to various social development risks at home and abroad. Uncertainties challenge China's social governance in the new era mostly. Global social risks and challenges brought about by global risk spillover account for the majority of new social risks under global integration. "In spite of achievements, we must be soberly aware that China, in its pivotal stage for transforming the growth model, improving economic structure and fostering new growth drivers, faces rising downward pressure on economy amid intertwined structural, institutional and cyclical problems, as well as the intensified impact of the slowdown in economic growth, difficult structural adjustments made and previous economic stimulus policies. We need to be well prepared with contingency plans because the global economy that continues to slow down is still undergoing profound adjustments due to the global financial crisis, leading to accelerated great changes and substantially increasing sources of turbulence."[1]

Contingency plans are required in view of the development situation at home and abroad. At a critical moment of China's development, the year 2020 marks not only a victory in the first Centenary Goal of building a moderately prosperous society in all respects and the concluding year of the 13th Five-Year Plan, but also a crucial year to create the pivotal underpinning for the 14th Five-Year Plan and the second Centenary Goal. To basically achieve modernization and develop China into a great modern socialist country are the Chinese Dream of national rejuvenation that countless dedicated patriots have been striving for since modern times. The modernization of social system and capacity for governance in the new era is bound to become an integral part of the modernization of China's system and capacity for governance in the new era. We must be aware that "as the sum of many ways in which individuals and public or private institutions manage their common affairs, governance is an ongoing process of reconciling conflicting or different interests and taking joint action".[2]

Globally speaking, social governance crises brought about by a series of institutional disorder and state governance disorder in western countries after the financial crisis in 2018 have hidden in all aspects of social operation, resulting in the arrival of a highly risky society caused by overall governance disorder or institutional collapse at state and society level due to internal social

---

[1] "Central Conference on Economic Work in Beijing, Capital of China", *Guangming Daily*, Page 1, Dec. 13, 2019.

[2] Yu Keping, "Introduction to Global Governance", *Marxism & Reality*, No. 1, 2002.

conflicts. The West or those countries and regions finishing industrialization or striding into post-industrial society are caught in a "crisis of order" in a highly risky society. In fact, "perfecting system and capacity for governance is a way out to many problems worldwide". ①

Profound changes accelerated and sources of turbulence increased substantially in 2019. The "Yellow Vest Movement" triggered by the increase in fuel oil tax has lasted for more than a year in France, thus making it a normal social phenomenon; moreover, the strike and march triggered by pension reform erupted throughout the winter. A compromise in sharing the fruits of social progress among different social strata could not be easily reached. International conferences such as APEC were cancelled due to the domestic riots in Chile caused by metro price adjustment. Similarly, there were persistent protests and riots in Colombia due to the pension-related affairs. "At present, the COVID – 19 outbreak worldwide is accelerating such changes. We are entering a period of turbulence and change and witnessing profound adjustments in the global economic, technological, cultural, security and political patterns amid protectionism and unilateralism on the rise, the world economy in the doldrums and the global industrial and supply chains challenged by non-economic factors." ②

Regardless of various reasons for the increase insources of turbulence, the social unrest in established capitalist countries and emerging economies is directly closely related to fuel oil tax, pension and the price of public transport such as subway. The deep-rooted contradictions in social progress are embodied primarily in the challenges in people's livelihood and the lack of social policies. Such social unrest thereby leads to the dilemma of state and social governance system, thus making it a major risk that affects the social operation.

---

① "Xi Jinping Meets with UN Secretary-General António Guterres", *Guangming Daily*, Page 1, Apr. 9, 2019.

② Xi Jinping, "Speech at the Symposium on Economic and Social Work", *People's Daily*, Page 2, Aug. 25, 2020.

The current uncertainties in social progress are far greater than in the past. In consideration of the uncertain risks, it would be difficult to tackle all kinds of potential and obvious risk factors today without modern system or capacity for governance. Risks often exist. A chaotic, disorderly, conflict and collapsed governance system and derived governance capacity cannot help to effectively address challenges of high-risk factors in a complex and fast-changing society at present. Actually, "social movement is both the original motivation of practical fighting and its manifestation, including the establishment of a positive social mechanism and the social movement itself". ①

Domestically speaking, China has embraced achievements in social development in endlessly. Chinese people feel satisfied, happy and secure to a larger extent and enjoy the fruits of social progress, for instance, per capita income, poverty elimination, tax reform, reduction in drug price, faster broadband and lower internet rates, as well as garbage sorting, thanks to stable national development. The economic growth and social progress in parallel as the two wheels help address the inadequacy and imbalance in development.

In 2019, China's gross enrolment rate of preschool education reached 83.4%, 37% higher than that in 2000; the completion rate of compulsory education was 94.8%, reaching the average level of high-income countries in the world; the gross enrollment rate of senior high school education was 89.5%, twice that of 2000; the gross enrollment rate of higher education was 51.6%, 4 times of that in 2000, marking that higher education is becoming universal. In 2019, the average years of schooling for new members of the labor force was 13.7 years, 1.29 years higher than that in 2010, of which 50.9% received higher education. ②

The health conditions of urban and rural residents have continued to improve by the end of 2019. The average life expectancy of Chinese people has

---

① [Germany] Scott Lash, "Risk Society and Risk Culture", *Marxism & Reality*, No. 4, 2002.

② Wan Donghua, "Achievements in Building a Moderately Prosperous Society in All Respects from the Perspective of Social Development", *People's Daily*, Page 11, Aug. 4, 2020.

rose from 71.4 years in 2000 to 77.3 years in 2019, and the infant mortality rate has dropped from 32.2 ‰ to 5.6 ‰. ①

Basic endowment insurance covered 968 million by the end of 2019, 7.1 times of that in 2000, with the coverage rate exceeding 90%. ②

The per capita disposable income of Chinese citizens in 2019 reached 30,733 yuan, 4.4 times higher than that in 2000, with an average annual real growth of 9.2%. It marks the new height of exceeding 30,000 yuan. ③

The Party has led Chinese people to make historic achievements amid social development, contributing to significant social progress enjoyed by the people. According to the Human Development Index (HDI) compiled by the United Nations Development Program, China's HDI reached 0.591 in 2000, lower than the world average of 0.641. In 2018, it rose to 0.758, making China the only country in the world to leap from "low level of human development" to "high level of human development" since 1990. ④

Despite historic achievements, China faces new tasks, challenges and difficulties at a new stage of development when it is about to finish the building of a moderately prosperous society in all respects and embark on a new journey towards a modern socialist country. As a result, swift actions must be taken to realize modern social development by tackling areas of weaknesses and breaking institutional barriers that affect social progress with greater courage and wisdom. Problems amid development can only be solved in the course of development. Social concepts, social psychology and social behavior are undergoing profound changes alongside profound changes in China's social structure. Around world's profound changes unseen in a century and the great

---

① Wan Donghua, "Achievements in Building a Moderately Prosperous Society in All Respects from the Perspective of Social Development", *People's Daily*, Page 11, Aug. 4, 2020.

② Wan Donghua, "Achievements in Building a Moderately Prosperous Society in All Respects from the Perspective of Social Development", *People's Daily*, Page 11, Aug. 4, 2020.

③ Fang Xiaodan, "Achievements in Building a Moderately Prosperous Society in All Respects from the Perspective of Chinese Citizens' Income and Expenditure", *People's Daily*, Page 10, Jul. 27, 2020.

④ Fang Xiaodan, "Achievements in Building a Moderately Prosperous Society in All Respects from the Perspective of Chinese Citizens' Income and Expenditure", *People's Daily*, Page 10, Jul. 27, 2020.

rejuvenation of the Chinese nation, a dialectical view should be adopted to look at the characteristics and tasks in difference phases of China's social development at new stage in line with new features and requirements, as well as new contradictions and challenges.

On the one hand, as China has ushered in the stage of high-quality development, the principal contradiction facing Chinese society is now the contradiction between imbalanced and inadequate development and the people's ever-growing needs for a better life. The profound changes in China's social development pattern lead to increasingly complex social interest relationship, more diverse value orientation and growing interest appeals. Alongside the mutual promotion of economic forms and social development pattern, the people are full of expectation for higher level of social development, call for higher efficiently modern governance, and put forward higher demand for material and cultural life. Additionally, the people passionately pursue fairness and justice as their demand for democracy, rule of law, fairness, justice, security, environment and other aspects is growing.

On the other hand, as China's social structure is undergoing profound changes, the overall operation mechanism of the society changes to a great extent. The medium and long-term social development is more likely to get affected by the changes of domestic and foreign economic situation. Social governance is confronted with complex situation amid various contradictions and risks interwoven and interest appeals intertwined. Therefore, efforts should be made to balance various demands in social development, reach a broader consensus on social development and achieve a higher dynamically balanced social interest regulation, thus maintaining social stability for medium and long-term economic growth and modernization.

"It turns out that difficulties after the development are no less than those before the development." [1] As the principal contradiction facing Chinese

---

[1] Xi Jinping, "Speech at the Symposium on Economic and Social Work", *People's Daily*, Page 2, Aug. 25, 2020

society now, inadequacy and imbalance in development have become increasingly prominent. Generally speaking, it is mainly because some pressing problems caused by imbalanced and inadequate development await solutions. For instance, many areas concerning public well-being require improvement; poverty alleviation remains a formidable task; the disparities in development between rural and urban areas, between regions, and in income distribution remain substantial; and Chinese people face many difficulties in employment, education, healthcare, housing, and elderly care……Moreover, "as China's social structure is undergoing profound changes, the Internet has profoundly changed the way of human communication, contributing to profound changes in social concepts, social psychology and social behavior. During the '14th Five-Year Plan' period, studies and plans are needed for adapting to the profound changes in social structure, social relations, social behavior patterns and social psychology, achieving fuller employment and creating better jobs, improving the nationwide and sustainable social insurance system, strengthening the public health and disease control system, as well as boosting the long-term and balanced population growth, enhancing social governance, resolving social contradictions and maintaining social stability."[1] The modernization of China's social governance in the new era is bound to help cope with the imbalanced and inadequate development efficiently.

China still faces new challenges brought about by new social risks amid the modernization of China's social system and capacity for governance in the new era. In fact, "new social risks pose new problems and challenges to social governance. Nowadays, the advancement of modernization, especially the continuous emergence of new technologies, leads to a modern 'risky society' besides economic growth and social progress. Modern risks are most different from traditional ones in their uncertainty and unpredictability, which may cause wide-ranging social panic because of their rapid and wide

---

[1] Xi Jinping, "Speech at the Symposium on Economic and Social Work", *People's Daily*, Page 2, Aug. 25, 2020.

spread." [1]

Efforts should be made to cope with the challenges of both traditional and modern social risks throughout the modernization of China's social system and capacity for governance in the new era. Alongside the rise of populism and the governance disorder in major developed economies under fast changing international situation, China's modern system of national governance and social governance in the new era, by virtue of its effective response, high synergy, structural reform driving capacity and strong organizational capacity, has become a crucial reference for the international community to address challenges and accelerate reorganizing and building the system and capacity for governance in the post financial crisis era. The "Governance of China" is hence becoming a significant system and a global public good for countries to learn from.

III. Innovation in Social Governance and the Building of a Community of Social Governance in the New Era

A modern society should be both vital and orderly. The well-rounded human development and social progress in all respects are integral to high-quality social development. Standing at a new historical starting point, China embraces accelerated new development pattern that is bound to greatly impact on the evolution of social development directly represented by employment. The rapidly developed new drivers will directly impact on social life, social psychology and social behavior at a more micro and specific level, and the micro changes in social progress will call for higher and more concrete requirements for governance capacity, thus making people live a more advanced and smarter life. The emergence of new development vitality will further stimulate passionate

---

[1] Li Peilin, "Guide Innovative Social Governance in the New Era with New Ideas", *People's Daily*, Page 7, Feb. 6, 2018.

social creation and innovation, thus achieving a higher level of public participation and carrying forward people's pioneering spirit to a greater extent; what's more, every one of our people has the chance to pursue career through hard work.

On the journey towards the second Centenary Goal and at the crossroads of the evolution of the times, the question of an era is the driving force of theoretical innovation. It is necessary to continuously explore new social development based on collaboration, participation and common interests to boost social progress in all respects.

First is to adhere to the general principle of pursuing progress while ensuring stability to constantly meet the people's new expectation for social progress, new yearning for a better life, and new requirements for governance capacity. It is necessary to maintain the overall development of the country moderately and seize opportunities to advance progress. Efforts should also be made to seek "qualitative" changes besides maintaining the stable "quantity", so as to continuously advance the transformation towards high-quality social progress. It takes time to transform from the traditional social development model to a high-quality one. The background of the times, the phased characteristics of the development course and the long-term development goal present us with the need to pursue progress in line with the principle of pursuing progress while ensuring stability. Imbalanced and inadequate development remains prominent. The basic dimension of the Chinese context that our country is still and will long remain in the primary stage of socialism has not changed. China's international status as the world's largest developing country has not changed. Hence at new stage of development, efforts should be made to pursue progress in line with the principle of pursuing progress while ensuring stability, remain firm in development determination, as well as improve people's livelihood and meet their yearning for a better life in continuous social progress; improve weak links concerning people's livelihood and enlarge the dividend of people's livelihood in continuous social progress; advance social progress with sustainable driving forces, enhance the synchronization and sustainability of social development, meet people's greater expectation for future social progress, and promote stable and higher-quality growth steadily.

Second is to advance social development with in-depth reforms in all respects in the new era. Deepening reform in all respects marks the development of our times. It helps enlarge the institutional dividend to drive continuous social progress. As a result, many institutional problems that have long troubled our development have been solved, and the growth has been driven further. The fundamental purpose of development is to endow people with happiness. We will unswervingly stay committed to economic construction, continuously transform the economic achievements into the driving forces for social progress, and synchronize economic growth and social progress. Reform and opening up has come a long way, but it has to overcome new challenges on its way ahead. Facing the development situation at home and abroad, swift actions are need to further deepen reform in all respects at new stage, so as to stimulate the vitality of China's social development with flexible institutions.

To advance social development in the new era, we must stay dedicated to the pioneering spirit advocated in the reform and opening up and the self-reform spirit advocated in deepening reform in all respects. Additionally, we must devote great efforts to the specific aspects of social development, such as priority in employment, innovation, starting businesses and creation, household registration system, equitable access to public services, reform of employment system, development of grassroots personnel, as well as upward flow of economically disadvantaged groups, priority in education development, fair employment, strengthening social assistance and healthcare. The reform in every aspect involves the vital interests of the people. We should stay focused on the key areas and dare to break restrictions and the impediments of vested interests, thus advancing social mobility and beautifying such a fast changing China.

Currently, people's needs and requirements for social development have undergone fundamental changes. To comply with their new requirements and changes for social development is to comply with their new expectation for development. Development is the Party's top priority in governing and rejuvenating the country, and it is also the primary expectation of the people. We should deepen reform in all respects at new stage to seek prosperity for the country, rejuvenation for the nation and wellbeing for the people, to advance sustainable and healthy economic growth, to ensure social fairness and justice and to safeguard long-term peace and stability.

Third is to advance social progress in the new area amid journey towards a modern socialist country. At present, alongside the great changes and adjustments in the world, the global economic, technological, cultural, security and political patterns are changing profoundly, leading to a period of turbulence and change worldwide. In consideration of more adverse external environment in the coming period, we must be well prepared to deal with a series of new risks and challenges. However, the basic trend of steady long-term growth for China's economy remains unchanged at present and for a period to come. So is the trend of the Chinese nation towards rejuvenation and prosperity.

China has to develop into a modern socialist country inevitably, which embodies the common aspiration of the Chinese nation. We should remain focused on modernization as required by the times amid journey towards a modern socialist country; moreover, we should further adapt to high-quality development and further keep pace with the modernization of China's system and capacity for governance, so as to achieve better, more efficient, more equitable, more sustainable and safer development.

We should formulate a good social development plan during the 14th Five-Year Plan period to meet the people's new expectation for development. Based on the new experience and new understanding of social development, as well as the new situation of internal and external changes, we must give full play to China's socialist system and enhance the adaptability to the characteristics of social development during the 14th Five-Year Plan period and in the longer term; besides, we should improve our capability to govern the country both macroscopically and microscopically, so as to find and solve problems, as well as discover new approaches and new experiences and summarize, refine and popularize them in a timely manner. Only in this way can China usher in continuous social progress with socialist system in its efforts against adverse development environment.

It is necessary to remain disciplined in steady policies towards social development at new stage. We will make ensuring stability a top priority, do a good job in fundamental and systematic work in a down-to-earth manner, and maintain strategic determination; we should also do everything within our capacity to meet people's basic and diversified needs, so as to make all the people get equitable access to the achievements. What's more, efforts should be made to maintain the stability, continuity and sustainability of social policies. In addition to meet the basic needs of the people, we should also explore the potential growth drivers, strengthen areas of weakness, tackle the longstanding and fundamental problems existing in the economic growth and social progress, and practice the Experience of Fengqiao in the new era.

Reform and opening up has constantly given birth to development vitality. Bearing in mind Xi Jinping Thought on Socialism with Chinese Characteristics for a New Era, we must continuously deepen the new understanding of social development, advance social progress in all respects at new stage amid journey towards a modern socialist country and constantly improve the social governance system based on collaboration, participation and common interests, so as to achieve a positive interplay of government governance, social regulation and residents' self-governance, and build a community of social governance under which everyone performs their duties and shares in the benefits. We should also strengthen and innovate the social governance at grassroots level to make each part of the society vital and resolve conflicts and disputes in harmony. Furthermore, more attention should be paid to safeguard social fairness and justice, thus advancing the well-rounded human development and social progress in all respects.

IV. Conclusion

The social governance pattern with Chinese characteristics is becoming a kind of Chinese solution and reflects Chinese wisdom, whose significance and advantages have been demonstrated in dealing with the crisis of high-risk development in the world. "The reform and opening-up in the new era has more new connotations and characteristics than the past, one of which is more focus on system construction. The reform faces more deep-rooted institutional problems. There are higher requirements for the top-level design of the reform and for the systematicness, integrity and synergy of the reform, leading to heavier task of putting in place sound frameworks and constructing systems accordingly."[①] The social governance pattern of Chinese style is characterized by efficient operation, stable core, strong coordination, consensus building, deep accumulation, effective participation and active response.

We must advance the modernization of social governance in the new era in view of new characteristics of China's social development and social construction. China is now undergoing adjustments, which is synchronized with its economic trends. The transformation of new and old driving forces in the economic sector also affects the social development. Global progress is inseparable from the government, market and society after the financial crisis in 2018. Although the invisible and visible hands play their role, social governance, with more prominent impact, becomes a new approach affecting economic growth. It has played a unique role to the emergence of a series of new economic and business forms. The settlement of structural contradiction in employment partly depends on the community. Laid-off workers affected by

---

① Xi Jinping, "Explanation on the Decision of the Central Committee of the Communist Party of China on Major Issues Concerning Upholding and Improving the System of Socialism with Chinese Characteristics and Advancing the Modernization of China's System and Capacity for Governance", *Guangming Daily*, Page 4, Nov. 6, 2019.

overcapacity can get access to safe haven through primary-level governance. The strengthening of social security and risk prevention help ensure economic growth, solve the "last mile" problem for government governance, address unsolved parts concerning social development, and bridge the social divergence. It can be said that social governance is not only productive forces, but also a "sharp weapon" to meet people's needs for a better life and to solve the imbalance and inadequacy in development.

Social Governance and Gender Equality in Belarus

Volha Davydzik

Sino-Belarusian Research Center of Philosophy and Culture,

Institute of Philosophy, National Academy of Sciences of Belarus

The social policy of Belarus is aimed, firstly, at achieving sustainable development of societies[1], secondly, at developing human capital[2], and thirdly, at supporting the most vulnerable groups of the population[3]. It is advisable to assume that the nature of social transformations should be pointwise, local, based on the actual state of things. It is assumed that such an orientation will be most effective in the process of achieving the goal of harmonious and sustainable development of society. It is also necessary to provide an algorithm for managerial decision-making procedures, which, first of all, should be based on rationality and a humanistic approach.

In Belarus, discussions around ensuring gender equality have become relevant as an effective tool for the modernization of all areas of national politics

---

[1] National Strategy for Sustainable Development (NSDS) for the period until 2020: - [Electronic resource]: Access mode: un. by. Access date: 08/01/2018.

[2] State program "Education and Youth Policy" for 2016 – 2020 – [Electronic resource]: Access mode: edu. gov. by. Access date: 08/01/2018.

[3] State program on social protection and promotion of employment for 2016 – 2020 – [Electronic resource]: Access mode: mintrud. gov. by. Access date: 08/01/2018.

and economics. The expert community, representatives of scientific and creative clusters are involved in this issue, and many events, exhibition projects, civic initiatives are conducted to intensify research interest and attract public attention to these issues. A new impetus to the development of gender was given by the *5th National Plan of Action for Gender Equality in Belarus for 2017 – 2020*, which was approved in February 2017 by the Decree of the Council of Ministers of the Republic of Belarus. ①This is a national policy document aimed at developing mechanisms for introducing a gender approach into the process of developing and implementing public policy measures in various areas of society. Key areas of gender mainstreaming are equality in socio-economic participation, family relations, gender education and enlightenment.

An important role in adapting national policies to gender-sensitive issues is played by the integration of these aspects into the legislative framework. In this case, first of all, we are talking about creating a legislative framework for the prevention of domestic violence, as well as a legislative framework for reproductive health. Thus, the issues of age restrictions of both donors and patients have become relevant (40 years for male donors, 35 years for female donors and 49 years for the patient). This restriction, experts believe, is excessive, given the need for a mandatory medical examination. "From the point of view of the feminist agenda, reproduction and sexuality are political categories that are constantly included in the struggle for power, since reproduction acts as a necessary condition for the existence of society. Therefore, it is a woman who is primarily controlled by the state, community, family, group. Criticism of the patriarchal system requires a rethinking of the question of which strategies of resistance and overcoming these power strategies we can develop." ②

---

① National action plan for gender equality in Belarus for 2017 – 2020: Electronic source: Access mode: http://www.government.by/upload/docs/file59fe04a05ce85ea9.PDF, Access Date: 11/10/2018.

② Schurko, T. Female body between feminism, pro-life and state politics// [Electronic resource]: – – Access mode: www.n-europe.eu. Access date: 11/12/2018.

The age limit applies to men who want to resort to the sterilization procedure. This procedure is intended for men after 35 years of age with at least 2 children. The exception is men with medical indications for this procedure. "… the adopted legislative norms indicate that reproductive freedom has a specific restriction in our country. In particular, we are talking about everything that, at least in some way, can undermine the norm of an active fertile body. Perceived as "reproductive potential" and "demographic reserve", a woman is forced to follow directions "from above", not being able to control the fullness of her reproductive rights by herself"[1].

The integration of gender-sensitive consciousness into the social body has a close relationship with humanitarian research and expertise. The concept of social production of gender, its interpretation as an ideological constant integrated into the social body and an element of social stratification, which hold social relations on the plane of the gender, is also a promising direction in modern socio-philosophical theory. The ideological commitment of the concept of gender leads to such social phenomena as the division of labor by gender, the consolidation of traditional social roles and behavioral stereotypes on the principle of courageous-feminine, the role of the body and corporality in social relations, etc. The deconstruction of this phenomenon, the study of the process of building this or that type of relationship, stable ties, structures are called upon to reveal the foundations of gender relations in a particular society, to identify those aspects that have become inherent in individuals and groups. They are reproduced in generative experience, but are, in fact, elements of usurpation and the continuation of abusive relations.

In the field of social practice, the problem remains extremely urgent, associated, firstly, with the weak representativeness of statistical data, their incompleteness, the inability to obtain objective information due to subjective factors from individuals involved in conflict situations, and the imperfection of

---

[1] Schurko, T. Female body between feminism, pro-life and state politics// [Electronic resource]: - - Access mode: www. n-europe. eu. Access date: 11/12/2018.

the system of government bodies and the legislative framework, from the other side. Secondly, there remains a high need for multidisciplinary research that can develop joint solutions in the field of conventionality of such concepts as "discrimination", "violence", "domestic violence", "victim", "aggressor", etc., clarification of the essence many phenomena, as well as analysis of domestic legislation, development of recommendations for its reform in terms of compliance with those provisions that were adopted in the National Plan. It should be noted the important role of the academic community in intersectoral cooperation for the implementation of the idea of gender equality in Belarus, the implementation of international conventions in national law. With all the diversity and fragmentation of topics and objects, local communities, gender studies in Belarus have a 20 - year history. Nevertheless, certain discourses have already settled at different levels of consideration of this problem, a fundamentally new discussion field has been created-overcoming the values of traditional society. At the same time, this area is both potentially containing many risks associated with the human factor, and is highly knowledge-based in terms of interdisciplinary research. In this regard, it is important to develop an understanding of the importance of expanding interagency cooperation with the participation of public organizations, government and the academic community in order to create an optimal approach to solving the problem of gender inequality in our country. All these measures and decisions will contribute to the sustainable development of the country, as well as the modernization of national identity, in terms of its correlation with trends in world practice and the relevance of the current situation in Belarusian society.

Some points of the national plan are crucial for the socio-economic sphere of the republic related to the need of integration a gender perspective in budget planning of social programs. Compliance with this aspect in the country's social policy implies equal access of men and women to social support resources, as well as considering the experience and needs of men and women in planning and approving programs.

Gender budgeting has been introduced in many European countries, as well as in some CIS countries, which has allowed more efficient spending of budget funds to support and develop significant initiatives in this area. Such a reorientation of the work of state bodies makes it possible to mobilize financial resources and direct them exactly as it is necessary in each specific case, considering the gender factor. To do this, it is necessary to conduct a gender analysis as far as the interests of specific groups that need government assistance. In this understanding of budget planning, issues of social justice and social solidarity are considered in terms of the distribution of benefits.

The procedure for introducing a gender budgeting strategy into the process of developing social programs to support the population of Belarus is of an important strategic nature. This aspect is important for the effective implementation of the entire gender policy of Belarus, which includes specification and adaptation of the *National Action Plan*; development of a legislative framework, in practice, preventing all forms of discrimination based on gender and age, as well as all forms of violence related to gender and age; creation of equal conditions for participation in political, economic, cultural and other spheres of public life, regardless of these aspects. The introduction of gender budgeting in the process of development and adoption of social programs in Belarus will allow more efficient planning and spending of budget funds for specific groups and for specific activities that are actually necessary at this stage of the existence of our society.

The peculiarity of gender budgeting is related to gender and age specifics of specific groups, and is not aimed at exclusively "female" financing. The main task is to observe the equality of all participants, to study how socio-economic factors affect different groups and participants. Gender analysis, as the basis for such planning, is aimed at understanding that, firstly, politics is directly related to social practice, and secondly, planning social programs directly depends on sociological data and studies in the field of humanities on target groups and the effectiveness of other programs. Such an orientation leads to an understanding of the need for a close fusion of the scientific approach with the process of state planning and management. Consequently, budget indicators are analyzed in terms of their effectiveness, considering the gender aspect. Thus, it is important to identify two areas in the analysis of gender budgeting: an indicator of gender budget sensitivity, the impact of budget indicators on the effectiveness of building a gender policy. ①

The implementation of gender policy in the process of implementing gender policy is important to ensure all development goals, as well as the harmonious development of society, in which successful self-government and regulation of the strategic needs of existing local groups are possible with observance of the rights and freedoms of each participant. A gender-sensitive budget involves the cancellation of the average representative of a society with anonymous needs, but the development of targeted programs aimed at solving specific problems. ②

Thus, the following can be noted. Gender-sensitive budgets are a tool for organizing the transparency of the spending process with the possibility of generating requests and monitoring effectiveness by civil society. The practice of introducing gender budgeting in the social policy of a number of countries not only in Europe but also in the CIS has made it possible to optimize expenditures, improve the social climate with regard to the involvement of local groups and participants in the socio-economic process, obtain a definite and effective result, rather than spend money on anonymous agents. In practice, gender-sensitive budgets can improve the level of well-being, education, social

---

① Salosina L. G. Gender Approach in Budget Planning // News. Volgogr. state un. – Series 3. – 2008. – № 2 (13). – C. 185 – 190. Kambariddinova N. What is gender budgeting // [Electronic resource]: Access mode: http://www.publicfinance.uz/upload/iblock/a7f/Gender _ overview _ NK. pdf. Access Date: 02/27/2019.

② Gender Responsive Budgeting // [Electronic resource]: Access mode: https://unwomen.org.au/our-work/focus-areas/what-is-gender-responsive-budgeting/. Access Date: 25.02.2019. Gender Mainstreaming and a Human Rights Based Approach, Budapest, 2017: [Electronic resource] / UN Food and Agriculture Organization. Access mode: http://www.fao.org/3/a - i6808r. pdf. Access date: 11/15/2018. Gender Mainstreaming: A Review, New York, 2002 [Electronic Resource] / Office of the Special Adviser on Gender Issues and Advancement of Women // UN. Access mode: http://www.un.org/womenwatch/daw/public/gendermainstreaming/Russian% 20Gender% 20Mainstreaming_full. pdf. Access date: 11/16/2018.

guarantees and protection of needy and vulnerable groups; it is an effective tool to support and optimize gender policy. The goals and objectives of gender policy should be promoted with the help of institutions and participants in civil society: NGOs, the women's movement, expert platforms, the media in equal partnership with government bodies and international organizations.

Implementation of gender policy allows to increase the level of the national economy, improve the socio-political climate, introduce effective tools for the equal participation of vulnerable groups. A platform has already been laid in Belarus to begin to effectively implement gender policy and introduce gender budgeting in the process of planning social programs, however, prolonged decision-making leads to a loss of effectiveness in the field of socio-political and economic growth, as well as to the outflow of human capital from the country.

It should be noted that the timely assessment of the effectiveness of a particular social program is a guarantee of improving the quality of life of the groups of the population whose interests it is aimed at. To implement this task, various monitoring and evaluation systems in Belarus are developed and improved, providing the opportunity for strategic analysis, revision and correction of social policy.

Sustainable Development Goals (hereinafter the SDGs)[1] are a large-scale framework for a comprehensive understanding of social policy areas, development of programs and subprograms aimed at improving the social climate. An important aspect of the implementation of the SDGs in Belarus is their implementation at various levels, from government to young leaders and NGOs. Thus, a favorable environment is created for including directly those leaders of opinions who interact with local groups and are stakeholders of social requests in work on social programs. For the most effective work to achieve the SDGs, it is necessary to take a number of measures that will be guaranteed:

---

[1] Belarus launched the Decade of Action to achieve the Sustainable Development Goals: [Electronic resource]: – Access mode: https://un.by/novosti-oon/v-belarusi/. Access Date: 02/10/2020.

firstly, provide access to civic leaders and initiatives to state resources, secondly, carry out processes of modernization of the economy and society, thirdly, realize the potential of civil society for implementing programs at different levels (from local governments to national representations). For example, the implementation of the *National Action Plan*. It was made possible through the interaction of many actors, some of which are represented by government, some by the scientific and expert community, some by NGOs and opinion leaders. ①

For example, within the framework of the implementation of SDGs No. 5 (Gender Equality), No. 8 (Decent Work and Economic Growth), No. 10 (Reducing Inequality), "Gender Perspectives" was conducted on gender discrimination in the labor market and in hiring. ②As part of the implementation of this study, tasks were set aimed at identifying explicit and latent (conscious and unconscious) cases of discrimination, a description of factors affecting discrimination and discriminatory behavior mechanisms. Targeting the respondents in terms of socio-demographic characteristics (education, place of residence, age, gender, etc.) made it possible to identify the level of discrimination in the labor market, to identify vulnerable groups and types of discrimination characteristic of the labor market in the Republic of Belarus. In particular, this study is indicative of revealing a willingness to assert one's rights and counter discrimination, barriers to protecting one's rights, and determining the level of awareness of one's rights during interviews and in the workplace.

References have already been made to gender budgeting as an effective mechanism for allocating funds for groups of people who really need additional

---

① Artemenko, E. K. Results of a study of the situation in the field of gender discrimination in the labor market and in hiring / Mr. sociologist. sciences E. K. Artemenko. – Minsk: Businessofset LLC. – 2019.

② Artemenko, E. K. Results of a study of the situation in the field of gender discrimination in the labor market and in hiring / Mr. sociologist. sciences E. K. Artemenko. – Minsk: Businessofset LLC. – 2019.

resources and support systems. Targeted funds and resources make it possible to efficiently budget for programs and subprograms of assistance to the population, monitor efficiency and consider the real needs of groups. Consequently, focusing on local groups, scaling up, developing assessment and monitoring criteria will optimize various types of resources and develop subprograms in such a way as to develop the most effective strategy regarding the formation of social policy in Belarus. In addition, the costs of evaluating and monitoring the work of social programs should be minimized by questioning experts directly interacting with population groups. This will allow you to adjust existing programs, and also predict new trends, target new groups and interests. ①

For example, the experience of introducing gender-sensitive budgeting in Ukraine and Kazakhstan showed that the analysis of financial costs for social programs allows both to optimize existing expenses and to identify shortcomings in covering all interests. So, women consume much more medical services, more often seek medical help, while the male population consumes them many times less, especially those that relate directly to male reproductive health. Thus, the identification of problem areas and insufficient or excessive funding through gender-sensitive budgeting is an effective social mechanism for the distribution of benefits in accordance with those factors that determine interests, for example, such as traditional roles of the distribution of labor in different places or the volume of consumption of services among male and female population. ②

The introduction of new mechanisms to increase efficiency also applies to

---

① Shadrina, L. Yu. Sociological monitoring as a means of information support for assessing the effectiveness of social technologies: – [Electronic resource]: Access mode: https://cyberleninka.ru/article/n/sotsiologicheskiy-monitoring-kak-sredstvo-informatsionnogo-soprovozhdeniya-otsenki-effektivnosti-sotsialnyh-tehnologiy/viewer. Access Date: 02/10/2020.

② Why gender budgeting is not "taken from men and given to women"?: – [Electronic resource]: – Access mode: https://forbes.kz//process/expertise/pochemu_gendernoe_byudjetirovanie_eto_ne_otobrat_u_mujchin_i_otdat_jenschinam/. Access Date: 02/12/2020.

education. Belarus enshrines the universal right to equal access to education (article 32, article 49 of the *Constitution of the Republic of Belarus*).[1] However, different population groups require different approaches, educational programs funded and designed in accordance with their needs. For example, the integration and socialization of ethnic groups in Belarus, such as the Roma population, has its own specifics and requires other methods and approaches. Girls in the Roma ethnic group as a teenager often leave school due to early marriage and motherhood, as well as the need to perform household duties on an equal basis with adult family members. In addition, there are a number of obstacles associated with the external environment and stereotypes. Thus, adolescent girls in the Roma ethnic group are more vulnerable in terms of equal access to social resources, least motivated to make independent professional choice[2]. This example is a clear illustration of how you can scale the focus of social programs, their duration, goals and objectives, the amount of financial costs, based on specific social realities. The above examples and many others in this series are the basis for the formation of strategies and approaches for creating social programs that will focus on local communities, consider specific needs, and make visible those small groups that fall outside the scope of existing standard approaches. A gender sensitive approach, in particular, is an excellent mechanism for identifying groups in the population that need different methods and methods for identifying their actual needs and ways to solve specific problems. In general, a series of opportunities can be offered that will create a favorable environment for such improvement, depending on what goals are currently being pursued.

---

[1] Constitution of the Republic of Belarus: [Electronic resource]: – Access mode: http://pravo. by/pravovaya-informatsiya/normativnye-dokumenty/konstitutsiya-respubliki-belarus/. Access Date: 02/12/2020.

[2] Social integration of the Roma population in the Republic of Belarus: [Electronic resource]: – Access mode: http://romaintegration. by/wp-content/uploads/2016/09/Roma _ socialintegration _ forsite. pdf. Access Date: 02/26/2020.

Modernization of Governance and Innovative Development of Governance

The Study of Macroeconomic Effect and Governance Effectiveness on the Reform of VAT in China

Lou Feng

Professor, Institute of Quantitative Economy and Technological Economy, CASS

From the view of economic system theory, according to the latest input-output table and the realistic characteristics of fiscal and taxation, this paper compiled the social accounting matrix of China's fiscal revenue and tax, and constructed the CGE model, and simulated and analyzed the influence of reducing the value added tax rate on the Macroeconomy and its structure. The simulation results showed that reducing the value-added tax rate of enterprises is beneficial to China's actual GDP growth and in favor of reducing the pressure ofinflation, and it has significant impact on import and export, especially on exports, and the tax rate of 1 percentage points can reduce the total revenue of government tax by 1.5 percentage points, and it can improve the general welfare of the society and thus to benefit the social harmonious development.

Ⅰ. Introduction

The 13th Five-Year Plan period is the key period for China to realize the transformation of economic growth mode, and is also the decisive stage for China to build an innovative country and a well-off society in an all-round way. For this reason, the Central Committee has clearly put forward a major development strategy of "structural reform on the supply side", and General Secretary Xi Jinping has repeatedly emphasized that structural reform on the supply side must be a definite one. to "reduce costs". At present, in terms of the domestic environment, the comprehensive tax burden of Chinese enterprises is too high, the burden is too heavy, and the profit margin of the real economy is constantly narrowing. As a result, the voice of "tax reduction" of enterprises, social organizations and academia is increasing day by day. In terms of the international environment, after the new President of the United States took office, the enterprise income tax has been greatly reduced to make the current income. Taxes fell from 35% to 15%; the UK also announced a plan to cut corporate income tax rates from 20% to less than 15% in 2016; India cut individual income tax, consumption tax and service tax rates in early 2017 to stimulate domestic demand. Therefore, under this international and domestic context, reducing tax burden is not only a key measure to promote the recovery of China's real economy, but also an urgent need to alleviate the pressure of capital outflow, stimulate economic vitality and improve the competitiveness of Chinese enterprises.

The structure of this paper is as follows: the second part reviews the existing literature, the third part introduces the CGE model of fiscal revenue constructed in this paper, the fourth part compares and analyses the simulation results, and the last part puts forward the policy recommendations based on the analysis conclusions.

Ⅱ. Literature Review

In the post-economic crisis era, the effectiveness of China's traditional monetary instruments and fiscal expenditure instruments has declined. On the one hand, there are some problems in monetary policy, such as limited space for interest rate reduction, weak directivity and poor transmission channels. On the other hand, the effectiveness of fiscal expenditure is facing obstacles such as financing difficulties, reduced return on investment, distorted economic structure and corruption.① Therefore, tax policy has become in progress. China's important options to reduce the burden of enterprises and stabilize economic growth. In theory, tax reduction can not only promote enterprise investment and increase real output by reducing the real price of factors, but also have a systematic impact on the labor market. Existing studies have focused on the macroeconomic effects of the decline of corporate tax burden mainly on investment and economic growth, labor market and international trade.

Firstly, the relationship between the decline of corporate tax burden and investment as well as economic growth. In theory, a lower tax rate would reduce the rent of rented capital or the reward rate necessary for investment, thereby increasing the scale of investment and thus increasing output. Most empirical studies also confirm that businesses respond positively to tax incentives. ②Most of the studies in China regard the transformation of VAT as a quasi-natural experiment to reduce the effective tax rate of VAT and investigate its policy effect. Most of these studies confirm that the tax reduction effect of VAT transformation has a significant positive effect on enterprise investment.③In addition, Li Linmu et al. (2017) found that reducing taxes and fees is conducive to promoting enterprises' R&D investment and innovation ability, thus promoting enterprises' transformation and upgrading.

---

① Shen Guangjun, Chen Binkai and Yang Rudai, "Can Tax Reduction Promote China's Economy? An Empirical Study Based on China's VAT Reform", *Economic Research*, No. 11, 2016.

② Hassett, K. A., Hubbard, R. G., "Tax Policy and Business Investment", *Handbook of Public Economics*, No. 3, 2002.

③ Nie Huihua, Fang Mingyue and Li Tao, "The Impact of VAT Transition on Enterprise Behavior and Performance", *Management World*, No. 5, 2009. Xu Wei and Chen Binkai, "Tax Incentives and Enterprise Investment: A Natural Experiment Based on VAT Transition from 2004 to 2009", *Managing the World*, No. 5, 2016. Shen Guangjun, Chen Binkai and Yang Rudai, "Can Tax Reduction Promote China's Economy? An Empirical Study Based on China's VAT Reform", *Economic Research*, No. 11, 2016.

The second is the impact on the labor market. Some studies focus on the policy effects of tax rate changes on employment. These studies also take the value-added tax transformation as the background, but the conclusions are not consistent. The transformation of value-added tax leads to the decrease of capital factor price relative to labor factor price. Enterprises will use more capital to replace labor input, which will have a negative impact on employment. Nie Huihua, Fang Mingyue and Li Tao (2009) tested the measurement of Northeast China and Chen Ye (2010) used CGE simulation to verify this conclusion. Chen Ye et al. (2010) further pointed out that the non-discriminatory production-oriented VAT tax reduction policy is conducive to promoting employment and economic growth at the same time. Shen Guangjun and others (2016) believe that the value-added tax transformation will lead to the replacement of capital for labor, but the reduction of unit product cost will promote enterprises to expand production and increase the demand for capital and labor. Therefore, the impact of tax reduction on labor input depends on the relative size of substitution effect and scale effect. Through the econometric model, this paper finds that the squeeze of tax reduction on employment is mainly concentrated in private enterprises, central and western regions and non-export enterprises. Generally speaking, tax cuts do not significantly squeeze out employment, but tend to improve employment.

Another part of the study focuses on the impact of tax rate changes on household income. Most of these studies use CGE model to simulate and analyze the tax reduction effect of "business-to-business" increase, and the conclusions are different. Ge Yuyu et al. (2015) found that the reduction of corporate tax burden can improve the income level of residents by promoting economic growth, promoting the development of secondary and tertiary industries and small and medium-sized enterprises, and reducing the price of consumer goods. Tax cuts can narrow the income gap between urban and rural areas, as income of low-income people grows faster. Wang Hao (2016) argued that although the decrease in the average tax burden caused by the "increase in business" was conducive to improving income distribution, the regressive increase in the tax system worsened the income distribution gap. Therefore, although the overall effect of the two is conducive to improving the income distribution of the whole country, as well as the urban and rural areas, it leads to an increase in the income distribution gap between urban and rural areas.

Finally, the impact on international trade. Empirical research on the background of value-added tax transformation shows that tax reduction can increase enterprise productivity and export by reducing the cost of technological upgrading and price distortion caused by tax. [1]

In view of the existing research, the study on the background of VAT transformation and "business increase" shows that the change of tax rate will have a significant systemic impact on China's macro-economy. However, there is no literature that directly simulates the reform plan of enterprise tax rate policy under the background that VAT has become the main tax burden of enterprises. It also lacks a comprehensive assessment of the macroeconomic effect of tax reduction based on a unified framework from the perspective of system theory. At the same time, due to the differences in the perspective of the study, the conclusions of different studies on some issues, such as the impact on the labor market, have significant differences. Therefore, a comprehensive conclusion needs more evidence from new studies. In addition, existing studies have noticed that due to the differences in competition, financing constraints and capital cost sensitivity, the tax reduction effect has significant differences among different industries, ownership enterprises and regions,[2] but there is still a lack of special investigation on the tax reduction effect of the subdivided industries. Therefore, based on CGE model, this paper makes use of its

---

[1] Liu, Q, Lu, Y, "Firm Investment and Exporting: Evidence from China's Value-added Tax Reform", *Journal of International Economics*, Vol. 97, No. 2, 2015. Wang Xiaoqin and Zeng Yu, "The Impact of VAT Transition on the Dual Margin of China's Export: Empirical Analysis Based on Gravity Model", *Economic Longitudes and Latitudes*, No. 6, 2016.

[2] Liu, Q, Lu, Y, "Firm Investment and Exporting: Evidence from China's Value-added Tax Reform", *Journal of International Economics*, Vol. 97, No. 2, 2015. Shen Guangjun, Chen Binkai and Yang Rudai, "Can Tax Reduction Promote China's Economy? An Empirical Study Based on China's VAT Reform", *Economic Research*, No. 11, 2016.

structural and systematic characteristics to simulate and analyze the macroeconomic effects of VAT tax reduction policy in China, and pays special attention to the impact of tax changes on the subdividing industries, which supplements the existing research.

III. Construction of CGE Theory Model of China's Fiscal Taxation

1. Compilation and Data Explanation of China's Financial and Tax Macro-Social Accounting Matrix (SAM)

Before simulating and analyzing China's fiscal and taxation profitability policy, it is necessary to construct China's fiscal and taxation social accounting matrix (SAM table). SAM table is a comprehensive and systematic description of the economic structure of a country (or region) in a certain period (usually one year). It is a matrix to express the transactions and their correlations between national economic accounting accounts. It systematically reflects the various economic associations among various social and economic entities (enterprises, governments, residents, foreign countries) in a certain period of time.

Based on the latest input-output table of China in 2015, this paper compiles the social accounting matrix (SAM) of China's fiscal and taxation, taking into account the main characteristics of China's fiscal and taxation, combining with *China's Taxation Yearbook*, *China Customs Yearbook*, *China's Financial Yearbook* and *China's Economic Statistics Yearbook*, etc. The model consists of 16 accounts: production, commodities, labor, capital, enterprises, government, domestic value-added tax, business tax, consumption tax, other indirect taxes, tariffs, enterprise income tax, personal income tax, savings-investment, inventory and foreign countries. The production and commodities are further subdivided into 42 industrial sectors. The macro-social accounting matrix of China's fiscal and taxation (SAM) is shown in Table 1.

Table 1 China's Financial and Tax Macro-Social Accounting Matrix (SAM) Table

Unit: 10 billion yuan

	Production	Commodity	Labor	Capital	Resident	Enterprise	Government	Value added tax	Sales Tax	Other indirect taxes	Tariff	Corporate income tax	Individual income tax	Investment	Stock	Other world
Production		14650														1367
Commodity	10648				1985		732							2340	327	
Labor	2641															
Captial	1991															
Resident			2679			398	16									
Enterprise				1991			23									
Government								265	157	314	225	220	58			
Value added tax	265															
Sales Tax	157															
Other indirect taxes	314															

(Contd.)

	Produ-ction	Commo-dity	Labor	Capital	Resi-dent	Enter-prise	Gover-nment	Value added tax	Sales Tax	Other indirect taxes	Tariff	Corporate income tax	Individual income tax	Invest-ment	Stock	Other world
Tariff		225														
Corporate income tax						220										
Individual income tax					58											
Investment					1050	1319	444							327		−146
Stock																
Other world		1221														

2. The Framework and Major Equations of CGE Theoretic Model of Fiscal Taxation in China

The CGE model of China's fiscal revenue includes 42 departments. According to international practice, the model assumes that enterprises make production decisions according to the principle of minimizing cost or maximizing profit under the condition of production technology with constant returns on scale. The production equation consists of two layers of nested structure, i. e. intermediate input and added value. The intermediate input is correlated by a fixed input-output coefficient (i. e. Leontief function). The added value equation is composed of two production factors (labor and capital). It is assumed that there is an incomplete substitution between the production factors, and the constant substitution bullet is used. Sex CES equation is compounded. The demand for factors in production activities follows the principle of maximizing profits or minimizing costs. Therefore, the marginal cost of factors (i. e. the price of factors) is equal to the marginal profit of products.

The CGE model of fiscal revenue in this paper includes eight modules: production module, consumption module, fiscal revenue module, income module, savings-investment module, price module, international trade module and equilibrium closed module.

Finally, based on the system equations derived from general equilibrium theory and fiscal and taxation theory, GAMS software is used to write programs independently and debug the system. The model has passed the feasibility test, consistency test, homogeneity test, WALRAS test and so on. Therefore, the model can be used for policy simulation analysis.

IV. Policy Simulation Based on Computable General Equilibrium (CGE) Model of China's Fiscal and Tax Revenue

Therefore, from the perspective of economic system theory, according to the latest input-output table and the realistic characteristics of tax structure in China, a social accounting matrix of China's fiscal and tax revenue is compiled, a computable general equilibrium (CGE) model of China's fiscal and tax revenue is constructed, and the reform of VAT tax related system is simulated and analyzed. After the overall "business-to-business" increase, VAT has become one of the main components of China's fiscal revenue. In 2017, VAT accounts for a large proportion of the total revenue of national fiscal revenue. Therefore, this paper carries out the following policy simulation.

The simulation hypothesis: reduce the enterprise VAT tax rate, reduce the existing four VAT tax rates (17%, 11%, 6%, 3%) to the original 13/17 that is, rvat (i) = 0.7647 * rvat 0 (i), rvat 0 (i) is the original industry VAT tax rate, and rvat (i) is the industry VAT tax rate after the change, other conditions remain unchanged. The effects of GDP, industrial structure, household income and household consumption, government income and government consumption, import and export, social welfare and other macroeconomic variables are simulated as shown in Table 2.

Table 2   Growth Rate of Major Macroeconomic Variables in Policy Simulation

Variable	Rate of change (%)	Variable	Rate of change (%)
Real GDP	0.4093	The actual total income of rural residents	1.4769
Nominal GDP	-1.0996	Actual total income of urban residents	0.4479
GDP index	-1.5027	Total savings of rural residents	-0.0484
Primary industry value added (nominal value)	1.1497	Total savings of urban residents	-1.0580
Second industry value added (nominal value)	0.4920	Value added tax	-21.1155

(Contd.)

Variable	Rate of change (%)	Variable	Rate of change (%)
Value added of tertiary industry (nominal value)	-3.3912	Sales tax	-4.0421
Total savings	-14.5901	Consumption tax	-1.2512
Total investment in fixed assets	-11.9886	Other indirect taxes	-1.3971
Total imports	-1.3987	Tariff	-1.8564
Total exports	16.2820	Individual income tax of urban residents	-0.0480
Trade surplus	83.5851	Individual income tax of rural residents	-1.0132
Nominal gross income of rural residents	-0.0480	Corporate income tax	0.5658
Nominal gross income of urban residents	-1.0615	Total government income	-5.8385
Social Welfare Variable Growth (Horizontal Value)			
Increase in social welfare	1110.1438 (10 billion Yuan)		

Table 2 shows that reducing the enterprise VAT tax rate and lowering the general VAT tax rate from 17% to 13%, and under the assumption that other conditions remain unchanged, China's real GDP will increase by 0.4%. This shows that the policy is conducive to promoting the real GDP growth rate and economic growth; from the industrial point of view, the nominal increase of the primary and secondary industries increased by 1.1% and 0.5% respectively, but the nominal added value of the tertiary industry decreased by 3.4 percentage points. This shows that although the policy will reduce the growth rate of the tertiary industry, thereby reducing the proportion of the tertiary industry in the national economy, the policy is generally composed of the primary industry and the secondary industry, which are mainly composed of the real economic sectors. It is conducive to the development of real economy and consolidation of the foundation and motive force of medium and long-term economic development. In addition, the GDP deflator index has dropped by 1.5%. As the policy reduces the production cost of enterprises, the selling price of products has declined, and finally the overall price level has declined. This shows that the policy is conducive to slowing down and restraining inflation pressure in China.

In terms of trade, under this policy, China's exports increased by 16.28 percentage points and imports decreased by 1.4 percentage points, which shows that this policy can effectively improve the competitiveness of international prices of products and promote the significant increase of exports. Because the exchange rate set in the model is fixed, with the dramatic increase of export level and the slight increase of import level, China's trade surplus in goods increased by 83.6%. The reason is that with the reduction of VAT tax rate, the production cost of Chinese enterprises decreases, and the price of domestic products also decreases, which makes the price of products relatively cheap, thus stimulating the demand for Chinese products in domestic and foreign markets, and because of the substitution of domestic and foreign products, the export of China increases, the imports reduced.

From the perspective of residents' income, although the nominal total income of rural residents and urban residents decreased by 0.05 and 1.1 percentage points due to the decrease of the total price level, the real total income of rural residents and urban residents increased by 1.48 and 0.45 percentage points respectively after deducting the price factor, which shows that the policy is beneficial to residents. Increasing income level is conducive to reducing the income gap between urban and rural residents.

In terms of tax structure, under this policy, the government's VAT income has been reduced by 21.1%, which has resulted in a decrease of 4.04%, 1.25%, 1.40%, 1.86%, 0.05% and 1.01% in business tax, consumption tax, other indirect tax, tariff, urban personal income tax and rural personal income tax, respectively, while the enterprise income tax has increased by 0.57%, resulting in a decrease of about 5.8 percentage points in the total revenue of government tax, which indicates that the policy will generally reduce government revenue, but the increase of enterprise income tax also reflects that the policy promotes the increase of enterprise profits, and it is conducive to the long-term development of enterprises, and conforms to the "cost reduction derelopment strategy" advocated by the structural reform of the state supply side.

In addition, under this policy, the level of social welfare increased by 1110.14, which shows that the policy can effectively improve the overall social welfare and is conducive to the harmonious development of society.

Table 3　　The Main Economic Variables in Policy Simulation are the Unit of Industry-specific Change Rate　　Unit: %

	Domestic output	Output price	Capital formation	Household consumption	Government consumption	Export	Import
Agriculture	1.27	-0.46	-12.91	-0.16	-5.41	3.15	0.31
Coal mining industry	0.52	-2.86	UNDF	2.42	UNDF	12.90	-5.28
Oil and gas exploitation industry	2.88	-2.23	UNDF	UNDF	UNDF	12.58	-1.85
Metal mining and dressing industry	1.63	-1.80	UNDF	UNDF	UNDF	9.29	-2.08
Non-metallic mines industries	-3.61	-1.47	UNDF	UNDF	UNDF	2.28	-6.70
Food manufacturing and tobacco processing industry	1.50	-1.22	UNDF	0.47	UNDF	6.59	-1.53
Textile industry	12.88	-1.63	UNDF	1.25	UNDF	20.56	5.13
Garment, shoes, caps, leather, down and its products industry	10.01	-2.05	UNDF	1.79	UNDF	19.50	0.28
Wood processing and furniture manufacturing	-2.06	-1.45	-11.79	0.81	UNDF	3.84	-6.76
Sports goods manufacturing industry	2.75	-1.65	-11.78	0.81	UNDF	9.83	-1.68

(Contd.)

	Domestic output	Output price	Capital formation	Household consumption	Government consumption	Export	Import
Petroleum processing, coking and nuclear fuel processing industry	0.51	−2.05	UNDF	1.04	UNDF	9.19	−3.90
Chemical industry	4.28	−1.68	UNDF	1.01	UNDF	11.58	−0.39
Non-metallic mineral products industry	−6.89	−1.70	UNDF	0.71	UNDF	−0.29	−10.15
Metal smelting and calendering industry	−0.06	−1.49	UNDF	UNDF	UNDF	6.11	−4.53
Metal products industry	0.87	−1.75	−11.60	1.00	UNDF	8.25	−4.07
Manufacturing of general and special equipment	−2.59	−1.87	−11.41	1.21	UNDF	5.04	−10.07
Transportation equipment manufacturing industry	−4.50	−2.08	−11.48	1.30	UNDF	3.86	−9.59
Electrical, machinery and equipment manufacturing industry	−0.06	−1.83	−11.46	1.20	UNDF	7.61	−6.52
Manufacturing of communication equipment, computer and other electronic equipment	31.93	−2.24	−10.83	2.12	UNDF	44.44	10.80
Instruments and instruments and cultural office machinery manufacturing industry	20.56	−1.93	−11.83	0.80	UNDF	30.31	1.53
Crafts and other manufacturing industries	0.61	−1.32	−12.27	0.26	UNDF	6.10	−3.20
Production and supply of electricity and thermal power	1.05	−2.21	UNDF	1.61	UNDF	10.95	−3.59

(Contd.)

	Domestic output	Output price	Capital formation	Household consumption	Government consumption	Export	Import
Gas production and supply industry	1.12	-1.65	UNDF	0.83	UNDF	8.09	-2.24
Water production and supply industry	1.90	-1.54	UNDF	0.83	UNDF	8.41	-2.51
Construction	-11.73	-1.17	-12.28	0.11	UNDF	-7.49	-13.84
Transportation and warehousing	-1.50	-0.79	-12.61	0.07	-5.08	1.68	-3.25
Postal industry	0.70	-0.95	UNDF	0.16	UNDF	4.62	-1.61
Information transmission, computer services and software industry	-2.69	-0.58	-12.79	-0.13	UNDF	-0.42	-3.96
Wholesale and retail trade	3.22	-3.01	-10.00	2.79	UNDF	16.66	-6.82
Accommodation and catering	-0.12	-0.72	UNDF	-0.25	UNDF	2.82	-1.91
Finance	1.36	-0.09	UNDF	-0.93	-5.76	1.71	1.17
Real estate industry	-3.29	0.04	-13.35	-0.75	UNDF	-3.45	-3.20
Leasing and business services	2.81	-0.96	UNDF	0.04	-4.81	6.84	-0.87
Research and experimental development industry	1.10	-0.95	UNDF	UNDF	-5.12	5.01	-0.92
Integrated technology services	-2.44	-0.59	-12.79	UNDF	-5.28	-0.10	-3.59
Water conservancy, environment and public facilities management industry	-2.66	-0.81	UNDF	-0.24	-5.07	0.56	-4.25
Resident services and other services	0.15	-0.69	UNDF	-0.26	UNDF	2.97	-1.76
Education	-3.91	-0.28	UNDF	-0.45	-5.57	-2.82	-4.45
Health, social security and social welfare	-1.69	-1.07	UNDF	0.14	-4.82	2.62	-3.79

(Contd.)

	Domestic output	Output price	Capital formation	Household consumption	Government consumption	Export	Import
Culture, sports and entertainment	-1.32	-0.65	UNDF	-0.26	-5.24	1.27	-2.96
Public administration and social organizations	-5.40	-0.40	UNDF	UNDF	-5.46	-3.87	-6.17

Note: UNDF indicates that the industry's initial value is zero.

Table 3 shows that, from an industry perspective, the gross domestic output of the primary and secondary industries has generally increased, while that of the tertiary industries has decreased. Domestic output of the communications equipment, computer and other electronic equipment manufacturing, textile, clothing, shoes, hats, leather and down industries and their products grew the most, with 31.9%, 12.8% and 10.0% respectively; output prices in almost all industries declined, with wholesale and retail trade, coal mining and washing, communications equipment, computer and other electronic equipment manufacturing industries falling the most, by 3.0%, 2.9% and 2.2% respectively. Because of the reduction of government revenue, the original government consumption of all industries has been reduced, generally falling by about 5 percentage points.

Table 3 also shows that most of China's exports have increased under this policy, with the largest increases in communications equipment, computer and other electronic equipment manufacturing, instrument and instrument manufacturing, and textile manufacturing, accounting for 44.4%, 30.3% and 20.6% respectively. It shows that this policy can raise Chinese products' comprehensive competitiveness, in particular communication equipment, computer and other electronic equipment manufacturing industry, instrument and cultural office machinery manufacturing industry, textile industry, which is conducive to Chinese enterprises to participate in international competition. From the view of economic theory, the growth rate of import and export mainly depends on the substitution elasticity coefficient of demand in these industries. Because the substitution elasticity coefficient of these industries is relatively large, when the production conditions change, these industries change greatly.

V. Suggestions

1. Aiming at "Steady Growth", We Should Pay Equal Attention to Both Supply-side Reform and Domestic Demand Expansion

First of all, we need to clarify the core objectives of the current active fiscal policy and its realization path. Economic theory shows that supply and demand are two basic forces to promote economic growth. Long-term economic growth can only be achieved if supply and demand are adapted to each other and coordinated and balanced. Therefore, the active fiscal policy with "steady growth" as its core objective should play an important role in both supply and demand. At present, supporting supply-side reform and expanding domestic demand are two main ways to achieve positive fiscal policy to promote economic growth. On the one hand, active fiscal policy should vigorously support supply-side reform, the core is to provide strong support for the real economy to reduce tax burden and economic restructuring. On the other hand, active fiscal policy should make great efforts to expand market demand and improve the demand environment for enterprise development. The motive force of enterprise development lies in market demand. If there is no market demand, there will be no space and power source for enterprise development. It needs to be emphasized that in the current complex economic situation, we should consciously strengthen the role of active fiscal policy in expanding domestic demand. How to effectively start market demand is a crucial issue.

2. Taking Effective Measures to Cut Taxes and Fees on Enterprises and Properly Reduce the VAT Tax Rate

On July 26, 2016, the meeting of the Political Bureau of the CPC Central

Committee clearly put forward the requirement of reducing the macro tax burden. The structural tax reduction policy implemented in recent years has undoubtedly played a positive role in reducing the tax burden of enterprises, and the proportion of tax revenue to GDP in China shows a downward trend; however, overall, the macro-tax burden of Chinese enterprises is still at a high level, which is embodied in the following aspects: the rapid growth of non-tax revenue and the increase of personal income tax. Excessive growth, excessive burden of enterprise value-added tax, etc. Under the situation of slowing down economic growth and declining profit growth rate of enterprises, one of the core contents of the current active fiscal policy is to lighten the tax burden of enterprises and reduce the tax burden of enterprises, which is conducive to enhancing the revitalization of enterprises, especially small and medium-sized enterprises, thus promoting enterprises to increase investment, expand production, increase employment and stimulate industries. The policy simulation also shows that the appropriate reduction of VAT tax rate is conducive to the growth of China's real GDP, to the reduction of inflation, to the improvement of exports and social welfare, and we should further vigorously clean up unreasonable charges to reduce the burden of enterprises.

The BRI and the Modernization of National Governance in Belarus

Dzmitry Smaliakou

Ph. D. Senior Scientific Fellow

Sino-Belarusian Research Center of Philosophy and Culture of

the Institute of Philosophy of National Academy of Sciences

of Belarus and Lingnan Normal University

I. Overview

National governing problems became more and more essential with the world bipolar system has been going to destruction in the end of the 20th century. New circumstances of the world cooperation and changed alliances of states restructured and rebooted economics in East Europe and Asia, following establishing new lines of collaboration between different states highly influenced on integration tendencies. This was expressed in the rapid rapprochement of states revealed in removing political, economic, trade and other barriers. International cooperation significantly accelerated that was interpreted as the absolute victory of globalization. The world political and economic collaboration have been started to concentrate around examples of regional integration, that was understood as the essential processes of the present situation and the sign of new level of global development.

However, the euphory of the end of 20 century was ruined in fire of "9·11" terroristic attack that clarify multisource nature of the world contradictions. The growth of terrorist activity in the early 21st century and subsequent wars showed that world globalization still has many problems to be solved. Probably, globalization was not right organized and regional cooperation was not properly arranged. Therefore, globalization should be reinvented on the new principles in order to continuing global cooperation activities that needed for father economic growth. The economic had to submit to the highest expediency, considering both regional imbalances and the willingness of various region players to strengthen regional and global cooperation.

Problems with terrorism strengthen at the beginning of the 21st century reinforced people's believe that globalization was not fair and had to be more balanced and inclusive.

In the same time Chinese economy rapidly grew. China's contribution to world development is increasing. The Belt and Road Initiative, implemented by China in 2013, is conducive to promoting a new type of globalization. For China the new initiative appears as the continuation of a successful policy of reform and opening up, which in many respects ensured the economic growth that made China one of the biggest economics of the world.

The Belt and Road Initiative has elicited warm responses and wide support from the world. The first Belt and Road Forum for International Cooperation was held in Beijing in May 2017.[1] The forum attracted more than 60 heads of countries, as well as numerous of politicians, scientists and experts. In general, the forum expressed the conviction that previous globalization needs to be deeply rethought and restructured, so far as significant number of the poor and developing countries did not fully participate in this processes, however rich countries of the Euro-Atlantic world became the main beneficiaries of globalization. The Belt and Road Initiative is a golden opportunity to bring about international integration, and build connectivity and institutions consolidating

---

[1] Official website of the Belt and Road Forum, http://www.beltandroadforum.org/.

the Eurasian landmass, and achieve a new model of globalization that is more equitable and balanced, which will surely have a positive impact not only on leader counties, but also on developing counties.

The Belt and Road Initiative will facilitate global economic growth, and serve as a new platform for all countries to achieve win-win cooperation. At the same time, the Belt and Road Initiative provides a platform for the building of a community with a shared future for mankind. China's development brings opportunities to the world and people wish to create a number of new growth points.

An important aspect of the Belt and Road Initiative is to achieve connectivity, and the transportation sector is undoubtedly the primary foundation. In this regard the reforming of national governance in order to suit to the new cooperation possibilities is important to ensure the success of international cooperation.

II. Situation in Belarus

As the Belarusian-Chinese relations developed, Belarus decided to balance cooperation with China through the increased joint projects.

As soon as Belarus chose a strategic approach to cooperate with China, the Belarusian government immediately began to take decisive steps to develop Belarusian-Chinese interaction. A lot of work was done on planning, to the moment of Belt and Road Initiative announcement in 2013. Belarus already has many government level plans in particularly all areas of politics, economic, military and social areas. ①The starting point of a joint activity on the implementation of the Belt and Road Initiative is the signing in September 2016 by Belarus and China the package of measures to jointly promote the

---

① 26. Смоляков, Д. А. Белорусско-китайское сотрудничество в области образования в контексте реализации инициативы "Один пояс, один путь" / Д. А. Смоляков // Вестник Минского государственного лингвистического университета: научно-методический журнал / Министерство образования Республики Беларусь. — 2017. - № 1. - С. 25 - 32.

construction of the Belt and Road Initiative that was held in the presence of two presidents, Xi Jinping and A. Lukashenko.① In the context of this document, numerous agreements were simultaneously signed in such areas as education, science, transport, investment, finance, security, etc.,② linking bilateral cooperation between Belarus and China with the implementation of the initiative. Subsequently, Belarus integrated plans for the implementation of the Belt and Road Initiative into national plans for socio-economic development until 2020,③ thereby confirming its importance for the national development and substanability of Belarus as independent state.

Since the signing of these documents cooperation between Belarus and China has grown significantly: "Mutual trade, large joint ventures have been created, logistics ties have expanded, in practice there are processes of 'conjugation' of not only business and politics, but also science and culture".④ Over time, it became understandable that without appropriate scientific support, cooperation cannot develop successfully and intensively. For this purpose, Belarus and China established the number of joint research centers. China, also, has allocated more scholarships for teaching Belarusian students, numerous bilateral conferences have been held, and Chinese financial assistance to Belarus has been increased.⑤

---

① Итоги развития проекта «Один пояс — один путь» /СОНАР/ 23. 08. 2018. Available at: https://www.sonar2050.org/publications/pervyy-yubiley-puti/.

② Ци Хуанюань. Беларусь и Китай активизируют взаимовыгодное сотрудничество по всем направлениям концепции «Один пояс, один путь» Available at: https://rep.bntu.by/bitstream/handle/data/39623/Belarus_i_Kitaj_aktiviziruyut_vzaimovygodnoe_sotrudnichestvo_po_vsem_napravleniyam_koncepcii_Odin_poyas_i_odin_put.pdf?sequence=1&isAllowed=y.

③ Программа социально-экономического развития Республики Беларусь на 2016 – 2020 годы. Available at: http://www.government.by/upload/docs/program_ek2016-2020.pdf.

④ Итоги развития проекта «Один пояс — один путь» /СОНАР/23. 08. 2018. Available at: https://www.sonar2050.org/publications/pervyy-yubiley-puti/.

⑤ Smaliakou, D. Sino-Belarusian Cooperation in Sphere of Education Faced the Challenges of the Belt and Road Initiative Between China and Belarus // Zhang Yi; Wang Lei / China and Belarus: Forge Ahead Together in the "Belt and Road" Construction. : Beijing, China Social Sciences Press, 2019. P. 201 –215.

Pretty soon Belarus adopted main criteria for the effectiveness of bilateral cooperation in the framework of the Belt and Road Initiative realization.[①] Firstly, the industries and projects with Chinese participation created in Belarus should provide goods and services for the domestic market of Belarus. Secondly, these industries and cervices should increase the quality so far enter to the markets of the Eurasian Economic Union and the European Union countries. On this stage, Belarus would not only consume joint products on its own market, but would also export it abroad.

Meanwhile, such conceptual foundations for the implementation of the Belt and Road Initiative ran into a number of problems that were associated with the previously described, false understanding of the essence of international cooperation. Accordantly with this understanding local problems in national governance should be minimized by Chinese support, while in reality, changes in Belarus's national governance should be only supported by external investments and increased partnership with China. In other words, Belarus should have been guided by business planning, and did not rely solely on the political factor, which is not capable of providing the necessary financial results on its own.

Firstly, in the framework of the first stage, the outflow of foreign currency from Belarus has intensified, tamounting to more than a billion USD a year, and credit conditions create a trade deficitas as well increase the external public debt of Belarus[②]. As far as Belarus has no perfect sustainability in financial resources and permanently needs external support to maintain national debt, the flow of foreign currency abroad has strong negative effect on national economic security.

---

① Итоги развития проекта «Один пояс — один путь» /СОНАР/ 23. 08. 2018. Available at: https://www.sonar2050.org/publications/pervyy-yubiley-puti/.

② Рудый, К. В. Беларусь-Китай: сдвиги в экономическом сотрудничестве // Белорусский экономический журнал. 2019 №2. С. 38 – 51. Available at: http://bem.bseu.by/rus/archive/2.19/2-2019_rudy.pdf.

During the 5 years, outflow of currency reached a difference of 10 billion USD.[①] Mutual structure of trade turnover has also changed. Thanks to the development of Belarusian-Chinese relations, China has increased technological exports to Belarus. China supplied mainly food products to Belarus early, now it supplies computers, vehicles, processing equipment, etc. Belarusian exports to China is increasing. Along with the traditional export of potash fertilizers has been accrued growth in food exports. These measures have raised the level of trade between China and Belarus.

III. Special Economic Zones—China's Development Experience

China recently became one of the leaders in setting up foreign zones of trade and economic cooperation. In 2016, China has been already launched 77 industrial parks in 36 countries with a total investment of 24.19 billion USD. At the same time, the total number of residents of these zones amounted to 1522, as far as gross output reached 70.28 billion USD.[②]

Creation of foreign zones of trade and economic cooperation positively affected on developing the sustainability of the host countries. In consider with this evidence there is possible confidently state that creation of this kind of zones on a national level perceived by the Chinese side as the fair assistantship provided by China with respect to transit states in accordance with understanding of fair globalization. Thus, Chinese integration assistance does not consist in the creation of supranational government bodies, financial subsidies or technological donations, but in the creation of jobs and taxes payment.

[①] Итоги развития проекта «Один пояс — один путь» /СОНАР/23.08.2018. Available at: https://www.sonar2050.org/publications/pervyy-yubiley-puti/.

[②] Яо Цзяхуэй. Беларусь и КНР: торгово-экономическое сотрудничество в контексте реализации стратегии «экономического пояса Шелкового пути» // Журнал международного права и международных отношений. 2017. № 1 - 2 (80 - 81). С. 122 - 129. Available at: http://elib.bsu.by/bitstream/123456789/183567/1/tsyahuey_Journal2017_1 - 2.pdf.

Such kind of foreign zone of technical and economic cooperation was created in Belarus as well. Belarusian-Chinese industrial park "Great Stone", which "does not stand out from the presentation of the specifics of the advantages of zones of trade and economic cooperation in relation to the region"①. This project is called in Belarus a pearl of the Belt and Road Initiative, that is to say the basement of Belarusian involvement into new globalization.②

The creation of an industrial park became possible after the signing of the agreement between the Belarusian and Chinese governments on state support and investment security. Both sides agreed to create a Belarusian-Chinese industrial park in March 2010, and the process of construction began in 2014 as long as the first residents were appeared. In 2017 President of Belarus issued Decree No. 166 that determined unprecedented conditions for doing business on that territory. The tax and law conditions of the Park became much more convenient for foreign investments and have no analogues among CIS countries as well as Baltic states. In order to emphasize the uniqueness of the industrial park, to confirm its difference from other territories with a preferential treatment (free economic zones, a high-tech park), the priority areas of investment projects were clearly defined: electronics, tele-communications, pharmaceuticals, fine chemicals, biotechnologies, engineering, new materials, integrated logistics, electronic commerce, activities related to the processing and storage of large amounts of data, socio-cultural activities, research and design work.③

In this regard, it is important to note that "Great Stone" was planned long

---

① Сазонов, С. Л. Экономическая парадигма формирования «пояса и пути» / С. Л. Сазонов // Стратегия Экономического пояса Шелкового пути и роль ШОС в ее реализации: материалы «круглого стола», 16 марта 2016 г. — М. : ИДВ РАН, 2016. — С. 131—148.

② «Великий Камень» — это «жемчужина» в китайском «Шелковом пути»? /REGNUM/ 13. 08. 2018. Available at: https://regnum.ru/news/2463458.html.

③ «Великий камень»-самый большой индустриальный парк, построенный Китаем за рубежом» /СТВ/02. 07. 2019. Available at: https://news.21.by/other-news/2019/07/02/1831256.html.

before the announcement of the Belt and Road Initiative, which testifies in favor of direct extension of China's previous policy that has already confirmed its effectiveness. Analyzing all economic and tax preferences of the park important to consider geography, as well. "Great Stone" is located on the capital and located near the National airport of Minsk, along the main economic artery of Belarus: the crossroad between Orša-Brest highway, connecting the borders of Russia and Poland and Homieĺ highway connecting the borders of Lithuania and Ukraine. The "Great Stone" industrial park set up the trade and logistics sub-park. This logistics center is constructing by China Merchants Group that plans to invest more than 500 million USD.[①] The logistics facility will include an exhibition center, a hotel, indoor and outdoor warehouses, retail space, offices and other facilities. A dry port accessed to Baltic countries will be constructed in the future, as well as high-speed rail road connected to China-Belarus-Europe corridor.

Logistic facilities of "Great Stone" industrial park should be understood as an element of Pan-Eurasian infrastructure. Technopark development is the part of regional cooperation plan for building integration structures in frame of new globalization. The development of logistics facilities along way from China to Europe primarily implies a network of railways and highways connections: "The Chinese part of the corridor includes highways from the eastern and central-southern provinces of China to Xinjiang Uygur Autonomous Region, accessed to Kazakhstan border. After China, a new land bridge passes through Kazakhstan, Russia and Belarus to Poland, and then branches into European countries and opens to seaports in the north and west of Europe".

There are several of international rail lines between China and Europe, including Chongqing-Duisburg (Germany), Wuhan-Pardubice (Czech Republic), Chengdu-Lodz (Poland), Zhengzhou-Hamburg (Germany),

---

① Торгово-логистический субпарк China Merchants Group в "Великом камне" обойдётся в $550 млн26 ноября 2015. Available at: http://www.logists.by/news/view/velikiy-kamen-obojdetsya-v-55-mln-doll.

Yiwu-Madrid. Along these directions there were simplified procedure for declaring goods and passing customs procedures that allowed to increase speed and reduce the cost of cargo delivery.

Inside this corridor Belarus is presented as a logistics hub on the way between China and Europe. In order to strengthen cooperation in 2018, Duisburger Hafen JSC (Germany) became the resident of the "Great Stone" industrial park. In the same time, Chinese government actively develop the infrastructure facilities of the countries along the Silk Road Economic Belt. China has already electrified 2 sections of local rail way system in Belarus: Maladziečna-Hudahaj and Homieĺ-Žlobin-Asipovičy. The total investment for the two projects amounted to 157.1 million USD. It has been electrified the 3rd section in 2018: Žlobin-Kalinkavičy. It is also important to note that Belarus railways directly involved in a number of projects in transport facilities development between the EU and the East-West of China that was positively influenced on local transport stability by using of emptied wagons returning from Europe.[①] In this regard the Belarus government created the customs clearance point of the Minsk Regional Customs in the "Great Stone" industrial park. In the days of Covid – 19 pandemic, the freight train services between China and Europe has shown strong resilience and became more important.

IV. Conclusion

Improving logistics infrastructure between China and Europe is an important part of the Belt and Road Initiative. Improving communications is aimed not only

---

① Папковская, В. И. Развитие международного транспорта Республики Беларусь в рамках инициативы «Один пояс, один путь» //Устойчивое развитие экономики: международные и национальные аспекты [Электронный ресурс]: электронный сборник статей III Международной научно-практической online-конференции, Новополоцк, 18 – 19 апреля 2019 г. / Полоцкий государственный университет. – Новополоцк, 2019. Available at: http://elib.psu.by/bitstream/ 123456789/23655/1/%D0%9F%D0%B0%D0%BF%D0%BA%D0%BE%D0%B2%D1%81%D0% BA%D0%B0%D1%8F%20%D0%92.%D0%98._%D1%81 1418 – 421. pdf.

at accelerating cargo, but also at filling traffic flow in both directions. Considering the opportunities for cooperation in the creation of zones of border technical and economic cooperation, Belarus should more actively work on joint implementation of the Belt and Road Initiative and more effectively use the growth of transport interaction between China and Europe. It is understood that this initiative could help Belarus in demand and employment at the stage of modernization of the Belarusian infrastructure, provide growth of trade on the EU border, due to supplies from China, provide profit from tax deductions and job growth.

In this regard Belarus has to optimize the business environment in order to strength private interactions between China and Belarus. Belarusian private business has to be more involved in joint activities as far as it could more attentively develop business planning in comparison with state bodies. Governance reform should make Belarus more adaptable to the implementation of the Belt and Road Initiative when necessary, and try more effectively at the national level in bilateral trade between Belarus and China. The national economic growth and modernization of local economy and legal system, the development of intellectual potential and the improvement of the social sphere are the part of Belarus' national responsibilities. Thereby, Belarus government has to focus on national and social governance as far as business interactions should be mostly developed by private sector and the government needs to provide them with good services.

Systems and Regulations and Action Construction on Ecological Civilization and Modernization of Ecological Environment Governance of China

Lin Hong
Assistant Professor, Institute of Sociology, CASS

In a risk society, any person can be both cause and effect, and there is an overall collusion among all components of the system.[1] In recognition of this risk, the international community and countries are taking diverse approaches to address the upcoming society fraught with ecological risk. As noted by *Global Environment Outlook 6*, the drivers and pressures leading to an unhealthy planet result from a continuing failure to internalize environmental and health impacts into economic growth processes, technologies and city design. The drivers include population growth and demographics, urbanization, economic development, new technological forces, and climate change. The pressures arise from massive use of chemicals (many with toxic health and environmental implications), huge waste streams (many largely unmanaged), committed and intensifying climate change impacts, and inequality which contributes to

---

[1] Ulrich Beck, *Risk Society*, translated by HE Bowen, Nanjing: Yilin Press, 2004, pp. 28 – 34.

demographic changes and other drivers and pressures.[1] To address these challenges, the report recommends countries establish ideas around a green, healthy and inclusive economy and systematically reflect these ideas in their existing national policies.

At present, at both the international and domestic levels, China is delivering on its pledge of protecting the global ecological environment, by actively implementing the *Transforming Our World: The 2030 Agenda for Sustainable Development*, the *Paris Agreement*, and by promoting ecological civilization. A review of China's environmental endeavors over the past few decades demonstrates that, China has been pursuing ecological civilization in a way that suits to its own national conditions. In 1978, the Constitution of the People's Republic of China confirmed environmental protection as one of national functions; in 2018, the requirements of the new development concept, ecological civilization, and of building a beautiful China were written into the amendments to the Constitution. In 1974, China established the State Council Leading Group on Environmental Protection; in 2018, China restructured the previous environmental authorities into the new Ministry of Ecological Environment. In 1979, China formulated the *Environmental Protection Law of the People's Republic of China* (trial); in 1989, China revised it and officially promulgated the *Environmental Protection Law of the People's Republic of China*. In 2014, after further revisions, China passed what was known as "historically the most stringent environmental protection law" —the new *Environmental Protection Law of the People's Republic of China* (trial). In the new era, China, guided by Xi Jinping Thought on Ecological Civilization, is pressing harder to build a beautiful China, thereby contributing more to building a more beautiful word.

---

[1] UN Environment. 2019. *Global Environment Outlook-GEO – 6: Healthy Planet*, Healthy People. Nairobi. DOI 10.1017/9781108627146. p. xxix – xxx.

I. Evolution of Thoughts on Ecological Civilization of China

Since 1949, China's environmental governance system has undergone many significant strategic transformations: startup, construction, and enhancement, evolving from "the outlook of pollution control concept" to "the outlook of ecological civilization". [1] Roughly, the development of the environmental governance has experienced five stages: firstly, early exploration prior to reform and opening-up focused on industrial pollution control; secondly, "prevention first and combination of prevention and control" in the early period of reform and opening-up; thirdly, "equal emphasis on pollution control and ecological protection" in the 1990s; fourthly, "protecting the environment while developing the economy and developing the economy while protecting the environment" in the early 21st century; and fifthly, "giving priority to ecology" since the 18th National Congress of the Communist Party of China.

In the 1970s, in favor of the international ecological protection ideas, China held its first National Conference on Environmental Protection and passed the *Several Provisions on Protecting and Improving Environment*, proposing that China needed to strategically look at environmental issues. The *Provisions* came as the first policy of China on environmental protection since 1949. In 1981, the State Council issued the *Decision on Strengthening Environmental Protection Work during Economic Adjustment*, which articulated that "environment and natural resources serve as the essential conditions for people to survive and as the material source to develop production and prosper the economy. To well manage our environment and rationally develop and utilize our natural resources

---

[1] Zhang Xiaojun, Liu Jiejiao, "Examination of Changes and Orientations in Environmental Regulatory Policies of China over the Past 70 Years", *Reform*, Issue 10, 2019.

is one basic task for modernization drive[①]". In 1982, the new *Constitution* promulgated and stipulated that "The government protects and improves the living and ecological environments, controls pollution and other public hazards". In December 1983, at the 2nd National Conference on Environmental Protection, Li Peng, then-time premier, noted that "Environmental protection is one strategic task towards China's modernization and it represents one basic state policy of the country". In 1990, the *State Council Decision on Strengthening Environmental Protection Work*, as an authoritative policy of the central government, officially established environmental protection as one basic state policy of China; in addition, environmental protection was incorporated into the *10 - year Plan and 8th Five-year Plan for Economic and Social Development* passed in 1991, through the expression of "it is one basic state policy of China to protect and improve the production and ecological environments and to prevent and control pollution and other public hazards". Afterwards, in 1992, the Report of the 14th National Congress of the Communist Party of China noted that "China will conscientiously carry out the basic state policy of controlling population growth and strengthening environmental protection". In 1996, at the 4th National Conference on Environmental Protection, then-time Chinese President Jiang Zemin underscored that "to control population growth and protect ecological environment represents a basic state policy that both the Party and the whole nation must maintain on a long-term basis". These policy texts and leaders' remarks from top-level design further established environmental protection as one basic state policy of China.

After environmental protection was established as one basic state policy, at the level of national development strategy, the idea of sustainable development was regarded as objectification of state policy awareness. In June 1992, the

---

[①] "Decision on Strengthening Environmental Protection Work during Economic Adjustment", China Network, February 24, 1981, http://www.china.com.cn/law/flfg/txt/2006 - 08/08/content_7058576.htm.

United Nations Conference on Environment and Development (UNCED), held in the Brazilian city of Rio de Janeiro, passed the *Rio Declaration*, *Agenda 21*, and other important documents—an indication that the international community established the core idea of sustainable development. The Chinese government actively participated in relevant activities relating to UNCED and signed the aforesaid documents. Moreover, in 1994 it took the lead to sign the *Agenda 21 of China*: *White Paper on Population, Resources, Environment, and Development of China in the 21st Century*, coming up with the overall strategy and policy for sustainable development, social sustainable development, economic sustainable development, rational use of resources, and overall planning for environmental protection, and identifying 78 concrete areas for actions. This not merely reflected China's inner demand for sustainable development, but also demonstrated the attitude and resolution of the Chinese government to actively perform its international commitment and to make due contributions to a common cause for all humanity. In 1995, the 5th Plenary Session of the 14th CPC Central Committee passed the *Suggestions of the CPC Central Committee on Formulating the 9th Five-year Plan for Economic and Social Development and the 2010 Long-term Objectives*, proposing that China would "shift from an extensive economic growth model towards an intensive one". In 2000, the 5th Plenary Session of the 15th CPC Central Committee passed the *Suggestions of the CPC Central Committee on Formulating the 10th Five-year Plan for Economic and Social Development*, which held that "implementing the sustainable development strategy represents a long-term approach that concerns the survival and development of the Chinese nation". In 2002, the Report of the 16th National Congress of the Communist Party of China systematically summarized the past basic experience and established the implementation of the sustainable development strategy to coordinate economic development with population, resources, and environment as the basic experience that must be followed by the Party while it leads the Chinese people to build socialism with Chinese characteristics. The Report underlined that, to realize the magnificent objective of building a moderately prosperous society in all aspects, we must constantly strengthen our sustainability, improve our ecological environment, significantly increase our resource utilization efficiency, and promote man-nature harmony, thus setting the entire society onto a civilization development path that features booming production, well-to-do life, and good ecology. From then on, sustainable development officially became a significant strategy for China to realize its goals of socialist modernization drive.

As the 21st century unfolded, the modernization process of socialism with Chinese characteristics faced a new situation of building on past achievements and striving for new progress. To a large extent, national development remained subject to traditional ideas and models of modernization. The CPC Central Committee with Comrade Hu Jintao noted that "We must bear in mind and conscientiously carry out the Scientific Outlook on Development and apply this outlook throughout our development process and all aspects", and we must use the Scientific Outlook on Development to guide the socialist modernization drive during the new decade for China (2002 – 2012). With respect to the ecological environment, the new leadership required that we must work hard to transform and upgrade our industries and technical structures and build an "energy-saving and environment-friendly" society. On June 25, 2003, the Decision by CPC Central Committee and the State Council on Accelerating Forestry Development noted that "We will work to build a society of ecological civilization with beautiful mountains". This was the first time that authoritative state media had expressly used the concept of "ecological civilization". Subsequently, the "Scientific Outlook on Development" and the "Building a harmonious society", respectively proposed at the 3rd Plenary Session and 4th Plenary Session of the 16th CPC Central Committee, both contained state-level expressions on the idea of ecological civilization as well as its policy implications. In 2005, the 5th Plenary Session of the 16th CPC Central Committee expressly noted that China would work faster to build an energy-saving and environment-friendly society, develop circular economy, strengthen environmental protection to effectively protect the environment, conscientiously resolve outstanding environmental issues affecting socio-economic development particularly those jeopardizing people's health, and establish an energy-saving growth pattern and healthy, civilized consumption pattern in society. In 2007, the Report of the 17th CPC National Congress officially came up with the concept of "ecological civilization" by saying "We will build ecological civilization and basically establish an industrial structure, growth pattern, and consumption pattern that conserves energy and resources and that protects our ecological environment". Obviously, under the development context for this period, building an "energy-saving, environment-friendly" society was the objectified connotation of "ecological civilization".

Since the 18th CPC National Congress, the CPC Central Committee with Comrade Xi Jinping as the core, standing at the new historical starting point towards the modernization of socialism with Chinese characteristics, systematically summarized China's experience in its socio-economic modernization drive as well as in the basic state policy of environmental protection, the sustainable development strategy, and in the building of an "energy-saving, environment-friendly society". The CPC Central Committee tries to systematically resolve the incomprehensiveness, inadequacy, and imbalances that are looming large in China's socio-economic development, from a higher view of political philosophy and a strategic vision level. Based on the series of important expressions from Xi Jinping about the Governance of China, the Xi Jinping Thought on Socialism with Chinese Characteristics for a New Era was gradually formed and this Thought, on the dimension of ecological environment governance, is expressed as "Xi Jinping Thought on Ecological Civilization". In fact, as early as in 2003, Xi Jinping proposed the important conclusion of "When ecology prospers, civilization prospers; when ecology decays, civilization decays".[①] In November 2012, the Report of the 18th CPC National Congress, for the first time, listed ecological civilization construction as one core element in the overall arrangement of modernization of

---

① Xi Jinping, "A Good Ecology Leads to Powerful Civilization: Advance Ecological Construction to Build a 'Green Zhejiang' ", *Qiushi*, Issue 13, 2003.

socialism with Chinese characteristics, alongside the construction of economy, politics, culture, and society, and required that we must carry out ecological civilization construction throughout "all aspects and processes".

In November 2012, the Report of the 18th CPC National Congress, for the first time, listed ecological civilization construction as one core element in the overall arrangement of modernization of socialism with Chinese characteristics, alongside the construction of economy, politics, culture, and society, and required that we must carry out ecological civilization construction throughout "all aspects and processes". In November 2013, the Decision of the 3rd Plenary Session of the 18th CPC Central Committee identified 60 reform tasks, one theme of which was to work faster to formulate regulations regarding ecological civilization construction so as to modernize the national governance system and capacity for ecological environment. In September 2015, the CPC Central Committee and the State Council jointly issued the *Overall Plan for Structural Reform in Ecological Civilization*, expressly requiring that we must advance core reforms in the framework system consisting of "multiple-pillar" systems on ecological civilization including "optimizing the property right system for natural resource assets; establishing a system for the development and protection of territorial space; establishing a space planning system; optimizing the system for managing total resources and conserving resources in all respects; optimizing the system for paid use of resources and ecological compensation; establishing an environmental governance system; optimizing the market system for environmental governance and ecological protection; and improving the performance assessment system and accountability system for ecological civilization". In October 2015, the 5th Plenary Session of the 18th CPC Central Committee came up with the vision of "innovative, coordinated, green, open and inclusive development" and proposed taking it as the guiding principle for formulating the 13th Five-year Plan for the socio-economic development of China. In October 2017, the 19th CPC National Congress, for the first time, expressly set forth the staged goals for ecological civilization construction of China. Specifically, by 2020, China will "win the battle against pollution"; from 2020 to 2035, China will realize "fundamentally improved ecological environment and a truly beautiful China"; from 2035 to 2049, China will "comprehensively enhance its ecological civilization". On October 24, 2017, the new version of *Constitution of the Communist Party of China* said that: "In the new century, our country has entered the new development stage of building a moderately prosperous society in all aspects and working faster to advance socialist modernization. In this stage, we must follow the 'five-in-one' overall plan and the 'four comprehensives' strategic plan for socialism with Chinese characteristics. We must orchestrate economic construction, political construction, cultural construction, social construction, and ecological civilization construction". In March 2018, Paragraph Seven of the newly amended *Constitution* said that "China will coordinate material civilization, political civilization, spiritual civilization, social civilization, and ecological civilization to build China into a modern socialist power that is strong, democratic, civilized, harmonious, and beautiful, thus rejuvenating the great Chinese nation". This indicated that ecological civilization was officially confirmed in the form of basic state law.

From 1973 to 2018, China has held a total of 8 national conferences on environmental protection. Symbolic achievements have been achieved in all these conferences, which embodies the development history of China's environmental protection in which the nation keeps forging ahead and innovating as the time goes by. In 1973, the State Council held the first National Conference on Environmental Protection, coming up with a 32 – (Chinese) character policy of "fully planning, rationally distributing, comprehensively utilizing, turn harming into good, relying on the masses, participating by everyone, and benefiting the people". In 1983, the second National Conference on Environmental Protection established environmental protection as one basic state policy of China and formulated the guiding policy of "We should synchronously plan, implement, and develop economic projects, urban-rural projects, and environmental projects to deliver economic, social, and environmental co-benefits". Additionally, the conference articulated the three major environmental policies of " 'Prevention first and combination of prevention and control'; 'Whoever causes pollution shall be responsible for its treatment'; and 'Intensifying environmental management'". In 1989, the third National Conference on Environmental Protection called on "staging a war against environmental pollution", noting that China would actively implement 8 environmental management systems including a target-oriented responsibility system for environmental protection, a quantitative assessment system for comprehensive improvement of urban environment, a license system for emission pollutants, a pollution centralized control system, a system of treatment within a prescribed limit of time, a "three simultaneous" system, and a pollution charges system. In 1996, the 4th National Conference on Environmental Protection noted that protecting environment is essential for implementing the sustainable development strategy; and that to protect environment, in effect, is to protect productive forces. In addition, the conference identified the implementation of the plan for controlling total pollutant discharge and the trans-century green project plan as two significant measures for improving environmental quality. In 2002, the 5th National Conference on Environmental Protection required that we must equal protecting environment to developing productive forces, and develop environmental undertakings according to economic laws by marketizing and industrializing such undertakings. In 2006, the 6th National Conference on Environmental Protection expressly said that to effectively protect our environment under the new situation hinges on working faster to achieve "three shifts": In specific, we should shift from more emphasis on economic growth and less emphasis on environmental protection towards equal emphasis on both; we should shift from environmental protection lagging behind economic development towards enabling both to move in lockstep; and we should shift from primarily using administrative measures to protect environment towards using a combination of legal, economic, technological means and necessary administrative measures to address environmental issues. In 2011, the 7th National Conference on Environmental Protection stressed that we should protect environment while developing the economy and we must develop the economy while protecting environment; we should actively explore a new approach to environmental protection that features less cost, more benefit, low emission, and sustainability; we should work hard to resolve outstanding environmental issues that affect scientific development damage people's health, thereby better protecting our environment. In 2018, at the 8th National Conference on Ecological Environment Protection, General Secretary Xi Jinping emphasized that, we should work faster to build an ecological civilization system; an ecological culture system held to the standard of ecological values; an ecological economy system piggybacking on industrial ecologicalization and ecological industrialization; a target responsibility system designed to improve ecological environmental quality; an institutional system for ecological civilization underpinned by governance system and governance capacity; and an ecological security system focused on virtuous cycle of ecosystems and effective prevention and control of environmental risk. [1]This marked the official establishment of Xi Jinping Thought on Ecological Civilization.

Since China's reform and opening-up, the Communist Party of China and the Chinese government under its leadership have gradually established an outlook on green modernization that is increasingly systematic theoretically and that embraces greater and greater environmentalism and even ecologism implications, as fleshed out with the thought of basic state policy of environmental protection, the thought of sustainable development strategy, the thought of building an "energy-saving and environment-friendly" society, and the current thought on ecological civilization. Ecological civilization as well as the "(socialist) modernization where man and nature co-exist in harmony" under its construction field and context can be the most concise expression of the

---

[1] Xinhuanet, 2019, Creating a New Situation in Building a Beautiful China—Important Remarks of President Xi Jinping at the National Conference on Ecological Environment Protection Evokes Great Enthusiasm, May 20 (http://www.xinhuanet.com//politics/2018-05/20/c_1122859915.htm).

thought on ecological civilization. ①

II. Establishment of Regulations and Systems of China Regarding Ecological Civilization

Since the 1970s, China has been making great efforts to protect its environment and has formulated various regulations and systems with respect to environmental protection. The introduction of these regulations and systems can largely fall into four stages.

Stage I (1973 – 1993): Point Source Treating and Establishment of Regulations and Systems

During this stage, by consistently establishing regulations and systems and controlling pollution in crucial regions, China started to protect its environment in accordance with laws and regulations. In August 1973, the first National Conference on Environmental Protection was held in Beijing. In December 1978, the CPC Central Committee endorsed and forwarded the *Essentials on Reporting of Environmental Protection Work*, passed by the 4th Meeting of the State Council Leading Group on Environmental Protection. In September 1979, the newly enacted *Environmental Protection Law of the People's Republic of China* (*trial*), for the first time, legally required all departments and governments at all levels to factor in environmental protection while they formulate plans on economic and social development, thus legally ensuring coordination between environment and economy and society. Single laws and regulations concerning environmental protection were successively enacted, including the *Law of the People's Republic of China on Water Pollution Control* (May 1984); the *Law of the People's Republic of China on Air Pollution Control* (September 1987); the *Grassland Law of the People's Republic of China* (June 1985); and the *Water Law of the People's Republic of China* (January 1988). In December 1989,

---

① Xun Qingzhi, "Evolution in the Green Modernization Discourse of the Communist Party of China Over Four Decades of Reform and Opening-up", *Journal of Yunmeng*, Issue1, 2019.

the Environmental Protection Law of the People's Republic of China was officially enacted. Since then, environmental protection laws, as important guarantee for environmental protection, have been a significant part of socialist legal system of China. In 1990, the State Council issued the *Decision on Strengthening Environmental Protection Work*, stressing that China would strictly enforce laws and regulations regarding environmental protection, would take effective measures to control industrial pollution according to law, and would fully implement 8 environmental management systems including a target-oriented responsibility system for environmental protection, a quantitative assessment system for comprehensive improvement of urban environment, a license system for emission pollutants, a pollution centralized control system, a system of treatment within a prescribed limit of time, a "three simultaneous" system, and a pollution charges system. In March 1993, the Environmental Protection and Resources Conservation Committee was set up and raised the "legal system framework for environmental protection and resources conservation of China". The successive establishment of the environmental protection theoretical system underpinned by environmental protection as one basic state policy, the environmental regulations predominated by pollution charges system, "three simultaneous" system, and environmental impact assessment system, and the legal system based on the *Environmental Protection Law* laid a solid foundation for massive environmental governance in the next stage.

Stage II (1994 – 2004): Basin Remediation and Intensified Law Enforcement

In the early 1990s, China entered the first wave of heavy chemical era. During this period, as urbanization picked up speed, the structure, compound, and compression characteristics of environmental pollution started to take shape, prompting this stage to become an important period for intensified law enforcement to control pollution and to protect ecology. In 1992, China officially started to prepare the national annual work plan on environmental protection and since the 9th Five-year Plan period, it has been officially preparing the national five-year plan on environmental protection, incorporating environmental protection plan into the overall economic and social development plan. As a result, environmental protection has extended from single industrial pollution control to many other important segments including treatment of domestic pollution, ecological protection, protection of rural environment, regulation over nuclear safety, and emergency response to sudden environmental events. Additionally, domestic pollution has gradually featured in the comprehensive decision-making with regard to economic and social development. In April 1998, as a department directly under the State Council, the former State Environment Protection Bureau was upgraded as the State Environmental Protection Administration (SEPA). To better coordinate with relevant departments for more effective environmental protection, SEPA took the lead to respectively set up inter-ministerial joint meeting systems. In March 2001, the first National Inter-Ministerial Joint Meeting on Ecological Environment Construction was held. In July 2001, SEPA established the national inter-ministerial joint meeting system on environmental protection. In August 2003, after approval by the State Council, SEPA took the lead to officially set up the inter-ministerial joint meeting system on conservation of biological species resources.

During this stage, the overall national approach was controlling pollution in key basins and regions and enabling these key basins and regions to help advance environmental protection across the country. In June 1994, SPEA, the Ministry of Water Resources, and four provinces along the Huaihe River: Henan Province, Anhui Province, Jiangsu Province, and Shandong Province jointly issued the first regulations with regard to water pollution prevention of big rivers—the *Decision on Preventing Sudden Contamination Accidents in the Watercourse of the Huaihe River Basin* (trial). In August 1995, the State Council issued China's first environmental regulations for a single basin—the *Provisional Regulations on Water Pollution Control of the Huaihe River Basin*, articulating the goals for water pollution control of the Huaihe River Basin. Due to the enforcement of relevant laws and regulations, more than 4,000 polluting enterprises were shut down in 1996 alone. The *Trans-century Green Engineering*

Program of China, which came into force in 1996, aimed to implement integrated treatment on basin water pollution and regional air pollution over phases, in accordance with the principle of highlighting priorities, technical and economic feasibility, and delivering comprehensive benefits. By 2010, under the Program, a total of 1,591 projects were implemented and 188 billion yuan was invested. The Program successively identified a few critical areas for pollution control during the 9th Five-year Plan period, namely the "3 rivers" (Huaihe River, Liaohe River, and Haihe River), "3 lakes" (Taihu Lake, Dian Lake, and Chaohu Lake), "2 control zones" (sulfur dioxide control zone and acid rain control zone), "1 city" (Beijing), and "1 sea" (Bohai Sea), trying to address those environmental issues that affected people's life, damaged their health, and restricted socio-economic development.

In November 1998, the State Council issued the *National Plan for Ecological Environment Construction*, launching a series of major projects on ecological protection. In 1999, China piloted returning farmland to forests and to grassland, giving priority to the return of farmland to forests in those ecologically sensitive regions taking an important position in ecological security. In 2000, the Natural Forest Protection Project (NFPP), in which China invested 100 billion yuan, was launched. The Project focuses its protection effort on the natural forest resources along the upper reaches of Yangtze River and Yellow River, as well as in Northeast China. In December 2000, the General Office of the State Council issued the *National Program for Ecological Environment Protection*. In March 2002, the State Council approved the *10th Five-year Plan for National Ecological Environment Protection*. In May 2003, SEPA issued the *Indicators for Building Eco-county, Eco-city, and Eco-province (trial)*, deepening the construction of ecological demonstration zones.

In the early 2000s, because water pollution in some basins started to spread from local river stretches to the entire basin, strengthening the prevention of sudden environmental events featured prominently in environmental protection during this stage. [1] In March 2002, SEPA started to set up the Environmental Emergency and Accident Investigation Center. In face of increasing numbers of sudden environmental events, the central government formulated and optimized a range of environmental emergency response plans with respect to water environments and air environments in critical basins and sensitive waters, hazardous chemicals (waste chemicals), as well as to nuclear and radiation. In 2005, the Chinese government formulated the *National Emergency Plan for Environmental Emergencies*, raising explicit requirements regarding the receiving, reporting, processing, and statistical analysis of information on environmental emergencies, as well as regarding the monitoring of early-warning information and information distribution. Meanwhile, China's investment in environmental protection grew rapidly, representing a higher and higher share of its GDP. During the 9th Five-year Plan period, China's environmental investment was 2.7 times of that during the 8th Five-year Plan period, hitting 351.64 billion yuan. In 1999, environmental investment as a proportion of GDP exceeded 1.0% for the first time; during the 10th Five-year Plan period, this figure rose to a further 1.19%. As governments at all levels take pollution control more and more seriously and spend more and more in environmental protection, pollution control has started to shift gradually from industrial sectors to urban areas, where positive progress has been made in comprehensive environmental improvement.

Stage III (2005 – 2012): Comprehensive Prevention and Control, Optimization of Growth

In 2005, China started to enter a high-incidence season for environmental pollution events. From 2005 to 2009, a series of significant pollution events broke out, including the serious water pollution in Songhuajiang River in Jilin Province, cadmium pollution in Beijiang River in Guangdong Province, blue

---

[1] Central People's Government of the People's Republic of China, Status of Environmental Protection, 2012 – 04 – 10 (http://www.gov.cn/guoqing/2012 – 04/10/content_2584066.htm) Login date: May 31, 2020.

algae eruption in Taihu Lake in Jiangsu Province, and arsenic pollution in Yangzonghai Lake in Yunnan Province. These events severely impacted regional economic development as well as local people's life. In December 2005, the State Council issued the *Decision on Applying Scientific Outlook on Development and Strengthening Environmental Protection*, establishing the environmental tenet of people-centricity and environment for everyone. This *Decision* came as the programmatic document guiding coordination between socio-economic development and environmental protection. Given mounting pressures on China's resources and environment, the 11th Five-year Plan came up with the strategic task and concrete measures for building an energy saving and environment-friendly society. In April 2006, the State Council held the sixth National Conference on Environmental protection, proposing the strategic thought of "three shifts". In specific, we should shift from more emphasis on economic growth and less emphasis on environmental protection towards equal emphasis on both; we should shift from environmental protection lagging behind economic development towards enabling both to move in lockstep; and we should shift from primarily using administrative measures to protect environment towards using a combination of legal, economic, technological means and necessary administrative measures to address environmental issues. From then on, environmental protection of China entered a new stage of protecting environment to optimize economic development. In October 2007, the 17th CPC National Congress, for the first time, established ecological civilization construction as one strategic task and a new goal for building a moderately prosperous society in all aspects. In 2009, *Macroeconomic Strategic Research on China's Environment* came up with a major theoretical and practical project of actively exploring a new path for environmental protection of China. In 2011, the State Council held the *Seventh National Conference on Environmental Protection*, issuing the *Opinions on Strengthening Priorities for Environmental Protection* and the *National 12th Five-year Plan for Environmental Protection*, which laid a solid foundation for promoting environmental protection in a scientifically sound fashion.

Stage IV (since 2013): Structural reform and overall transformation

Since 2013, there has been a growing public awareness for ecological environment in China. Subjective perception about ecological environment has become an important factor for the Chinese people to define a good life. *The Decision on Several Important Issues Regarding Fully Deepening Reform*, passed at the 3rd Plenary Session of the 18th CPC Central Committee, further elevated ecological civilization construction by formulating regulations to promote it, more explicitly raising the task of applying rules and regulations to protect ecological environment. The 4th Plenary Session of the 18th CPC Central Committee passed the *Decision of the CPC Central Committee on Several Important Issues Regarding Fully Advancing Rule of Law*, legally raising higher requirements for ecological civilization construction by stipulating "applying more stringent laws and regulations to protect ecological environment", thereby promoting ecological civilization construction. In April 2015, the CPC Central Committee and the State Council issued the *Opinions on Accelerating Ecological Civilization Construction*, comprehensively and systematically proposing the guiding thought, basic principles, major objectives, major tasks, and crucial measures for ecological civilization construction. In September 2015, the CPC Central Committee and the State Council issued the *Overall Plan for Structural Reform in Ecological Civilization*, raising an approach of "1 + 6" to structural reform in ecological civilization. These programmatic documents have formed the strategic arrangement and the system framework featuring "multiple-pillar systems" for deepening structural reform in ecological civilization, in terms of ideas and strategies, objectives and tasks, and systems, regulations, and structures. The "1 + 6" scheme filled the gap in basic systems and regulations for ecological civilization construction at different levels. In addition, as the special plan that features clear reform orientation, clear reformers, and clear reform measures and that covers important fields and critical elements including reform experiment, space planning, delimitation of property rights, responsibility assignment, environmental monitoring, environmental damage, ecological compensation, evaluation, and accountability was advanced, the

"1 + 6" scheme started to play an important role in practice. So far, 79 reform tasks determined by the overall scheme for completion during 2015 – 2017 have been completed.[①] "Environmental Inspection" has immensely deterred environmental polluters. The introduction of the "river chief system" and the lake chief system" has allowed for full-process regulation from water sources to water faucets. The "ecological conservation redline" has enabled delimitation of ecological conservation redlines across the country. The "national park system" is contributing to a new pattern for nature conservation. The "off-office auditing on leaders for natural resource assets" has generated a strong warning effect. The "assessment on objectives for ecological civilization construction" reflects a new vision for regional development. From top-level design and overall arrangements to subsegments and functional structure, China's systematic regulations and systems structure for ecological environment governance is gradually taking shape.

Since the 3rd Plenary Session of the 19th CPC Central Committee, structural and mechanism reforms in ecological civilization have been deepening. First, state-level structural and mechanism reforms in ecological environmental regulatory system are progressing in an orderly manner. The reforms aim to set up the Ministry of Ecological Environment by integrating discreet ecological protection responsibilities of relevant departments. The Ministry of Ecological Environment is responsible for formulating and implementing plans, policies, and standards for the ecological environment, monitoring the ecological environment, and for carry outing pollution prevention and control and environmental protection law enforcement. In addition, by integrating the responsibilities of relevant departments for natural resources protection, these reforms aim to set up the Ministry of Natural Resources, which is concerned with defining and determining the property rights of natural

---

① Yang Weimin, "20 of 38 Meetings of the CPC Leading Group on Deepening Reform Discussed Issues on Structural Reform in Ecological Civilization", October 23, http://cpc.people.com.cn/19th/n1/2017/1023/c414536 – 29604149.html.

assets, with distributing and transferring such assets, and with maintaining and adding their values. The reforms on ecological protection institutions have intensified the functions with respect to the formulation of regulations, monitoring and evaluation, supervision and law enforcement, as well as inspection and accountability with respect to ecological protection. Reforms in vertical management for monitoring, supervision, and law enforcement in environmental protection institutions below the provincial level are progressing in an orderly manner. Meanwhile, the reforms of "streamlining administration, innovating regulation, and optimizing service" in ecological environment are constantly deepening, contributing to high-quality economic development and high-level ecological protection. The environmental tariff system has been precisely implemented, thanks to three innovative measures including fee-to-tax reform, tax amount increases, and environmental tariff belonging to local governments. The third-party governance mechanism is becoming increasingly market-based. The accountability system chain where the Party and the government share the same responsivity and where rights and obligations are clear-cut prompts the government, businesses, and society to share their joint responsibility for green development. The objective assessment using both incentives and constraints plays a robust role in guiding and constraining behaviors. Additionally, the reform aims to build a comprehensive enforcement team for ecological environment, unify enforcement in ecological environment, and inspect ecological protection, so as to forcibly deter illicit behaviors that damage the ecological environment. Second, both supportive regulations and explorative practices are carried out at the local level. For instance, when it comes to the ecological redline system, some provinces, depending on priorities, differentially manage redline areas by grading them; whereas some other provinces are exploring setting up punishment and accountability system for ecological redline. As another example, in terms of piloting projects, Guizhou, Fujian, Jiangxi, and other regions national pilot zones for ecological civilization have conducted testing on 38 of the 47 key tasks raised by the *Overall Plan* to explore the system models for ecological civilization construction at different development stages, and have established productive reform experience and system results[1]. As China consistently presses ahead with its systematical, integral, and reorganizational structural reforms in ecological civilization, the environmental governance system with Chinese characteristics is being gradually modernized, which has laid a solid foundation for realizing the objective of "building a new modernization landscape where man and nature develop in harmony"[2] as raised by the *Overall Plan for Structural Reform in Ecological Civilization*.

III. Actions of China on Ecological Civilization

The year 2018 marked a new era for ecological environmental protection of China, in which the local governments are strengthening ecological protection with unprecedented determination and intensity.[3] As China works harder and harder to protect its ecological environment, the quality of the country's ecological environment continues to improve. Due to further declines in the total emissions of major pollutants and carbon dioxide emissions per unit GDP, China's rankings in international development index on ecological civilization has substantially moved up.[4] Over recent years, from the central government to local governments, from environmental elements (air, water, soil, etc.), China tries to apply and deepen the idea of ecological civilization, by taking ecological environment governance actions at different levels and in different

---

[1] Chen Ying, "A Review of Structural Reform in Ecological Civilization of China and Its Future Direction", *Reform of Economic System*, Issue 6, 2019.

[2] Xinhuanet, "CPC Central Committee and the State Council Issues the Overall Plan for Structural Reform in Ecological Civilization", September 21, 2015, http://www.xinhuanet.com//politics/2015-09/21/c_1116632159.htm.

[3] Editors-in-chief: Li Peilin, Chen Guangjin, Wang Chunguang, *Analysis and Prediction of Social Situations of China for 2020* (Social Blue Book), Beijing: Social Sciences Academic Press, January 2020, p. 312.

[4] Chen Jia, Wu Minghong, Yan Geng, "Evaluation and Research on Ecological Civilization Construction and Development of China", *Chinese Public Administration*, Issue 6, 2016.

types. This is mainly reflected in the following aspects. ①

Press ahead with Blue Sky Protection Campaign. In July 2018, the State Council issued the *Three-year Action Plan for Winning the Blue Sky Protection Campaign*, articulating the overall approach, basic goals, major tasks, and guarantee measures with respect to air pollution control and raising the timetable and road map for winning the Blue Sky Protection Campaign. The Standing Committee of the National People's Congress (NPC) has organized inspection on enforcement of the Law on Air Pollution Control; intensified regional joint prevention and control by setting up the Air Pollution Control Leading Group for Beijing-Tianjin-Hebei and Surrounding Areas; set up the Air Pollution Control Coordinating Mechanism for Fenhe River Plain-Weihe River Plain Basin; and optimized the air pollution control coordinating mechanism for the Yangtze Delta region. In addition, the NPC Standing Committee has intensified supervision on key regions for the Blue Sky Protection Campaign. It has assigned 23,000 new environmental issues relating to air pollution to local governments and in 2017, all of the total 38,900 issues assigned were fully rectified. Nationwide, there have been approximately 810 million kilowatt of coal power units with ultra-low emissions, representing 80% of installed gross capacity of coal power. The consumption proportion of non-petrochemical energy hits 14.3%. The number of pilot cities covered by the project of clean energy heating for winter in northern China has increased from 12 to 35. Over 4.8 million households have been ordered to regulate their use of scattered coal. China has issued the *Action Plan on Tackling Pollution from Diesel-powered Trucks*, and formulated the Chinese emission standard at phase VI for heavy-duty diesel vehicles. Additionally, China fully supplies automotive gasoline and diesel oils adopting the Chinese emission standard at phase VI, realizing the alignment of automotive diesel oil, general diesel oil, and marine oil. Moreover, China works to push ahead with

---

① Ministry of Ecological Environment of the People's Republic of China, Communiques on Environment Status of China for 2018 and 2019, May 29, http://www.mee.gov.cn/hjzl/zghjzkgb/lnzghjzkgb/.

the project on the study of the cause for serious air pollution and treatment, and popularizes the work model of "one policy for one city" tracking study across "2 + 26" cities, Fenhe River Plain-Weihe River Plain Basin, and Xiong'an New Area. All of such concrete campaigns are designed to realize the target of "By 2020, total emissions from sulfur dioxide and from nitric oxides will decline by over 15% from 2015. The PM2.5 concentration of prefecture-level cities and above that fail to meet the standard for this indicator will fall by over 18% from 2015; prefecture-level cities and above will see their proportion of number of days with good air quality reach 80% and will see their proportion of days with serious pollution and above drop over 25% from 2015"[①].

Work hard to advance the Green Water Protection Campaign. In April 2015, the State Council issued the *Action Plan for Controlling Water Pollution*, which serves as the action guideline for China's water pollution control. In 2018, China issued the *Implementation Plan on Reward Policy by State Revenue for Ecological Conservation and Restoration of the Yangtze River Economic Belt*, under which China would rectify 1,361 illegal wharfs along the main line of the Yangtze River and would set up the Joint Research Center on Ecological Conservation and Restoration of the Yangtze River. China has issued the action plans or implementation plans for the treatment of black and odorous water bodies in urban areas, pollution in rural areas, the conservation and restoration of the Yangtze River, the comprehensive treatment of the Bohai Sea, and for the protection of water sources. Among the 1,062 black and odorous water bodies in 36 key cities, 1,009, or 95% of the total, have had blackness or odor removed of them. Moreover, comprehensive environmental improvement has been completed in 25,000 incorporated villages. China has pressed ahead with environmental improvement in centralized sources of drinking water across the country. So far, 99.9% of the 6,251 issues in 1,586 water sources have

---

① Central People's Government of the People's Republic of China and the State Council, *Three-year Action Plan for Winning the Blue Sky Protection Campaign*, July 3, 2018, http://www.gov.cn/xinwen/2018-07/03/content_5303212.htm.

been fully rectified. Nationwide, 97.8% of industrial agglomeration areas at provincial level and above have built centralized sewage treatment facilities and installed automatic online monitoring apparatuses. In 2018, the "Demonstration of 1,000 Villages and Improvement of 10,000 Villages" project in Zhejiang Province won the Champions of the Earth of the United Nations. All of these actions are aimed to realize the environmental objectives of "By 2020, across the nation, the quality of water environments will be improved; the seriously polluted water bodies will dwindle; safety guarantee of drinking water will be constantly improved; groundwater overdraft will be strictly controlled; the trend towards worsening groundwater pollution will be preliminarily curbed; the environmental quality of offshore areas will improve amid stability; aquatic ecological environments in Beijing-Tianjin-Hebei, the Yangtze River Delta, and the Pearl River Delta will improve. By 2030, the overall quality of water environments nationwide will improve and the functions of water ecosystems will preliminarily resume. By 2050, the quality of ecological environment will be comprehensively improved and the ecosystems will enjoy virtuous circles."[1]

Steadily advance the Soil Protection Campaign. In August 2018, the NPC Standing Committee passed the *Law of the People's Republic of China on Soil Pollution Control*, legally supporting the "phenomena of a certain substance entering surface soil of the land due to human factors, resulting in changes in the chemical, physical, and biological properties of land, affecting soil functionality and effective utilization, harming public health or damaging ecological environment[2] (soil pollution)". In 2018, 31 provincial regions and Xinjiang Production and Construction Corps completed detailed survey on pollution of farmland soil and 26 provincial regions set up the interconnected regulatory mechanism for polluted plots. China has conducted risk investigation

---

[1] Central People's Government of the People's Republic of China, The State Council Issues the *Action Plan for Controlling Water Pollution*, April 16, 2015, http://www.gov.cn/xinwen/2015-04/16/content_2847709.htm.

[2] NPC website, *Law of the People's Republic of China on Soil Pollution Control*, August 31, 2018, http://www.npc.gov.cn/npc/c30834/201808/13d193fc25734dee91da8d703e057edc.shtml.

and remediation on farmland pollution by heavy metal industries including in cadmium-related ones. As a result, the trend towards worsening farmland soil pollution in a few regions has been preliminarily curbed. China has conducted pilot project on the classification of the environmental quality of farmland soil and the application of the nationwide information system on the management of soil environment of polluted plots. China has set up the national platform for the management of information on soil environment. In addition, it constantly advances the construction of the 6 comprehensive pilot areas for soil pollution control as well as the 200 - plus pilot projects on the application of technology for soil pollution control and restoration. China is advancing household garbage sorting and rectification of irregular garbage dumps. Meanwhile, it is advancing the work of prohibiting imported foreign garbage. The nationwide total imports of solid waste declined by 46.5% compared with 2017. Furthermore, China cracks down on illicit transfer and dumping of solid waste and hazardous waste. So far 1,304, or 99.7%, of the 1,308 outstanding issues registered for handling in the "Waste Removal Action 2018" have been fully rectified. These actions exemplify the legal force of the *Law of the People's Republic of China on Soil Pollution Control*.

Conduct ecological conservation and restoration. In January 2012, China launched the "National Investigation and Evaluation on Changes in Ecological Status". In 2016, China published the *National Investigation and Evaluation Report on Changes in Ecological Environment over 10 Years (2000 – 2010)*. In February 2017, China launched the "National Investigation and Evaluation on Changes in Ecological Status (2010 – 2015)". The significant investigation and evaluation concerning basic status on nationwide ecology, covered 31 provincial regions and Xinjiang Production and Construction Corps, and aimed to "ascertain the basic status, detect issues, find out causes, and come up with countermeasures". In August 2016, the General Office of CPC Central Committee and the General Office of the State Council issue the *Opinions on Establishing Unified and Formal National Ecological Civilization Pilot Zones*, according to which China would select Fujian Province, Jiangxi Province, and

Guizhou Province that enjoy good ecological foundation and strong carrying capacity for environment and resources as the first pilot zones to conduct comprehensive testing on structural reforms in ecological civilization and regulate demonstration of various pilot projects, thus exploring path and accumulating experience for optimizing the regulations system for ecological civilization[①]. In 2008, across the country, the number of national nature reserves increased to 474; Beijing-Tianjin-Hebei and Yangtze River Delta regions, and 15 provincial regions including Ningxia preliminarily delimited the ecological protection redlines; 16 provincial regions including Shanxi basically formulated the delimitation plan; the pilot project of the delimitation of ecological protection redlines was started; and the national regulatory platform for ecological protection redlines was built. China continues to implement the projects of returning farmland to forests or grassland and returning grazing land to grassland. It tries to take massive greening actions across the country, having achieved 106 million mu in afforestation. China presses ahead with the pilot project of the third batch of ecological conservation and restoration of mountains, waters, forests, farmland, lakes, and grassland. So far 1.07 million mu of degraded wetland has been restored; 56 plots of important international wetland have good ecological protection status as a whole. China has named and commended the second batch of innovation bases for practicing "lucid waters and lush mountains are invaluable assets" and the second batch of national demonstration cities and counties in ecological civilization construction. These actions have, in terms of practice, responded to the issues found in "National Investigation and Evaluation on Changes in Ecological Status".

Intensify supervision and enforcement in ecological environment protection. In 2018, China completed the establishment of the new Ministry of Ecological Environment, which integrated the relevant functions of the previous 7

---

① Gu Yang, Xiong Li, "What Are the First Batch of 3 Ecological Civilization Pilot Zones of China Tasked with?" *Economic Daily*, October 3, 2017, https://baijiahao.baidu.com/s? id = 1580232816825073136&wfr = spider&for = pc.

departments and combined pollution control and ecological protection. China has issued the *Guiding Opinions on Deepening Reforms in Comprehensive Administrative Enforcement for Ecological Environment Protection*, integrated the enforcement duties and teams in ecological environment protection, and fully introduced reforms in vertical management system for monitoring, supervision, and enforcement in ecological environment protection institutions below the provincial level. China has issued the *Regulations on License for Discharging Pollutants* (trial), cumulatively approved and issued pollutant discharging licenses to more than 39,000 enterprises in 24 industries, and has approved and issued pollutant discharging licenses to sewage treatment plants in built-up areas of 36 key cities in advance. China has fully implemented the *Reform Plan for Compensation System on Ecological Environment Damages*, fully adopted off-office auditing on leaders for natural resource assets, and has conducted the pilot project of preparation of the balance sheet for natural resource assets. The ranking scope of air quality has expanded to 169 cities. The lists of better-performing cities and the lists of worse-performing ones in air quality and in improvements are released on a regular basis. From 2015 to 2018, the Central Environmental Inspectorate, initiated by the Ministry of Environmental Protection and joined by relevant leaders of the Central Commission for Discipline Inspection and the Organization Department of the CPC Central Committee, staged multiple waves of "inspection firestorms", the first of which resolved roughly 150,000 environmental issues related to people's everyday life and prompted local governments to have tackled over 2,100 major ecological environment issues[①]. In June 2019, the General Office of the CPC Central Committee and the General Office of the State Council issued the *Provisions of the Central Government on Inspection on Ecological Environment Protection*, and in July 2019, they officially embarked on the second wave of "Inspection of

---

① "2019, Ministry of Ecological Environment: First Wave of Environmental Inspection Resolves a Total of Approximately 150, 000 Issues", China News, September 29, 2019, https://m.chinanews.com/wap/detail/sp/sp/shipin/cns-d/2019/09-29/news8968837.shtml.

Central Government on Ecological Environment Protection". As of January 5, 2020, the inspection project group had concluded 13,319 cases, temporarily concluded 2,748 cases, ordered 8,776 enterprises to rectify, investigated and prosecuted 3,288 enterprises, imposed a fine of some 254.0006 million yuan, registered and investigated 169 cases, administratively detained 38 persons, criminally detained 70 persons, interviewed with 1,935 persons by appointment, and held 359 persons accountable. Specifically, the inspection project group resolved 8,707 public environment management issues in urban areas concerning garbage, dust, undesirable odor, noise, among other undesirables; resolved 1,559 cases concerning direct sewage discharge and black and odorous water bodies; rectified 1,050 cases concerning destruction of forests and grassland, enclosure and occupation of lakes, mine exploitation, and other ecological damages. [1]

Enable social forces to participate in ecological civilization construction. In 2018, the national "12369" environmental reporting platform accepted and concluded on time a total of over 710,000 cases reported by the public. Multiple departments, led by the Ministry of Ecological Environment, jointly issued the Code of Ecological Environment Conduct for Citizens, which was designed to "guiding citizens in performing their responsibility for ecological environment". In addition, the Ministry of Ecological Environment has started the practice activity on the theme of "I take action towards a beautiful China". Moreover, the Department has formulated the *Regulations on Public Participation in Environment Environmental Impact Assessment*, encouraging and regulating public participation in environment environmental impact assessment. The first batch of 124 national environmental facilities and urban sewage and garbage disposal facilities have been opened to the public for 5,218 times. Additionally,

---

[1] Ministry of Ecological Environment of the People's Republic of China, *Progress on Handling of First Batch of Issues Reported by the People in the Second Wave of Inspection by the Central Government on Ecological Environment Protection* (as of January 5, 2020), January 10, 2020, http://www.mee.gov.cn/home/ztbd/rdzl/msqhqzlywtzxzz/gzdt/202001/t20200110_758567.shtml.

social organizations are actively involved in ecological civilization construction by taking advantage of their own strength. The "Plastic Smart Cities" Initiative, initiated by WWF in 2019, was officially carried out in China in 2020, with Sanya and Yangzhou becoming the first batch of cities joining the initiative[1]. On the annual Earth Day of April 22 in 2020, environmental organization Friends of Nature and its partners jointly initiated an initiative of "green office", encouraging the public and businesses to opt for more environment-friendly behaviors in office scenarios.

Enable co-construction of regional ecological civilization. The Belt and Road Initiative is continuously powering sustainable development of the countries and regions covered by it, becoming an example par excellence for regional co-building, co-governance, and sharing of green, sustainable future[2]. In 2015, China issued the *Vision and Actions on Jointly Building Silk Road Economic Belt and 21st Century Maritime Silk Road*, articulating that concerned countries should highlight the idea of ecological civilization, strengthen cooperation in ecological environment, biodiversity, and in addressing climate change, so as to co-build a green Silk Road. Later, China successively issued policy documents such as the *Planning on Ecological Environment Protection for the 13th Five-year Plan Period* (2016), the *Guiding Opinions on Enabling Green Belt and Road Initiative* (2017), and the *Planning on Cooperation in Ecological Environment Protection under the Belt and Road Initiative* (2017)[3], laying a solid political and system foundation for building a green Belt and Road and articulating the overall approach, objective, and task from the top

---

[1] "Yangzhou Becomes One of China's Plastic Smart Cities, CPC Jiangsu Provincial Committee News, April 22, 2020, http://zgjssw.jschina.com.cn/shixianchuanzhen/yangzhou/202004/t20200422_6612955.shtml.

[2] Editors-in-chief: Li Peilin, Chen Guangjin, Wang Chunguang, *Analysis and Prediction of Social Situations of China for 2020* (Social Blue Book), Beijing: Social Sciences Academic Press, January 2020, pp. 296–310.

[3] Ministry of Environmental Protection of the People's Republic of China, *Notice on Issuing the Planning on Cooperation in Ecological Environment Protection under the Belt and Road Initiative*, May 12, 2017, http://www.mee.gov.cn/gkml/hbb/bwj/201705/t20170516_414102.htm.

perspective. In addition, according to these policy documents, China will, over the next 3 - 5 years, build a practical, efficient cooperation and exchange system, a supportive and service platform, and an industrial technical cooperation base for ecological environment protection, and will formulate a series of policies and measures to prevent the risks associated with ecological environment. China will, over the next 5 - 10 years, build a sound service, supportive, and guarantee system for ecological environment protection, implement an important batch of ecological environment protection projects, and will yield good results. [1] By signing over 50 cooperative documents with ecological environment protection departments of countries and regions covered by the Belt and Road Initiative as well as with concerned international organizations, China has led the official setup of the International Coalition for Green Development on the Belt and Road and is consistently optimizing the mechanisms for cooperation. In addition, China has launched the platform of Belt and Road green supply chain, set up the Lancang-Mekong Environmental Cooperation Center and China-Cambodia Environmental Cooperation Center, and is actively preparing to build China-Africa Environmental Cooperation Center. China is constantly building and expanding environmental cooperative platforms in an effort to enable co-building of regional ecological civilization.

IV. Conclusion

China is facing a "compressed modernization". This "compressibility" makes risk more likely, but it leaves no ample time for system expectation and management of risk. [2] To cope with the scenario of risk society derived from ecological environment risk, China is establishing systems and taking actions,

---

[1] Central People's Government of the People's Republic of China, *Four Departments Jointly Issues the Guiding Opinions on Enabling Green Belt and Road Initiative*, May 27, 2017, http://www.gov.cn/xinwen/2017 - 05/27/content_5197523.htm.

[2] Ulrich Beck, Deng Zhenglai, Shen Guolin, "Risk Society and China—Dialog with German Sociologist Ulrich Beck", *Sociological Study*, Issue 5, 2010.

trying to "build a new modernization landscape where man and nature develop in harmony" through ecological environment construction. ① "Socialist outlook on ecological civilization", as a core concept or category of China's ecological civilization and its construction theory or discourse system, can be summarized as the following four interconnected elements or links: Stringent natural value concept or man-nature relationship notion based on ecology thinking; Overall orchestration and rule of law ecosystem and its governance system as well as ecological environment protection system; Green production and living style and civilization development path that take into full account of rational requirements or objectives of production, living, and ecology; A strong sense of responsibility for striking a balance between building a beautiful China and protecting global ecological security②. As can be seen from top-level design to local practice and from policy documents to individual actions, China is proactive to "welcome various emergency reforms needed for faster shift towards a more equitable, environmentally more sustainable economy and a healthier society. By enacting top-down policy guidance and bottom-up initiatives, China seeks to consolidate the well-being and prosperity of different countries and their people, both now and in the future". ③ The *Decision of the CPC Central Committee on Several Important Issues Concerning Adhering to and Optimizing System of Socialism with Chinese Characteristics and Promoting Modernization of National Governance System and Governance Capacity* clearly notes that China will build a social governance community where everyone has a responsibility, everyone fulfils his or her responsibility, and everyone enjoys the results of social governance. In March 2020, the General Office of the CPC Central

---

① "CPC Central Committee and the State Council Issues the Overall Plan for Structural Reform in Ecological Civilization", Xinhuanet, September 21, 2015, http://www.xinhuanet.com//politics/2015-09/21/c_1116632159.htm.

② Xun Qingzhi, "Triple Visions Illustrated by Socialist Outlook on Ecological Civilization", *Journal of Beijing Administrative College*, Issue 4, 2018.

③ UN Environment (2019). Global Environment Outlook-GEO – 6: Healthy Planet, Healthy People. Nairobi. DOI 10.1017/9781108627146. p. XXX.

Committee and the General Office of the State Council issued the *Guiding Opinions on Building a Modern Environmental Governance System*, which noted that China will "optimize the public action system for environmental governance",[1] further articulating the responsibility of the public (everyone) for taking action for environmental governance. Guided by the "socialist outlook on ecological civilization", China is "encouraging a green development model and lifestyle and conducting a profound revolution in development outlook"[2].

---

[1] "General Office Of the CPC Central Committee and General Office Of the State Council Issue the Guiding Opinions On Building a Modern Environmental Governance System", Website of The Central People's Government of the PRC, March 3, 2020, http://www.gov.cn/zhengce/2020-03/03/content_5486380.htm?trs=1.

[2] "Remarks of Xi Jinping While Presiding over 41st Collective Study of the 18th Political Bureau of the CPC Central Committee", people.cn, http://theory.people.com.cn/n1/2018/0103/c416126-29743660.html.

Personality Identity in the Process of Modernization of Belarusian Governance

E. V. Kuznetsova

Senior Research Fellow, Center of Globalization, Integration and Sociocultural Cooperation, Institute of Philosophy, National Academy of Sciences of Belarus

The process of identification is investigated in many sciences: philosophy, sociology, psychology, anthropology, ethnography, cultural studies. And each of these sciences has its own methodological principles, allowing to explore various components in the identification's process from different perspectives. The more researchers interact with each other, the more completed examination of this issue we get, because identity is also a result of different interactions at cultural, ethnic, linguistic and other levels. And we will do our best in our article in order to provide a variety of approaches to the problem of self-identification of a person.

In order to make conclusions concerning the problem of a subject's identity we use a comparative and typological method in our investigation as we compare different types of the identity on different stages of civilization. Also we use systematical method as it helps to produce the analysis of the problem from different points of view.

But first of all let us determine the notions of " identity " and "identification". We suppose that the distinction between these notions is not essential, but it's semantic and practical, because both of them mean the same phenomenological reality. Usually, the first one means a result, the second one means a process. According to social and cultural conditions on different historical stages of human existence we distinguish the following types of identity, formed and dominant in one or another historical epoch. There are ethnic identity, linguistic identity, religious identity, national identity, cultural identity, transcendental identity.

Ethnic identity is one of the fundamental types of the subject's identity. Thus, ethnic identity means the relations of a subject with his blood ties, "roots", that is, of course, a process of self-determination of each person. The main theoretical approaches to the analysis of the concept of ethnic identity are implemented mainly through psychological and socio psychological studies. Historically, one of the main approaches to the problem of identification is based by the founder of psychoanalysis Z. Freud. The problem of identification is also investigated in the psychoanalysis by G. S. Sullivan (interpersonal psychoanalysis), E. Fromm (humanistic psychoanalysis), E. Erixon (epigenetic analysis).

One of the most recent approaches in psychology to the explanation of ethnic identity is founded by behaviorism. Behaviorists believe that the process of identification is the result of inter-group conflict. Their studies confirm that in some cases because of his external resemblance a man can identify himself simultaneously with two ethnic groups. But these ethnic groups must be similar to each other externally, for example, the Belarusians and the Russians. But if ethnic groups are not similar to each other, especially if they belong to different races, the child of a mixed-race family will be a stranger for both races.

Representatives of the activity approach believe that identification's process is determined by activities between different groups. Formation of ethnic identity is a dynamic process, and different factors may influence this formation. Any changes lead to its transformation, especially in a case of change of a residence or environment. Ethnic identity has become the object of a careful study during the last decades. Political events of the 1990s significantly stepped up processes on the basis of relations between peoples, and not only in Russia, but throughout the whole world. Because of the influence of several factors (globalization, integration, erasing of different boundaries, etc.) ethnic situation in a contemporary society on a personal level, and on a level of a group requires a responsible and deep analysis of many concepts and categories. If ethnic identity is forced out by other kinds of social identity, for example, by civil identity, it can be very dangerous for a human identity in general. It threatens to destroy the" I-image, to lose ties of a subject with his native culture in the world. A man can lose himself in this world. This kind of identity is a key for forming of personality and interaction of people with each other.

One more important factor for us in this discussion about subject's identity is language. Language and people are closely linked with each other. V. Humboldt believes that meditation and mentality of the nation form the structure of the language in a certain way. In particular, he believes that the inflectional languages are typical for those peoples who have embarked on a "path of a concentrated meditation". [1] Under the formula "language is a spirit of the people", Humboldt understands "a special form of sound materialization of mental and psychic activities which is special for all national language speakers"[2]. In any case, individual interpretation of the language is always defined by the prevailing linguistic stereotypes of the nation.

In each language we deal with the so-called "free" units. Thus, each individual's speech includes both "formulas" and "free" units. But best of all mental peculiarities of the nation can be clear by means of "formulas", which can include not only set phrases, but various kinds of phraseological units. Understanding of phraseological units is impossible without knowledge of culture of the people. Actually, all language units have some cultural fullness

---

[1] Humboldt, V., *Language and Philosophy of Culture*, Moscow: Progress, 2007. p. 78.
[2] Humboldt, V., *Language and Philosophy of Culture*, Moscow: Progress, 2007. p. 78.

only in varying degrees. A. F Losev rightly notes that "the word and, in particular, the name includes the whole cultural wealth accumulated during the centuries".

The subject's identity is formed also by nonverbal tools. It's a paralanguage. Formation of paralanguage is determined by the same factors as the formation of the language itself. There are culture and mentality of the nation. So, a paralanguage includes the following media: facial expressions, gestures, the distance between communicators, various peculiarities of kinesics. All these media are quite different in different nations and manifest themselves differently. Let's take the most famous example. In Russia when we nod by our head, we mean "Yes", but in Bulgaria it means "No". Thus, linguistic identification is a process which is as complicated as ethnic or national identification. And if we deal in communication with verbal and nonverbal characteristics of the subject's speech, we must take into account all the variety, identifying this or that subject. Linguistic identification is connected with national identification, because language is one of the most important factors that define the subject's belonging to a specific national community.

The transition from feudalism to capitalism, according to the theory of Marxism, led to the formation of such ethno-social forms of community of people as nation. Many studies emphasize that nation is a phenomenon of modern times. In foreign studies the term "nation" gets a political meaning. Scientists define people as a nation if they belong to one (national) state. In domestic literature we find another definition of nation. Russian scientists define economic factors in the formation of this type of social community as the most important. But we choose the position of those scientists who lean towards the so-called post-modern concept and invest political content in the concept of "nation". It is more modern in comparison with Marxist approach and more applicable for Russia, because in our country there are many different peoples and native culture is a complex amalgam of diverse ethnic elements. From this point of view, we'll look at the problem of national identity in this work. So, according to our understanding, national identity is an equivalent of civil identity.

Many researchers rightly indicate (M. Semluk, S. Walker) that the end of the cold war and changes in the political map of the world of the last decades have led to a crisis of identity in many states, since all countries have been forced to re-examine their role and status in the international arena. [1] W. Bloom underlines the connection between national identity and influence of political behavior and determines three types of relations between these phenomena. [2]

Type 1: national identity is a resource of foreign policy. A messianic nationalism is an example of this kind of identity. Messianic vision of the world usually leads to aggressive actions of the nation vis-à-vis other countries. As a rule, a propaganda of "messianism" lies at the heart of imperialism (Russia, Poland, the United Stated).

Type 2: foreign policy is an instrument of building of a nation. Foreign policy plays a special role to determine the identity of the state.

Type 3: national identity, formed by non-state actors, determines foreign policy. This happens when some public ideas receive the status of state and they affect the country's foreign policy.

Already quite evident today is the fact of destruction of economic borders between states, erasing of the political and cultural controversies. The image of the state is changed and national identity of the state's citizens is also changed.

Now is a time of constant changes and disasters, upheavals and explosions. Many views collapse including those views on which the traditional identity is based. Human identification is rather complicated today, and it happens primarily because of the complexity of interpersonal relations in our society. Such factors as professional activity, social mobility, social affiliation begin to influence the identification's process. Development of culture and

---

[1] Kiselev, I., *Evolution of the Image of the State in International Relations*, St. Petersburg: Publishing House of St. Petersburg University, 2006. p. 42.

[2] Bloom, W., *Personal Identity, National Identity and International Relations*, Cambridge: Cambridge University Press, 1996, p. 89.

society has led to widening of the range of identification. We mean here the emergence of new kinds of identities and new forms of research in this area.

One of the most prominent figures of sociological science, dealing with issues of identity, is E. Durkheim. Social factor is considered by him to be the most important in the process of subject's identification, based on collective views of large communities of people. Durkheim relates such views with an integral system of ideas, customs, religious beliefs, moral attitudes, public institutions. [1] They are models and elements for identification's purposes in the course of subject's life. Durkheim says that there are two creatures in each of us, one of which consists of mental positions. They mean a private life of subject (individual "I"). Social "I" is the second creature in a man. It is a set of attitudes, feelings, and habits. E. Durkheim notes that it is important to add a social creature for a new born selfish and asocial creature. "The process of adding of this substance to personal merits, of connecting them into a coherent unit means a process of personal identification".

K. Horney affects in her studies the role of sociocultural dominants. Thereby, she believes that cultural conditions have a profound effect on the development and functioning of the individual. [2] Sociocultural factors, from her point of view, explain relations between people. American scientist F. Boas undertook a comparative study of processes of maturation of different peoples living in different cultural contexts. He was sure that the behavior of younger generations is determined by biological factors, and by properties of a specific culture. [3]

Self-determination is the most important act for any person in his life for a famous philosopher, psychologist and methodologist G. Schedrovitsky. He writes: "If the circumstances are composed in a way that self-determination

---

[1] Durkheim, E., *Sociology of Education*, Moscow: Science, 1996, p. 57.
[2] Horney, K., *Our Internal Conflicts*., April – Press; Exmo-press, 2000, p. 340.
[3] Boas, F., *Some Problems of Methodology in the Social Sciences*, Chicago: University of Chicago Press, 2002, p. 238.

does not occur, the person never becomes a personality."[1] He believes that the most important thing for a man in the process of self-determination is a reflection. Schedrovitsky supposes that a consideration by a man of the former frameworks of his life as the subject of his action is the first level of reflection. The second level of reflection is a position of a reflecting person towards himself. The form of the reflection is an intellectual form, which means speech expression. So, the communication according to the concept of Schedrovitsky is a basic condition for reflection and self-determination.

Reflection is considered to be an internal mechanism of cultural identification also by some other authors. V. Slobodchikov and E. Isaev note that reflection is directed to self-determination and is caused by multiple real and practical situations of social existence, requiring from a person an ability to communicate with others.[2] Only by becoming a part of the universe or world culture, people become personalities. So, meditation or transcendental self-identification is the ultimate form of self-identification of the individual.

Communication, as G. P. Schedrovitsky writes, is a condition for the realization of the self-identification of the individual. Modern people always communicate, they have to understand each other, they are eager to pass something new to others. To live, according to M. Bakhtin, is to engage in a dialogue, to ask questions and to answer them. The main purpose of all processes taking place in the modern world can be formulated as a constructive dialogue in a common cultural and communicative space. And A. Vasilenko characterizes this space as "a common space of thoughts". It's a set of common ideas and concepts that are formed in the course of the discussion, they do not belong to any of the parties, they exceed the subjective opinions of interlocutors

---

[1] Schedrovitsky, G. P., "On the Boards. Public lectures on Philosophy", School of Political Culture, 2004, p. 58.

[2] Slobodchikov, V. I., *Foundations of Psychological Anthropology*, Moscow: School-Press, 2005, p. 94.

and become a common partners' status[1]. This dialogue is an art of a formation of new political and sociocultural concepts, which can explain a common field of political interactions.

But the main objective of this dialogue is the self-realization of partners. In the context of the actual dialogue of cultures, this problem becomes a problem of the self-realization of each culture in a communicative space in the modern world. Various institutes of communication help to analyze such a dialogue, to identify ways and means of interaction.

Communication is a necessary condition for the existence of an individual in a society because, as Aristotle says, an individual is a political animal. The phenomenon of communication has already been investigated during the centuries by many scientists at the intersection of sciences, such as: philosophy, sociology, psychology, linguistics. Very often the term "interaction" is replaced by the term of communication by many scholars. The term of communication, according to our point of view is broader than the term "interaction". Let us try to differentiate these two concepts.

The term "communication" comes from Latin. To communicate means to share, to talk, to discuss. The dictionary "Modern Western Sociology" (1990) provides the following definition of communication: firstly, means of communication of objects of material and spiritual peace; secondly, information's transmission from one person to another; thirdly, communication and sharing of information in a society (social communication). Thus, the term "interaction" is included into the term "communication". Webster's New Word Dictionary (1989) gives the following interpretation: firstly, the act of transmission; secondly, exchange of information, signals, messages in the conversation; thirdly, information or message; fourthly, closerelations based on the sympathy; fifthly, means of communication.

V. P. Konetskaya underlines the following modern variants of the

---

[1] Vasilenko, I, "About the Possibilities of Political Hermeneutics", *The Questions of Philosophy*, No. 6, 1999, p. 5.

understanding of the term of "communication" as a means of communication, as a synonym for the concept of interaction, "an exchange of information in a society in order to influence it. [1] We must enter here a term such as social communication, theoretical aspect of which is represented in the works by K. Jaspers, A. Toffler, J. Habermas, M. Buber, J. G. Mead, D. Bell, T. Shibutani, D. Watson. If we summarize the research data, we can conclude that social communication is a common activity of people determined by specific situations, regulations, rules of communication, it's a spiritual and informational exchange among actors in a society.

The transformation of the world into a communicative space ruins today many moral norms, values, moral guidance, on which the previous generations are relied. Thanks to the growth of technology and the emergence of new ways of communication a man gets completely new opportunities, but at the same time he finds himself one by one with the surrounding world. Serious transformations are connected with all spheres of a society. Reconstruction of traditional values, a large-scale meditation, new principles in management mean a complete transformation of a society. The above trend is unfolded against the backdrop of the intensification of communicative-discursive exchange. Interaction between private individuals and peoples defines a contemporary cultural world's view, its existence and development. It is obvious that we cannot talk about the identity of the subject of transitional sociocultural development stage as something permanent and unchangeable. A modern man can have several identities that compete with each other or are complementary. His identity is in crisis now, it is in the process of changing. For a number of people there is a risk of loss (total or partial) of identity at the individual or group level, identity can be false, which threatens to destroy the "I" image, to lose human relations, to lose culture itself. The real identity of a subject can be defined only as a result of his participation in the cultural and communicative processes. Communication allows us to determine a

---

[1] Konetskaya, V. P., *Sociology of Communication*, Moscow: Science, 2007, p. 121.

real identity of the person. The more meaningful and rich is the interaction between the actors themselves, the more correct, but at the same time complicated is the process of identifying them.

Among all types of identity (ethnic, religious, linguistic, national, transcendental) transcendental identity is the ultimate form of identity and is the most significant on a contemporary social-civilizational stage. On the one hand, the transition epoch, in which the world community exists now, initiates the need for knowledge based on rationalization (science) . On the other hand, if an individual gets a great personal freedom he needs an internal mechanism of moral self-regulation that provides socially responsible ethical behavior of this individual (reflection) . A communication can become a mechanism of this kind, it provides the link between state and society; society, state and individual. It forms a new ideological concept of the modern international community. Rethinking of a communicative reality, approval of its new structure is a condition for development of cultural pluralism.

China's Enterprises Democratic Management Researches

Sun Zhaoyang

Associate Professor, National Institute of Social
Development, CASS

I. The Beginning in 1980s

Reform and opening up has relaxed the constraints on enterprises, the efficiency and enthusiasm of production has been improved via the market mechanism, correction of factor price distortion, recovery of individual labor compensation and other institutional reforms, the vitality of enterprises has been released to a great extent, and entrepreneurs power and managers to control and control enterprises has also been greatly enhanced on the other hand. In July 1981, the CPC Central Committee and the State Council forwarded *Interim Regulations on the Staff Congress of State Enterprises* to promote the staff congress system. In September 1986, the *Regulations of the Workers' Congress of Industrial Enterprises Owned by the Whole People* (the *Regulations of the Congress*) were promulgated, which established the nature, powers and contents of the workers' Congress. The *Law of the People's Republic of China on Industrial Enterprises Under the Ownership System of the People's Republic of China* (Enterprise Law), adopted in April 1988, officially established the legal status of the system of the Congress.

Articles in this stage mainly starts from the socialist nature of the enterprise and emphasizes the necessity and inevitability of the enterprise democracy system, the vocational congress in particular. For example, Chen Wenyuan[1], Qi Jicheng[2], Tian Mei, Zhou Gui[3], etc. But the primary goal of the reform is to establish and open the market to play its main role of market allocation of resources, stimulate the market main body vitality and promote production efficiency and economic margins. With a view to stimulating enterprises' market vitality, the government gradually withdraws from the direct management of the business activities, and implements the factory director / manager responsibility system, and the managers of the enterprise are given more power. The *Decision on the Reform of the Economic System* formulated by the Third Plenary Session of the 12th Central Committee in 1984 pointed out: "Modern enterprises embrace a fine division of labor, a high degree of continuity in production, strict technical requirements and complex relations of cooperation. A unified, strong and efficient production command and management system must be established. Only by implementing the factory director (manager) responsibility system can we adapt to this requirement." Therefore, more scholars turned to discuss the power distribution and the power and responsibility relationship between the factory director/manager responsibility system and the enterprise democratic management system, such as Liu Zhongyao[4], Shi Tianjing[5], Sang

---

[1] Chen Wenyuan, "The Basic Form to Achieve Democratic Management in Enterprises——Analyse System of Workers and Staff Congress", *Journal of China University of Political Science and Law*, No. 3, 1981, pp. 63 –69.

[2] Qi Jicheng, "Brief View of Enterprise Democratic Management", *Journal of Jiangxi University Of Finance And Economics*, No. 1, 1981, pp. 77 –80.

[3] Tian Mei, Zhou Gui, "On the Democratic Management of Enterprises", *Business Management Journal*, No. 4, 1983, pp. 40 –41.

[4] Liu Zhongyao, "Some Theoretical Problems about Implementing the System of Overall Responsibility by Factory Manager", *Research on Finance and Economic Issues*, No. 6, 1984, pp. 24 –32.

[5] Shi Tanjing, "On Labor Contract and Labor Contract System", *Chinese Journal of Law*, 1987, No. 4, pp. 71 –78.

Weijun, Guo Hongjun[1], Zhang Kun[2], An Miao, Cui Yi[3] and so on. Because of the supervision and restraint of management power, the democratic management of enterprises is regarded as the practice that affects the efficiency under the promotion of the reform tide.

II. The Development of 1990s

With the advance of the state-owned enterprises reform after the 1990s, in addition to the former state-owned enterprises and state-controlled enterprises, there are also the congress, many new foreign enterprises, private enterprises have refused to set up staff congress in the organization, especially "invigorate large enterprises while relaxing control over small ones" of State-owned enterprises since 1998. While some large state-owned enterprises have been restructured into joint-stock systems, a large number of small and medium-sized state-owned enterprises have become non-public enterprises through restructuring, contracting, combining, annexing, leasing and auctioning. Against impact of the market mechanism, the profit evolved as the main production target of the enterprise and the private enterprise after the reform, and most of the business operators and the private enterprise owners had established the centralized management system to change the situation of the former state-owned enterprises and improve the production efficiency.

Some scholars hold the view that the democratic management system of enterprises makes its role in supervision and management, and the staff congress system and so on may play a greater role in perfecting the performance of enterprises and improving the distribution of income. At this stage, foreign

---

[1] Sang Weijun, Guo Hongjun, "A Discussion about the Role of Labour Union in Promoting Enterprise Democratic Management", *Social Sciences Review*, No. 3, 1989, pp. 54 – 57.

[2] Zhang Kun, "A Discussion about the Democratic Management of Enterprise at This Stage", *Lanzhou Academic Journal*, No. 2, 1989, pp. 103 – 106.

[3] An Miao, Cui Yi, *Study on the Status quo of the Working Class and the System of Workers' Congress*, Shenyang: Liaoning People's Publishing House, 1990.

theories have entered China in large numbers, and the study of enterprise democracy has the following three main sources.

One is economic democracy or industrial democracy theory. These theories emphasized that the establishment of a modern enterprise system reflected the principal position of the staff and workers and emphasized the spirit of "ownership", thus highlighting the legitimacy of democratic management and participation. Because the main force of absorbing urban employment in this period is still state-owned enterprises and collective enterprises, private and foreign-owned non-public-owned enterprises, self-employed enterprises have just emerged and have not become the main force of the market, so the focus of the study lies on the state-owned enterprises embody the status of workers under the premise of public ownership. For example, as the main body of the enterprise is the key to distinguish between the socialist enterprise and the capitalist enterprise, workers shall realize the democratization of the respect such as labor system, property right system, management system, distribution system, leadership system, such as: right to speak, participate in management, participate in profit distribution and other democratic rights, with a view to reflecting the principal position of the workers. ①This democratic right, as industrial democracy defined by the International Labour Organization (ILO), is a policy or measure that promotes the participation of workers in business management decisions, thereby enabling workers' rights and interests to be respected by employers or managers and to break down the monopoly of employers or managers. ②In general, economic democracy within the enterprise

---

① Jiang Yiwei, "Theory of Staff and Workers as Main Body of Enterprise", *Labour Science of China*, No. 9, 1991, pp. 3 – 8. Du Yi, Zhang Yanchun, "The Economic Participation System of Enterprises in Western Countries", *Foreign Economies and Management*, No. 10, 1994, pp. 20 – 24. Wu Guangbing, "On Laborers Participation in the Distribution of Surplus Value of State – owned Enterprises", *Labour Science of China*, No. 8, 1995, pp. 8 – 10. Feng Tongqing, "Economic Democracy in Enteprise: An Option of Going with Nature", *Journal of China University of Labour Relations*, No. 8, 2001, pp. 4 – 8.

② Qi Huaqing, "The Industrial Democracy Form Abroad and China's Staff and Workers' Participation System", *Academy Journal of Zhongzhou*, No. 3, 2002, pp. 18 – 21.

means that employees have to share the right to manage and have the same control over economic interests.

While the "master theory" of industrial democracy has been impacted by market competition, and corporate democracy is considered to be detrimental to the improvement of enterprise production efficiency and the rapid identification and utilization of opportunities in incentive competition. With the gradual deepening of the reform of state-owned enterprises, the logic of "shareholder supremacy" has replaced the "master theory" and occupied a dominant position, so to speak, maximizing the interests of owners or shareholders is the standard to measure the efficiency of enterprise system. Some scholars argued that this "master theory" is mainly derived from the political angle, it has been separated from the market economy practice formed after the reform and opening up, and the democratic management of enterprises must attach greater importance to the economic law and social development.[1] But the logic of "shareholder first" is not valid in theory and practice in that the enterprise system is essentially composed of capital and labor, serving stakeholders who shall have equal opportunity to participate in the distribution of enterprise ownership. Scholars criticize this "shareholder first" view from two other aspects.

The second is the theory of labor property right or human capital property right. According to Marx's Surplus Value, the laborer's labor creates the value, it also the only source of the surplus value, the surplus value is deprived by the capitalist to become its profit, therefore, laborer, as the owner of the labor property right, shall share the profit as the capital, this is the enterprise democracy root. In the 1950s, the Human Capital theory put forward by Theodore W. Schultz, Gary Stanley Becker, was that, in addition to the traditional elements of land, capital, resources and so on, human factors were of great importance for economic development. As for enterprise operation, both labor and capital enterprises have invested special assets, the enterprise has

---

[1] Qin Zhongzhong, Zhao Feixue, "A Re-understanding of Industrial Democracy Theory in Enteprises", *Journal of China Institute of Industrial Relations*, No. 1, 2005, pp. 34 – 36.

invested the material capital of land, plant, equipment and so on, the laborer is the owner of the labor force put into production, both sides are bearing the business risk of the enterprise, their interests are affected by the result of enterprise operation, so the ownership and income distribution right of the enterprise shall be shared by both sides, with same rights and status. ①In state-owned enterprises, the assets are owned by the whole people, the government is entrusted to hold them on their behalf, the managers are put into labor to carry out the operation, the workers are also put into labor to carry out the production and operation, and the two sides are also put into the production and operation of the enterprise. At the same time, the rise of private enterprises and foreign-funded enterprises pose a new challenge to corporate democracy, so to speak, corporate assets do not come from the state or government, whether workers can still demand the same democratic rights. The stakeholder theory offers some new insights to this end.

Third, stakeholder theory, based on the theory of stakeholders and common governance that emerged in the West in the 1980s, discusses industrial democracy and employee participation from the perspective of human rights. Among many modern enterprises, shareholders and managers only assume limited liability, and some of their risks are transformed by diversification of investment, and the other part is transferred to the creditors, employees, government, suppliers and other stakeholders of the enterprise, so they cannot monopolize the profit surplus. ②And the interests of these groups are directly related to the survival of the company, without their support, the operational efficiency of the company will be reduced to a great extent, which determines that all kinds of groups should actively participate in the company's business decisions. ③This determines that a

---

① Zhou Qiren, "Enterprises in Market: A Special Contract between Human Capital and Non-Human Capital", *Economic Research Journal*, No. 7, 1996, pp. 71–80.

② Blair, Margaret., *Ownership and Control: Rethinking Corporate Governance of the Twenty-first Century*, translated by Zhang Ronggang, Beijing: China Social Science Press, 1999.

③ Liu Lianyu, *Corporate Governance and Social Responsibility*, Beijing: China University of Political Science and Law Press, 2002.

enterprise shall not only attach importance to the interests of shareholders, but also the participation of employees, suppliers, creditors and so on in its management and decision-making, so that it can achieve success via the loyal support and cooperation of the vast number of employees. ①They hold that it works for state-owned companies, the efficiency of the enterprise first hinge on stakeholders on the basis of equality and equal participation in enterprise decision-making through each property, the original state-owned enterprises "unilateral governance" to "common governance", and supervise each other equally, to improve the efficiency of the state-owned enterprise governance structure.

Although democratic management is an important part of the modern enterprise system in theory and the demand of socialization of mass production,② it can arouse the enthusiasm of the staff and improve the management efficiency while dealing with the property rights well,③ it is inevitable that the conflict between workers and managers becomes more serious because of the weakening of workers' congress. To this end, the government has sought to strengthen the scope of application of the workers' congress and expand the forms of enterprise democracy. For example, in September 1991, *the Regulations of the People's Republic of China on the Collectively Owned Enterprises in Cities and Towns* have been promulgated, specifying the nature, functions and powers, organization system and work system of the workers' congress of the enterprises under collective ownership in cities and towns. In December 1993, the *Fifth Session of the Standing Committee of the Eighth People's Congress adopted the Company Law of the People's Republic of China* (the *Company Law*), which stipulated that corporate enterprises should adhere

---

① Yang Ruilong, Zhou Yean, "On the Joint Governance Mechanism of Enterprises under the Cooperation Logic of Stakeholders", *China Industrial Economics*, No. 1, 1998, pp. 38 –45.

② Zheng Xianhua, "Legal Thinking on Congress of Workers and Staffs", *Modern Law Science*, No. 2, 1997, pp. 38 –45.

③ Zhang Haijun, Wang Wangsheng, "The Establishment of Modern Enterprise System Must Attach Importance to and Strengthen Enterprise Democratic Management", *Journal of Central Normal University (Humanities and Social Sciences)*, 1995, No. 2, pp. 13 –16.

to the democratic management system, and proposed the implementation of the staff and workers' representative system in the board of directors and the board of supervisors, and added new contents such as the disclosure of factory affairs with the main objective of supervision power and democratic management of enterprises such as staff and workers' directors and supervisors. The form and content of democratic management of enterprises under different forms of ownership are stipulated in the Labour Law issued in 1994. The introduction of the *Company Law* and the *Labour Law* greatly stimulated scholars' attention to the democratic system of enterprises, so the amount of periodical articles reached 76 in 1994, the highest in 1990s.

Although the proportion of state-owned and collective enterprises in urban employment has been declining since the reform and opening up, from 99.8% in 1978 to 71.6% in 1996, it is still the main force for accommodating non-agricultural employment before the restructuring. At this stage, therefore, the issues that scholars pay most attention to are still mainly related to state-owned enterprises.

One is the entrusted agency of state-owned enterprises. Although the reform of state-owned enterprises has established the perfect internal management system in its process of gradually clear property rights, the entrusted agency relationship in the resulting flow of principal-agent is not properly treated, for example, the malicious management of factory directors and managers of some state-owned enterprises. In view of this, some scholars believe that it is necessary to establish the mechanism of "good agent" of state-owned enterprises to effectively cope with the malicious encroachment in operation to ensure the property security of the state and people. The underlying guarantee arising from this mechanism is economic democracy. [1]Some of the more radical views have argued that the people's consciousness must be legalized, and that the government should be empowered by law to regulate their behavior in a

---

[1] Ren Biyun, "Economic and Democratic System: The Basic Guarantee of Searching for the Good and honest Trustees of SOEs", *Journal of Shanxi University* (*Philosophy & Social Science*), No. 1, 2000, pp. 62–65.

democratic way. ①Or "socialized" and "democratized" reforms in state-owned enterprises are implemented to eliminate the benefits of a few managers and special interest groups via post-fordism modes of production and a wider range of democratic participation and oversight. ②These viewpoints gradually dissipated after the reform of the state-owned enterprises.

The second is the standardization of the benefit distribution and company management of state-owned enterprises. The workers' rights and interests have not been effectively guaranteed in the process of the reform of the state-owned enterprises, one of the main reasons is the lack of commercial democratic management system tradition, thus forming a high degree of insider control, and the distribution of the interests of state-owned assets is concentrated in the hands of managers. In the late 1990s, as state-owned enterprises were restructured, scholars who supported privatization argued that "who invests, who owns, who benefits" and defined investment as material capital, thus excluding employees from the beneficiary group. Many scholars, however, have criticized this view, some scholars believe that human capital (including operators) should participate in the profit distribution of state-owned enterprises like material capital, which is a necessary way to carry out the theory of labor value and realize the prosperity of one country. ③Although the initial reform of capital shortage and labor surplus, capital gains account for the majority of corporate profits, with the increasing capital accumulation, human capital has become increasingly prominent, science and technology has improved the knowledge of labor, workers' contribution to corporate profits is constantly increasing as well, they shall be recognized in a wider range of human capital

---

① Qiao Xinsheng, "Are State – owned Enterprises Owned by the Workers and Staffs Themselves—Reflections on Property Rights and Democracy", *Faren Magazine*, No. 1, 2005, pp. 29 – 30.

② Cui Zhiyuan, "Two Meanings of Economic Democyacy", *Dushu*, No. 4, 1997, pp. 79 – 82.

③ Wu Guangbing, "On Laborers Participation in the Distribution of Surplus Value of Stateowned Enterprises", *Labour Science of China*, No. 8, 1995, pp. 8 – 10.

returns. ①Once the interests of employees are ignored, it will distort the ownership allocation of state-owned enterprises, and managers will grasp the actual control, which leads to the loss of surplus control and residual claim of employees. ②

As a matter of fact, the entrusted agency and the state-owned enterprise worker's rights and interests are two related aspects. From the ownership of the whole people and the state-owned enterprises to the state-owned enterprises, it is not only the transform of the name, but also the right to dispose of assets such as enterprises, resources and capital. Article 6 of the *Constitution* stipulates that "The socialist economic system of the People's Republic of China is based on the socialist public ownership of the means of production, so to speak, ownership by the whole people and collective ownership by the working people". A state is therefore entrusted by the general public to administer the assets under ownership by the general public, the first tier of entrusted agency. A state, as an abstract concept, needs to rely on its present carrier in practice, so to speak, the central and government at all levels authorize the chairman and general manager to operate the assets on behalf of the specific form, or all kinds of state-owned economy, which is the second layer of entrusted agency. According to Article 7 of the *Constitution*, "State-owned economy, a kind of socialist economy owned by the whole people, is the leading force of national economy." The whole people into state ownership here. The entrusted agency relationship at the first level is further eroded, emphasizing the income derived from individual labour and the absence of references to "ownership" and the distribution of entrusted income, for example, the establishment of the modern enterprise system requires that the legal person's representative of the corporate enterprise be decided by the asset owner, and the state becomes the investment subject of the solely state-owned

---

① Li Shuyun, On Labour's Participation in Surplus Value Distribution, *Inner Mogolia University of Finance and Economics*, No. 2, 2002, pp. 10 – 13.

② Chen Zhonglian, Zhao Xueqing, "Labor Participation in Governance: The Basic Way that State – owned Enterprises Realize System Innovation", *Journal of PLA Nanjing Institute of Politics*, No. 3, 2004, pp. 49 – 52.

company and the state-owned investment company, so to speak, it has the right to appoint the enterprise leader as the "shareholder", and the voting right of the staff and workers' congress loses the basis of existence. [1] In the state-owned enterprises, the internal managers are responsible to the entrusting party, that is, the government. In the case of the failure of the first entrusted agency to carry out the supervision, the staff and workers lack the channels to supervise and balance the authority of the managers.

Third, the coordination of the "Old Three Committees" and the "New Three Committees". After the introduction of the *Company Law*, some scholars have turned their research focus to the establishment of modern enterprise system and the design and relationship between the "Old Three Committees" and the "New Three Committees" in the corporate governance structure. "Old Three Committees" means the party committee, the trade union, the workers' congress, and "New Three Committees" means the board of directors, the board of supervisors, the general meeting of shareholders under the *Company Law*. Some scholars hold that the highest legal authority of the company is the general meeting of shareholders, and it is easy to cause confusion in the organization of the company. [2] From the stakeholder point of view, the state-owned enterprises are in the fierce market competition, and are bound by many legal, social and political conditions, and the mode of "New & Old Three Committees" mixed together has too many constraints on the enterprise, which will inevitably reduce the operational efficiency of the enterprise. [3] But most scholars do not share this view. Feng Tongqing believes that since the reform and opening up, workers and staffts congress system reconstruction has become an

---

[1] Liu Wenyuan, "Concord and Confrontation: Research on the Extent of Democracy in Enterprise in Contemporary China", Beijing: China Labour and Social Security Publish House, 2004.

[2] Yang Ruilong, Zhou Yean, "On the Joint Governance Mechanism of Enterprises under the Cooperation Logic of Stakeholders", *China Industrial Economics*, No. 1, 1998, pp. 38 – 45.

[3] Zheng Haihang, Xiong Xiaotong, "Corporate Governance under Fames of Different Theories: With Discussion of China State-owner Enterprises", *China Industrial Economy*, No. 6, 2005, pp. 105 – 111.

important choice for the development of state-owned enterprises, and the staff director and supervisor system also follows company's growth under market economy, and also the extension of the staff congress system. The relationship between the two is not contradictory and conflicting, but a system of intersecting at different stages of development. ①Lu Chongchang agrees that the party committee is not in conflict with "New Trees Committees". From the point of view of enterprise organization system and incentive mechanism, although there is a contradiction of unity of opposites between workers' congress, trade union and "New three Committees" and managers, the relationship between them can be coordinated by establishing the mechanism of material interests convergence among workers, operators and shareholders. ②The contradiction of "New & Old Three Committees" in some enterprises is not essentially the cause, but rather the system is biased in its implementation, for example, Jane believes that "Old Three Committees" and "New Three Committees" are not simply superimposed relationships, otherwise the two leadership systems and organizational management systems will coexist and lead to confusion in management, the two should reasonably divide and cooperate, and include party committee members and staff and workers' representatives in the board of directors and the board of supervisors. ③More specifically, deal with the following "three relationships". The first is to integrate the relationship between the manager responsibility system under the leadership of the board of directors and the central role of the party committee politics. The second is to sort out the relationship between the staff Congress and the general meeting of shareholders, the board of directors and the board of supervisors. The third is to straighten out

---

① Feng Tongqing, "A Tentative Discussion on the Relationship beteen the System of Worker's Sitting in the board of Directors & Board of Supervisors and the Workers' Congress System", *Journal of China University of Industrial Relations*, No. 4, 2000, pp. 7 – 11.

② Lu Chongchang, "On the Relationship between Enterprise Governance Institutions and the New & lod Three Committees", *Economic Research Journal*, No. 111994,, pp. 101 – 17.

③ Jian Xinhua, "The Risk of Principal-agent and State-owned Enterprise Reform", *Economic Research Journal*, No. 9, 1998, pp. 44 – 49.

the relationship between the board of supervisors of the company and the discipline inspection committee. [1]

In the 1990s, China is in the special period of economic system transformation, industrial structure adjustment, sufficient labor relations and change of interest pattern, against many difficulties for workers, the traditional ideology insists on the loss of ownership of the working class, which can easily lead to the lack of democratic management and the legitimate rights of workers. [2]Researches at this stage focuses mainly on the convergence of the restructuring of state-owned enterprises and the "New & Old Three Committees", which, driven by the central government's efforts to accelerate reform and opening up, has created a nationwide climate of alignment with GDP, efficiency and margin.

III. Struggling of the First Decade of the 21st Century

After joining the World Trade Organization in 2001, China further integrated itself into the international division of labor. The private economy and the individual economy, spurred by the export-oriented economic policies, have made remarkable achievements, with hundreds of millions of rural workers flowing to towns and southeast coasts. The enterprise democratic management system has been challenged unprecedentedly, which is manifested in the following two aspects in the academic field.

The first is the impact of human resource management and employee participation. At the beginning of the 21st century, the theory of human resource management was sought after by the government and enterprises for its emphasis on

---

[1] Xu Huilan, "Straighten out the Relationship between 'New Three Committee' and 'old Three Committe' and Establish Chinese-style Enterprise Leadership System", *Finance and Trade Research Resaerch*, No. 3, 1995, pp. 49 – 51. Wang Quanxing, "Research on Employee Participation Srstem", *Labour Science of China*, No. 7, 1995, pp. 12 – 15.

[2] Zhao Lijiang, Zhang Yuanfeng, "Democracy Participation in Development of Workplace", *Journal of Beijing Administration Institute*, No. 6, 2007, pp. 63 – 67.

the nature of performance management and the more novel and fashionable concept, and was rapidly popularized in China. Enterprises have changed the personnel department to the Ministry of Human Resources, colleges and universities have opened a human resources management major. The concept and practical characteristics of employee participation in human resource management theory have attracted the attention of scholars, some believe that democratic management is different from employee participation in nature and cannot be mixed, for example, Chen Xiangcong argues that democratic management in China refers to the system whereby enterprise employees participate in the management of their own enterprise affairs as owners of means of production and owners of enterprises, which means that the people are masters of the country, which is fundamentally different from the employee identity, clear ownership of property rights and democracy between labor and capital in the participation of employees.[1] But most scholars deem that the democratic management and employee involvement on the mechanism and rules shares non-substantial difference between the concept of different mainly theoretical framework of the subjects and the expression, management, especially in human resource management is to use employee involvement, and sociology, political science, especially the labor relations subject more adopts the industrial democracy, democratic participation, enterprise and staff, etc. From the aspects of content, purpose, procedure, method and so on, the democratic management of Chinese enterprises is the same as the mechanism and rules of employee participation in western countries, which describes the position and role of workers in enterprise management from different angles, and its connotation and extension are not substantially different.[2] Some scholars have analyzed the similarities and

---

[1] Chen Xiangcong, Probe into the Definition of Participation of Workers, *Journal of Fujian College of Political Science & Law*, No. 1, 2002, pp. 22 – 23.

[2] Cheng Yanyuan, "Consideration of Legislation of Democratic Management of the Enterprise", *Journal of Beijing Federation of Trade Union Cadre College*, No. 3, 2006, pp. 14 – 16. Hu Fangzhi, "Employee Participation and Wage Determination – Based on the Enterprise Empirical Analysis of the Collective Wage Negotiations", *Scientific Decision*, No. 9, 2010, pp. 35 – 45. Xie Zengyi, "The Position and Function Remolding of Employee Representation Committee", *Chinese Journal of Law*, No. 3, 2013, pp. 110 – 121.

differences of the forms of enterprise democratic management and employee participation via national comparison or historical comparison. ①

In fact, enterprise democratic management can be a realistic compromise to the concept of employee participation to some extent. Although the central government has continued to emphasize the positive role of democratic corporate governance, its use scope is shrinking in practice, such as: the *Trade Unions Act of 2001* emphasizes the functions of trade unions and explains the functional relationship between workers' congresses and trade unions. In 2006, All-China Federation of Trade Unions promulgated the *Regulations on the Work of Enterprise Trade Unions*, which regulate the work of the workers' congresses as the working mechanism and enterprise trade unions system. *The Labour Contract Law of 2007* defines the staff congress as the institutional basis for the basic forms of democratic management of all enterprises for the following two reasons: one is that the enterprise is unwilling to support the democratic supervision and restriction of the management power, the other is that the human resource management and employee participation strengthen the management power in essence, with user-friendly operation. The living space of corporate democracy will be further compressed by over-emphasizing the differences between the two, as evidenced by the year-on-year decline in the number of journal articles in 2002 – 2007.

Second, the enterprise democratic management system legislation. Although the democratic management of Chinese enterprises needs to be improved both in content and form, scholars note that the lack of legislation has

---

① Liu Wenyuan, Cunwu gongai, "Open Village Affairs, Make Public the Affairs of Enterprises and Democratic Political Construction", *Theory & Practice of Trade Unions*, No. 6, 2000, pp. 40 – 44. Qi Huaqing, The Industrial Democracy Form Abroad and China's Staff and Workers' Participation System, *Academy Journal of Zhongzhou*, No. 3, 2002, pp. 18 – 21. Su Xiaohong, Hou Chaoxuan, "A Comparative Analysis of Employees in China and Abroad Participation in business Management", *Journal of Henan Normal University (Philosophy and Social Sciences)*, No. 5, 2004, pp. 94 – 97. Gao Yulin, "Laborer's Participation in Firm Governance: A Review in Western Economcis and Marxist Economics", *Theory and Practice of Finance and Economics*, No. 4, 2005, pp. 11 – 16. Xie Yuhua, He Baogang, "Industrial Democracy and Employee Participation: An Eternal Topic - - A Review of Research on Industrial Democracy and Employee Participation in China", *Socialism Studies*, No. 3, 2008, pp. 86 – 93.

led to the passivity of democratic management. In particular, firstly is that the level of legislation is low, the legal provisions are vague and the legal responsibilities are weak. Although there are more than a dozen national-level laws dealing with the content of democratic management, there is not a systematic and comprehensive special law. The *Regulations of the Staff and Workers Congress* and the *Regulations on Democratic Management of Enterprises* will conflict again because of its upper and lower positions. Secondly is the provisions of the law are vague, the provisions emphasize the principle too much, with narrow scope of application. Thirdly, the legal responsibility is unknown, the execution is insufficient, the *Labor Law*, the *Labor Contract Law*, the *Company Law* only stipulates the staff and workers, the trade union reports, the government investigates the processing, but does not have the legal responsibility and the punishment to the illegal democratic management stipulation behavior. Fourthly, the trade union independence is weak, the membership fee is paid by the enterprise, the trade union chairman is concurrently appointed by the management, and the trade union duty is formalized. Fifthly, there are no rigid regulations on the proportion or number of staff and workers' directors, relatively low regulations on the proportion of staff and workers' supervisors, and unclear procedures and qualifications for staff and workers' directors and supervisors to be elected and dismissed. [1]Given the

---

[1] Luo Peixin, "On the Legislation of Staff's Participation in Management in China: Its Omissions and Perfection", *Journal of Shanghai University (Social Sciences)*, No. 4, 2000, pp. 73 – 78. Zhang Rongfang, "On the Legal Perfection of the Democratic Management System for Staffs in China", *Law Review*, No. 2, 2000, pp. 108 – 112. Wang Yicheng, Yuan Jie, "Establishment of Chinese Grass – Roots Democracy since Reform and Opening up", *Journal of Political Science*, No. 2, 2004, pp. 26 – 33. Shou Jiguo, "A Positive Analysis of a System Building of Democratic Management in Enterprises", *Journal of China Institute of Industrial Relations*, No. 2, 2006, pp. 40 – 43. Chen Waihua, "On the Participation of Workers in Corporate Governance: From the perspective of Economic Democracy", *Journal of Political Science and Law*, No. 4, 2008, pp. 97 – 101. Liu Yuanwen, "On the Democratic Participation and the Construction of the Workers Congress System", *Labour Union Studies*, No. 6, 2011, pp. 7 – 9. Wu Yaping, "On the Improvement of Legislation on Democratice Management in Enterprises", *Journal of China Institute of Industrial Relations*, No. 1, 2013, pp. 72 – 76. Liu Wenhua, Zhao Lei, "Research on Legal Regulation of Enterprise Democratic Management", *China Labor*, No. 10, 2017, pp. 4 – 10.

legal defects of democratic management of enterprises, many scholars have put forward suggestions, mainly including improving the level of legislation, expanding the coverage, perfecting the legal content, clarifying the legal responsibility and so on.

Democratic management, as an aspect of modern management system, is bound to play greater role in deepening of enterprise and market reform. As things stand, democratic management can provide institutionalized and regular channels for employees to participate in different links and levels, so that both labor and capital can express, communicate and coordinate each other's interests,[1] it is conducive to forming a community of interests, enhancing corporate cohesion, and promoting employee fairness and satisfaction.[2] Whether in foreign-funded enterprises,[3] or in private enterprises,[4] trade unions, workers' congresses and other systems can stabilize the workforce and promote the role of harmonious interpersonal relations, labor relations construction.

IV. New Era & New Development

In April 2012, the SASAC, All-China Federation of Trade Unions and other six ministries jointly issued the *Regulations on the Democratic Management of Enterprises*, which stipulated the guiding ideology, basic principles and

---

[1] Wu Jianping, Chen Ziwei, "The Empirical Basis for Democratic Management Enterprises", *Journal of China Institute of Industrial Relations*, No. 4, 2010, pp. 71 – 75.

[2] Lin Yufang, "On the Relationship between Democratic Management in Business and Harmony in Labour Relationship", *Journal of Yunnan Provincial Committee School of the CPC*, No. 2, 2009, pp. 115 – 117.

[3] Zhao Wei, "Workers and Trade Unions in the New Type of Labor Relation: An empirical investigation of Workers and Trade Unions in a Wholly Foreign – Owned Enterprises", *Chinese Cadres Tribune*, No. 6, 2003, pp. 24 – 27.

[4] Yang Yong, Gao Ruxi, "On the Construction of Harmonious Labor Relations in Private Enterprises", *Human Resources Development of China*, No. 3, 2007, pp. 34 – 37. Xie Yuhua, "The System and Functions of Chinese Industrial Democracy and Employee Participation", *Comparative Economic & Social System*, No. 1, 2009, pp. 129 – 135.

organizational system of democratic management, and set up a special chapter on the staff congress system, the open system of factory affairs and the staff and workers' supervisor system. The report of the 18th National Congress of the CPC also regards the system of democratic management of enterprises and institutions such as the workers' congresses as an important part of democracy at the grassroots level, pointing out: "Rely whole heartedly on the working class, improve the system of democratic management of enterprises and institutions with the workers' congress as the basic form, and safeguard the democratic rights of workers to participate in management and supervision."

With the sluggish world economy and the pressure upon deepening domestic reform, China's economy presents the "three superposition" of the period of changing the growth rate, the period of structural adjustment and the period of early stimulus policy digestion. The CPC Central Committee, with Comrade Xi Jinping at its core, has vigorously deepened its reform, thoroughly implemented its strategy of innovation-driven development, and continued to push forward the widespread entrepreneurship and innovation; vigorously promoted the structural reform on the supply side, vigorously promoted the upgrading of the industrial structure, phased out the labor-intensive processing enterprises, and made great efforts to develop the equipment manufacturing and high-tech manufacturing industries. The implementation of "Made in China 2025", "Internet" and other planning and action, platform economy, sharing economy, collaborative economy and other new models of rapid growth. From 2014 to 2016, there were more than 44 million households in the new registration market, of which 13.62 million were newly registered enterprises, an annual increase of 30 percent. Against the backdrop of the downward economic pressure, how to eliminate backward production capacity to achieve industrial upgrading, to reduce the tax burden to enterprises, stimulate economic vitality has become the most imperative issue, and academic research on democratic management is no longer a major contradiction in corporate survival.

V. Conclusion

With a view to stimulating the production enthusiasm of the business operators, on the one hand, the government in the early period of reform and opening up lets the managers benefit from the business operation through the incentive mechanism, on the other hand, it gradually liberalizes the restriction of the management authority while establishing and perfecting the market mechanism. From the factory director responsibility system under the leadership of the party committee to the factory director (manager) responsibility system to the contract responsibility system to the implementation of the joint-stock system and the current enterprise system.

As a matter of fact, on the basis of inheriting the tradition, China's enterprise democratic management system continuously absorbs advanced management experience and gradually explores an enterprise democratic managemant system suitable for China's national conditions. In the report of the 19th National Congress of the Communist Party, General Secretary Xi Jinping pointed out that "we should improve the consultation and coordination mechanism of government, trade unions and enterprises and build harmonious labor relations". Academic circles shall take Xi Jinping Thought on Socialism with Chinese Characteristics for a New Era as the guidance, thoroughly implement the spirit of the Nineteenth National Congress of the Party, strengthen the construction of enterprise party organizations, strengthen the construction of enterprise democratic system, strengthen the study of enterprise democratic management, and improve the position of democratic management in the structure of enterprise management, so as to contribute to the healthier development of enterprises and the better interests of employees.

Modernization of Governance and People-to-people Bond

The Characteristics of the Development of China's Cultural Industry and the Modernization of Governance in the Cultural Field

Zu Chunming

Associate Professor, Institute of Philosophy, CASS

China's cultural industry has developed for nearly 20 years since the concept of "cultural industry" first appeared in supreme documents of the Chinese government in 2000. From striving for legitimacy to being identified as a pillar industry by the state in 20 years, China's cultural industry has gone through three key development stages, namely, the initial period, the period with trend-bucking surge of growth and the period with the new normal. Since the new era, China's cultural industry has shifted from scale expansion based growth to innovation-driven growth alongside the continuous marketization of digital technology, and has gradually presented a new intertwined situation with progress in various fields of national economy and social development.

I. Analysis of the Concept of "Cultural Industry"

"Culture" itself is an extremely complex concept with hundreds of definitions; however, it is difficult to find a connection with the concept of "industry" in so many definitions. Hence, it is necessary to figure out the relationship between culture and industry with two logical clues from economy to culture and from culture to economy before clarifying the concept of "cultural industry".

1. The Logical Clue from Economy to Culture

According to the viewpoints of economists, sociologists and futurologists, the economic development since pre-modern times can be divided into five stages: the agriculture-based stage, the industry-based stage, the service-based stage, the knowledge-based service stage, and the stage based on the arts and cultural knowledge services. Here I would like to focus on the fourth and fifth stages of economic development instead of the first three that have little to do with this paper.

Amid the progress in emerging information industry in the 1970s and 1980s, the industrial sector in the service industry specialized in information products and labor services was called "knowledge-based economic sector". According to the statistics on the economic development of its member states made by the Organization for Economic Co-operation and Development (OECD) in the 1990s, the output value of the aforementioned sector accounted for more than 70% of the national economy, thus marking a new phase in "knowledge-based economy".

After the 21st century, the products and services that specifically meet people's spiritual and cultural needs have become increasingly salient in the knowledge-based service industry, contributing to a shift in their consumption from material needs to spiritual needs, as well as from science and technology to psychological and emotional satisfaction. Therefore, it can be said that the economy is continuously developing towards culture.

2. The Logical Clue from Culture to Economy

Alongside the trend of continuous integration with economic life, the development from culture to economy can also be divided into five stages compatible with the five stages of development from economy to culture. The first stage is marked by the elite culture independent of the masses which matches to the agriculture-based economic development, fitting with the industry-based economic development; the second stage marks a shift from traditional culture to commercial culture thanks to glorious modern media technology and created cultural market, keeping with the service-based economic development; the third stage witnesses a progress from commercial culture to cultural industry by building commercial culture with mass media, in accord with the knowledge-based economic development; the fourth stage represents the transformation from cultural industry to content industry due to industrial restructuring and the change in overall pattern caused by media convergence, in sync with the economic development based on the arts and cultural knowledge services; the fifth stage ushers in creative industry upgraded from content industry, thus leading to the national economy characterized by cultural added value.

Emphasis should be placed on the third, fourth and fifth stages. The invention of telegraph is of epoch-making significance during the progress from commercial culture to cultural industry. Alexander Bell invented the telegraph in 1876, contributing to a great leap forward from print media to electronic media, followed by radio and television. Such kind of electronic media available to the masses helps create and preserve various cultures on an industrial scale basis, hence a foundation for the emergency of cultural industry.

The fourth stage represents the transformation from cultural industry to content industry primarily because of media convergence and unification after the emergence of digital technology and computer networking technology. Media convergence has changed the structure of traditional media and the entire cultural industry, and even the appearance of the entire economic life. There will be a surplus of media means when all media converge on the Internet, and the content of communication thereby will become the key factor determining the survival of media resources. This is the so-called era of "King of Content".

The creative industry is upgraded from the content industry. The further trends towards the creative industry in the digital network era are presented as follows. First, powerful digital media technology can help digitize traditional cultural heritage and spread it worldwide; second, digital technology contributes to an increasingly "media-oriented" life and as a result, more and more consumer goods have become carriers of meaningful cultural symbols with high price. For instance, all Donald Duck related products will be priced relatively high since it is a cultural symbol with higher brand value. The third is the network-based trend. The role and cost of replication and dissemination are declining and reducing respectively under the impact of the global network, thus making innovative parts valuable most. Therefore, the market players will remain disciplined in creation and innovation for their strategic transformation.

3. The Connotation of the Concept of "Cultural Industry"

It can be seen that cultural industry is a concept formed in the integration of cultural progress with economic growth; however, countries in different development stages understand cultural industry differently. For example, the cultural market in a country such as the United States with fully developed market-oriented economy flourishes in all respects. Therefore, the cultural industry is defined as the "commerciable information content product industry" with a complete market-based trend around "products" highlighted. Although the European Union has mastered the same technology as the United States, the Europeans highlight the particularity of "meaningful content" in their definition of emerging cultural industry thanks to diverse national cultures, thus defining it as "meaningful content based production activity". As a rising force in the cultural industry, South Korea is undergoing upgrading from cultural industry to content industry, thus defining it as "content industry".

In summary, we have an overall understanding of cultural industry, that is, an industry that produces cultural symbols on the basis of material production activities in modern society. Around the accumulation, production, exchange and consumption of cultural symbols with cultural significance and in line with different parts of industrial development chain, it can be classified into triple circle, namely "producing and reproducing cultural significance itself", "replicating and disseminating products with cultural significance" and "attaching all production activities and products with cultural marks".

In this regard, we can make clear three levels of "cultural industry". In the narrowest sense, it refers to the "creation, accumulation and display of cultural content" at the "basic level of industry", including literary and artistic creation, music creation, photography, dance, industrial design and architectural design, as well as other creative art activities.

The second level is about expansibility. Cultural industry refers to "cultural production and communication industry" at the "core level of industry", covering press and publishing industry, broadcasting industry, film and television industry, recording and video industry, telecommunications industry, network industry, etc.

The cultural industry at the third level commonly refers to the industry based on cultural significance. Such definition is close to the concept of anthropology, that is, all spiritual and material activities of human beings act as a "symbol" to convey social significance. It involves the "extended level of industry" and covers all products with cultural marks and modern trademarks in clothing industry, building industry, etc. For a country like China still in a stage of industrialization, its understanding of cultural industry is still between the first level and the second level.

II. Background of the Rise of China's Cultural Industry

The year 2000 is of great epoch-making significance for China's cultural field. At the Fifth Plenary Session of the 15th CPC Central Committee held in October 2000, the concept of "cultural industry" appeared for the first time in China's "supreme policy document", marking a new journey towards China's cultural system reform.

There have been divergences on the rise time of China's cultural industry. Judging from paid services rendered by cultural institutions, it can be said that "cultural industry" runs through the reform and opening up launched in 1978. Judging from using "cultural industry" by government departments concerned in official documents as policy language, it can be traced back to 1992 during the 8th Five-Year Plan period when the concept of "cultural industry" first appeared in the *Decision of the State Council of the CPC Central Committee on Fostering Progress in the Third Industry*. Judging from appearing in the "supreme policy document" of the plenary session of the CPC Central Committee, it can be traced back to 20 years ago when the Fifth Plenary Session of the 15th CPC Central Committee adopted the *Proposal of the CPC Central Committee on the 10th Five-Year Plan* in October 2000. The above landmark events can be used as the basis for three kinds of opinions about the rise time of China's cultural industry. Here we prefer the third one.

China's cultural industry ushers in a marked rise in the world at the turn of the century. This is inevitably the result in the course of modernization driven by China's reform and opening up and the trend of a new round of globalization, as well as the active measures taken by the Chinese government to cope with the challenges of globalization after joining the WTO.

Firstly, in view of domestic development trends, China's cultural industry rises amid economic growth, social progress, growing personal income and changes in the consumption structure. Reform and opening up marks a new phase in China's economic and social development. According to the statistics of authoritative departments, China's per capita GDP has been close to 1,000 USD from the 6th Five-Year Plan in the early 1980s to the end of the 9th Five-Year Plan in 1999, leading to fundamental changes in the consumption structure of residents.

Changes in the consumption structure are prominently characterized by a tendency towards "non-concrete object", that is, a faster growing proportion of consumption in culture and education sectors. During this transition, the expenditure on daily necessities continued to decline steadily, while that on the service sector increased fast. For the first time, the expenditure on entertainment, culture and education spheres exceeded that on supplies, marking a change in Chinese residents' priority from "food, clothing, and daily necessities" to "food, clothing, entertainment, culture and education". A considerable number of residents began to spend money on education, science and technology, tourism, as well as intellectual and artistic products. In a word, the growing income level and changes in the consumption structure, as well as the burning demand for culture related goods have become a decisive essential driver of the rise of China's cultural industry.

Secondly, in view of international trends, alongside the overall improvement of the emerging service industry thanks to the progress in the knowledge-based economy, the trend of economic globalization to cultural globalization was obvious and the cultural industry once again flourished worldwide from the 1980s to the 1990s, thus reshaping the globalization.

The knowledge-based economy is primarily driven by digital information technology and modern media convergence caused by digital technology, thus advancing the knowledge-based economy towards "culture-based economy". The United States, a pioneer in digital information technology, has led this transition. The US Congress passed the new *Telecommunications Act* in 1996, contributing to fewer restrictions on American media industry and American media giants going world.

The United States exported consumer audio-visual technology based cultural products worth 60 billion USD in 1998, higher than the export value of the aerospace industry, thus making it the biggest export. So far, the United States has once again gained an upper hand in international industrial upgrading after completing a new round of industrial restructuring and advanced globalization to a new stage by shaping a new round of globalization with American characteristics—the so-called "McDonaldization".

Thirdly, in view of the direct cause, China's cultural industry is an active policy promulgated by the Chinese government to tackle the challenge of China's accession to the WTO in its course of industrialization.

Cultural industry is the product of developed countries striding into "post-industrial" society in all respects. Developing cultural industry represents a reshaping of global cultural progress and economic growth by developed countries such as European countries and the United States that have already stridden into "post-industrial" society. The primary task of China is to complete industrialization against the backdrop of global industrial upgrading and restructuring. Besides a significant opportunity to undertake global industrial transfer after its accession to the WTO, China still faces the challenge of opening trade in cultural services.

China's accession to the WTO has brought multiple challenges to Chinese cultural institutions, such as competition in cultural industry, impact by cultural capital and conflicts between cultural values; however, it is definitely a very rare opportunity through which China can usher in a historic progress in developing and reforming the culture sector and further transform the overall economic structure based on the boom in the cultural industry. The Chinese government has formulated a significant policy to boost the cultural industry after weighing the pros and cons.

III. Characteristics of China's Cultural Industry Development

1. The Initial Stage Characteristics: Industry Start-up and Reform Pilot

On October 11, 2000, the Fifth Plenary Session of the 15th CPC Central Committee adopted the *Proposal of the CPC Central Committee on the 10th Five-Year Plan*, mentioning "advancing the integration of information industry with the cultural industry concerned"; it was proposed to "perfect cultural policies and strengthen the construction and administration of cultural market to boost relevant cultural industry" in the Section XV: Promoting Socialist Cultural and Ethical Progress.

In the Report on the Outline of the 10th Five-Year Plan for Social and Economic Development delivered by then Premier Zhu Rongji at the Fourth

Session of the 9th National People's Congress in March 2001, the relevant suggestions at the Fifth Plenary Session of the 15th CPC Central Committee were expressed as "deepening the reform of cultural system, perfecting cultural and economic policies, and boosting the relevant cultural industry". The proposal for developing "cultural industry" appeared in China's supreme policy documents—the resolution of the plenary session of the CPC Central Committee and the five-year plan of the National People's Congress, marking the completion of "legalizing" China's cultural industry. It represents a new historic start for China's cultural industry, which is of great strategic significance.

In the report to the 16th CPC National Congress in 2002, the statement on the reform of cultural system was specified as "quickly formulating an overall plan to reform cultural system". Accordingly, the "pilot reform of cultural system" started in 2003. 35 units and 9 provinces and cities were involved in this pilot reform that covered fields such as news media, publishing houses, libraries, museums, cultural centers, art troupes, film and television production enterprises, printing, distribution and screening companies, etc. The units involved in the pilot reform were categorized as "non-profit public institutions" and "commercial entities". They put forward the objectives of and approaches to the reform and formulated corresponding policies. The reform was launched nationwide after the pilot program ended in 2005.

2. "Trend-bucking Surge of Grouth" Stage Characteristics: "Trend-bucking Surge of Growth" and "Pillar Industry"

China's cultural industry has been developing rapidly since 2000. After the pilot reform of cultural system started in 2003, supporting policies were introduced to give preferential treatment to the enterprises involved, thus speeding up cultural industry advancement. The scale of the industry has been further expanding due to more participants benefiting from preferential policies since the reform was launched nationwide in 2005.

In particular, since China's accession to the WTO, its economy has been growing at a high speed with a peak growth rate of 13% in 2007 thanks to the reform and opening up; however, the economic growth rate dropped to less than 9% in one year after the international financial crisis in 2008. At that time, there was an extraordinary growth in such fields of film and television and new media of the cultural industry. Such a rare bright spot in economic growth is known as "trend-bucking surge of growth" and "lipstick effect".

This has attracted the attention of the comprehensive economic management departments and led to the deliberation and approval of the *Plan to Revitalize Cultural Industry* at the executive meeting of the State Council in September 2009, through which the cultural industry was incorporated into the 11th national industry revitalization plan. In October of the next year, the Fifth Plenary Session of the 17th CPC Central Committee adopted the *Suggestions for the 12th Five-Year Plan*, emphasizing "developing the cultural industry into a pillar industry for economic growth" during the 12th Five-Year Plan. So far, the cultural industry is officially incorporated into the national strategic pillar industries.

3. New Normal Stage Characteristics: "Turning Point" and "Transition"

There is a market demand in China, a country with a long-standing shortage of cultural products, to develop the cultural industry into a pillar industry for economic growth. The only problem is whether the development model is reasonable and whether cultural enterprises can make effective production and creation under the current cultural management system and policies. In this regard, China's cultural industry has not yet well prepared.

Since the 12th Five-Year Plan, China has entered a new normal with the macroeconomic growth at "medium-high speed", instead of "high speed", and has presented increasingly obvious institutional and policy changes after transforming the development model and conducting economic restructuring substantially. Since cultural industry is originally a part of macro-economy, changes in the economic situation will help improve the consumption environment in the long run, which is conducive to the progress in cultural industry; however, such changes will definitely affect the cultural industry adversely in the short and medium term. Additionally, the cultural system reform came to an end at this time and the policy effect related to the reform has gradually declined, resulting in a year-by-year drop in development speed. Therefore, during the 12th Five-Year Plan period, a "turning point" arrived in the cultural industry developing at "fast speed" in the past 10 years: an increase of 21.96% in 2011, 16.5% in 2012, 11.1% in 2013, 12.1% in 2014, and 11% in 2015.

The essence of "turning point" is "transition". A major policy statement of "ensuring that the market plays the decisive role in allocating resources" appeared in the *Decision of the Central Committee of the Communist Party of China on Major Issues Concerning Deepening the Reform in All Respects* adopted by the Third Plenary Session of the 18th CPC Central Committee. In the section on cultural policy, the first key word was changed from "cultural industry" to "cultural market" —to establish a sound modern cultural market system. China's cultural industry has been stepping forward towards a new stage that relies on the endogenous driving force of the market after the government-led initiation stage.

IV. Promote the Modernization of Governance in the Cultural Field

According to the data of the cultural industry included in the three economic censuses in 2004, 2008 and 2013, there were 318 thousand impersonal entities and 8.73 million employees in China's cultural industry in 2004, with an added value of 344 billion yuan, accounting for 2.15% of GDP; while there were 918, 500 impersonal entities and 17.59 million employees in 2013, with an added value of 2008.1 billion yuan, accounting for 3.42% of GDP. The number of impersonal entities has tripled, the number of employees has doubled and the added value has increased by 4.8 times in the past 10 years. However, China's cultural industry is still at the initial stage of development by taking into account the macro situation of reform and opening up and the comparison with the international community.

1. The Motivation of Development has Changed from Government Investment to Social Investment

China's cultural industry was once an industry that was extremely in short supply. After approximately three five-year plans, the continuous rapid growth exceeding 20% per year has greatly eased the supply shortage, and even over-investment and bubbles have emerged in some areas (for instance, the "animation industry"), leading to a new phase of coexistence of shortage and surplus.

The coexistence of shortage and surplus can be further defined as the coexistence of shortage and surplus amid a relatively low-level development in a limited open market. First of all, generally speaking, China's level of cultural consumption is still much lower than the average of the same countries in the world. Therefore, the so-called surplus is only a "relative surplus" when cultural consumption is not really met.

Secondly, the coexistence of shortage and surplus lies in the limited openness of cultural market, resulting in excessive investment and competition in the open market, as well as insufficient investment and supply in the unopened market. Besides, false prosperity emerged because of a large number of invalid investments in areas in short supply caused by limited openness and overdependence on financial support.

It is an inevitable trend to get rid of the coexistence of shortage and surplus. Through over ten years of effort, the government-led investment boom has come to an end. China's cultural industry will further be driven by social investment instead of government investment, consumption instead of investment, and will develop towards a quality-oriented, not quantity-oriented objective. In the coming new stage of development, the ground-breaking progress will be made in relatively open emerging cultural fields with vibrant culture and technology integrated innovations, thus contributing to a large-scale technological innovation driven restructuring, optimization and upgrading.

2. Promote the Modernization of Governance in the Cultural Field

Since the turn of the century, the GDP growth rate in China's cultural industry has been impressive primarily thanks to the accommodative institution (cultural system reform) and policy support (supporting preferential policies for cultural system reform). The government has played a leading role in boosting China's cultural industry; unfortunately, the growing personal income and cultural consumption demand itself have contributed less to driving China's cultural industry.

China's cultural industry is characterized by "reforming while developing" because it has developed alongside cultural system reform. Under the new situation, China needs to transform its cultural industry by virtue of the reform of the national macro cultural management system—reconstructing the relationship between the government and the market.

The same is true as far as the logic of cultural system reform is concerned. The reform has emphasized more on "creating market entities" and "separating undertakings from enterprises" since 2003, and thus has achieved phased results. The next is to build a "modern cultural market system", so that the transformed enterprises get access to a fair and open market with free competition. This laid the foundation for the overriding task of "establishing a sound modern cultural market system" proposed in the report to the Third Plenary Session of the 18th CPC Central Committee.

3. Prospects for the Modernization of China's Cultural Industry in the New Development Stage

There are five growth potentials for China's cultural industry development.

Firstly, as a for-profit service industry, cultural industry will present us with a huge development space. In the new development stage, the substantial transformation of the macroeconomic development model and the further improved consumption environment will contribute to the substantially activated cultural consumption, thus greatly driving the cultural industry that meets people's cultural consumption needs.

Secondly, as a productive service industry, cultural industry will become a major fulcrum of national economic transformation and restructuring. The transformation of China's macroeconomic development model and its economic restructuring and upgrading during the 13th Five-Year Plan period will drive the related industries, thus contributing to explosive growth in the demand for the cultural industry, the trend of large-scale integration of cultural industry with real economy and the penetration of the cultural industry into more and more areas of the national economy.

Thirdly, as a brand new technology industry, cultural industry will be greatly driven by the integration of cultural progress with technological advances. Moreover, the technological revolution will contribute to significant restructuring and upgrading of cultural industry. It can be seen clearly now that the next five to ten years witness fundamental changes in cultural development brought about by technological advances.

Fourthly, since the modern cultural industry is an urbanized industry, the construction of new-type urbanization continues to bring great opportunities for cultural development. China's urbanization is further deepening, and a large number of people will be transferred from rural to urban areas. Therefore, the developed cities have a huge need to expand the population capacity, while the boom cities have a huge need to enlarge the population, both of which are conducive to widened space for cultural development.

Fifthly, the advancement of cultural trade in all respects will push forward the global culture development towards a new phase dominated by China. China's international cultural trade has surged amid the progress in cultural industry and cultural system reform in a dozen years. Alongside such a stronger momentum of development, the next five to ten years may witness fundamental changes in China's international cultural trade. China will no longer "import copyright and export manufactured goods". Instead, it will be seen as a country of "exporting copyright and importing manufactured goods", and make contributions to the international cultural market with large-scale cultural consumption.

The Prospects and Innovation in Governance of China-Belarus Tourism Cooperation under the Belt and Road Framework

Zhang Yanlu

Associate Professor, Institute of Russian, Eastern European & Central Asian Studies, CASS

Nowadays, tourism, as one of the fastest growing industries in the world economy and contributing a lot to the global GDP, has played a significant role in boosting the world economic growth. Moreover, tourism cooperation is becoming an important direction in bilateral cooperation between countries and multilateral cooperation among regions. In the latest *Strategy for Stable Social and Economic Development of Belarus before 2030*, tourism has been identified as one of the main driver of Belarus' economic growth. Despite the difficulties in infrastructure and development funds, and deficiencies of Belarusian tourism in contribution to the national economy, popularity, form and quality of service, etc., Belarus' tourism has built sound foundation in resource, tourism infrastructure construction and policy support, and has great potential and broad prospect. Despite the obstacles to China-Belarus tourism cooperation, desirable cooperation conditions in terms of resource, policy, market, etc. are available now. If promoted by such means as joint development of third party market, regional tourism cluster construction, convenient consumption payment methods, innovative products, etc., China-Belarus tourism cooperation is likely to become a highlight in practical cooperation between China and Belarus after the China-Belarus Industrial Park, and a new model under the Belt and Road cooperation framework.

Over the past decades, the world tourism has developed rapidly. In particular, the number of international tourists has grown year after year. As of 2017, tourism has become one of the fastest growing industries in the world economy. According to estimates of the World Tourism Organization (UNWTO), about 1.4 billion trips were made by international tourists in 2018, up by 6%.[1] Over the past decades, tourism and the economic system formed around it have become the major driver of the world economic growth, and contributed more than 10% to the global GDP, namely, about one out of every ten jobs comes from tourism.[2] Tourism, as a universally recognized industry with low resource consumption, more job creation and high comprehensive benefit, has been identified by many countries as the focus of industrial structure adjustment and major way to enhance the comprehensive competitiveness of a country. It has become increasingly important in the national economy. Simultaneously, the role of tourism in promoting mutual understanding of people from various countries has been further revealed. Tourism is no longer confined to an economic concept showing the collection of tourist relations, but evolves into a social phenomenon in contemporary relations between countries (regions), an active cultural cooperation manner between countries and a natural result of the general trend of strengthening relationship between countries (regions). It has played a significant role in people-to-people exchanges and cultural spread. Nowadays, tourism cooperation is becoming the trend of bilateral cooperation between

---

[1] World Tourism Organization of UN, World Tourism Barometer, Volume 17, Issue 1, January 2019. http://cf.cdn.unwto.org/sites/all/files/pdf/unwto_barom19_01_january_excerpt.pdf.

[2] Cheryl Martin, Richard Samans, Preface in the Travel & Tourism Competitiveness Report 2017.

countries and regional multilateral cooperation.

On December 1, 2017, while the prime ministers of China and Belarus met in Sochi, Russia, Andre Kobayakov, the then-Prime Minister of Belarus, officially proposed to the Chinese side to set 2018 as "China-Belarus Year of Tourism". Chinese Prime Minister Li Keqiang expressed his support to this proposal on behalf of the Chinese side, and said that the Chinese side will carefully consider all proposals advanced by the Belarusian side. According to the report of Xinhua News Agency released on December 23, 2017, China and Belarus reached consensus on hosting the 2018 year of tourism in each country. On January 10, 2018, China held a solemn opening ceremony of "Belarus Year of Tourism" in Chongqing, China, and simultaneously hosted the "Belarus-China Friendship" Tourism Forum. Mr. Rudd, the then Belarus ambassador to China pointed out at the forum that cultural ties and tourism played a special role in the bilateral relations between China and Belarus. It has brought closer the relationship between people of the two countries, enhanced mutual trust, and paved a solid foundation for partnership between the two countries.[①] On January 12, Deputy Director Du Jiang of China National Tourism Administration and Vice Minister Portnoy of Belarusian Ministry of Sports and Tourism concluded the Memorandum of Cooperation for 2018 China-Belarus Year of Tourism in Beijing. The tourism cooperation between China and Belarus has been pushed to a new level since opening of the direct flight route in May 2015, which has become another highlight in the economic cooperation between China and Belarus after the "China-Belarus Industrial Park". During the 2nd Belt and Road Forum for International Cooperation, leaders of China and Belarus listed tourism, trade, investment, education and local cooperation as the focuses of future cooperation between the two countries when meeting with

---

① Торжественная церемония открытия Года туризма Беларуси в Китае состоялась в Чунцине, http://www.belta.by/society/view/torzhestvennaja-tseremonija-otkrytija-goda-turizma-belarusi-v-kitae-sostojalas-v-chuntsine-283842-2018/.

each other.[1] Along with the continuous improvement and enhancement of China-Belarus relations, the China-Belarus tourism cooperation has warmed up, but a series of problems, such as the foundation, problems and prospects of China-Belarus tourism cooperation, is subject to further exploration and research.[2]

Ⅰ. Conditions and Basis for China-Belarus Tourism Cooperation

Despite the remote distance and remarkable differences in natural landscape and customs between China which is located at the east coast of the Pacific Ocean and east of Aisa, and Belarus which is located at the hinterland of Europe and the Central European Plains, the tourism cooperation between the two countries has accumulated certain basis.

Firstly, the China-Belarus relationship has created good political environment for the tourism cooperation and cultural and people-to-people exchange between them. The stable and friendly bilateral relationship between China and Belarus has paved a solid foundation for the tourism cooperation between them.

China is one of the first countries acknowledging the indepenence of Belarus. The China-Belarus relationship has developed steadily since establishment of China-Belarus diplomatic relations on January 20, 1992. The two countries executed a joint declaration in 2005, declaring that the China-Belarus relationship has entered a new stage for comprehensive development and strategic cooperation. Thereafter, especially after 2013, the China-Belarus relationship has warmed up continuously. President Lukashenko of Belarus

---

[1] Xinhuanet, "Xi Jingping met with President Lukashenko of Belarus", Apr. 25, 2019.

[2] So far, domestic research results on the tourism development of Belarus and the status quo and prospects of China-Belarus tourism cooperation are scarce, and only the *Analysis on the ABC-XYZ and Influence Factors of Belarus' Tourist Trade* issued by Nahi-ZadaSabina (2016 master's thesis of East China Normal University), the *Analysis and Thinking on China-Belarus Relationship* issued by Zhao Huirong (*Foreign Theoretical Trends* 2017 Issue 11) and some other articles discussed relevant issues.

visited China in 2013. During his visit, China and Belarus executed the *Joint Declaration of the People's Republic of China and the Republic of Belarus on Establishment of a Comprehensive Strategic Partnership*; President Xi Jinping of China visited Belarus in 2015. During his visit, both sides executed the *Treaty of Amity and Cooperation between the People's Republic of China and the Republic of Belarus* and the *Joint Declaration between the People's Republic of China and the Republic of Belarus on Further Developing and Deepening the Comprehensive Strategic Partnership*; in 2016, while President Lukashenko paid another visit to China, the two sides executed the *Joint Declaration between the People's Republic of China and the Republic of Belarus on Establishing a Comprehensive Strategic Partnership of Mutual Trust and Win-win*, and announced to develop an all-weather friendship.

Secondly, the Chinese and Belarusian governments have devoted to developing their respective tourism, developed and implemented relevant planning and policies for development, and achieved phased results, which have paid a material foundation for their tourism cooperation.

Since its independence, especially in the 21st century, Belarusian government has cared about and supported development of its tourism. It not only promulgated and implemented the *Tourism Law of the Republic of Belarus* on November 25, 1999 to regulate tourism-related activities, but also formulated and implemented four national plans for tourism development since 2001. As for the lastest *National Tourism Development Planning of Belarus 2016 – 2020*, the former Primte Minster Andre Kobayakov of Belarus pointed out that the current comprehensive planning of Belarus for tourism development has not only taken tourism as an industry, but also deemed it as a major impetus to the national economic development of Belarus. [1]The *Strategy of the Republic of Belarus for Economic and Social Development before 2030* promulgated in May 2017 listed tourism as a key sector for Belarus' service development, and set relatively

---

[1] Годом туризма Беларуси в Китае будет объявлен 2018 – й, http://www.belta.by/society/view/godom-turizma-belarusi-v-kitae-budet-objjavlen – 2018 – j – 278487 – 2017.

high goals: making Belarus rank among the world's top 50 tourism powers before 2030, and raising the proportion of tourism service exports in the national service exports to 3.5%. According to the *Report on the Implementation Results of "Hospitable Belarus" National Planning 2018* published by the Ministry of Sports and Tourism of the Republic of Belarus, the tourism of Belarus overfulfilled the goals (see Table 1 for details) set in the *National Tourism Development Planning of Belarus 2016 – 2020* in 2018, realized the tourism service exports of 0.2305 billion USD, and accumulatively completed 39 marketing campaigns for promoting the tourism of Belarus. Moreover, the Belarus government also formulated and passed the *"Belarusian Castle" National Planning* in 2012 for extensive renovation of more than 30 historical and cultural buildings within the territory of Belarus.

Table 1   Progress Chart of 2018 "Hospitable Belarus" National Planning

	Completed	Planned	Excess
Number of newly-added licensed guides	138	—	—
Including: Guides	106		
Guide interpreters	32		
Number of newly-added and updated tourist routes	11	—	—
Foreign visitors (in thousands of visitors)	4781.9	4654	127.9
2018 tourism service exports (in millions of USD)	230.5	208	22.5

Source: Информация о реализации в 2018 году Государственной программы "Беларусь гостеприимная" на 2016 – 2020 годы.

Besides national planning for tourism development, local governments of Belarus also devleoped corresponding plans for tourism development in light of their realities. For example, the Minsk Council passed the *Planning of Minsk for Tourism Development 2006 – 2010* on December 31, 2005. The municipal government expected that this planning could mine the tourism potential of Minsk most effectively, develop the tourism infrastructure, improve the contribution of tourism to the economic development of Minsk, and create conditions to foster tourism to the key industry to the economy of Minsk. Grodno State Council also approved the *Local Planning of Grodno State for Tourism Development 2002 – 2005* in 2002.

Meanwhile, Belarus also promulgated a series of presidential decrees, such as the Presidential Decree No. 371 *Measures for Tourism Development of Belarus*, Presidential Decree No. 372 *Measures for Developing Agricultural Eco-tourism in Belarus*, Presidential Decree No. 462 *Provisions on Visa-free Formalities of Foreigners' Entry and Exit*, etc. The tourism of Belarus has undergone remarkable changes and developed rapidly in recent years due to attention of Belarus. Especially in 2016, Belarus was ranked among the fastest growing countries by investment in tourism by the ranking released by the World Travel & Tourism Council (WTTC). According to the estimate of WTTC, the growth of Belarus' investment in tourism reached 12% in 2016, ranking the 6th among the 185 assessed countries, far above the world (4.7%) and European (4.1%) average, and substantially above its neighbours: Lithuanis (160th), Poland (171st), Russia (180th), Ukraine (183rd), etc.

In China, the *Opinions of the State Council on Accelerating the Development of Tourism* (No. 41 [2009] of the State Council) promulgated on December 1, 2009 proposed to develop tourism into a strategic backbone industry of the national economy and a more satisfactory modern service industry to the people. Thereafter, the State Council of the People's Republic of China further defined May 19 as China Tourism Day in 2011. According to the latest statistics released by the Data Center of China National Tourism Administration, the growth of domestic tour exceeded expectations, and the inbound and outbound tours realized steady growth. As of the first half of 2018, China had 69.23 million inbound tourists, including 14.82 million foreign inbound tourists, up 4%. The international tourism revenue reached 61.8 billion USD, up 2.8% year on year. Meanwhile, Chinese citizens took a total of 71.31 million outbound trips, up 15% year on year[1]. Besides, the *Overview of 2018 Tourism Market* showed that the integration of culture and tourism started well in 2018. Adhering to the thoughts of integrating those fit for or capable of integration, promoting tourism through culture and manifesting culture through tourism, expand the development space of the tourism economy via culture, promote the development of high quality tourism via the supply side reform, and continuously enhance the public's sense of gain in tourism. Domestic tourism market has maintained the rapid growth. The inbound tourism market has steadily entered the slow recovery channel, while the outbound tourism market has developed steadily. The number of domestic tourists reached 5.539 billion, up 10.8% year on year; the number of inbound and outbound tourists reached 0.291 billion, up 7.8% year on year; the total tourism revenue amounted to 5.98 trillion yuan across the year, up 10.5% year on year. In 2018, the comprehensive contribution of tourism to GDP was 9.94 trillion yuan, accounting for 11.04% of the total GDP. The number of people directly employed in tourism reached 28.26 million, while the number of people directly and indirectly employed in tourism amounted to 79.91 million, accounting for 10.29% of the total employees in China. In terms of outbound tourism, about 149.72 million Chinese citizens travelled abroad, up 14.7% year on year[2].

Finally, despite the differences in tourism resources, the characteristic and varied tourism resources of China and Belarus have provided space and potential for their tourism cooperation.

Similar to China, Belarus also possesses abundant tourism resources. Belarus, a landlocked country in the East European Plains, is adjacent to

---

[1] *Statistics on Tourism in 2018H1*, website of the Ministry of Culture and Tourism of the People's Republic of China, Aug. 22, 2018, http://zwgk.mct.gov.cn/ceshi/lysj/201808/t20180822_834337.html? keywords =.

[2] Profile of the Tourism Market in 2018, website of the Ministry of Culture and Tourism of the People's Republic of China, Feb. 12, 2019, http://zwgk.mct.gov.cn/auto255/201902/t20190212_837271.html? keywords =.

Russia in the East and North and to Polland, Lithuanis and Latvian in the West, and borders on Ukraine in the South. It covers an area of 207,600 km², ranking the 13th in Europe, and has a population of 9.50 million. Belarus has a flat landscape, considerable wetland, and a temerate continental climate with warm and humid climate and comfortable temperature. Besides abundant late and river resources, Belarus also has well preserved complete natural landscape. Two remains, namely, Belovezhskaya National Forest Park and Struve Geodetic Arc, have been selected into the world natural heritage list. Besides natural resources, Belarus also enjoys rich and unique historical and cultural resources. The civilzation history of Belarus can be traced back to the stone age. Historical relics belonging to the Stone Age, such as stone plates, pottery, etc., used to be unearthed within its territory. The Belarusian culture began to form gradually in the 7th – 8th century on the basis of Slavic tradition and the cultural tradition of the Baltic tribes. There are some fine works of religious architecture art within the territory of Belarus, such as the Hagia Sophia, St. Yevrosinia Church, Boris and Gleb Monastery (Berechtz Monastery) of Borook, Cathedral of Annunciation in Vitebsk, Boris and Gleb Cathedral (Crowe Cathedral) in Grodno, etc. Among others, the first stone cathedral-Hagia Sophia built in the 11th century in Belarus has become one of the national symbols of Belarus.

Meanwhile, the tourism resources possessed by China and Belarus vary remarkably in kind, type and founction. In terms of natural resources, Belarus known as "land with 10,000 lakes" is famous for its abundant animal and plant resources, while China's natural tourism resources are featured by magnificent and changeable geographical sceneries and climate wonders due to its vast territory and large latitudinal span. In terms of cultural resources, Belarus' relevant tourism resources bear distinctive features of Eastern Slavic civilization and Soviet culture, while China, as the center of the East Asia cultural circle, its relevant tourism resources have distincitive features of Confucian culture. Moreover, from the perspective of function, the resources of Belarus make it enjoy strengths in the development of cross-border tourism, eco-health tourism, sports and business tourism①, while China is better suitable for development of various modern tourism products due to its comprehensive tourism resources. The differences in tourism resources make China and Belarus rarely compete with each other while developing their respective tourism, and can realize strength complementarity, and thus provide vast space for their tourism cooperation.

II. Continuously Tap the Potential of China-Belarus Tourism Cooperation

Up to now, the China-Belarus tourism cooperation has achieved initial success. For example, in terms of visa facilities, visa-free has been available for Chinese citizens with passport for private affairs when entering Belarus since August 10, 2018. According to the *Policy of 144-hour Visa-free Transit for Foreigners from Some Countries* promulgated by the Exit-Entry Administration of China upon approval of the People's Republic of China, Belarusian citizens may enter or exit from any of the 15 ports including Shanghai Pudong International Airport, and enjoy a 144-hour visa-free transit in 7 administrative regions, namely, Shanghai, Jiangsu, Zhejiang, Beijing, Tianjin, Hebei and Liaoning. In terms of the development of concrete tourism projects, China Tourism Group has listed the tourism projects of Belarus as key development projects in 2017 under the Belt and Road Initiative framework. Meanwhile, the "7 – day First Experience of Belarus", a unique characteristic tourism product developed by China Travel Service Head Office Co., Ltd., was launched officially, and the first tour group made their trip in September 2017. Moreover, according to the *Report on China-EU Tourism Market Data 2017* jointly released

---

① Национальная туристическая индустрия. Обеспечение доступности услуг по организации внутреннего туризма для Белорусских граждан. Безвизовый порядок въезда в Беларусь. http: // oshmiany. gov. by/uploads/files/IPG/IPG-ijun – 2017 – material-s-dopolnenijami-upravlenija-sporta-i-turizma –. pdf.

by China Tourism Academy and Ctrip Group, Belarus has become one of the European destinations with the largest growth in Chinese tourists, ranking the 7th place. Despite certain results, the China-Belarus tourism cooperation has just started up, and there is still room for further expansion.

Firstly, there is a certain gap between China and Belarus in tourism development, and the potential of tourism cooperation needs to be tapped in depth.

Though Europe is the world's largest destination of international tourism, and almost holds a 50% stake in the world's tourism, and tourism economy is also one of the pillar industries of European economy, and occupies a leading position in the global tourism market, the tourism of Belarus which is a member of the European family is far below the average level of European countries, also fails to occupy an important position in the domestic economy, and stays at a low position in the global tourism market. According to the latest statistics released by WTTC, the direct output value and total output value of Belarus' tourism in 2017 were 2.2 billion Belarusian roubles (or 1.1108 USD) and 6.8 billion Belarusian roubles (or 3.4082 billion USD), respectively accounting for 2% and 6.2% of Belarus's gross domestic product (GDP) in 2017. In terms of job creation, the tourism of Belarus created about 86,000 direct jobs in 2017. As for the export of tourism service, Belarus realized the export of tourism service of 2.1 billion Belarusian roubles or 1.0423 billion USD in 2017, accounting for 3.0% of its total exports in 2017. Moreover, Belarus invested 0.6 billion Belarusian roubles (or 0.3128 billion USD) in tourism in 2017, accounting for 2% of its total investments in 2017. Despite the growth of Belarus' tourism indicators, the major indicators were still far below the average of the world and Europe where it is located (see Table 2), and both the input and output growth slowed down. [1]

---

[1] World Travel and Tourism Council. Travel and Tourism Economic Impact 2018 – Belarus. https://www.wttc.org/-/media/files/reports/economic-impact-research/countries-2018/belarus2018.pdf.

Table 2 Comparison of Belarus' Major Tourism Indicators and the World and European Average in 2017

	Belarus	World average	European average
Direct contribution of tourism to GDP	1.1 billion USD	21.5 billion USD	5.9 billion USD
Contribution of tourism to GDP	3.4 billion USD	62.9 billion USD	19.5 billion USD
Direct jobs	85,900	937,500	158,500
Total jobs	259,200	2,341,000	582,100
Tourism investment	0.3 billion USD	4.8 billion USD	2.6 billion USD
Tourism export	0.1 billion USD	8.1 billion USD	5.7 billion USD

Source: World Travel and Tourism Council. Travel and Tourism Economic Impact 2018 – Belarus, https://www.wttc.org/-/media/files/reports/economic-impact-research/countries-2018/belarus2018.pdf.

As shown in Table 3, except for the relatively low investment in tourism, there is a big gap between China and Belarus in major indicators regarding tourism development, such as tourism competitiveness, contribution to national economy and jobs, export of tourism service, absolute value of tourism investment, inbound and outbound tourists, spending power, etc.

Table 3 Simple Comparison of Major Tourism Indicators between China and Belarus (subject to the data in 2017)

	Belarus	China
Ranking by tourism competitiveness (among 136 countries)	Not on the list	15th
Ranking by tourism contribution (among 185 countries)	97th (ranking by absolute contribution); 146th (ranking by relative contribution)	2nd (ranking by absolute contribution); 75th (ranking by relative contribution)

(Contd.)

	Belarus	China
Direct contribution to GDP	1.1108 billion USD, 2% of GDP	402.3 billion USD, 3.3% of GDP
Comprehensive contribution to GDP	3.4052 billion USD, 6.2% of GDP	1,349.3 billion USD, 11% of GDP
Contribution to direct jobs	86,000, 1.9% of total jobs	28.25 million, 3.6% of total jobs
Contribution to comprehensive jobs	259,000, 5.8% of total jobs	79.90 million, 10.3% of total jobs
Exports of tourism	1.0423 billion USD, 3% of total exports	125.3 billion USD, 5.2% of total exports
Investment in tourism	0.3128 billion USD, 2% of total investments	154.7 billion USD, 2% of total investments
Inbound foreign tourists	282,700	139.48 million
Outbound tourists	727,536	130.51 million
Spending of outbound tour	0.6124 billion Belarusian rubbles (or 0.288 billion USD)	115.29 billion USD

Source: prepared according to relevant data released by the Ministry of Culture and Tourism of the People's Republic of China, Statistical Commission of Belarus, World Economic Forum and WTTC in 2017.

Secondly, the attractiveness of the tourism products of China and Belarus in each other's tourism market needs to be improved.

Foreign tourists to Belarus are primarily for business affairs, sports and leiture, and most of them select team tour without individuality. Moreover, one of the characteristics of Belarus' tourism is the provision of comprehensive tourism service, but tourism activities completely organized by travel agencies have increased the spending of tourists, which does not comply with the prevailing tourism concept of emphasing personablity and pursuing autonomy and cost saving.

Besides, China and Belarus are not each other's main source of tourists and tourist destination. Though the number of Chinese tourists to Belarus has grown due to the relaxed visa system, according to the statistics of the National Statistical Commission of Belarus, in 2018, the number of Chinese tourists to Belarus was 3,277, 1,698 above that in 2016, there was still a big gap with 207,400 tourists to Russia (2018). Belarus ranked the 5th after Lithuanis, Poland, Latvia and Germany by the number of inbound tourists from countries other than CIS countries in 2018. ①The audiences of Belarus' tourism products are relatively fixed, and mainly spread in former Soviet Union republics and Some Central and Eastern European Countries. Despite the slight growth in its market share in other countries and regions, it was still on the low side. Meanwhile, for Belarusian tourists, China is not a preferred tourist destination. According to the statistics of the National Statistical Commission of Belarus, 1,411 Belarusian tourists took group tour to China in 2018, which is basically the same as that in 2017. China ranked the 25th among the 27 non-CIS countries counted, slightly higher than Britain and Israel.

III. Deepen the China-Belarus Tourism Cooperation

The two countries shall change potential into result and practically promote practical cooperation in tourism.

Firstly, promote China and Belarus to jointly develop the third party market of international tourism under the Belt and Road Initiative multilateral frameworks. Market is one of the key factors handicapping the China-Belarus tourism cooperation.

The inbound tourists of Belarus mainly come from CIS countries like Russia and its neighbouring countries, such as Poland, Latvia, Lithuania, etc. The tourism products of Belarus do not have strong enough competitiveness in

---

① Национальный статистический комитет РБ. Туризм и туристические ресурсы в Республике Беларуси (статистический сборник). Минск, 2019 г., С. 30.

China's internaional tourism market, and are less attractive to China's outound tourists. Though Belarus has implemented the visa-free policy to Chinese citizens traveling to Belarus since August 10, 2018, the number of Chinese tourists to Belarus has not surged. The lack of market momentus and expectation on low profitability in the future have directly resulted in the weak attractiveness of investment in China-Belarus tourism cooperation projects. Under such circumstance, Given the development conditions of Belarus' tourism and the features of the audiences of its tourism products, while developing each other's market, strengthening China and Belarus' joint development of the third party market of international tourism products by relying on the multilateral mechanisms, such as the Belt and Road Initiative, Eurasian Economic Union, etc., will be an effective way to expand the market channel of China-Belrus tourism cooperation and enhance the attractiveness of the cooperation projects.

Secondly, make good use of the geography of Belarus to promote cross border and regional tourism cooperation, and build characteristic regional tourism cluster.

Belarus' geographical location as the east-west transportation hub and its geographical attributes as a "transit place" and "transit country" can facilitate its cross border or region tourism cooperation projects. Meanwhile, a number of cross border tourism resources including the world natural heritages like Belovezhskaya National Forest Park and Struve Geodetic Arc within the territory of Belarus provide Belarus and its neighbouring countries with reliable natural carrier for joint dvelopment of regional tourism cluster, also make its cross border/region tourism cooperation possible. The development of tourism projects across borders and regions cannot only partially solve the homogenization of tourism resources between Belarus and Central and Eastern European countries, such as Russia, Lithuania, Latvia, etc., but also reduce redundant construction of similar projects, which can reduce even avoid unnecessary cutthroat competition and further deepen regional economic cooperation while cutting down the international tourism costs and raising the performance-price ratio to a certain extent.

Thirdly, introduce third party payment platform and promote Internet payment to facilitate payment of tourism consumption.

Tourism is a comprehensive economic activity integrating food, accommodation, transportation and entertainment, in which, one of the most important links is consumer payment. So far, though UnionPay International has concluded a comprehensive cooperation agreement with the largest commercial bank of Belarus-Bank of Belarus in 2017, and all ATMs and merchants of the Bank of Belarus could accept the UnionPay card business in that year, the service scope is still limited and cannot meet the demand of Chinese consumers for easy consumption payment, who have already got used to mobile payment. Therefore, China and Belarus may strengthen cooperation in finance, especially the cooperation in Internet payment while carrying out tourism cooperation, introduce third party payment platforms like Alipay and WeChat payment to Belarus, and promote more covenient mobile payment methods, and thus indirectly stimulate the spending power of tourists.

Finally, emphasize marketing, and take new approaches like new media and popular TV shows to recommend respective tourism products. Neither the tourism products of China nor the tourism produts of Belarus are attractive or competitive in each other's tourism market, which, for one thing, is because the tourism products do not meet the market demand; for another, or the most direct reason, is that the product publicity channel is comparatively traditional, uneffective and untargetted, which makes potential consumers lack of knowledge and understanding of products. Given this, it is suggested to try new media more, such as Internet and mobile APP, to promote respective tourism products, as well as make use of popular variety shows, films and TV dramas to enable potential tourism product consumers from China and Belarus to get a preliminary understanding of each other's culture and tourist spots, and thus boost the consumption of tourist products.

Cooperation and Prospects of Society, Sports and Humanity between China and Belarus in the Context of the BRI

Fang Zhengwei

PhD of the Institute of Philosophy, National Academy of Sciences of Belarus

I. Significance of Sports Cultural Exchanges between Belarus and China

With the comprehensive development of economic and cultural exchanges between China and Belarus, how to carry out further exchanges and development is a critical issue. The social sports activities, as a part of cultural exchanges, just can answer this question.

Social sports cultural activities, as a carrier of various exchanges, can realize exchanges not only in ideology and culture, but also in national economic development and social thoughts. Such special carrier makes sports cultural exchanges play a significant role of China's exchanges with the rest of the world.

It is not too much to say that sports cultural exchanges have become the most important exchanges next to normal political and economic exchanges among modern countries, and on the basis of the Olympic Games and other championships, just this kind of exchange promotes the understanding and cooperation among countries. Therefore, sports cultural exchanges are of great significance to Belarus and China. ①

II. The Course of Cultural Exchanges between Belarus and China

The sports cultural exchanges between Belarus and China have started since their establishment of the diplomatic relations. Belarus declared independence on August 25, 1991. China is one of the first countries acknowledging Belarus. Thereafter from January 19 to 24, 1992, Kebich, the then-Chairman of Ministerial Meeting of Belarus (i. e., Prime Minister) paid an official visit to China. On January 20, the two countries established the diplomatic relations.

In January 1993, Shushkevich, the then-President of the Supreme Soviet of Belarus paid an official visit to China, and executed documents including the Sino-Belarus joint declaration. It is not only the first official visit made by president of Belarus, but also indicates that the two countries will further strengthen the cooperation in such aspects as sports cultural exchange.

In January 1995, Lukashenko, President of Belarus, paid an official visit to China which is the first country beyond the former Soviet Union that Lukashenko visited after being elected as president. In June of the same year, Li Peng, then-Premier of State Council, paid an official visit to Belarus. While leaders of the two states met with each other cordially, the states declared that the sports cultural cooperation between China and Belarus will be strengthened further.

In April 2001, Lukashenko, President of Belarus, paid a state visit to China. Leaders of the two states executed the *Sino-Belarus Joint*

---

① Yu Dawei, Yuan Lei and Zhu Jinghong, " Review and Enlightenment of China's Sports Diplomacy in the 1980s", *Journal of Nanjing Sports Institute*, Vol. 1, 2017, pp. 24 – 28.

Declaration. Other documents, such as the *Agreement between Chinese and Belarusian Governments on Protecting Intellectual Property Rights*, *Cooperation Agreement between the People's Bank of China and National Bank of Belarus*, *Cooperation Agreement between the Ministry of Justice of the People's Republic of China and the Ministry of Justice of Belarus*, etc., were also concluded. In July 2001, Jiang Zemin, the then-President of China, paid a state visit to Belarus, which is the first visit made by head of China to Belarus. The conclusion of a series of documents indicated that the two states had a clear direction of cooperation in economy, politics, science and technology, sports and culture, etc.

In December 2005, Lukashenko, President of Belarus, paid a state visit to China. During his visit, heads of the two states executed the *Joint Declaration between the People's Republic of China and the Republic of Belarus*, declaring that the relations between China and Belarus enter a new stage of comprehensive development and strategic cooperation. Heads of the two states also attended the signing ceremony of 12 documents in respect of the economic and technological cooperation between the two countries. In the same year, the two states executed a working conference protocol between them, showing that they agreed on the practice of holding regular meetings of heads of the administration of sports for negotiation on joint actions. Shortly after that, Liu Peng, the then-Minister of the General Administration of Sports of China and President of the Chinese Olympic Committee, met with the delegation headed by Gligorov head of the Minster of Sports and Tourism of the Republic of Belarus. Both sides held talks on the sports exchanges and cooperation between the two countries. The convention of these conferences shows once again that China cherished the friendly sports partnership with Belarus, and would further strengthen the sports exchanges and cooperation with Belarus to jointly improve the athletic performance and promote mutual understanding and friendship between athletes and people of the two countries.

In November 2007, Wen Jiabao, the then-Premier of State Council, paid an official visit to Belarus. During this visit, both sides executed a series of bilateral cooperation documents, and declared once again the prospects of both countries in politics, economy, science, society, sports, culture, etc. Moreover, in this visit, Premier Wen Jiabao extended a warm welcome to Belarusian athletes' attention to the 2008 Beijing Olympic Games, and wished the Belarusian athletes good results in the Beijing Olympic Games.

On July 2, 2008, Belarusian Olympic Committee and Belarusian Sports Journalists' Association held a ceremony in Minsk and issued qualification certificates to Belarusian sports journalists for their interview during the Beijing Olympic Games. Alexeyenko, the assistant to Belarusian President, said that the people of Belarus would know the Beijing Olympic Games through reports of these journalists. He hoped that the 33 Belarusian journalists to China could give an objective, comprehensive and in-depth report of Beijing Olympic Games. Minister Gregorov said that about 200 athletes from the sports delegation of Belarus would attend 26 events of Beijing Olympic Games, which topped the history of Belarus since its independence in 1991 by the number of athletes and events attended. He hoped that the journalists could perform their duties faithfully to present the most wonderful competition and the whole social life of the host country to the Belarusian audiences.

In March 2010, Xi Jinping, the then-Vice President of China, paid an official visit to Belarus. In October, Lukashenko, President of Belarus, came to China to attend the Shanghai World Expo, celebrated the National Pavilion Day of Belarus, and visited China. During his visit, the leaders of both sides repeatedly declared the friendship between the two countries, and expected further exchanges and progress in social culture and other aspects.

In June 2017, invited by Belarusian Boxing Federation, Chinese National Boxing Team sent 6 female players to visit Belarus and attend the contest. All of them had excelled themselves. The female players of the Chinese team have not only verified their previous special training effect in this contest, but also recognized corresponding deficiencies and problems.

In November 2017, the first International Electronic Sport Tournament was held in Minsk, capital of Belarus. FC Dynamo Brest held several international

E-sports competitions under the support of Belarusian E-sports Association. China sent five teams to attend this tournament. A number of Chinese live broadcasting platforms gave a full range of live broadcast of this tournament.

In January 2018, the 14th Belarus President Cup Christmas Ice Hockey Championship was opened as scheduled in Minsk, capital of Belarus. This is a traditional annual international ice hockey event of Belarus. The Belarusian delegation was headed by President Lukashenko. Most of the teams participating in this event came from ice hockey powers in Europe and North America. This year, the oval office of Belarus and Belarus Ice Hockey Association invited Kunlun Hongxing National Ice Hockey Club under China International Culture Communication Center (CICCC) through CICCC to attend the event on behalf of China.

In July 2018, Sergey Kovaichuk, Minister of the Ministry of Sports and Tourism of Belarus said at the opening ceremony of Chongqing Culture and Sports Day held in Minsk that Belarus and China have actively carried out cooperation in sports and further establish a relationship of mutual trust between the two countries in accordance with the direction of cooperation deterned by the two heads of state.

In 2019, the Belarus Open Wushu Championship of "European Confucius Institute Cup" was held officially at Belarus National Sports University. This event was jointly hosted by Belarus Wushu Development Center, Belarus Wushu Association and Confucius Class of Belarus National Sports University, and attracted more than 600 athletes and sports enthusiasts from Belarus, Russia, Ukraine, Latvian, Poland, Italy and China. The contest is divided into two parts, namely, Wushu routine and Sanda. During the Wushu Open, the host also held cultural experience activities, such as Chinese tea art, calligraphy, promotion of Chinese, etc.

On April 25, 2019, during the 2nd Belt and Road Forum for International Cooperation, the Chinese President Xi Jinping met with President Lukashenko of Belarus at the Great Hall of the People, and unveiled the models of Belarusian National Football Stadium and International Standard Natatorium projects which were completed under the aid of China. At the ceremony, President Xi Jinping exchanged opinions on the models with President Lukashenko, and praised the design concept of the scheme with the characteristics of Belarus. Belarus National Football Stadium is located in downtown Minsk, covers an area of 12.43 hectares, with a floor space of 48,000 m^2 and a total capacity of 33,000 seats. This project has not only filled in the blanks of China in design of professional football stadium, but also paved a way for domestic design institutions to completely design a standard UEFA stadium located in Europe. It is a milestone project for China's sports architecture design.

III. Significance of Sports Cultural Exchanges in Modern International Community

In today's world, sports cultural activities have become an important symbol of social development and progress of human civilization, and played an increasingly important role in the international community. Meanwhile, sports cultural exchanges also constitute an integral part of contemporary international relations and cultural exchanges, serve as an emissary of spreading peace and friendship and an important method to solve conflicts and disputes. Since under certain circumstances, sports cultural activities, especially athletic sports, can transcend national politics and realize fair competition, they can break boundaries easily and transcend the differences in system, belief and concept for exchanges and cooperation. The sports cultural activities have played an active role in promoting reconciliation. Such role is particularly obvious in nowadays when athletic sports face the world, while the reason to this is the characteristics of sports cultural activities.

Sports cultural activities can be integrated and developed together with other cultural activities. First of all, the combination of sports cultural activities with education can make up the teaching deficiencies. Practical activities in sports activities, such as physical training, organizational disciplines, competition and cooperation, etc., can shape and perfect people's physical and mental harmony, social adaption, ideal ad morality, willpower, etc. All these cannot be replaced or made up by other educational means and approaches. Secondly, the combination of sports and arts activities can fuse and unfold static and dynamic beauty. The dynamic and physical beauty of sports activities make sports activities very ornamental. The combination of sports activities and arts can be presented from stadium, such as the Bird's Nest and Water Cube built for Beijing Olympic Games, which are the treasures of architectural art. The National Football Field of Belarus built under the aid of China is not only the perfect embodiment of this treasure, but also unfold the friendship between Belarus and China beyond politics. All these demonstrate that arts can be expressed more thoroughly and comprehensively via the carrier-sports; meanwhile, such combination and integration of modern science and technologies, such as news reports on sports activities, live broadcast of sports events, film arts regarding sports activities, etc., have made the sports cultural exchanges more direct and attractive. People can get direct or indirect knowledge of each other's cultural connotation, characteristics and value orientation via these cultural forms with substantial content, and thus narrow the gap and realize cultural exchange. ①

Sports cultural activities can be easily accepted by the social public because body language is the simplest and most intuitive form of expression; moreover, this form of expression is free of effect of too many other factors. As long as being communicated and exchanged via certain channels, people who have some knowledge of this form of realization will accept and recognize this form, which is just an important feature of sports cultural activities. Secondly, the development of modern society makes sports cultural activities easier be accepted and recognized by people. In today's society where material and science are developed, the spiritual thoughts conveyed by sports exist in everyone's

---

① Zhang Haili, Liu Xiaohai and Zhang Haijun, "Sports as an Important Carrier of Chinese Culture in Exchange with the Rest of the World", *Sports Culture Guide*, Vol. 10, 2018, pp. 11 – 14.

thoughts. In leisure sports activities, the yearning for physical and mental health, people-to-people emotional communication and cosy life is the common needs of everyone; while in competitive sports, everyone can feel and accept the pursuit for human limit and winning and display of human nature in games. The simple rules and action requirements of mass sports activities and the popularity of sports venue and equipment in modern society enable everyone to participate in sports cultural activities; the reports on competitive sports events and live broadcast of TV also enable everyone to recognize such form of sports, and enjoy spiritual pleasure by watching sports events, and then join this form of sports. The developed information technology bridges the cultural gap between countries, and enables people across the world to enjoy the same viewing and involvement. All these have made modern sports cultural activities be integrated into social life easier, also made sports cultural activities become a means of cultural exchange.

Sports cultural activities are the expression of different cultural traits. Just because of this, sports cultural exchanges are taken as an important supplementation to and a pioneer in international exchange. The characteristics of natural environment and national history have created different countries and societies and formed various cultural and sports activities. What's more, different understanding and development of the spiritual core of sports culture is an important aspect in the cultural exchange between the East and the West. Various attitudes towards leisure sports and competitive sports, and different policies towards national and social sports are associated with the characteristics of each country and nationality. The exchange and development of sports cultural activities just forms the bridge and tie to know these differences. Knowing these is helpful to promote the development of national and ethnic culture, and form the focus of international exchanges. Nowadays, a major trend in the world is diversified common development. The ethnic cultural and sports activities have also become a trend in international exchange because these non-Olympic events and ethnic sports cultural activities can promote better understanding and integration of nations and social public. The traditional

Chinese sports cultural activities held in Minsk, Belarus, and the important Belarus Open Wushu Championship Wushu of "European Confucius Institute Cup" show that sports cultural activities, as a means in exchanges with the rest of the world, go before political and economic exchanges. Such sports cultural exchanges and contests will firstly stir up the public's interest in learning, and then actively guide the future social cultural exchanges. The existence of sports cultural exchanges has enabled countries to carry out more perfect political and economic exchanges and cooperation.

Sports cultural activities are an important reflection of national development, culture is the product of society, and sports culture is an important product of social and economic development. The launch of and performance in sports cultural activities enables to understand the political and economic direction of a country better. Nowadays, China has also accelerated the perfection and development of its sports industry, league system, sports education, social sports, etc. while comprehensively developing its politics and economy. China launched the reform of professional football leagues in 1994. In 2016, the General Administration of Sports of China promulgated the 13th Five-Year Plan for sports development, which marks that China has started the transformation from a sports nation to a sports power, and the focus of China's sports has been swift from competitive sports to school sports and mass sports. With regard to the sports industry, China has achieved comprehensive development and success in sports science and technology, development of sports culture, stadium construction, sports equipment, holding of sports events, etc. All these will be deemed as important direction of future sports cultural exchanges and important direction of economic cooperation and development between China and the rest of the world.

IV. Prospects of the Sports Cultural Exchanges between Belarus and China

Firstly, in view of the current sports cultural exchanges between Belarus and China, it is expected that the two countries can further consolidate and strengthen the sports exchanges between them, continuously expand the exchanges in the sports and culture fields and groups of exchange, continuously intensify communication and contact on the basis of the Sports Cooperation Framework Agreement between Belarus and China, step up exchanges between colleges and universities of the two countries in sports education and scientific research and exchanges between twin cities in sports cultural activities, expand the scope of youth sports cultural activities, and on this basis, promote the political and economic exchanges between the two countries. [1]

Secondly, it is expected to strengthen the cooperation and exchanges between Belarus and China in athletic sports. The invitational boxing and ice hockey tournaments hosted by Belarus have made China recognize its deficiencies in comprehensive sports events. In order to make up and strengthen the development of competitive sports, it is necessary to carry out cooperation and exchanges with Belarus.

Finally, it is expected to strengthen China-Belarus exchanges and cooperation beyond sports cultural activities. In terms of cooperation in sports information media, promote and strengthen the two sides' sharing of sports news information and communication on media reports, and thereupon form good public opinion. There is still much room for exchange and cooperation in the sports industry and sports derived economy. China-Belarus exchanges may be enhanced further via stadium construction and holding of sports events. The emerging and development of these exchanges and cooperation will substantially influence the political and economic status of Belarus and China in the international community, and demonstrate the friendship and win-win between countries to the most extent.

---

[1] Han Xiaolan, "Research on Sports Exchanges between China and Russia", *Sports Culture Guide*, Vol. 8, 2014, pp. 12 – 15

New Pattern of China's Talent Development and Governance

Ge Yanxia
Associate Professor, National Institute of
Social Development, CASS

Over the past four decades since the reform and opening up, China has notably improved its human resource quality and entered a new era when a new pattern of talent development has been established. A nationwide strategic system on talent work has been preliminarily formed, which is helpful to forge greater synergy of talent policy with the strategic planing for industrial, economic and social development, enhance the concept of regional comparative advantage, strengthen interregional coordinative, opening, mutual benefit and win-win talent cooperation, and establish the concept of attracting talents at home and abroad.

Talent is the prime resource driving innovation. [1]From "widening channels to attract talents" proposed at the 18th CPC National Congress to "the strategy of reinvigorating the country through talent cultivation" set at the 19th CPC National Congress, the CPC Central Committee with Comrade Xi Jinping as the

---

[1] CCCPC Party Literature Research Office (compilation), *Excerpt of Xi Jinping's Exposition on Scientific and Technological Innovation*, Beijing: CCCPC Party Literature Press, 2016.

core has continuously released the strong signal of strengthening talent cultivation. ①

In recent years, under the stress of labor supply decline and industrial transformation and upgrading, attracting and retaining talents has become critical to boost the core competitiveness of a city. Currently, major cities in China have all attached great importance to talents. Governments at various levels have devoted unprecedented attention to talents, proposing to take talents as the most valuable resource for scientific development and focus on talent introduction and cultivation.

In 2018, at least 35 cities issued more than 40 talents introduction policies, and most of these policies were attractive. For example, Tianjin released the "Haihe River Talent" program: graduates of 40 years below may directly settle down in Tianjin. About 130,000 people were introduced in that year. ②Chengdu issued the *Program of Chengdu for Prioritizing Talent Development* in 2017, announced that young talents with bachelor degree or above may go through the household registration procedure against their diploma, and offered graduates starting business in Chengdu within 5 years after graduation with full soft loan of no more than 500,000 yuan and no longer than 3 years, which attracted more than 130,000 people with bachelor degree and above to settle down in Chengdu for development. ③Wuhan initiated the "Program for Millions of Graduates Staying in Wuhan for Entrepreneurship and Employment" in 2017, namely, graduates may settle down in Wuhan against diploma. More than 700,000 graduates stayed in Wuhan for entrepreneurship and employment. ④ Xi'an launched the move of "online household registration

---

① Cheng Xiang, "Identify, Gather and Use Talents-Xi Jinping Creates a New Style of Talent Work", July 17, 2018, http://politics.people.com.cn/n1/2018/0717/c100130152 708.html.

② Data source: *Report on the Work of Tianjin Government* 2019 issued by Tianjin Municipal People's Government, Jan. 14, 2019.

③ Data source: *12 New talent policies issued by Chengdu attracted about* 130,000 *talents of bachelor degree and above to settle down for development last year*, NEWSSC.ORG, Feb. 25, 2018.

④ Data source: *Wuhan issued citizen cards to college students in Wuhan*, Wuhan Municipal People's Government, Sep. 30, 2018.

for nationwide college students against student card and ID card" in 2018, and realized the record high household registration per day of 8,050, and annual household settlement of more than 300,000. ①Both first-tier cities in the East and second and third-tier cities in the central and western regions have remarkably lowered the household registration threshold, and offered preferential policies, such as housing subsidies, bonus, subsidies, etc., to attract talents, and formed a new pattern of talent development. Along with the deepening of the reform and opening-up pattern, China's talent introduction will be expanded further.

Ⅰ. Background of the New Pattern of Talent Development in China

1. Robust Demand for Talents Spawned by the Transformation of Economic Development Pattern and Industrial Transformation and Upgrading

The world history of science and technology since the modern times shows that talents are of great significance to the national scientific and technological innovation and economic and social development. Since the 18th CPC National Congress, the CPC Central Committee has demanded transformation and upgrading of China's economy by virtue of scientific and technological innovation and all-round innovation, while the core resource of innovation is human resource, especially high-level talent resource. The 19th CPC National Congress advanced the objective of economic development from high-speed growth to high-quality growth, which further the consciousness of resorting new development and new growth to talents.

---

① Data source: *Development of Permanent Population in Shaanxi Province* 2018, Shaanxi Provincial Bureau of Statistics, May 15, 2019.

2. Local of Ficials' Strong Sense of Talent Seeking Since the 18th CPC National Congress

General Secretary Xi Jinping has stressed for times that China needs talents more than ever. Currently, local officials as various levels have deeply recognized it and taken practical measures to value talents because most of them are graduates after the reform and opening up. They have an instinctive desire for knowledge and a genuine recognition and acknowledgement of the importance of talents. Therefore, they will definitely place more emphasis on talents and naturally have special recognition to graduates.

3. Inevitable Requirement to Improve Urban Development Quality

Since the reform and opening up, Chinese cities have made substantial advances. The focus of urban development since the 18th CPC Central Congress has been shifted to quality and benefit-oriented improvement. Urban development is not only extensive expansion of urban size and single economic scale, but also connotative and idiosyncratic development in respect of industrial cluster, innovation ability, high-tech and population quality, while all these all-round improvement in urban development quality cannot be realized without talent support and guidance, which has further aroused cities and city administrators' strong desire for talents.

4. Demand of Second-tier Cities for Being Upgraded to New First-tier Cities

The data released by the National Bureau of Statistics showed that after Tianjin, Chongqing and Suzhou, from 2014 to 2017, some second-tier cities, such as Hangzhou, Chengdu, Wuhan, Nanjing, Qingdao, Changsha, Wuxi, etc., successively joined the "1 trillion yuan club" by economic output",[1] with the economic growth constantly above the national average, and expected to be

---

[1] Data source: *China Statistical Yearbook 2014 – 2017*, published by the National Bureau of Statistics.

qualified for new first-tier cities. Given this, these second-tier cities are eager to accelerate their development and capable to attract talents from all over the world. For example, the resident population of Hangzhou hit a record high in 2017, which were 280,000 over last year. Besides the original cities, such as Beijing, Tianjin, Shanghai, Guangzhou and Chongqing, some new cities were seen in the 2017 list of "central cities of the state" determined by the state, such as Hangzhou, Chengdu, Wuhan, Nanjing, Zhengzhou, Qingdao, Xi'an, etc., which has undoubtedly increased the redevelopment impetus and competitive pressure of these cities.

II. Effect of the New Pattern of Talent Development in China

While carried out the talent-oriented policies of General Secretary Xi Jinping and the guiding principles of the 19th CPC National Congress, some local governments in China have promulgated their respective talent introduction policies.

Talent introduction is of great significance to improve the innovation ability and promote the social and economic development. Talents may come from home or abroad. In science and technology innovation powers like the United States and Germany, talents introduced from abroad account for a large proportion. According to the *World Migration Report 2018*, as of 2015, United States had the introduced talents and other migrants of about 46 million[1]; as of 2018, Germany had about 13.50 million migrants.[2] According to the *World Migration Report 2013*, foreign-born people residing in China was only 848,500, accounting for 0.06% of the total population, basically the lowest level across the world, far below the average 10.8% in developed countries and

---

[1] Data source: *World Migration Report 2018*.
[2] Data source: released by the Federal Statistical Office of Germany in August 2019.

regions, and the world average 3.2%. ①

According to the human capital flow theory, human capital flow is one of the ways to rapidly increase human capital investment. In an opening market economy, the value of talents is realized through the market mechanism. Talents flow to get good employment opportunities and more economic benefits, as well as non-monetary satisfaction. Talent cultivation needs not only personal cost but also social cost. Among others, the term "personal cost" means the education cost born by individuals or families, while the term "social cost" means the public education facility cost born by the society.

The development experience of major cities at home and abroad indicates that a city has to solve employment opportunity, living quality and public service supply well if it intends to attract and retain talents. ②The construction of socialism with Chinese characteristics is in urgent need of high-quality workers and technical personnel. ③Since the national and regional demands for talents are diversified, we must advocate diversified talent-oriented policies to inspire talents from all nationalities, all walks of life and all aspects to the most extent, so that gather a great force for the rejuvenation of the Chinese nation.

III. Comprehensively Promote the New Pattern of Talent Development in China

According to the "scientific, efficient and precise" principle, establish and perfect the new talent system giving priority to efficiency with due consideration to fairness, strengthen macro control of talents, improve the talent benefit policies and promote efficiency improvement.

---

① Data source: Annual Report on Chinese International Migration (2015).
② Garmise · S, *People and the Competitive Advantage of Place: Building a Workforce for the 21st Century*, New York: Routledge, 2006.
③ The compilation group of this book: *Assemble the Best Minds across the Land and Draw fully on Their Expertise-Learning from Xi Jinping's Important Exposition on Talent Work*, Beijing: China Social Science Press, 2017, p. 34.

Build a nationwide integrated talent system. Talent resource is of great significance to national development. The constitution and implementation of talent policies shall always be planed as a whole by the CPC central committee, consciously practice the talent-oriented policies reflecting the Xi Jinping Thought on Socialism with Chinese Characteristics for a New Era, plan the direction and task talent work in light of the Five-sphere Integrated Plan, the Four-pronged Comprehensive Strategy and realization of the "three-step" strategic objectives; always adhere to the principle of the Party exercising leadership over talent administration, assemble the best minds across the land and draw fully on their expertise, and step up efforts to make China a talent-strong country; deeply understand the scientific connotation and great significance of "talent is the primary resource" and "innovation-driven is talent driven in essence"; build a nationwide integrated strategic system for talent work, strengthen top-level design and systematic planning, and define the general idea of talent work.

Improve the precise connection between talent policies and the strategic planning for industrial, economic and social development. Talent is not only the primary resource, but also a scarce resource urgently needed in national social and economic development. Therefore, it is necessary to use talents preciously to avoid waste brought by mismatch of talent resource. It is suggested to design the talent policies in light of the Five-sphere Integrated Plan, the Four-pronged Comprehensive Strategy and realization of the "three-step" strategic objectives to make the talent policies exactly gear to the strategic planning for regional development, and bring talent resource into full play. [1] The "Seven Strategies" advanced at the 19th CPC National Congress aim at different regions and industries. These strategies cannot be implemented effectively without matching talent resource. For example, the talents needed in the strategy for Guangdong-Hong Kong-Macao Greater Bay Area are definitely different from those needed in

---

[1] Ma Ziliang, "Industrial Cluster and Urban Population Agglomeration in Northwest Region: Interactive Collaboration and Geographic Coupling-spatial Statistical Analysis from the Evolutionary Perspective", *Journal of Southwest Minzu University (Humanities and Social Science)*, Vol. 5, 2016.

the strategy for Beijing-Tianjin-Hebei integrated development. Therefore, corresponding factors shall be considered when developing strategies and talent policies. Both the central government and local governments shall consciously connect strategy planing and implementation with talents because strategies without support from talents can hardly be realized and is unsustainable.

Bring the role of market in talent allocation into full play to promote smooth and orderly flow of talents. Since market is the primary channel for talent flow, a perfect market mechanism plays a significant role in guaranteeing smooth and orderly flow of talents. We shall fully respect the development law of market economy and the law of talent cultivation and flow, and bring the role of market in talent allocation into full play. It is necessary to carefully implement the arrangements for the *Opinions on Deepening the Reform of Talent Development System and Mechanism* issued by CPC Central Committee, and perfect the talent flow market mechanism, regulate the talent flow order and improve the talent flow service system by focusing on the strategy of reinvigorating China through talented people and the innovation-driven development strategy, activate the market mechanism, break down the institutional barriers and other barriers hindering the flow of talents, continuously promote the smooth and orderly flow of talents, and energize talented people's innovation, entrepreneurship and creation.

It is necessary to strengthen interregional talent cooperation in an efficient, coordinated, opening, sharing and win-win way. Uneven development is a problem that China's economy and society has faced for a long time. It is also one of the important judgments of the 19th CPC National Congress. Local governments shall firstly build the "four consciousnesses" firmly, thoroughly implement the *Opinions of the General Office of the Communist Party of China Central Committee on Encouraging Talented People to Remote Areas with Harsh Conditions and Frontlines*, intensify support to talented people-dominated projects in remote areas with harsh conditions and frontlines, promote interregional talent cooperation in an efficient, coordinated, opening, sharing and win-win manner, and advance interregional coordinated development of economy and society.

Strengthen the concept of regional comparative advantage. Since the 18th CPC National Congress, the CPC Central Committee has attached close attention to regional economic integration and economic development strength. Therefore, the planning of some regions for industrial, social and economic, and talent development shall adhere to the principle of applying advanced experience according to local conditions. Develop talent policies pursuant to the regional position set by the CPC Central Committee, carry out talent attraction measures fit for local conditions, improve industry and talent disposition efficiency, and realize the optimum talent disposition across the country.

We should assemble the best minds across the land and draw fully on their expertise. Over the past 40 years, China cannot make remarkable achievements in its economic development if it had not opened up. Just as opening up is indispensable for economic construction, talent work also demands opening up to attract talents across the world. Talent work shall be based on domestic talents, and eye on the global talents. Since one of the features of the era of globalization will definitely be the globalization of resources, China shall also review talent, the first resource, from a global perspective.

The "accuracy" idea shall be carried out thoroughly in formulation of local talent policies and implementation of talent work because different regions and cities need different talents at various stages of development, only when this idea is followed, can the objectives of talent accuracy, industrial accuracy and cause development be accomplished, or low-level, homogeneous and fragmented urban competition, idleness, waste, mismatch and inefficiency of talent resource will be brought on.

A hierarchical, classified and step-by-step idea and methodology shall be set up when developing local talent policies and carrying out the talent work. Since cities demand talents at various levels; different fields and industries also demand different talents; the demand for talents also varies by stages of development, the differentiation consciousness must be fostered to avoid waste of resources like residency right and manning quota due to blind introduction, and new weaknesses and problems in urban management due to scramble for talents.

The long-term development planning shall be kept in mind when developing local talent policies and carrying out the talent work. Local governments of China may borrow ideas from each other in formulation and implementation of talent policies, master the characteristics and laws of industrial development, take building industrial chain and ecological chain as the organic goal of talent policy formulation and implementation, and thus make the policy formulation have certain relevance and periodicity.

It is necessary to practice the policy of "respecting knowledge and talent", actively carry out the strategy of reinvigorating the country through science and education and the strategy for talent development, create a social atmosphere of respecting talent and knowledge, gradually improve the treatment of talents, and improve their working and living conditions to bring their wisdom into full play. In order to solve the talent shortage in frontlines and remote areas with hash conditions, we shall solve the talent flow difficulty from the system perspective, support talent-dominated projects in frontlines and remote areas with hash conditions, improve the talent support and coordination mechanism, and actively create conditions to cultivate, attract and make full use of talents, and pave a solid talent foundation for building a moderately prosperous society in all respects and realizing the great rejuvenation of the Chinese nation.